NUCLEAR ABOLITION

A SCENARIO

Timmon Wallis

Indispensable Press
Northampton, Mass. USA

Nuclear Abolition: A Scenario

Indispensable Press, 59 Gleason Rd, Northampton, Massachusetts 01060
www.indispensable.press

Printed and distributed by IngramSpark

This book includes substantially revised and rearranged sections of Chapters 7-11 from ©2023 Timmon Wallis, *Warheads to Windmills: Preventing Climate Catastrophe and Nuclear War*. It also includes excerpts from ©2016 Timmon Wallis, *The Truth About Trident: Disarming the Nuclear Argument*, published by Luath Press, Edinburgh, Scotland, and from ©2017 Timmon Wallis, *Disarming the Nuclear Argument: The Truth About Nuclear Weapons*, also published by Luath Press.

The Doomsday Clock is created and maintained by the *Bulletin of the Atomic Scientists* but the *Bulletin* is not a part of or endorser of the content of this book.

Other material is as quoted and cited in the text, including graphics and photographs.

World maps created with free and open source QGIS. US map data from OpenStreetMap: openstreetmap/copyright.

An audiobook version of this book is forthcoming.

Cover design: Vicki Elson

ISBN 979-8-218-69718-1 (paperback)
ISBN 979-8-218-60945-0 (hardback)

Second printing (July 28, 2025)

Praise for *Nuclear Abolition:*

"More than a story of how we might achieve a world free of nuclear weapons, Timmon Wallis has given all of us some serious homework. There is something for everyone to do here, from young people raising awareness, to ordinary citizens calling on their local and national leaders to take action, to those in position to change the status quo doing exactly that. Achieving total elimination of nuclear weapons won't be easy. But it is necessary if humanity is to continue, let alone thrive. By reading this book, you'll be ready to do your part. "

— from the Foreword by Ivana Nikovic Hughes

"In *Nuclear Abolition - a scenario*, Timmon Wallis brilliantly elaborates some of the ways in which the total elimination of nuclear weapons may be achieved in our lifetimes. In doing so, he gives nations, campaigners, and members of the public valuable information and tools to avert the global catastrophe foretold in Annie Jacobsen's *Nuclear War - a scenario*. A timely and essential resource for everyone interested in human and planetary security - that means all of us!" **— Melissa Parke, Executive Director, ICAN**

"Here we have a surprisingly powerful argument – a world without nuclear weapons would be a better world in many ways – combined with the most powerful argument possible that ought to be no surprise: a world with nuclear weapons would be a world without life. Understanding the need for nuclear abolition, Wallis details a perfectly plausible step-by-step path to success. It's hard to imagine a more useful book." **— David Swanson, author of *War Is Never Just***

"Wallis shows vividly how many, many people, each taking a small step, working together, can result in enough pressure for companies to give up producing weapons of mass destruction. Although often the job we've taken on seems overwhelming, Wallis's organized and clear exposition makes it seem within our capabilities."

— Jeanne Trubek, Mass Peace Action

"What a good read. I typically would not have sought out a book on the nuclear threat as it has always seemed so exasperating and overwhelming. I'm relieved you and others see a way out for humankind. Thank you for writing it."

— Mary Finn, Northampton, MA

This book is dedicated to the thousands of nuclear abolition campaigners around the world who are not mentioned by name in this book. (You know who you are!). They have worked tirelessly to get us to the starting point of this scenario, and all that remains now is to keep pressing on until nuclear abolition is achieved!

TABLE OF CONTENTS

FOREWORD *by Ivana Nikolić Hughes*

Speaking at the United Nations General Assembly in 1961, US President John F. Kennedy stated, "Today, every inhabitant of this planet must contemplate the day when this planet may no longer be habitable. Every man, woman and child lives under a nuclear sword of Damocles, hanging by the slenderest of threads, capable of being cut at any moment by accident or miscalculation or by madness. The weapons of war must be abolished before they abolish us."

Echoing his words more than 56 years later, as she accepted the 2017 Nobel Peace Prize on behalf of the International Campaign to Abolish Nuclear Weapons (ICAN), then Executive Director Beatrice Fihn asked, "The story of nuclear weapons will have an ending, and it is up to us what that ending will be. Will it be the end of nuclear weapons, or will it be the end of us?"

Of course, President Kennedy and Beatrice Fihn are not the first nor the only luminaries to have come to the conclusion that nuclear weapons must be eliminated. This is the only logical and rational conclusion one can arrive at once they know even just the basic facts about these extraordinarily powerful and extraordinarily harmful arms.

The International Committee of the Red Cross called for the abolition of nuclear weapons in September of 1945. The winner of the 1943 Nobel Prize in Physics, I.I. Rabi and Robert Oppenheimer, the father of the atomic bomb, called for nuclear weapons to be put under international control in December of 1945. The 1955 Einstein-Russell Manifesto sought to denounce not just nuclear weapons, but all war. Countless people have recognized the madness and advocated for sanity.

It has been many decades since those earliest calls for elimination of nuclear arms. It is time to get the job done.

The enormous energy nuclear weapons can produce was apparent from the very start of the nuclear age. Their devastating effects on people and other life came into sharp relief with the bombings of Hiroshima and Nagasaki, and have continued to reveal themselves over the decades since in the many illnesses and ailments that the Hibakusha - survivors of the bombings - have suffered.

As nuclear weapons became bigger, especially with the advent of hydrogen bombs, the first of which was detonated by the United States in Enewetak Atoll in the Marshall Islands in 1952, their potential for causing harm globally was also revealed step by dangerous step. With radiation fallout devastatingly impacting local populations, but also spreading around the planet, the ability of nuclear weapons to affect communities far away and far into the future began to be widely recognized.

President Kennedy was painfully aware of this unique feature of nuclear weapons. What he didn't know was that nuclear war, in which hundreds or even thousands of warheads are used in attacks, could give rise to nuclear winter as a consequence of the enormous fires and soot released in the atmosphere, which would lower temperatures around the globe and impair production of food, leading to global famine. At the same time, such widespread use of nuclear weapons could produce nitric oxide, which would destroy the ozone layer at levels that would make every corner of the planet unsafe for all of its life forms. The risk we are living with is much greater than even President Kennedy could have imagined.

The humanitarian consequences of nuclear weapons - past, present, and future - gave the impetus for negotiating the Treaty on the Prohibition of Nuclear Weapons (TPNW), which bans all activities having to do with nuclear weapons. This historic treaty is the result of a collaborative effort between civil society and countries that are not nuclear armed. Those countries understand how they, too, would be impacted by nuclear war. As the TPNW continues to garner more and more support from UN member states and actors at all levels of public life, the big question is whether it can achieve its ultimate goal of removing all nuclear weapons from the face of the planet.

Timmon Wallis has now given us a manual on how the TPNW can achieve this goal, small step by small step, leading to ever bigger and bigger steps, all the way to a world free of nuclear weapons.

Nuclear Abolition: A Scenario focuses on the United States, the country that was the first to develop nuclear weapons, the only one to ever use them in attacks on cities full of women and children, and the one that wrote the playbook for the nuclear testing era. Timmon recognizes that the US must lead the world when it comes to eliminating all nuclear arsenals. But he is not naïve in thinking that we can just wish this and it will happen. He recognizes that the persistent existence of nuclear weapons is deeply intertwined with monetary interests of the so-called military industrial complex. Therefore, Timmon's scenario involves pressure on the United States both from the outside (the international community) and from the inside (local and state governments), focused on the companies that are engaged in the business of making nuclear weapons.

An introductory section on Nuclear Abolition sets the stage. Then Timmon gives a plausible scenario, narrating it in sections devoted to Global Pressures, US Pressures, and the Endgame. Under Global Pressures, we witness countries as they (1) vote for non-binding UN resolutions, (2) sign the TPNW, (3) ratify the TPNW, (4) write obligations into national laws, (5) define financing of nuclear weapons manufacturers as "assistance," (6) commit to divesting from corporations involved in making nuclear weapons, and (7) ban contracts with them. In each chapter, we are given an Example of a country that is already doing something, a Next Up for a state that is primed to act, and a Prize, a state whose actions would be ambitious and yet not inconceivable. By the time you catch on to the pattern, you are curious to know who is next and how it all unfolds. Finally, we watch as non-supporters start to join the TPNW, and nuclear hosting states like Italy, Germany, Belgium, and the Netherlands get rid of the US arsenals on their soil.

In the US Pressures section, we watch as towns and cities (1) commit to nuclear abolition, (2) call on the US to act, (3) take action, (4) turn resolutions into city ordinances, (5) commit to divesting from nuclear weapons, and (6) refuse nuclear weapons manufacturers from city contracts. Then states take action, and prominent politicians, including Alexandria Ocasio Cortez, Bernie Sanders, and the Democratic National Convention, all put their weight behind nuclear abolition.

Along the way, we learn about history of the nuclear age (yes, indeed there are 50 nuclear warheads at the bottom of the ocean!), international relations (from Sierra Leone to Norway, from Mexico to the Philippines), and local politics (from "Sewer Socialists" in Milwaukee to the Northampton Home Rule Petition). We also learn about prominent activists and organizations from around the globe and the US who have been carrying the torch of abolition, often working against the grain and with low or minimal funding. They are the true heroes of this story. They are the reason why we can even envision the elimination of nuclear arsenals.

More than a story of how we might achieve a world free of nuclear weapons, Timmon Wallis has given all of us some serious homework. There is something for everyone to do here, from young people raising awareness, to ordinary citizens calling on their local and national leaders to take action, to those in position to change the status quo doing exactly that. Achieving total elimination of nuclear weapons won't be easy. But it is necessary if humanity is to continue, let alone thrive. By reading this book, you'll be ready to do your part.

Ivana Nikolić Hughes
New York
May 19, 2025

AUTHOR'S PREFACE

What if there were no nuclear weapons in the world? What would that world look like, feel like, taste like, smell like? Take a moment to savor that vision. Imagine yourself in a world whose continued existence does not depend on the whims of a few narcissistic old megalomaniacs with their fingers on The Button.

It shouldn't be that hard to imagine, since everyone alive before 1945 lived in such a world. And most people today go about their daily business *as if* there were no nuclear weapons even now, completely oblivious to the existential threat these weapons pose to all of us.

Of course, even without nuclear weapons, we would still have the threat of climate catastrophe hanging over us. But what if getting rid of nuclear weapons was a key to ending the climate crisis?

Imagine all that money, energy, brainpower, and infrastructure that is going into nuclear weapons going instead into addressing the climate: Trillions of dollars going into mass transit, tree planting, a decentralized electricity grid. Our best scientists and engineers hard at work to create better, safer, cleaner solar panels, wind turbines and batteries. Global cooperation to wean the world off fossil fuels and to enable affected communities around the world to move to safety as habitats are threatened.

We have been conditioned to believe that this kind of talk is just naïve poppycock. Such a world could never exist. Humans are too violent and warlike to live together in peaceful harmony with each other. What about all the conventional weaponry and ongoing wars and armed conflict everywhere? Wouldn't it be so much worse without nuclear weapons keeping the "lid" on conflicts between countries?

After all, we are told that nuclear weapons are somehow "keeping the peace" and preventing even more conflict and war than we already have. This is nonsense!

The world is more violent today than ever before. As many as 100 million people died in, or as a result of, the two World Wars. Thankfully, there has not been a third one. But, by some accounts, at least that many have died in, or as a result, of all the wars since 1945.[1]

In other words, nuclear weapons have not kept the lid on violence. On the contrary, nuclear weapons have enabled the countries that have them to bomb and kill with impunity. Most recently, it has been Russia using their nuclear weapons to keep other countries from interfering with their war in Ukraine. But for most of the last 80 years, it has been the US, UK, France and Israel who have used their nuclear weapons to enable them to launch wars all over the world - and get away with it.

Without nuclear weapons, these same countries would be much more likely to stay at home and out of other people's business. Conventional (non-nuclear) weapons are a much more effective "deterrent" against military adventurism, because (as we have seen in Ukraine and in so many other modern wars) big countries don't always win wars against smaller countries. Modern conventional weaponry favors the defender more than the attacker.

So there will likely be *fewer* wars in a world without nuclear weapons, not more. There will be fewer excuses for big countries who won't play by the rules, and fewer opportunities for them to bully smaller countries. That means the world will be more fair and a bit more balanced in a post-nuclear-weapons world.

And although countries will continue to want conventional weaponry for their national defense, at least for the foreseeable future, the elimination of nuclear weapons will drastically affect *how much* conventional weaponry they will want. European countries, for instance, are undergoing a massive military build-up, supposedly to defend themselves from Russia.

But without nuclear weapons, Russia would be no more of a threat to Western Europe than a nuclear weapons-free North Korea would be to Japan. They would not need massive military might to protect themselves from Russia. They would need a bare minimum for self-defense, and even less if they decide to work cooperatively with Russia to reduce the likelihood of either side attacking the other.

The United Nations and the system of international laws that has been in development since 1945 will finally have a chance to really flourish in a post-nuclear-weapons world. There is so much potential for the countries of the world to work together, to cooperate, to build a more just and peaceful world. Nuclear weapons have been one of the biggest barriers to a more cooperative world system.

And the money freed up from nuclear weapons can do more than transform our collective efforts to halt and reverse global warming. Countries like India and Pakistan have staggering levels of poverty to address, and the money released from their nuclear weapons programs could utterly transform living standards in those countries.

Of course, in the United States, other things will need to change before we can start to call it normal or sane again. But if the US can't point to Russia or China (or North Korea) as posing an existential threat to the United States, that would undermine a key factor in the US political psyche.

US politicians have always relied on an external enemy to maintain their grip on the US-American public. Fear of Russia – and now of China – has kept the US population from demanding what every other country has demanded of their governments: free healthcare, better working conditions, affordable housing, public transportation systems, safe cities…

Imagine the United States no longer in the pocket of giant military corporations. Nuclear weapons are the biggest racket of all time – billions of dollars going from taxpayers to giant corporations to produce things everyone hopes will never be used! Once that gravy train dries up, these corporations would suddenly have to compete in the normal marketplace like everyone else. And that in turn means becoming more open, more accountable, more humane enterprises.

And finally, when the dust has settled, and people take in the fact that the world is no longer on the brink of annihilation with every breath they take, imagine how the world's mental health would improve. Imagine people breathing freely and living each moment in the certain knowledge that life will go on. Maybe not your own personal life or mine, but *life* - children, families, grandchildren, organizations, communities, societies, humanity, nature – will go on!

Unfortunately, that is not the world we live in at the moment. But what would it take to reach that point? How hard could it be? And why hasn't the world gotten rid of these weapons by now?

In fact, since the end of the Cold War, nearly 50,000 nuclear warheads, along with thousands of bombers, missiles and other related hardware, have been dismantled and destroyed. Technically, it is totally doable to eliminate the remaining 12,000 warheads.

We know how to disarm nuclear weapons, safely and irreversibly. We know how to monitor and verify that the disarmament has taken place. And we have the global infrastructure already in place to make sure no one can cheat or build a new nuclear weapon without the whole world knowing about it.

The only real challenge to nuclear abolition, therefore, is political. And in the United States, the political challenge is directly related to the power that a few very large corporations have over our elected politicians.

These corporations spend millions lobbying the White House, the Pentagon and Congress to ensure continued bipartisan support for multi-billion dollar nuclear weapons programs. They directly finance re-election campaigns to keep their friends in power and to dispose of their enemies. And they use an array of think-tanks, academics and non-governmental organizations to ensure that there is a steady drip of propaganda and misinformation hitting every form of media to convince the rest of us that nuclear weapons are somehow our best guarantee of security – and that we have no choice in the matter.

There are many possible pathways to nuclear abolition. This book focuses on a pathway that goes through these corporations, not because that is necessarily the most likely scenario, but because it is perhaps the easiest and most direct. It's also a pathway that has worked in the past, at least partially.

In the 1980s, several major corporations got out of the nuclear weapons business following boycotts and divestment campaigns that swept across the United States. Similar efforts have successfully helped to dismantle apartheid, win rights for farmworkers, and change the discourse on climate.

Today, some of the nuclear weapons corporations are feeling the pinch again, as global divestment movements are growing, especially in Europe. The Treaty on the Prohibition of Nuclear Weapons (TPNW, or "Nuclear Ban Treaty") provides a legal framework for divesting from and boycotting these corporations in the countries that have joined this treaty.

To create the conditions necessary for a major shift of policy on nuclear weapons in Washington, additional pressure on these corporations will be needed. As more and more countries join the TPNW and take additional steps to strengthen its prohibitions, the pressure on the corporations is going to increase. And that pressure will increase even more as cities, states, faith communities, colleges and other institutions across the United States launch divestment campaigns, boycotts and other forms of stigmatization.

The combination of these two pressure points – one coming from other countries and the other coming from within the US – creates a kind of "pincer movement" that can finally bring the nuclear age to an end. And that's because these corporations do not exist to make nuclear weapons. They exist to make a profit. And they will, without hesitation, ditch nuclear weapons in order to save their businesses – and their profits.

Once these corporations see the writing on the wall, they will come running to the US Congress. They will *beg* Congress to cancel nuclear weapons contracts and instead fund these corporations to produce products and services that are acceptable to the US public and the rest of the world.

It will take some further steps to convince the other nuclear-armed countries to give up their weapons. But those steps are totally doable once those US corporations have moved out of the nuclear weapons business. That is how, in a nutshell, the world – in this scenario – will abolish nuclear weapons.

NOTE: In the pages that follow, facts are written in normal typeface. There are numerous notes at the end of the book that give more details and provide references to back up those facts.

And what is written in bold is fiction. This is just one scenario that lays out what *could* happen at unspecified times in the future. And hopefully it's a convincing one.

INTERVIEWS

Rosalie Anders,
Mass Peace Action Board member, Cambridge, MA

Jeroen Beirnaert,
Political Director, International Trade Union Congress, Brussels

Reiner Braun,
Executive Director, International Peace Bureau, Berlin, Germany

Keith Brumley,
President, Veterans for Peace, Chapter 102, Milwaukee, WI

Jackie Cabasso,
US Coordinator, Mayors for Peace, Oakland, CA

Tom Charles,
Veterans For Peace, Spokane, WA Chapter #35

Kevin Clements,
Public Advisory Committee on Disarmament and Arms Control, Aotearoa/New Zealand

Jean-Marie Collin,
Director, ICAN-France, Paris, France

Kate Dewes,
Former Director, Disarmament and Security Centre, Christchurch, Aotearoa/New Zealand

Sharon Gaya Dolev,
Executive Director, Middle East Treaty Organization, Jerusalem, Israel

Anthony Donovan,
Nuclear abolitionist and filmmaker, New York, NY

Joseph Dube,
Director, Disarmament and Arms Control, South Africa

Florian Eblenkamp,
ICAN Advocacy Officer and Board Member, ICAN Germany

David Hutchinson Edgar,
Chair, Irish Campaign for Nuclear Disarmament, Dublin, Ireland

Abdul M. Fatoma,
Director, Campaign for Human Rights and Development International, Sierra Leone

Janet Fenton,
Organizer, Secure Scotland,
Edinburgh, Scotland

Victor Gaute,
Vice President, Cuban Institute of Friendship with the Peoples,
Havana, Cuba

David Gibson,
Peace, Justice and Sustainability Now, Philadelphia, PA

Rob Green,
Commander (Retired),
British Royal Navy

Walae Hayek and **Malika Sud,**
Coalition for Responsible Investment, Jamaica Plain, MA

Ivana Nikolić Hughes,
President, Nuclear Age Peace Foundation, Santa Barbara, CA

Josefin Lind,
Secretary-General,
Swedish Physicians Against Nuclear Weapons, Stockholm, Sweden

Clara Levin,
Communications Manager,
Swedish Physicians Against Nuclear Weapons, Stockholm, Sweden

David Mackenzie,
Secretary, Secure Scotland
Edinburgh, Scotland

Carolina Barrios Martinez,
Deputy Manager, Disarmament Affairs, Colombia Campaign to Ban Landmines

Girish Menon,
Chairman, NADA Foundation,
India

John McDougall,
350 Mass and Mass Peace Action,
Cambridge, MA

Susan Mirsky,
Chair, Nuclear Disarmament Working Group, Massachusetts Peace Action, Cambridge, MA

Alejandra Muñoz,
Senior Project Officer, PAX,
Utrecht, the Netherlands

Grethe Østern,
Editor, Nuclear Ban Monitor,
Norwegian People's Aid,
Oslo, Norway

Pamela Richards,
Peace Action Wisconsin

Paula Rogge, MD,
Physicians for Social Responsibility,
Madison, WI

Gem Romuld,
Director, ICAN Australia

Seth Shelden,
General Counsel and
United Nations Liaison, ICAN

Susi Snyder,
Program Coordinator, ICAN

Ann Suellentrop,
Vice Chair, PeaceWorks Kansas City, and Program Director, Kansas City PSR, Kansas City, MO

Carlos Umaña,
President, IPPNW Costa Rica

Francesco Vignarca,
Campaign Coordinator, Italian Peace and Disarmament Network

Maria Eugenia Villarreal,
Co-Founder, SEHLAC Guatemala

Cristian Wittman,
SEHLAC Brazil

Prologue: A World Turned Upside Down

As this book goes to print in the spring of 2025, the world has gone topsy-turvy – especially the United States. The people most opposed to the work of various government departments in the US are now running those departments. The US government is busily dismembering and dismantling itself. Former adversaries of the US are now friends, and former allies are now adversaries. The US ideological commitment to "free trade" is now replaced by a reign of tariffs. And European governments, previously very much under the thumb of the US, are now giving it the middle finger.

All of this is, of course, the direct result of Donald Trump's re-election as President of the United States in November 2024. Nationally, Trump received 2.3 million more votes than Kamala Harris. But, as in previous US elections, the election was actually decided in just three states: Wisconsin, Michigan and Pennsylvania. If Harris had received just 330,000 more votes in those three states, she would be President right now, even if she still had fewer votes nationally.[1]

It is also the case that only 63.9% of eligible voters in the United States bothered to vote in that election, compared to a record high of 66.6% in 2020, when Joe Biden beat Trump by more than 7 million votes nationally. The lower turnout in 2024 means that more than 6 million people across the country who voted for Biden in 2020 did not vote at all in 2024.[2]

Post-election opinion polls have shown that US-Americans voted for Trump primarily because of two (in their view related) issues: the price of eggs and the number of immigrants entering the United States.[3] To the extent that Trump can stem the flow of immigrants and bring down the price of eggs, the people who voted for him should be happy.

But those people did *not* vote for the wholesale dismantling of the federal government. They did *not* vote for a trade war that will inevitably increase the cost of everyday goods for US families. They did *not* vote for increasing oil and gas production as the planet continues to heat up. And they did *not* vote for many of the other policies that Trump is now attempting to implement.

Generating reactions

According to Newton's Third Law of Motion, for every action there is an equal and opposite reaction. This applies to politics as much as to physics. Attempts to suppress protest with increasing force have often resulted, not in crushing the protest, but simply in escalating the protest. And building up military forces against an opponent has generally led, not to achieving military superiority, but simply to an increased build-up of military forces by the opponent.

If there is one thing that Trump's current actions are guaranteed to create, it is a powerful galvanizing of opposing forces across the US which will not accept what is going on. These are likely to be spearheaded by students and young people, many of whom are being directly affected by deportations, threats directed at the LGTBQ community, rising costs of living, indebtedness, and the backward movement on so many other fronts.

As prices continue to rise for US households, especially on eggs and other basic foods, the reaction is likely to spread well beyond students. Trade unionists, journalists, teachers, health professionals, lawyers, judges, university administrators and many other sectors of society, when facing open hostility from the government, are going to respond. That is likely to mean strikes, boycotts and many of the other tools described in this book.

Internationally, the response to many of Trump's policies is likely to be even more marked. We are already seeing a trade war in response to the imposition of US tariffs. European governments are trying to appease Trump but at the same time they are making their own plans for a new world order that does not include the USA as a friendly ally.

As in the 1980s, European governments are going to face enormous resistance to cutting public services in order to pay for huge increases in military spending. And the idea of a nuclear war in Europe is likely to make a movement grow even stronger.

So while the scenario played out in this book may have seemed far-fetched to some only a few months ago, it may soon seem to be overly cautious, as massive global social movements rapidly coalesce to confront the Trump agenda.

And it is also possible that Trump himself will surprise us all by taking up the cause of nuclear abolition. That scenario is provided in the epilogue at the end of the book, and if things seem to be moving in that direction by the time you are reading this, feel free to skip to the end!

PART I: NUCLEAR ABOLITION

Setting the scene: As of January 2025, the *Bulletin of the Atomic Scientists'* Doomsday Clock stands at 89 seconds to midnight. And yet we are no closer to eliminating the weapons that could end human civilization than we have ever been. The reason? Follow the money. The United States got us into this predicament and it will take the United States to get us out of it. The corporations that make enormous profits from nuclear weapons are pulling the strings in the US Congress to keep it that way.

1 Turning back the Doomsday Clock

Our story begins on January 28, 2025, at the handsome concrete and glass structure that for decades has housed the United States Institute for Peace (USIP), just off the National Mall in Washington, DC. Founded by Congress in 1984, under Ronald Reagan's presidency, the USIP has had strong bipartisan support for most of its existence. It is home to research and publications on the status of violent conflicts around the world. It hosts confidential behind-the-scenes diplomatic efforts to try to end some of those conflicts.

The USIP building is like a fortress. It's heavily protected against covert eavesdroppers, whether from other embassies in DC or from other US government agencies who might want to pry into the confidential discussions that go on inside. Once inside, the building is surprisingly light and expansive, a breath of life and fresh air, unlike in the movies where backroom deals take place in dark smoke-filled rooms.

To get to the USIP Briefing Room, one passes along a corridor of giant photographs of every US President, whether Democrat or Republican, doing at least one thing right during their Presidency: President Carter shaking hands with Menachem Begin and Anwar Sadat in 1978; President Reagan shaking hands with Mikhail Gorbachev in 1987; President Clinton shaking hands with Yitzhak Rabin and Yasser Arafat; President George W. Bush shaking hands with Ariel Sharon and Mahmoud Abbas. (At least that's how it was until January 2025, when these pictures were suddenly removed.)

In the Briefing Room, the official Doomsday Clock is facing backwards. At exactly 10 am eastern time, it will be revealed to the media, invited guests, and online viewers around the world.

It's not a real clock. Since 1947, two years after nuclear weapons were unleashed on Hiroshima and Nagasaki, it has served as a metaphor for how close humanity is to doomsday, according to a committee of nuclear scientists and other experts.

Each year, the *Bulletin of Atomic Scientists* invites a special guest to take part in the unveiling, and this year it's Juan Manuel Santos

Calderón, former President of Colombia and Nobel Peace Prize laureate. Mr. Santos and his fellow speakers from the *Bulletin's* Scientific Advisory Panel gently swivel the clock until it faces the audience: the time is 10am, but **the time on the clock is 11:58:31pm** - just 89 seconds to midnight. That's closer than ever before.[1]

Members of the Bulletin of the Atomic Scientists, together with President Santos (second from left) reveal the 2025 Doomsday Clock, Jan 28, 2025.

PHOTO: T. Wallis

An abolition scenario

This book is about moving that clock back, away from midnight, and away from doomsday - not just by a few seconds, but by many hours - bringing the hands of that clock all the way back as far as they will go.

Perhaps you have read Annie Jacobsen's realistic bestseller, *Nuclear War: A Scenario.* Her book starts with the launch of a single bomb and ends 72 minutes later with much of North America, Europe and Asia destroyed. A frozen, radioactive wasteland awaits any survivors. It's a page-turner, and it's very important for people to understand the risks we are facing.

But it's equally important to understand that *we are not doomed to nuclear extinction.* The scenario that unfolds in the following pages may not be as gripping as the one in Jacobsen's book. But step by thoughtful step, we can actually get rid of these weapons. This book explores one way it can happen.

1947: **11:53:00pm**

The Doomsday Clock was launched just two years after the US bombed Hiroshima and Nagasaki. It was originally an artist's impression that set the symbolic Clock to seven minutes to midnight. A group of nuclear scientists, many of whom had worked on the Manhattan Project, took this on as a warning to the world: nuclear weapons represent an existential threat to all of us, and if we do not eliminate them, *they* will eliminate *us*.

At the time, only the US had nuclear weapons, and it only had a few of them. As the nuclear scientists feared, that was soon to change.

1949: **11:57:00pm**

The hands of the Doomsday Clock were moved four minutes closer to midnight when the Soviets exploded their first atom bomb.

1953: **11:58:00pm**

The US exploded the world's first thermonuclear bomb, 700 times more powerful than the bomb dropped on Hiroshima and and 500 times the Nagasaki bomb. Two minutes to midnight.

—

During the Cold War, the Doomsday Clock has moved back and forth with the times, but never as close as it was in 1953, even during the Cuban Missile Crisis of 1962 – until 2018.

—

1989: **11:43:00pm**

When the Berlin Wall came down, followed by the dissolution of the Soviet Union, the Clock went backward all the way to 17 minutes before midnight.

This was an indication that the world was in a much safer place than it was in the 1950s and 60s, and yet not *so* much safer that we could afford to get complacent about it.

Even with the apparent end of the Cold War between the US and the Soviet Union, nuclear weapons remained. And even when many of those weapons were taken off the highest level of alert status, a large number of them still remained dangerously ready to be fired at a moment's notice. And many still are.

And even at that "safest" point in the last 80 years, the stark reality was that the very existence of nuclear weapons, with the readiness and willingness to use them "if necessary," was still the gravest threat to the entire human race. Since then, the Doomsday Clock has been inching back toward midnight, with the world seemingly asleep at the wheel.

1998: **11:51:00pm**
India tested its first nuclear weapon and became the seventh country to build a nuclear arsenal. Nine minutes to midnight.

2007: **11:55:00pm** North Korea became the ninth nuclear-armed country. Five minutes to midnight:.

2018, **11:58:00pm**
Trump pulls out of the INF Treaty. For the first time since 1953, two minutes to midnight. Since then the clock has just kept moving closer to midnight, counted no longer in minutes but in seconds...

2025: **11:58:31pm**
We're 89 seconds to midnight. The Clock's committee didn't leave itself much wiggle room. Even significant changes can only be allotted a second or so.

The myth of nuclear deterrence

Most people, if they think about nuclear war at all, assume it *can't* happen. Nuclear weapons are there to "keep the peace," we're told. And the biggest lie of all: "Nuclear weapons are so effective as a 'deterrent,' *they will never have to be used.*"

But in fact "deterrence" is just a psychological game, involving a threat that you hope will scare away your opponent. But a threat is only scary if your opponent believes you will actually carry it out. So it turns out that nuclear weapons are not a very good deterrent *unless* they are used, sooner or later.

And the more time goes by after the only time nuclear weapons *were* used in war (80 years ago now), the weaker the deterrent effect of *threatening* to use them becomes. [2]

How nuclear war could start

Annie Jacobsen's nuclear war scenario begins with a "bolt out of the blue," in this case a single missile fired from North Korea and heading for Washington, D.C. She doesn't give a reason why the North Korean supreme leader might launch such a missile, apart from the assumption that he is a "nihilistic madman" who apparently doesn't need a reason.

Of course, it *is* possible that a nihilistic madman might launch a nuclear weapon out of the blue for no apparent reason. But that is probably the *least* likely of all the possible scenarios that could lead to nuclear annihilation.

First of all, it might not be North Korea that sets nuclear disaster in motion. But if it were, a far more likely scenario is that Kim Jong-un or his military advisors come to believe that a nuclear attack by the United States on North Korean missile sites is imminent. North Korea's entire nuclear capability could potentially be destroyed by such an attack, so rather than waiting for incoming missiles to destroy their nuclear arsenal, they might decide to fire off their missiles before that happens. (And, of course, that might also appear to the US as a "bolt out of the blue" if there were no obvious signals given by the US that could be interpreted as imminent preparations for an attack.)

An even more likely scenario, in the case of North Korea, is that a US President or his military advisors come to believe that a nuclear attack by North Korea is imminent. Rather than waiting for North Korean missiles to rain down on Washington, D.C., the United States decides to launch *its* missiles to try to destroy North Korea's nuclear arsenal before it can be launched towards the United States.

That latter scenario, of course, could be the precursor to the former, or vice versa. The point is that nuclear arsenals aimed at each other are inherently dangerous and unstable. Flying time for an ICBM from North Korea to the United States is only 33 minutes, according to Jacobsen's sources. That allows very little time for making any decisions before it's too late to respond. And there are numerous opportunities for mistakes or misunderstandings to get in the way.

Close calls

There are many possible scenarios that end up with doomsday because of people making assumptions that seem rational at the time and then *deciding* to launch nuclear weapons. But there are far more likely scenarios in which doomsday happens *by mistake.*

There have been concerns for the past three years, for example, that Russia might decide to use nuclear weapons in Ukraine. This possibility cannot be discounted.

However, the real danger is that the war in Ukraine makes the unintended launch of nuclear weapons far more likely, through misunderstanding, miscommunication, computer error, or simple human error.

These kinds of errors have happened many times before and they can happen again at any time. The chances increase enormously when there has been a breakdown of communication, a major loss of trust, increased tensions, and/or open hostilities between nuclear-armed states.

The 2014 Chatham House report, *Too Close for Comfort: Cases of Near Nuclear Use and Options for Policy,*[3] examined 13 incidents between 1962 and 2002 when the world came perilously close to a nuclear war. The most famous of these was the Cuban Missile Crisis of 1962, which brought the world to the brink of nuclear war in a very public way.

But there have been several other times that human civilization almost ended in a nuclear conflagration. Each case illustrates how simple human errors can be compounded by multiple failings into a dangerous scenario that can quickly spiral out of control. With missiles on hair-trigger alert, and automatic systems of "mutually assured destruction," there is no room for error.

For example, in November 1983, a large NATO exercise called "Able Archer" took place in central Europe. It involved a simulated NATO attack on the Soviet Union with nuclear as well as conventional forces.

This was during a period of heightened tensions between the Soviets and the West: A Korean Airlines flight with many US-Americans on board had been shot down after flying directly into Soviet territory. The first nuclear cruise missiles had arrived at Greenham Common in England. The Soviets were especially nervous about a possible "first strike" by NATO against the Soviet Union.[4]

The Soviets were looking for specific warning signs – and they found some. Soviet forces were immediately raised to high alert, and the Chief of Soviet General Staff was scurried to a wartime command bunker ready to issue instructions. In the end, a Soviet double-agent in London warned NATO commanders to tone down the exercise before it led to a nuclear war.[5]

Another example: In January 1995, a research rocket was launched in Norway. The Norwegians had officially informed the Russian government about the launch, but the message had not been passed on to the appropriate people by the time the launch took place.[6]

Nuclear weapons are not just very large conventional weapons. They produce effects that no other type of weapon has ever produced, including temperatures of tens of millions of degrees Celsius that can vaporize human beings and shock waves that can flatten skyscrapers.

Just one detonation in a large city today, by accident or on purpose, would kill millions. The immediate casualties would overwhelm the response capacity of the entire global humanitarian system and potentially overfill every burn bed in every hospital on the planet. Women, girls and fetuses would suffer the most from ionizing radiation. Food and water would remain toxic for millions of survivors.

The smallest radioactive particles rise up into the upper atmosphere and are dispersed across the entire globe. Even these tiny radioactive particles can be fatal if they enter the food chain and are ingested by humans.

The effects of relatively small doses of radiation are still disputed. However, medical professionals have suggested that as many as 2.4 million people worldwide will have died from leukemia and other cancers as a direct result of radiation from those nuclear tests.[7]

This means that if nuclear weapons were ever used again in war, they could do more than cause cruel and unnecessary suffering to those immediately affected by high doses of radioactivity near to, and downwind of, the explosions. They could also cause large amounts of radioactive materials to enter the earth's upper atmosphere and cause birth defects, leukemias, and other cancers to people hundreds and even thousands of miles away.

Nuclear winter and nuclear famine

Nuclear explosions produce fires and intense heat, with dust and soot rising into the upper atmosphere. Most nuclear tests in the 1950s and 60s took place on Pacific islands, barren (but not unpopulated!) atolls, or in the deserts of the western US, central Australia or the steppes of Kazakhstan. Without forests or cities as fuel, these explosions didn't cause major fires, and therefore the soot content was less apparent.

But if a nuclear explosion takes place over dense forest or a densely populated city, fires could be expected to burn out of control for many days over a large area. This happened with nuclear bombs in Hiroshima and Nagasaki, and with conventional explosives that caused firestorms in Hamburg, Dresden, Tokyo, and other cities during WWII.

During the 1980s, concern arose that an all-out nuclear war between the Soviet Union and the West could push so much soot into the atmosphere that it would block sunlight from reaching the earth. Such a "nuclear winter" would lower global temperatures precipitously, causing widespread famine, disease, and death of large numbers of people not already killed by the nuclear weapons themselves or from the after-effects of radiation.

Using the same modeling techniques, scientists a few decades later tried to estimate the climatic effects of just 100 Hiroshima-sized bombs, for example in a regional war between India and Pakistan. Given the population densities in those two countries and the vulnerability of crops to radiation damage, it was concluded that even a "limited" nuclear war in that region would have devastating consequences for all the countries across the whole Northern Hemisphere. This study was updated in 2022, taking into account the larger nuclear arsenals in both countries and larger size of warheads. That study concluded that as many as two billion people could starve to death within two years of a nuclear exchange between India and Pakistan today.[8]

See footnotes[7,8]

On Russian radar screens, it looked like an incoming nuclear missile was aimed at the Kola Peninsula, where Russia's nuclear submarines are based. The radar operators immediately informed the commander of Russian Radar Forces, who immediately informed President Yeltsin. Yeltsin was handed the nuclear "briefcase" and was on the phone with another general to decide the response when it was calculated that the rocket would land outside Russian airspace and therefore did not pose a threat. And so, we are still here.

Table 1.1 List of "close calls" that almost led to nuclear exchange[9]

Date	Incident	Countries involved	Cause
October 1962	Operation Anadyr	Soviet Union	Miscommunication
October 27, 1962	British nuclear forces during the Cuban missile crisis	United Kingdom	Conflict escalation
October 27, 1962	Black Saturday	United States	Conflict Escalation and miscommunication
November 22, 1962	Penkovksy false warning	Soviet Union	Espionage
October 1973	1973 Arab-Israeli War	Israel	Conflict escalation
November 9, 1979	NORAD: exercise tape mistaken for reality	United States	Exercise scenario tape causes nuclear alert
June 3, 1980	NORAD: Faulty computer chip	United States	Faulty computer chip
September 25, 1983	Serpukhov-15	Soviet Union	Technical error
November 7-11, 1983	Able Archer – 83	Soviet Union, United States	Misperception of military training exercise
August 18-21, 1991	Failed coup	Soviet Union	Loss of command-and-control structure
January 25, 1995	Black Brant scare	Russia	Mistaken identity of research rocket launch
May-June 1999	Kargil crisis	India, Pakistan	Conflict escalation
December 2001-2002	Kashmir standoff	India, Pakistan	Conflict escalation

Accidents and near-detonations

Thankfully, in over 70 years of handling nuclear weapons, there has never been an accidental detonation of a nuclear weapon. But the number of times that accidents *nearly* caused a detonation is alarmingly high.

The most serious accidents involving nuclear weapons took place in the 1950s and '60s, when US bombers were routinely flying around the world with nuclear weapons on board.

In 1961, a B-52 bomber on routine patrol had a leaky fuel tank, caught fire, and broke up in mid-air.[10] Two 4-megaton bombs were on board and landed outside Goldsboro, North Carolina. One of the bombs was recovered, and it was discovered that five out of six arming mechanisms had been activated, but the sixth, a cheap little low-voltage switch, prevented it from exploding and creating "a very large Bay of North Carolina."[11]

The other bomb plunged into muddy ground at 700 mph and broke up without detonating. More than 50 years later, it's still there, 180 feet underneath a cordoned-off field, because it would be too dangerous to try to remove it.[12]

In 1966, another B-52 collided in mid-air with a fuel tanker over Palomares, Spain. Four hydrogen bombs were released on that occasion. One fell into the sea and was later recovered, one landed intact with no explosion, and two exploded but only with the outer conventional explosives. Fortunately, though some radioactive materials were released, a full nuclear explosion did not take place.

In 1968, a B-52 crashed in Thule, Greenland, after some foam cushions caught fire in the navigator's compartment. Four hydrogen bombs were released, but again, the final arming mechanisms prevented them from detonating. Nevertheless, large amounts of radiation were released, requiring a major clean-up operation. Parts of at least one of the bombs were never recovered.[13]

Eric Schlosser, in his 2014 book *Command and Control*, recounted some chilling moments when some of the largest and most powerful ICBMs ever produced suffered multiple simultaneous malfunctions and came dangerously close to exploding. Some were carrying multiple nuclear warheads, each a thousand times more powerful than the Hiroshima bomb.

The book details the 1980 "Damascus Incident:" A worker accidentally brought the wrong socket wrench with him into a missile silo. The 8-pound socket fell off, dropped 80 feet, and pierced the skin of the missile, causing a fuel leak that led to an explosion. One worker was killed, 21 were injured, and the entire complex was destroyed. The 9-megaton warhead was found nearby the next morning in a ditch. Its safety features held, and it did not detonate.[14]

Table 1.2 Nuclear weapons lost at sea[15]

Date	**Event**	**Warheads Lost**
July 28, 1957	C-124 Globemaster II cargo plane jettisoned two nuclear weapons off coast of New Jersey	2
December 5, 1965	A-4E Skyhawk carrying B-43 thermonuclear bomb sank into ocean near Ryukyu Islands	1
January 21, 1968	B-52 crashed and two nuclear bombs fell to ocean floor, one still lost	1
April 11, 1968	Soviet K-129 submarine with three ballistic nuclear missiles and two nuclear torpedoes sank	5
May 21, 1968	USS Scorpion, carrying one nuclear reactor and two nuclear-tipped torpedoes, sank in Atlantic Ocean	2
April 12, 1970	Soviet K-8 submarine potentially carrying 4 tactical atomic torpedoes sank	4 or more
October 6, 1986	Soviet K-129 submarine carrying 2 nuclear torpedoes and 15 nuclear missiles with two warheads each sank north of Bermuda	32
April 7, 1989	Soviet K-278 submarine carrying two torpedoes with nuclear warheads sank off northern coast of Norway: it was successfully hermetically sealed by Russia in 1996 but this seal was expected to degrade by 2025	2

Warheads lost underwater

As many as 50 nuclear weapons currently lie at the bottom of the sea.[16] They have rolled off ships, sunk with submarines, and been jettisoned from airplanes. For example, in 1959, a US Navy aircraft dropped a nuclear depth charge[17] by mistake off Puget Sound, Washington. The bomb sank and was never recovered.

In 1968, the nuclear-powered USS Scorpion sank in the mid-Atlantic with nuclear-tipped torpedoes on board. It's still down there.

In 1986, the Soviet submarine K-219 sank in the mid-Atlantic following an explosion in one of the missile tubes, probably caused by a leaky seal that let salt water mix with the missile fuel, creating an explosive chemical reaction. The K-219 apparently had 15 nuclear missiles on board, each one containing either two or three individual 200 Kiloton (Kt) warheads. All were lost at sea.[18]

In 2000, a Russian nuclear-powered submarine, *The Kursk*, suffered an explosion on exercise off Norway, probably due to leaking torpedo propellant. The ensuing fire caused seven other (non-nuclear) torpedoes to detonate in a massive explosion detected as far away as Alaska and measuring 4.2 on the Richter scale. Russia claimed at the time that no nuclear weapons were on board, but this has since been disputed.[19] The wreckage of the *Kursk* was eventually recovered after an enormous salvage operation. None of the men on board survived.

The human factor

Nuclear weapons are made by human beings and they are managed by human beings. They break down, they have faulty parts, they malfunction, and they get lost. And the people who look after them make mistakes.

Personnel fall asleep on the job, they drink on the job, they take drugs on the job, they forget how to do their tasks and they cheat on tests.[20] In 2003, half of the Air Force units responsible for nuclear weapons in the US failed their safety inspections despite being given a three-day warning that the inspectors were coming.[21]

In 2007, 6 US nuclear weapons went "missing" for several hours because they were loaded onto the wrong plane and sent to the wrong air base in the wrong state.[22] In 2013, 17 officers with the authority to launch nuclear weapons were stripped of their duties because of a "pattern of weapons safety rule violations, possible code compromises and other failings over an extended period."[23] In 2016, 14 airmen responsible for guarding America's ICBM nuclear missiles were disciplined for drug offenses.[24] And in 2023, six officers were fired from Minot Air Force Base after a "failed nuclear safety inspection."[25]

What is the actual level of risk?

Risk is normally defined in terms of the *probability* of something happening times the *consequences* of it happening. If the probability is very, very low, but the consequences are catastrophically high, the overall risk would be considered very high. As long as the probability is greater than zero, the risk is that something potentially catastrophic is likely to happen sooner or later.

This is the case with nuclear weapons. No matter what precautions are taken and no matter how many failsafe systems are in place to prevent a catastrophe, no government can claim that the probability of something going wrong is zero.

There is a parallel with civil nuclear power. In 1975, the US Nuclear Regulatory Commission produced a detailed study of the probability of a major accident at one of the 100 US civil nuclear power stations. They calculated the stress factors of different materials used, the likelihood of different parts malfunctioning, the redundancy built into the system to ensure that if one safety component failed another would kick in, and so on.

The report concluded that the probability of a major nuclear generator accident occurring in the United States in any given year, with 100 nuclear power stations operating at once, was one in five billion.[26] Four years later, the worst nuclear accident in US history happened at the Three Mile Island nuclear plant.[27]

The chance of an accidental nuclear weapon detonation in any given year may likewise be claimed to be one in five billion or some other wildly small number. But it is not zero.

Is doomsday inevitable in the long run?

As long as nuclear weapons exist, the possibility of their use remains, and with it the possibility that these weapons will destroy human civilization as we know it. But even if these weapons are abolished, isn't it likely that sooner or later someone will rebuild them and we will end up with the same doomsday scenario? "You can't put the genie back in the bottle," as some would say, implying that nuclear weapons *cannot* be eliminated and neither can the ultimate threat of a nuclear doomsday.

It is clearly true that the *possibility* of nuclear doomsday can never be completely eliminated, no matter what steps we take to reduce the likelihood. The ability to cause massive explosions is built into the physics of the universe we live in. That was Einstein's great discovery: every atom of matter contains an enormous amount of energy, and under certain conditions, that energy can create an explosion.

The *potential* to use the energy stored in the very heaviest of atoms, like uranium and plutonium, will always be there. And the knowledge of how to do that will probably always be there. But does that mean that countries will inevitably build arsenals of nuclear weapons and that sooner or later they will be used?

The case of poison gas

The poison gas that was used in World War I is also a product of the chemical properties of our universe. That fact can never be undone, nor can the knowledge of how to use that fact to produce deadly canisters of poison gas.

And yet poison gas was *not* used in WWII, even though both sides had vast stockpiles of it. All chemical weapons have now been banned by international treaty. Although they were allegedly being used as recently as 2018 in Syria, those weapons have now largely been removed from the world's arsenals under the terms of the CWC.

Numerous countries, including the US, Russia and most of Europe once maintained stockpiles of chemical weapons and continued to develop new ones right up to the time of the Convention, but they have since destroyed those stockpiles and ceased to develop chemical weapons (as far as we know).

The truth is that even if something has been invented and cannot be uninvented, that does not mean we have to live with it. Even in the nuclear weapons field, many different types of weapons and delivery systems have been tried and even deployed in the field before being withdrawn as unworkable, too dangerous, outmoded or just plain crazy.

Ward Wilson, in his book *Five Myths about Nuclear Weapons*, describes all sorts of technologies that have become obsolete and long-since abandoned. Why should nuclear weapons not share the same fate as these?

Most countries do not have nuclear weapons

Out of 193 member states of the United Nations at present, only nine are known to have nuclear weapons.[28] That means 184 countries do not. Thirty-five of those countries are in NATO or other nuclear "umbrella" relationships with the US, but still they do not have nuclear weapons of their own, even though, according to the International Atomic Energy Agency (IAEA), they have the capacity to build them.

Eleven countries have started nuclear weapons programs and then abandoned them over the last several decades. South Africa, for example, built several nuclear weapons before dismantling them.

Thirty-one countries have civil nuclear power stations from which they could, if they wished, obtain weapons-grade plutonium. Another 46 countries have uranium deposits from which they could, theoretically, obtain weapons-grade uranium.[29]

So why have so few countries chosen to build and possess nuclear weapons? One reason is the expense. Nuclear weapons are extremely expensive to build and maintain. The US is currently investing trillions of dollars to "modernize" (expand) its nuclear weapons arsenal.

Not many countries have that kind of money to spend on nuclear weapons, and those that do have so far chosen to spend it on other priorities. Some historians have argued that it was the cost of keeping up with the US in the nuclear arms race that "broke" the Soviet bank account and caused the collapse of the Soviet Union.[2]

There are many other reasons why the vast majority of countries have chosen not to develop their own nuclear weapons capacity, including legal, moral, practical, utilitarian and security reasons.

Most of all, there is a large and growing consensus throughout the world that nuclear weapons simply make the world less safe.

Verifying disarmament

Many wonder, "What if we agree to get rid of our nuclear weapons, and somebody cheats?" Fortunately, it's much easier to ensure compliance than it is with chemical weapons or landmines.

Because nuclear explosions are so massive, they are very hard to hide. While it is conceivable to produce nuclear weapons without ever testing one,[30] most countries that would want to produce a nuclear weapon would want to test it out, not only to see if it works but also to show the world that they have one.

There is no place left on earth, under the earth, or even under the sea, where a nuclear explosion is not immediately detectable by infrared satellite imaging and/or by seismic equipment used for detecting earthquakes. So it is literally impossible for a country to secretly test a nuclear weapon.

Nuclear weapons also require a delivery system, a long-range bomber or a missile of some kind. While there may be some rather crude delivery systems available for detonating a nuclear device *in situ*, in most cases delivering a nuclear weapon requires very sophisticated technology that most countries do not have. Once again, it's very hard to test medium or long-range missiles or aircraft in the modern world without detection.

By far the biggest challenge of building a nuclear weapon is not the design, which can be obtained from the internet, but obtaining the raw (fissile) materials for making the bomb: either highly-enriched uranium or plutonium. The enrichment of uranium is a very expensive and complicated process that requires high precision equipment.

Plutonium can be created from uranium (it does not exist naturally) in certain designs of nuclear power plants. But those power plants are closely monitored by the IAEA, so it is extremely difficult to stockpile plutonium undetected.

The entire world knows how close Iran is to being able to build a nuclear weapon. That's a good example of how difficult it is for any country to produce nuclear weapons without being noticed. Of course, any country can choose to go ahead anyway, but there may be global consequences for doing so.

In the 1980s, following the INF Treaty,[31] which abolished all intermediate range nuclear weapons in Europe, Russian inspectors were invited onto US bases to verify withdrawal and dismantling of nuclear weapons systems. And US inspectors were invited onto Soviet bases to verify the same thing on the other side.

In the case of the START Treaty, which required destruction of a certain number of existing long-range nuclear bombers on both sides, the US and Russia both chopped up planes into pieces and left them spread out on the ground so that satellite reconnaissance from the other side could verify that they had been destroyed.

So while it is not possible to 'uninvent' anything, it is certainly possible to get rid of things we no longer want or need, including obsolete weapons systems. All that is needed is the political will, and then ways can be found to verify and monitor compliance.

As the world declares nuclear weapons unacceptable under any circumstances, it establishes a global norm. Once they have been eliminated, it is unlikely that any country will choose to spend its resources re-endangering itself.

The complete elimination of nuclear weapons is the only sure guarantee that these weapons will not be used sooner or later. And yet most people seem convinced that abolition is either unnecessary or impossible. What is going on?

2 Why abolition?

Why talk about "abolition" rather than "arms control" or "non-proliferation?" Why not focus on realistic, doable steps that can be taken to reduce the likelihood of nuclear annihilation?

Nuclear weapons pose an existential threat to humanity just as assuredly as climate change does. And while it may be decades before the effects of climate change make life impossible for millions or even billions of people, an exchange of nuclear weapons could take place at any moment, and civilization as we know it could end within a matter of minutes.

Ever since the dawn of the nuclear age, people have been trying to find ways to reduce the threat posed by nuclear weapons – without actually eliminating them. Some of these efforts have been more successful than others.

It is encouraging, for instance, to know that the total numbers of nuclear weapons in the world has gone down significantly from a peak of more than 60,000 warheads in the 1980s to around 12,000 today. But like many of the other steps that have been taken to reduce the nuclear danger, those numbers can be misleading.

The numbers game

Most people looking at the chart below could be forgiven for thinking that the problem of nuclear weapons was solved almost 40 years ago, when the number of nuclear weapons started to decline. They may also assume that we just need a little more patience to see those numbers continue to go down until they reach zero.

Unfortunately, the raw numbers in this chart are grossly misleading. The reality is that nuclear arsenals have been carefully weeded and pared down to a level that the nuclear-armed countries are comfortable with *and want to maintain more or less indefinitely.* Old, rusty, leaky, less reliable and less "usable" nuclear weapons have been taken out of the arsenals, while newer, more sophisticated, more "usable" ones remain.

Figure 2.1 Global stockpiles of nuclear weapons[1]

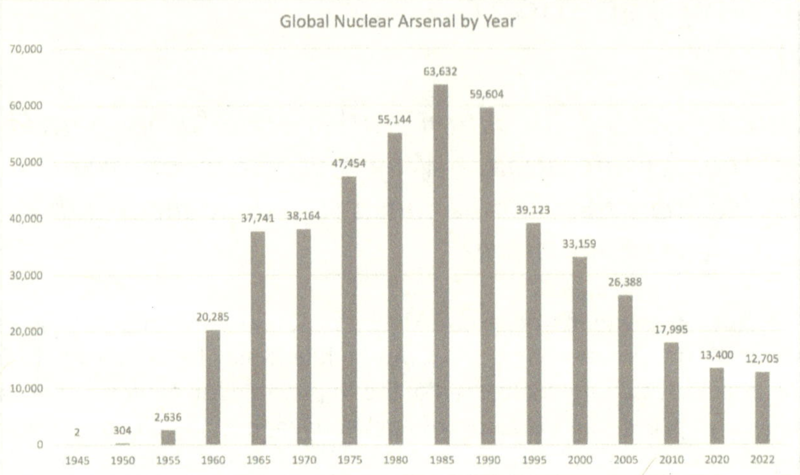

Eliminating the smallest weapons

The vast majority of nuclear weapons that have been taken out of service since the 1980s are the smaller, so-called "battlefield" weapons.

The WE-177A, a nuclear depth charge, was designed to be dropped by Sea King helicopters flying over Soviet nuclear submarines. Former Royal Navy Commander Rob Green, who was responsible for a Sea King helicopter crew, described it as a "suicide mission," since the nuclear explosion below the sea would assuredly destroy the helicopter above it before the crew could get out of range.[1]

Even worse, the W54 warhead, or Special Atomic Demolition Munition (SADM), was designed to be strapped on the back of a soldier and carried into battle, where it could be set up at the desired location and detonated (hopefully after the soldier ran far, far away).

At 6 Kilotons, these portable little bombs could explode with nearly half the destructive power of the Hiroshima bomb. Less powerful versions were also available, with some deployed on jeeps or on portable gun tripods. The W48, a 155mm nuclear-tipped artillery shell, was designed to be fired by NATO troops in the heat of battle.

As many as 20,000 of these and other battlefield nuclear weapons were withdrawn by the US alone in the late '80s and early '90s. We can celebrate that these weapons were withdrawn from service. However, they were withdrawn primarily because they were too dangerous to have lying around, and they were no longer seen as useful or appropriate by the military themselves.

The real question is how they could ever have been considered useful or appropriate in the first place.

Moving away from the biggest weapons

Most of the *biggest* nuclear weapons ever built have also been removed from arsenals, not because the military doesn't like "big," but because these weapons were simply too unwieldy – and dangerous – to be usefully deployed. The goal nowadays is to have the fastest and most accurate weapons possible. And that means delivering them to their target on top of a missile, not dropping them from an airplane that may require refueling in mid-air to reach its destination halfway around the world, and may risk being shot down on the way to its target.

And even the gigantic missiles of the 1950s, like the Titan ICBMs, with their massive 9 Megaton warheads (9,000 Kilotons, or equivalent to 9 million tons of TNT), were considered too slow as other weapon advances were speeding up. Replacing these was not a "sacrifice" in terms of nuclear capacity, since the newer, smaller Minuteman missiles were far more accurate, far more reliable, and far more sophisticated.

The quality of today's nuclear weapons

There is a measurement available to compare older nuclear weapons with newer ones. It's called the "circular error probable," or CEP. This describes how accurately a missile is likely to reach its target (how near it will land to the center of the circle it's aiming at), and therefore how *many* missiles are needed to destroy a particular target.

It turns out that destroying a hardened nuclear missile silo requires *either* a lot of very big missiles that don't necessarily land all that near the center of the silo *or* a smaller but much more accurate missile that strikes right in the middle of the target.[2]

The CEP of the Trident I submarine-launched nuclear missile, for example, was 380 meters, while the CEP of the newer Trident II missile is only 90 meters. The CEP of the Minuteman II ICBM was 480 meters, while the CEP of newer Minuteman III is 120 meters.[3] These differences in CEP allowed the US to deploy far fewer missiles and still get the same – or even better – "bang for the buck" in terms of destructive effect.

Other technological advances compensate for reduced numbers of nuclear weapons by increasing the "kill capability" of each missile. A new "super-fuze," for example, has enabled US nuclear weapons to explode at just the right height above a hardened silo to achieve maximum effect.[4] These new super-fuzes have already been retrofitted to existing weapon systems, but more developments are on the way, each one giving the US a key technological advantage with fewer numbers of nuclear weapons.

Focusing on reductions of total nuclear warheads has been the name of the game in arms control since the 1980s, but for all the reasons just given, it is not enough. Getting from "smaller" nuclear arsenals to "zero" nuclear weapons is impossible as long as the belief remains that we need these weapons for "deterrence."

The minimum number needed for "deterrence"[5]

The idea that nuclear weapons are purely a "deterrent" and therefore will never be used is so ingrained in popular thinking that it provides the rationale for *reducing* the number of nuclear weapons while at the same time providing the rationale for *never reducing that number to zero* (see Chapter 1).

A great deal of time and energy has been spent over many decades on the question of what constitutes the minimum number of nuclear weapons needed to effectively deter one's adversaries.

In 1988, then-Prime Minister of the UK Margaret Thatcher famously announced that the "minimum credible deterrent" needed to keep Britain safe from nuclear attack was 512 nuclear weapons deployed at sea and ready to launch at a moment's notice. In 1995, she revised that number down to 300, and in 1998, her successor reduced it still further to 200. In 2006, it was reduced to 160 and in 2015 it was reduced to 120.[6]

The United States currently has 1,550 warheads deployed and ready to launch, and according to sources at the Department of Defense, that is already the bare minimum necessary to deter Russia. But at the height of the Cold War, when the whole concept of nuclear deterrence was being developed, the US had, as we've seen, tens of thousands more warheads in its arsenal than it has today. At that time, it was clearly believed that a lot more than 1,550 warheads were needed to deter the Soviet Union.

The truth is that there is no such thing as a "minimum deterrent." A government possessing nuclear weapons *hopes* that the nuclear weapons they have will act as a deterrent. But deterrence is actually a psychological concept, not a military one. And, once again, there is no evidence at all that nuclear deterrence "works" or has ever worked.[7]

When we refer to nuclear weapons as a deterrent, or when we seek to reduce the number to the minimum "needed for deterrence," we merely reinforce the idea that deterrence is real. Absurdly, we think that it's okay to reduce the number of nuclear weapons as long as we retain some imaginary number of them for deterrence purposes.

Members of Congress continue to rely on the "minimum deterrence" argument as a rationale for reducing nuclear stockpiles – but not eliminating them. "The sole purpose of nuclear weapons [is] to deter their use by others," said Rep. Adam Smith in 2021.[8]

Non-proliferation

Non-proliferation means stopping the further growth of nuclear arsenals, but says nothing about reducing or eliminating existing arsenals. "Horizontal" proliferation refers to the spread of weapons to more countries, and is what most people mean when they use the word. But there is also "vertical" proliferation, meaning further growth of nuclear arsenals in the countries that already have them.

The Nuclear Non-Proliferation Treaty (NPT) was signed in 1968, supposedly to curtail any further spread of nuclear weapons beyond the five countries that had them at the time. Now there are nine. That might be considered a success, since there are "only" four more, or an abject failure, because there are "already" four more.

But this treaty referred only to *horizontal* proliferation, and as we have seen, the nuclear-armed states just kept on increasing their nuclear arsenals without limit for another couple of decades after that.

The NPT was actually adopted as a "grand bargain" between the countries that did not at that time have nuclear weapons and promised never to acquire them and the countries that at that time *did* have nuclear weapons and promised to get rid of theirs "in good faith" and "at an early date." There would have been no treaty without this *quid pro quo* designed to ensure that *no* countries would end up possessing nuclear weapons (see box).

The US and the other nuclear-armed countries have conveniently forgotten about this part of the deal and pretend that they can keep the weapons they already have, continue to "modernize" them, and even expand their arsenals, as long as *other* countries do not acquire them. This makes non-proliferation a dirty word in many parts of the world, where it is associated with bad faith and the determination of a few powerful countries to maintain their domination over everyone else.

The **Nuclear Non-Proliferation Treaty (NPT)** refers, in various places, to the different responsibilities of "nuclear-weapon states" and "non-nuclear-weapon states." This has allowed the countries *with* nuclear weapons to claim that they are the nuclear-weapon states, and all others are non-nuclear-weapon states, as if this is a permanent state of affairs and gives the nuclear-weapon states that status *for all time*.

There is nothing in the NPT, however, that says anything of the kind. Indeed, it is clear from the wording in the Preamble to the treaty that the goal of the NPT is "to facilitate the cessation of the manufacture of nuclear weapons, the liquidation of all their existing stockpiles, and the elimination from national arsenals of nuclear weapons and the means of their delivery pursuant to a Treaty on general and complete disarmament under strict and effective international control..."

The wording of Article VI of the NPT also clearly states that "each of the Parties to the Treaty undertakes to pursue negotiations *in good faith* on effective measures relating to cessation of the nuclear arms race *at an early date* and *to nuclear disarmament*, and on a treaty on general and complete disarmament under strict and effective international control." (emphasis added)

In order to get the NPT extended indefinitely after the initial 25-year term expired in 1995, the US and the other four "official" nuclear-armed states (Russia, China, UK and France) gave the rest of the world their "unequivocal undertaking" that they would fulfil their promise in Article VI to negotiate the elimination of their nuclear weapons.

Since then, there have been no such negotiations and three of the last four 5-year review conferences have ended with no agreed outcomes. The failure of the nuclear-armed countries to fulfil their solemn NPT obligation was a major factor in why so many countries decided to support the TPNW.

The NPT nevertheless remains the favorite nuclear weapons treaty of the United States and the other four "official" nuclear-armed states, precisely because of its ambiguity.

Nuclear testing

On June 10, 1963, President Kennedy announced to the world that the US would unilaterally stop testing nuclear weapons in the atmosphere. He invited the Soviets to do the same, and by October, the

US, UK and Soviet Union had signed the Partial Test Ban Treaty banning nuclear tests in the atmosphere. It was Kennedy's publicly stated hope that the partial test ban would so restrict further development of nuclear weapons that the US and the Soviets would soon be willing to negotiate a complete ban on these weapons.[9]

Unfortunately, after JFK's assassination and Khrushchev's fall from power, what happened instead was that testing just went, quite literally, underground. Underground nuclear testing allowed nuclear arsenals in both the US and the Soviet Union to continue growing at an fast clip. It was not the slightest impediment to continued development and "improvements" in nuclear weapon design.

Three decades later, it was Mikhail Gorbachev of the Soviet Union who announced a unilateral halt to *underground* nuclear testing. The US followed suit and by 1996, both countries had signed the Comprehensive Test Ban Treaty (CTBT), banning all explosive testing of nuclear weapons, whether above or below ground.

Although almost all countries of the world have by now signed the CTBT, the US and seven other countries have still not ratified it, and in 2024 Russia rescinded its ratification. Thus it cannot enter into force as a treaty.[10] Nevertheless, underground nuclear testing has stopped for all existing nuclear-armed countries except North Korea.

But, once again, that hasn't slowed development. The nuclear-armed states have continued to refine existing nuclear weapons and to develop new capabilities for them.[11]

The United States has engaged in sub-critical testing (just shy of actual explosion) ever since signing the CTBT, and can now combine those tests with the use of advanced supercomputers to simulate how a bomb would behave. The US can thus obtain all the data they need to continue monitoring existing nuclear weapons and developing new ones without violating the terms of the CTBT.[12]

China and Russia have also conducted sub-critical tests and are believed to be capable of computer simulations.[13] The UK has access to US data and has used US equipment to conduct its own sub-critical tests.[14] And France is now working with the UK to share data on sub-critical tests. So the nuclear weapon developments continue, even in the absence of underground testing.

Arms limitation treaties, complete with loopholes

The first Strategic Arms Limitation Treaty (SALT I), signed in 1972, limited the number of nuclear weapon launchers (ICBM missiles, submarines and planes) on both sides, but there was a loophole: it did not address the number of warheads on each launcher.

Multiple Independently-Targeted Re-entry Vehicles (MIRV) allowed several nuclear warheads to be launched from a single missile, each one going to a different target. So both sides continued their relentless expansion, simply adding multiple warheads onto their existing missiles.[15]

The SALT II Treaty, signed in 1979, tried to limit MIRV warheads as well as delivery vehicles, but there were numerous loopholes in that agreement too, and it was never ratified by the US Senate. So the arms race continued right up to the dissolution of the Soviet Union in 1991. US warhead numbers remained static during the SALT II period, but that disguised enormous technical advances that were taking place at that time (as discussed above).[16]

The next treaty to limit nuclear arsenals, START I, was signed in 1991, and it is credited with eliminating up to 80% of the world's entire nuclear arsenal by the time it expired in 2009.[17] This claim, however, is misleading, because a large number of those warheads were eliminated through *unilateral* Presidential Nuclear Initiatives (PNIs) undertaken by Presidents George Bush Sr., Mikhail Gorbachev, and Boris Yeltsin in 1991-1992.[18]

But once again, many of the warheads that were eliminated on both sides were ones that were outdated and/or being replaced anyway. For example, START I eliminated the entire US Minuteman II ICBM force of 450 missiles and their associated launch facilities.[19] Installed back in 1967, they were developing various technical problems.[20] Eliminating these now outdated weapons was counted under the START I treaty as "disarming" 450 missiles, and yet the whole system was subsequently replaced with 450 *new* Minuteman III missiles and their associated launch facilities, which are still in place today.

Nuclear freeze

In the 1980s, it became popular to call for a "nuclear freeze." Up until then, the peace movements in the US and Europe were mainly calling on their governments to "ban the bomb" entirely. Freezing things as they were seemed like a more palatable message for politicians who for 30 years had shown no interest at all in actually banning the bomb.[21]

The Freeze, like the Partial Test Ban Treaty, was believed by many at the time to be a step that would start the ball rolling inevitably toward complete nuclear disarmament. If governments would only stop developing and building *new* nuclear weapons, they hoped, perhaps the arms race could then be put into reverse gear.

As palatable as the freeze message was, it still wasn't mild enough to get enacted into law by the US Congress.[22] The net effect of the Cold War ending and all the nuclear treaties being signed during that period was a freeze of sorts, but it was only a freeze in terms of raw numbers, not, as we have seen, in terms of stopping the unabated development of new and more advanced weapons.

Now, 40 years later, the idea of a nuclear freeze has returned, with calls to stop production of new nuclear weapons under development – without eliminating all of the existing nuclear weapons.[23] Calling for a freeze still seems more palatable to some than calling for the abolition of these weapons.[24] But is stopping construction of an entire new generation of nuclear weapons any more likely now than it was in the 1980s?

One problem with the freeze concept is that existing nuclear weapons are getting older and more dangerous to handle. The military will always argue that they need new nuclear weapons purely for "safety" reasons and that it is irresponsible to continue deploying weapons that are well past their supposed "expiration" date.[25] They use names like "Life Extension Program" and "Stockpile Stewardship" to justify their "modernization" (build-up) of the arsenal.

The other problem with a nuclear freeze is that by leaving all the current weapons intact, a freeze does not in any way challenge the logic of deterrence used to justify their continued existence, as discussed above. In fact, it's written into some of the bills currently in Congress that we don't need more or newer nuclear weapons because the ones we have would still provide "an assured retaliatory capability."[26]

Not all "steps" are steps in the right direction

Of course, every campaigner wants to support actions that are politically "doable" – that might actually be enacted into law. And every journey begins with a single step. We all know that. But that doesn't mean that every step is taking us where we're trying to go.

For example, many climate activists got sucked into the Beyond Coal campaign, which was about replacing coal-fired electricity plants with gas-fired ones. Sure, gas emits less carbon than coal. People *thought* that was a step forward that might lead to more climate-friendly changes. But gas is also a fossil fuel, and the world will never end its dependency on fossil fuels simply by replacing coal plants with gas.

Similarly, calls to reduce the nuclear arsenal to a minimum level "necessary for deterrence" will never reach the goal of eliminating these weapons altogether. There are numerous other policy initiatives that merely reinforce and validate the myth of nuclear deterrence, and the idea that we can somehow hold onto nuclear weapons forever.

These initiatives are all potentially worthwhile. They can potentially draw needed attention to the danger we are in. But they can also potentially give people a false sense that the problem has been solved – just as arms reductions at the end of the Cold War allowed so many of us to become complacent, just as the Doomsday Clock continued to tick away. And they can potentially diffuse the energy and resources needed for the more important goal of actually eliminating these weapons.

The rest of this book explains how and why the elimination of nuclear weapons is both possible and necessary. It lays out one possible scenario for that to happen. And every step in that scenario is based on the assumption that it will take pressure to achieve nuclear abolition.

3 The politics of pressure

Nuclear weapons pose an existential threat to the planet. Efforts to eliminate them have so far failed. So what will it take to abolish these weapons?

This chapter explains why:

1. The focal point for abolishing nuclear weapons must be the United States;
2. The corporations that develop, build and maintain nuclear weapons have so much power over US politicians and US policy on nuclear weapons;
3. It will therefore take an enormous amount of pressure *on the nuclear weapons corporations* to achieve abolition;
4. Divestment, boycotts, and stigmatization are some of the most effective tools for putting pressure on powerful corporations.

The scenario that follows in the rest of this book lays out one pathway for the abolition of nuclear weapons, based on the above assumptions and further assuming that:

1. The Treaty on the Prohibition of Nuclear Weapons (TPNW) provides countries around the world with a legal framework to divest, boycott and stigmatize these corporations (Chapters 4-12).
2. The TPNW also provides campaigners in the US with a powerful incentive to build campaigns focused on these corporations (Chapters 13-20).
3. The combination of external and internal pressures on the nuclear weapons corporations is what will ultimately push them, and through them, the US government, to abandon their addiction to nuclear weapons (Chapter 21).
4. Once the US agrees to sign the TPNW, the other nuclear-armed countries will also come around and nuclear weapons will be abolished (Chapters 22-26).

Why focus on the US?

The US invented nuclear weapons, is the only country to have used them in war, and has led the way on every nuclear weapon advancement since then. The US has direct and powerful influence over three of the other nuclear-armed countries (the UK, France and Israel). It also has influence, to a lesser extent, over the other five (India, Pakistan, China, Russia and North Korea). If, alternatively, one of the other nuclear-armed countries were to take the lead in eliminating its nuclear arsenal, there is less chance that the US would follow suit.

The reality is that no other country possessing nuclear weapons is likely to give them up *unless and until the United States does.* Russia, China and North Korea have nuclear arsenals primarily because they feel threatened by US nuclear weapons. Pakistan has nuclear weapons primarily because they feel threatened by India's nuclear weapons. And India has nuclear weapons primarily because the other big countries (US, Russia and China) have them.

France and the UK have nuclear weapons primarily because they feel threatened by Russia's nuclear weapons, although those cases are more complicated than that (see part IV). And that leaves Israel, which will never give up its nuclear weapons without intense pressure that only the United States can apply.

Furthermore, it is only the US that is so heavily dependent on private corporations to develop, produce and maintain its stockpile of nuclear weapons. It is therefore more vulnerable to the pressures described in this chapter than other nuclear-armed countries.

These corporations are also the driving force behind the US nuclear weapons agenda. But these corporations don't exist to make nuclear weapons. They exist to make a profit. And that means they will move on to something else if making nuclear weapons is no longer profitable for them.

So if these corporations are under sufficient pressure to move away from nuclear weapons, it is ***the corporations*** who will convince the US government to abandon their nuclear addiction. It's happened before, and it can happen again.

Why focus on the corporations?

Corruption is legal in the United States. Corporations spend a relatively small amount of money lobbying, supporting politicians' election campaigns, advertising, influencing the media, and funding think-tanks. They offer politicians "revolving door" jobs. Their lobbyists ease lawmakers' workloads by writing legislation themselves. In return, corporations get awarded government contracts worth billions of dollars.

In some cases, this can amount to a return on investment of over 100,000%.[1] That's not a typo. For example, in 2022, Bechtel invested $0.9 million lobbying Congress. They were awarded defense contracts that year worth almost $1.7 *billion* (see table below). That's not unusual.

Figure 3.1 The Congressional-Corporate Complex[2]

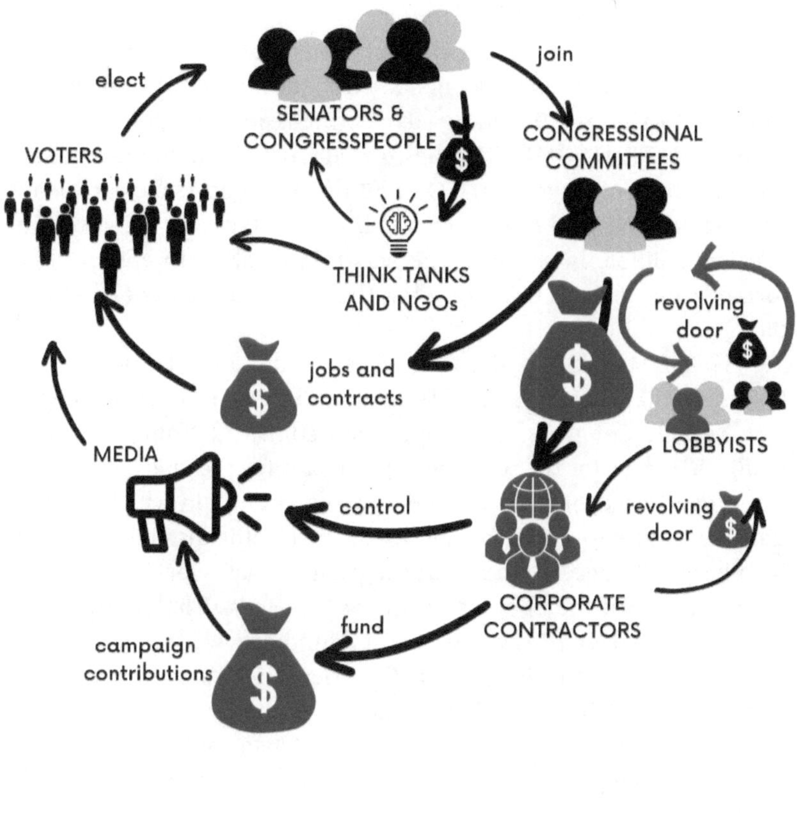

How they do it: Election financing

According to OpenSecrets, the top 10 companies in the "defense" industry gave over $50 million to candidates during the 2024 election cycle.

These campaign contributions included $4.5 million from Lockheed Martin, $3.4 million from Northrop Grumman, $2.8 million from RTX (Raytheon), $2.5 million from L3 Harris, $2.1 million from General Dynamics, $1.4 million from Leidos, and over $1 million from BAE Systems.[3] These are not just some of the top contractors for the US military. They are also some of the top US *nuclear weapons* contractors (see table below).

How they do it: Revolving door

Four-star General Lloyd Austin went from the Pentagon to the corporate world and back again. First, he served in several high-ranking positions, including as Commander of the US Central Command (CENTCOM). Then he retired from the military and served on the board of Raytheon/RTX, one of the biggest nuclear weapons contractors. Next, he served as US Secretary of Defense under President Biden. In that role, he was in a position to ensure that his former colleagues at RTX got what they wanted – and of course, they did.[4]

This is typical of the 3-way revolving door between jobs in Congress, the Departments of Defense and Energy, and the companies who receive Congressionally-approved contracts from the DOD and DOE. (DOE pays for the warheads. DOD pays for the delivery systems.)

OpenSecrets.org identified 672 cases in 2022 in which the top 20 defense contractors had former government officials, military officers, Members of Congress, and senior legislative staff working for them as lobbyists, board members, or senior executives.[5] That year, Congress gave the DOD over $851 billion in total funding.

A report by the Project on Government Oversight found that a quarter of the DOD officials that moved to the private sector in 2016 went to work for one of the top five US defense contractors (Lockheed Martin, Boeing, Raytheon/RTX, General Dynamics and Northrop Grumman).[6]

Table 3.2 Top Nuclear Weapons Industry lobbying costs and income from government contracts[7]

Nuclear Weapons Companies	Lobbying 2023	Nuke Related Income 2023 (in millions of dollars)
Airbus	3.07	951.20
Babcock International	-	883.90
BAE Systems	4.16	3306.70
Bechtel	0.90	1,682.60
Boeing	14.49	586.80
Fluor	3.72	unknown
General Dynamics	12.16	2,706.70
Honeywell International	9.31	6,184.40
Huntington Ingalls Industries	4.96	1282.60
Jacobs Solutions	0.87	357.70
L3Harris Technologies	3.02	82.40
Leidos	2.46	830.00
Leonardo	1.47	281.20
Lockheed Martin	14.06	2,894.00
Northrop Grumman	10.86	5,978.00
Peraton (portfolio of Veritas Capital)	3.07	42.30
Rolls Royce	0.94	unknown
RTX (Raytheon)	11.42	489.10
Safran	0.44	623.20
Textron	4.41	unknown
Thales	0.51	771.50

How they do it: Lobbying

A vast army of corporate lobbyists in Washington provides a lot more than free lunches for their Congressional targets. They provide an array of technical expertise and assistance in writing complex budget authorization bills. They provide technical briefings. They do the work that Members of Congress simply do not have the time to do themselves (in large part, because they are so busy raising money for their re-elections[8]). In 2024, defense contractors spent $150 million on lobbying expenses in Washington, DC, according to OpenSecrets.org.[9]

How they do it: Dark money

We can more or less track the corporate money spent on election funding, revolving doors, and lobbying. But it's harder to count so-called "dark money."

The former head of the Federal Election Commission recently estimated that more than $600 million was being funnelled to Members of Congress through unaccountable non-profit organizations with innocuous names like "Patriot Majority," "American Future Fund," "Americans for Prosperity" and "Crossroads GPS."[10]

All of this adds up to a situation that most US-Americans understand intuitively, reinforced by a 2014 Princeton study:[11] big corporations have much more influence over what becomes US policy than do ordinary citizens.

The corrupting influence of big corporations on the US Congress is much greater since the 2010 "Citizens United" Supreme Court decision. That ruling overturned meager attempts to control the influence of corporations over Congress, and gave corporations the legal right to unlimited spending on elections.[12]

How are the corporations vulnerable?

Some academic studies have suggested that divestment, boycotts and other attempts to put pressure on large corporations are futile and ineffective.[13]

For example, if for moral reasons one person sells their stock in a given company, someone else with fewer moral scruples can simply buy it, cancelling out any possible effect the first person might have. Similarly, boycotting goods or services matters little to a company if others are willing to continue buying from them.

But corporate profit does not come solely through the selling of goods and services. Corporations have to care about their public image, because that affects their corporate reputation ("reputational risk") and the bottom line value of their brand ("brand equity").[14]

They also have to care about who is buying and selling their stock, because if even a small number of investors lose confidence in the corporation ("investor anxiety"), it can cause a sudden drop in its overall value ("market capitalization").[15]

And they have to care about intangibles, like whether their activities carry any risk of being considered illegal or unacceptable at some point in the future ("legislative risk"), or whether they may be forced to abandon resources they are currently including on their balance sheet as valuable assets ("stranded assets").[16]

The people who run and invest in these companies are also human beings. They all have families, friends and colleagues, people they listen to and care about. They may be influenced by religious figures, academics, or media personalities.

Today these corporations maintain a presence on social media. That's one place they're especially vulnerable to public attitudes towards them, even when these do not directly translate into customers or sales.[17]

Divestment, boycotts and shaming are proven tools that have worked in various campaigns, including nuclear disarmament. Here's an example.

How do we know these pressures work?

The most dramatic political success we've had so far on the road to nuclear abolition was when President Ronald Reagan switched from being gung-ho about the most expansive nuclear weapons program of the Cold War to eliminating a whole class of nuclear weapons - and nearly eliminating all of them.[18]

What changed Reagan's mind? During his first term, from 1981-1984, there were extraordinarily massive protests, to no apparent effect. *The Day After* TV movie about nuclear apocalypse petrified the public, and it made Reagan himself "depressed," but he still didn't budge.

The Nuclear Freeze campaign almost got a resolution passed in Congress. It won 60% of referendum votes *and* a solid majority of House votes - but it failed to pass in the Senate. And the Freeze hadn't even asked for abolition - it was designed to be palatable to politicians, so it asked them only to stop paying for *new* nuclear weapons.

The Executive Director of the Nuclear Weapons Freeze Campaign at that time, Randy Kehler, who had worked so hard to try to get the Freeze enacted into law, was appalled by the corrupting power of the defense industry and their iron grip on Congress (or at least on the Senate), despite what citizens wanted. He went on to spend the next 14 years of his life working on campaign finance reform instead.[19]

The marches, the movie, the Freeze – each of these were important contributions (along with Gorbachev's personality, and other factors we may never know).

But by the time of Reagan's second term, 1985-1988, other tactics were coming to the fore: consumer boycotts, divestment campaigns, and Nuclear Free Zones that directly targeted the corporate makers of nuclear weapons.

Nuclear Free Zones

By 1985, there were already over 100 municipal Nuclear Free Zones across the country. Most were in the form of non-binding resolutions that simply declared nuclear weapons (and anything to do with nuclear weapons) to be unwanted in that locale.

But a significant subset of these NFZs directly targeted the nuclear weapons companies through legally binding ordinances and statutes. These *forbade* the companies from operating within their city limits or jurisdictions. They ordered city funds to be divested from these companies. They prohibited any further city contracts with these companies. That got the companies' attention.[20]

Divestment

Divestment in the 1980s was largely focused on companies doing business with apartheid South Africa. However, divestment also became a major tool in the anti-nuclear movement when these NFZ municipalities (and counties) started to add divestment to their portfolio of tools.

Oakland, Berkeley and other cities in California (and the County of Marin) committed to removing nuclear weapons companies from their investments, as did a small number of other towns and cities across the country.

Ironically, it was the cities and counties in California that continued to invest in these companies that ultimately got into trouble for it. Only a few years after Marin County divested from nuclear weapons, Orange County declared bankruptcy because of speculative investments that had gone wrong. California law was subsequently changed to prohibit local governments in California from engaging in many kinds of private investment, meaning that today, *no* cities or counties in California have investments in nuclear weapons corporations![21]

Boycotts

In 1986, there was a national consumer boycott of Morton salt. The **Morton Thiokol Corporation** was involved in nuclear weapons – and it also made the table salt that almost all Americans had in their kitchens. (Their motto: "When it rains, it pours.") Twelve months later, Morton claimed that the boycott was having no effect on their business and that they remained "proud to be part of the defense industry."[22] But soon after that, they disappeared from the Department of Defense list of nuclear weapons contractors.[23]

In 1987, there was a boycott of telecoms giant **AT&T.** ("Reach out and touch someone.") The chairman of the board himself went on a public relations offensive, claiming that AT&T played "but a small part" in the nuclear industry.[24] In 1992, AT&T cut its ties with the nuclear weapons business by pulling out of the management of Sandia Labs.[25]

Morton and AT&T caved to grassroots citizen pressure and got out of the nuclear weapons business forever. They still make salt and phone systems.

Ford Motor Company filed a lawsuit against Marin County, CA, for their divestment policy, claiming the company was being unfairly targeted. They lost. **IBM** and **Hewlett-Packard** were also launching lawsuits. **Dupont** was threatened with a boycott of their household paints.

All of these household-name corporations pulled out of the nuclear weapons business and never returned. They clearly *care* what the public thinks about them.

But the most successful boycott of them all was against **General Electric**. ("We bring good things to light.") GE was a big player in nuclear weapons – and also the producer of everyone's light bulbs. GE was the largest corporation in the US *and* the largest nuclear weapons contractor at that time.

Ronald Reagan had also previously been the public face of GE, so this one was personal.

GE lost millions of dollars from the national boycott. Stores were refusing to stock their products. GE offered them all kinds of special deals, but they stood firm. One chain store manager said they wouldn't stock GE products "even if they gave them to us for free."[26]

To this day, you can visit GE's website and read "*We do not manufacture, assemble, sell or service cluster bombs, land mines or nuclear weapons.*"

And while there is no direct evidence to link the pressures on these corporations to Reagan's turnaround on nuclear weapons, there is ample evidence that it was having an effect on him (see chapter 20).[27] Just as these corporations prioritize profit over making nuclear weapons, so too did Ronald Reagan prioritize keeping big corporations in business over his infatuation with nuclear weapons.[28]

What is beyond dispute is that a combination of political, social and economic *pressures* were brought to bear on the Reagan administration in the 1980s and that these contributed to the most wide-ranging curbs on the nuclear arms race that had taken place up to that point – or since.

The Treaty on the Prohibition of Nuclear Weapons

Today, the situation in the United States is not what it was in the 1980s, although there are certain similarities between Reagan's agenda and Trump's. One factor that makes the abolition of nuclear weapons *more* possible now than in the 1980s is the Treaty on the Prohibition of Nuclear Weapons (TPNW).

The TPNW bans everything to do with nuclear weapons in the countries that join it, including all "assistance, encouragement and inducement" in support of these weapons. That phrase, in other recent treaties, has been interpreted to also mean a prohibition on *financing* the prohibited weapons.[29]

Most of the nuclear weapons corporations that are controlling the nuclear agenda in the US also have branches, offices, projects, suppliers – and investors – in numerous other countries. This includes many of the countries that are already parties to the TPNW. That means these countries now have an opportunity not previously available to them for pressuring the nuclear weapons corporations.

If they choose to, they can enforce the prohibition on assistance, cutting into the supply chain of these corporations. They can enforce the prohibition on financing and seriously curtail the corporations' access to capital. And these countries can, above all, create both legislative and reputational *risks* for these corporations that directly affect their market value and balance sheets.

The new treaty also provides a powerful rationale for cities and other institutions in the United States to boycott, divest and stigmatize these corporations. How is this possible when the United States itself is not party to the TPNW?

Despite the best efforts of the Trump administration to stop them, more and more cities, institutions and private investors in the US want to invest their money and do business with companies that share their social and civic values. And much of what goes under the name of "ethical investment" or "socially responsible investment" is based on global norms that get established over time.

There is already a developing global norm against "controversial weapons." This category includes both landmines and cluster munitions, which have been banned by recent international treaties. For an increasing number of investors, this category also includes nuclear weapons, since these too have now been banned by international treaty.

The TPNW thus gives investors in the US, including cities, pension funds, banks, faith communities and other institutions, a *reason* for divesting from nuclear weapons that was also not previously available to them.

A "pincer movement" against the corporations

Pressures on the nuclear weapons corporations from countries in the TPNW can be powerful and important, but probably not enough to seriously threaten these corporations. Their primary financial backers are mostly in the United States (as well as in Europe and Japan) and are not yet as directly impacted by the TPNW.

Pressures from cities and other institutions in the United States can also be powerful and important, but so far they have been insufficient to achieve the goal of nuclear abolition. And that's partly because the nuclear weapons corporations also have financial backers, customers, etc. who are *not* in the United States.

By combining pressures from outside the US with those coming from inside the US, there is at least a chance that the nuclear weapons corporations will bend, and with them, the US government.

This strategy may not work, but there is little chance of anything else working. And the choice before us is to *make* it work if we want to survive.

As former Director of ICAN Beatrice Fihn said as she accepted the Nobel Peace Prize on behalf of the organization, "There *will* be an end to the nuclear weapons story. Either it will be the end of nuclear weapons, or it will be the end of us."

The Treaty on the Prohibition of Nuclear Weapons (TPNW, or "Nuclear Ban Treaty") was adopted in July, 2017, by a vote of 122 to 1 (with one abstention) after lengthy negotiations at the UN.

The treaty outlaws everything to do with nuclear weapons in the countries that have ratified it. This includes development, testing, production, manufacturing, acquiring, possessing, or stockpiling nuclear weapons. It includes transferring control of nuclear weapons, stationing, installing or deploying nuclear weapons. And most significantly, the TPNW commits its parties not to "assist, encourage or induce, in any way, anyone to engage in any activity prohibited to a State Party under this Treaty" (see full text of the treaty in Appendix I).

Once the treaty was adopted, it took another three and a half years before it entered into force as an international agreement. Treaties generally set their own rules as to how and when they enter into force, or become legally binding on the treaty parties. In the case of the TPNW, it was agreed that it would enter into force 90 days after 50 countries had signed and ratified it.

The fiftieth country to ratify the TPNW was Honduras, who deposited their instrument of ratification with the UN on October 24, 2020. The treaty duly entered into force on January 22, 2021. This was generally in line with the time it has taken other treaties to get that many ratifications.

Signing a treaty is rather straightforward and is normally done by a President or Prime Minister or other senior official assigned by the Head of State to sign treaties. For most countries, ratification is a much more cumbersome process, requiring a majority (or even a two-thirds majority) vote in one or more legislative chambers. In the US, for instance, treaties must be ratified by a two-thirds majority in the Senate, which can be an impossible barrier to cross for any matter that does not have very widespread bipartisan support.

In this scenario, a very small island in the South Pacific takes a very small step that leads, ultimately, to nuclear abolition.

PART II: GLOBAL PRESSURES

There are many possible pathways to the abolition of nuclear weapons. The pathway chosen for this book involves putting pressure on the nuclear weapons companies to get *them* to push for nuclear abolition in the US, with the other nuclear-armed countries following along afterwards. And that pathway in turn involves pressures coming from both inside and outside the US.

Pressures from outside the US come largely from countries progressively voting for, signing, ratifying and implementing the Treaty on the Prohibition of Nuclear Weapons (TPNW), in this scenario. None of these countries have nuclear weapons of their own, but they can apply all kinds of pressure on the countries that do - and especially on the private companies that develop, produce and maintain nuclear weapons for the countries that have them. These companies operate all over the world, and they have offices, plants, projects, suppliers, customers and investors in the very countries that are joining the TPNW.

PRESSURE FROM THE WORLD

- [x] VOTE FOR UN RESOLUTION
- [ ] SIGN THE TPNW
- [ ] RATIFY THE TPNW
- [ ] IMPLEMENT LAWS
- [ ] INCLUDE FINANCE
- [ ] COMMIT TO DIVESTMENT
- [ ] BAN CONTRACTS
- [ ] ADD NATO COUNTRIES
- [ ] US BOMBS OUT OF EUROPE

4 From Mali to Australia: Getting to a yes vote on a UN resolution

For the vast majority of countries around the world who support the abolition of nuclear weapons, the first and simplest step they can take is to vote Yes on a United Nations resolution. Of the 195 countries who can vote at the UN, 127 of them voted in favor of the most recent resolution calling on all countries to join the TPNW. Another 13 countries abstained in that vote. What will convince those countries that abstained – because they don't actually oppose *the treaty – to actually vote in favor of it?*

In 1946, not long after the first atomic bombs destroyed the cities of Hiroshima and Nagasaki, the very first resolution of the United Nations General Assembly (UNGA) was a call to abolish nuclear weapons. It passed unanimously. Virtually every year since then, there have been numerous resolutions calling for nuclear disarmament measures of one kind or another. These have all passed with overwhelming support from governments around the world.[1]

The TPNW Resolution

Since 2018, among the many resolutions voted on in the UNGA each year is one that specifically calls on all countries to join the TPNW. The text of the resolution varies slightly from year to year, but in 2024, it included the following line:

> *... Calls upon all States that have not yet done so to sign, ratify, accept, approve or accede to the Treaty [on the Prohibition of Nuclear Weapons] at the earliest possible date...*

Like most of the other nuclear-related resolutions, this TPNW resolution passes by a huge majority every year. And even though a few of the countries that originally voted for adoption of the treaty in 2017 have since dropped off, others who were not part of those original negotiations have since been added.[2] A total of 134 UN members[3] have been voting fairly consistently in favor of this resolution in support of the TPNW, even if some of them occasionally miss one of the votes.[4]

How does a vote at the UN help abolish nuclear weapons?

Voting in favor of a UNGA resolution is nothing major. UNGA resolutions are non-binding and carry no legal force.[5]

This particular resolution is also what we are calling in this book a *recommendatory* resolution: It calls on some other body, over which it has no control (in this case the governments of countries that have not yet joined the TPNW), to do something. This, as we shall see in future chapters, is very different from a *decisional* resolution, in which the body making the resolution is committing *itself* to do something.

Still, this TPNW resolution sends a powerful signal: Most of the world is definitively rejecting these weapons. The TPNW is gaining momentum and it's here to stay.

The countries that still support nuclear weapons hear that message. Importantly, so do the companies that develop, produce and maintain those weapons: their boards, their employees, their shareholders, their suppliers, their customers, and the banks and investment houses that keep them in business.

What those companies hear, with every added vote at the UN in support of this treaty, is a risk to their business model.

As noted in the previous chapter, companies that rely too heavily on nuclear weapons contracts face a risk that those contracts could suddenly dry up, shutting down their source of revenue and competitive advantage.

Companies that spend their capital (and borrow money) to invest in new plants, equipment, hiring and training new workers could end up with "stranded assets." Companies whose brand is an important part of their value face a "reputational risk."

And companies who rely on a complex set of sub-contractors and supply chains that span the globe are at risk of losing contracts and revenue if those supplies are interrupted by growing compliance with the TPNW.

None of these risks are suddenly going to materialize just because one more country votes for a resolution at the UN. But if the companies are paying attention, they know that each country that votes Yes on the TPNW resolution might sooner or later sign it, and ratify it, and pass laws and take other steps to implement it. With every step, countries are building more and more pressure on those companies with the tools available to them in the TPNW.

Yes, No, or Abstain?

While 134 UN members can be counted on to continue voting Yes on the TPNW resolution, another three dozen countries vote No. These are the nuclear-armed countries and their allies who claim to be protected by the "nuclear umbrella" (otherwise known as Extended Nuclear Deterrence, or END).[6]

But what about the 13 countries that continue to abstain on this resolution? They are clearly not *opposed* to the treaty, or they would vote No, like the nuclear and umbrella countries. They even vote in favor of other nuclear-related resolutions that fall short of supporting the TPNW. So what's stopping them from voting Yes on this one?

Perhaps some are responding to pressure from the nuclear-armed countries, which is indeed significant and ongoing. Perhaps some small countries simply don't have the administrative bandwidth (a theme in the next chapter). Perhaps there are reasons we don't know about.

The current abstainers:

- Armenia
- Australia
- Belarus
- Bosnia and Herzegovina
- Georgia
- Kyrgyzstan
- Marshall Islands
- Moldova
- Saudi Arabia
- Serbia
- Singapore
- Switzerland
- Tajikistan

The example: Mali

The West African country of Mali did not take part in the negotiations for the TPNW, and thus did not participate in the vote for its adoption in 2017. When the first resolution in support of the TPNW came up for a vote in the UN General Assembly in 2018, Mali abstained. Mali abstained again on the resolution in 2019.

Then in 2020, Mali changed its vote from Abstain to Yes, and has voted Yes on the resolution every year since then. Mali has not yet signed the TPNW itself (that is coming in the next chapter!), but by voting Yes on the UN resolution, it is stating to the world its intention to do so. Mali's decision to change their vote to Yes is an unmistakable sign that this treaty is building momentum and is here to stay.

Like Mali, the Pacific island of Tonga also abstained on the UNGA resolution before changing theirs to a Yes vote in 2024. Tonga had already voted for adoption of the TPNW in 2017, so for them to abstain in the first place was a bit of a surprise.

These countries can have many different reasons for their voting behavior (including mistakes that are made somewhere along the chain of command from the decision-makers back home to the vote count on the floor of the UN). Nevertheless, in the case of Tonga, as in the case of Mali, switching from Abstain to Yes is almost certainly a precursor to signing the treaty.

Tuvalu also abstained on the UNGA resolution in 2018, but they had in fact already signed the TPNW by then. Nauru, which was not present for the treaty adoption in 2017, did not vote at all on the UNGA resolution until 2020, after they, too, had signed the TPNW.

It is also true that countries have gone the other direction, and changed their vote from Yes to Abstain, as Saudi Arabia has done, or even from Abstain to No, as have Sweden, Finland, Ukraine and Argentina.

In the case of Sweden and Finland, at least, this change goes against very long-standing anti-nuclear traditions in those countries and is likely to be short-lived (see Chapter 11). As with all the other No votes, it remains to be seen how long the nuclear-armed countries and their allies can continue to hold out against the growing chorus of countries voting Yes – and eventually going on to sign and ratify the treaty.

Of all the countries that continue to abstain on the TPNW resolution, the most likely to switch to a Yes vote in the near future is the Marshall Islands.

Next up: Marshall Islands

The Republic of the Marshall Islands (RMI)[1] is one of the countries most affected by radioactive fallout from nuclear testing that took place in the South Pacific between 1946 and 1996.[2] The fallout from these tests left behind a legacy of sickness, anxiety, displacement, radiation and environmental damage that continues to this day.[3]

But the people of RMI received more than fallout. A total of 67 nuclear weapons were detonated by the US on Bikini and Enewetak Atolls during this period. The people living on Bikini Atoll were "temporarily" removed by the US Army in 1946, but high levels of radioactivity are still being recorded on the island today.

Tony DeBrum was a Marshallese politician who played a key role in awakening the world to the humanitarian consequences of nuclear weapons. He was variously the RMI's Minister of Education, Minister of Foreign Affairs, Minister of Finance and Assistant to the Prime Minister.

When Tony was nine years old, he was out fishing with his grandfather when he witnessed the sky turning "blood red" during one of the nuclear tests on Bikini Atoll. He became a lifelong campaigner for nuclear disarmament. Tony documented the cancers and other effects of nuclear testing on Pacific islanders. He was an outspoken critic of every attempt to justify the continued existence of these weapons.[4]

Like survivors of Hiroshima and Nagasaki, the people of RMI have every reason to stop this from ever happening to anyone ever again. But the US has set up a system that has made it very hard for the RMI to participate in abolition efforts.

Nuclear abolition as self-determination

Under the terms of the so-called "Compacts of Free Association," the Marshall Islands and a few other Pacific islands are granted access to Medicaid and university scholarships in the US, in exchange for granting the US military continued access to bases on those islands. In the case of the Marshall Islands, this includes a major US base on the Kwajalein atoll, now housing the Ronald Reagan Ballistic Missile Defense Test Site.

Minuteman III ICBM missiles (minus the nuclear warhead) are routinely tested by launching them from Vandenberg Air Force Base in California to a target at the US base on Kwajalein. US Navy ships also stop at Kwajalein on their way to other destinations in the Pacific. It has been the policy of the US Navy for decades to "neither confirm nor deny" the presence of nuclear weapons on US ships or planes travelling through other countries. And RMI's Compact of Free Association basically gives the US the right to do whatever it wants with its base on Kwajalein.

Tony deBrum championed the TPNW despite this enormous pressure from the US. The RMI lost a strong voice for abolition when Tony himself died of cancer, just weeks after the TPNW was adopted in 2017.

Since Tony deBrum's death, the RMI has declined to join the TPNW and has abstained on all UN votes in support of the treaty. The official reason is that they are unhappy with certain phrasing in Article 6 of the treaty, which in their view does not sufficiently lay the blame for nuclear testing squarely at the door of the countries that did the testing – and expects the victims to help shoulder the costs of caring for the victims and repairing the damage done.

Article 7 of the TPNW in fact obligates *all* the parties to the treaty to help with the process of victim assistance and environmental remediation, by providing financial, technical and material assistance to the countries that are faced with this legacy. Since none of the countries *responsible* for the damage are currently parties to the TPNW, and parties to the TPNW have no power to force them to pay for it, this is a more pragmatic approach to getting the job done. But that is not good enough for the Marshall Islands.

"Some of the Treaty's provisions, while noble, do not go far enough to address the very real and harmful impacts that people affected by nuclear weapons continue to live with on a daily basis. The treaty... still wrongfully absolves responsibility for the consequences of nuclear weapons testing from those states which conducted the nuclear testing. And instead leaves us responsible to pay for billions of dollars of adjudicated impacts which we did not choose," said the Marshall Islands Ambassador to the UN during the Third Meeting of States Parties to the TPNW (the 3MSP) in March, 2025.

But the Ambassador went on to say that the RMI wants to work with the States Parties to amend the wording of Article 6. And he made a big announcement: at long last, RMI has signed the Treaty of Rarotonga, which makes the South Pacific a Nuclear Free Zone.

Most of the islands in the region, including Australia and New Zealand, signed the Rarotonga Treaty way back in 1985 when it first opened for signatures. But RMI was inhibited from signing it by the conditions of the Compacts. RMI's recent signature is a breakthrough, an expression of willingness to now stand up to the US.

In our scenario, RMI acknowledges frustration that they don't have official input on amendments because they're not yet a party to the TPNW. So it's in their direct interest to join the TPNW, and fast. The TPNW Review Conference takes place in

2026, and that's the first time that amendments will be considered.

Even before joining the TPNW, RMI stops abstaining on votes at the UN, and instead aligns itself with the majority of the world, including almost all of its Pacific island neighbors. They vote Yes on the TPNW resolution in the UNGA.

It's not a huge step, just one more country voting in favor of the TPNW, so it's only worth one second on our imaginary clock. But every step matters.

> **The clock we are using in this scenario moves back by one second to 11:58:30pm** when the Marshall Islands vote Yes on the General Assembly resolution calling on all states to join the Treaty on the Prohibition of Nuclear Weapons (TPNW).

By the time you read this book, RMI or one of the other abstainers may have already changed their vote. **Switzerland**, for example, voted in favor of the TPNW at the negotiations in 2017, but has abstained on every UNGA TPNW vote since then. **Saudi Arabia**, as mentioned above, also voted in favor at the negotiations and in subsequent votes, but has since switched their vote to abstain.

A number of other countries (like **Armenia**, **Bosnia**, **Georgia, Kyrgyzstan, Moldova, Serbia, Tajikistan**) continue to abstain, more because they do not want to upset a powerful, nuclear-armed neighbor than because they necessarily oppose the TPNW as such. Kyrgyzstan, for instance, announced in April 2025 that it would sign – and ratify – the TPNW in the coming months.[5]

In our scenario, four of these countries, all formerly part of the Soviet Union, all decide to join the Marshall Islands and vote in favor of the TPNW. As with the Marshall Islands, these votes are not in themselves particularly significant, but they show that momentum is building, and that, ultimately, *is* significant.

Our clock moves back a further 4 seconds to **11:58:26pm** when Armenia, Kyrgyzstan, Moldova, and Tajikistan also vote "yes" on the General Assembly resolution calling on all states to join the Treaty on the Prohibition of Nuclear Weapons (TPNW).

The prize: Australia

The nuclear weapons companies are not going to be overly concerned about the Marshall Islands or Bosnia or Tajikistan voting for the TPNW, or even joining it. But Australia is a different matter altogether.

Australia is another country that abstained on the most recent vote at the United Nations. That was a step forward, however, from previous votes on the TPNW resolution, which until 2022 were a consistent No.

Australia is a key military ally of the United States, with a joint intelligence facility at Pine Gap and other forms of military cooperation. The new AUKUS Treaty involves purchasing nuclear-powered submarines from the US, and then building more with technical help from the US and the UK.

Like the Marshall Islands, Australia is party to the NFZ Treaty of Rarotonga but allows US military planes and ships to come and go without questioning whether they may be carrying nuclear weapons in contravention of the treaty. And like the Marshall Islands, Australia is tied to the concept of "Extended Nuclear Deterrence" that many in Australia believe is their ultimate protection against potential adversaries.

Nevertheless, Australia had a change of government in 2022, and with it, a change of approach, if not yet a change of policy, with regard to nuclear weapons.

Gem Romuld and ICAN Australia

Gem Romuld is the Director of ICAN Australia. She is the one who must convince the Australian government to change their vote – again – this time from Abstain to Yes. Luckily, she is not alone.

ICAN Australia is just one of 650 partner organizations of ICAN internationally. But ICAN also started out in Australia and has deep roots there.

The **International Campaign to Abolish Nuclear Weapons (ICAN)** was founded in 2007 with help from International Physicians for the Prevention of Nuclear War (IPPNW), which was awarded the Nobel Peace Prize in 1985 for "creating an awareness of the catastrophic consequences of atomic warfare."

ICAN took on the goal of building a global movement with the specific goal of banning and abolishing nuclear weapons. It was itself awarded the Nobel Peace Prize in 2017 for those efforts which lead to the adoption of the TPNW.

In 2025, ICAN consists of 650 partner organizations in 110 countries. All are committed to getting their own countries to sign and ratify the TPNW if they haven't already.

In countries that have not yet joined the TPNW, ICAN campaigners are working to get cities to join the ICAN Cities Appeal, and to get elected officials to sign the ICAN Parliamentary (or Legislative) Pledge. These commit the city or the legislator, respectively, to push for their country to join the TPNW.

And in those countries that are already in the treaty, partner organizations are busy trying to get their governments to take additional steps to strengthen the treaty and to use it as a tool for putting pressure on the nuclear-armed countries to disarm.

In this scenario, the most effective way they can do that is by pushing for divestment and other pressures that directly impact the companies responsible for nuclear weapons, especially in the United States.

It was a group of Australians (including Tilman Ruff, Dimity Hawkins and Bill Williams) who took the original inspiration from IPPNW to start a new organization dedicated to abolishing nuclear weapons. They set up an office in Melbourne, and for the first few years of ICAN's existence, the international headquarters were based there (before moving to Oslo and then to Geneva, where it is now based).

Another Australian, Tim Wright, became one of ICAN's most effective international campaigners, and remains very prominent in the organization as ICAN's Treaty Coordinator.

And in 2023, ICAN chose another Australian, Melissa Parke, to be their new Executive Director. Melissa worked as a human rights lawyer for the UN before being elected to the Australian parliament in 2007. In 2013, she was appointed Minister for International Development by the previous Labor Prime Minister, Kevin Rudd. Melissa is thus in a very strong position to assist Gem in her efforts with the current Labor Prime Minister.

Gem works with more than 70 organizations across Australia, including faith groups, lawyers, students, trade unions, medical professionals, affected communities and veterans. Like 76% of Australians (according to a 2022 poll), they all want to see Australia join the TPNW.[6]

ICAN Australia has successfully gotten over 50 towns and cities to pass resolutions in support of the ICAN Cities Appeal, including Sydney, Melbourne, Canberra, Brisbane, Adelaide and Hobart. It has gotten over 300 national and regional parliamentarians to sign the ICAN Parliamentary Pledge (including the current Prime Minister, Anthony Albanese, and several members of his Cabinet).[7]

Gem and her colleagues work directly with some of the more supportive parliamentarians who have formed a "Parliamentary Friends of the TPNW" group. This group includes people in the present Cabinet, and there are constant discussions about strategies and tactics for getting the government to join the TPNW.

Anthony Albanese, before becoming Prime Minister of Australia, at an ICAN Australia rally. PHOTO: ICAN Australia

Anthony Albanese and the Australian Labor Party

The Australian Labor Party has been committed on paper to joining the TPNW since its annual conference in 2018.[8] This in itself was a huge success story, after years of getting commitment for this from local Labor Party branches on up to the provincial levels of the Party and finally reaching the federal level.

Before he was Prime Minister, Albanese authored the resolution that finally made it national Labor Party policy to join the TPNW. He held up ICAN's Nobel Peace Prize as he gave the speech that won the party over to the resolution.

The Labor Party was not in power at that point. But the policy was reaffirmed in 2023, after Labor won the election and became the party of government.

The Labor policy commits the party, when in government, to sign the TPNW, "taking into account" the need to:

1. Have an effective verification and enforcement architecture;
2. Ensure interaction of the TPNW with the NPT;
3. Work to achieve universal support for the Ban Treaty.

The Labor Party insists these are not "conditions" but only factors to be taken into account before signing the TPNW. Nevertheless, it is now coming to the end of their term in office and they have not yet done so.

The Prime Minister himself was deeply affected by his relationship with Tom Uren, an Australian WWII veteran who saw the sky turn "crimson" when he witnessed the atomic bombing of Nagasaki from a nearby prisoner of war camp where he was being held. Uren called the atomic bombing a "crime against humanity." He went on to become a campaigner for nuclear abolition and a mentor to Albanese.

When ICAN Australia met with Albanese in 2023 to discuss his promise to join the TPNW, they talked about how joining the TPNW is compatible with an ongoing military alliance with the US, the dangerous fallacy of a "nuclear umbrella" and why Australian nuclear submarines would undermine the NPT.

Ironically, much of the discussion in Australia about nuclear submarines has suddenly shifted since Trump's return to the White House. There is now some serious buyer's remorse about being too dependent on the US at a time when the US is changing all the rules and reconsidering its own commitments to other countries like Australia. Nevertheless, Albanese's government wants nuclear-powered submarines and that is a higher priority right now than joining the TPNW.

Submarines and weapons-grade uranium

There was already considerable controversy surrounding the AUKUS nuclear submarine agreement.[9] These are not nuclear *missile* submarines, but they are powered by highly-enriched uranium (HEU), which is the same grade of uranium used in nuclear weapons. This would be the first time HEU is being transferred from a nuclear-armed state to a non-nuclear armed state, potentially in breach of the NPT.[10]

Australia has insisted it will not use the HEU or any of the waste fuel (which also contains plutonium) for making nuclear weapons, but this deal clearly sets a precedent for the transfer of HEU to other states, risking further proliferation of nuclear weapons.

One obvious solution to this problem would be for Australia to sign and ratify the TPNW, making it clear to the world that it will *not* make nuclear weapons, and setting the precedent for any other state accepting HEU that they should also commit to the TPNW before doing so.

Gem is doing her best to make this case. She is supported by a very strong network of campaigners across Australia (and across the world), as well as by 35 prominent lawyers and former government Ministers who recently signed an open letter calling on Australia to join the TPNW.[11]

A more immediate step that Australia could take to indicate its *support* for the TPNW, as well as its intention to find a way to sign and ratify it sooner or later, would be to vote in favor of the UNGA TPNW resolution. It's still a small step in the grand scheme of things. It commits Australia to nothing in the immediate term.

In this scenario, Gem and her colleagues convince Albanese to change Australia's vote at the UN from Abstain to Yes. And Australia goes on to sign and ratify the TPNW (but this happens in later chapters). For now, our clock moves back by just a little bit – but it's a big deal to the nuclear weapons profiteers.

Our clock moves back another second to 11:58:25pm when Australia votes "yes" on the next General Assembly resolution calling on all states to join the Treaty on the Prohibition of Nuclear Weapons (TPNW).

Impact of Australia's moves towards the TPNW

The US had already raised the alarm when Australia changed its vote at the UN from No to Abstain, telling the Australian government that joining the TPNW "would not allow for US extended deterrence relationships, which are still necessary for international peace and security" and that joining the treaty risked "reinforcing divisions" within the international community.[12]

Virtually every US and European corporation involved in nuclear weapons work has some kind of stake in Australia. **This single little vote on a UN resolution alerts them to the fact that Australia *could* go on to sign, ratify and further implement the TPNW. That potential is deeply troubling for these corporations.**

Boeing Australia

Boeing, for instance, has its largest subdivision outside the United States in Australia, with seven wholly owned subsidiaries, consolidating and co-ordinating Boeing's businesses and operations there. While aircraft components are made in Japan, Canada, UK, Sweden, France, and Italy before being assembled in the US, only Australia produces one crucial piece, the complex wing parts called "moveable trailing edges," for Boeing 787 Dreamliners.[13]

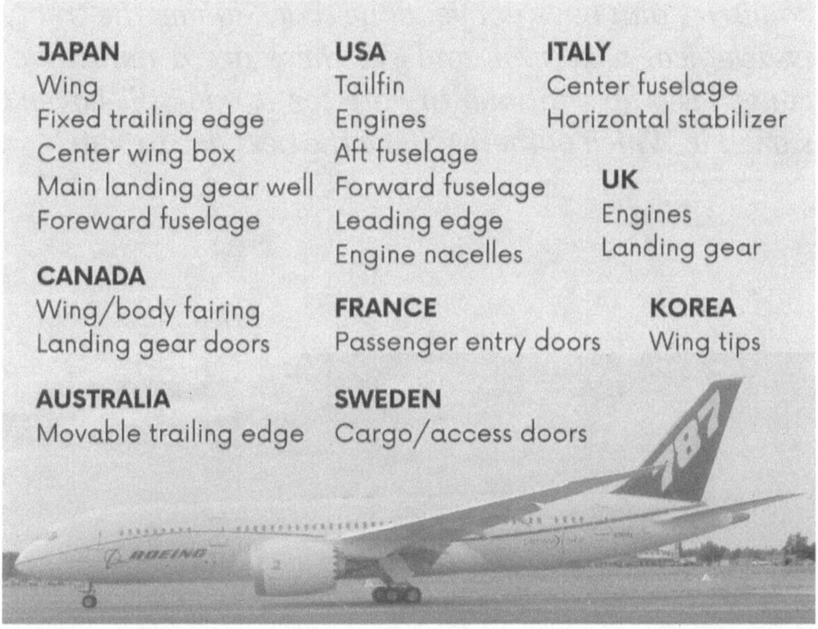

Parts for the Boeing 787 are made in 9 countries and then assembled in the US.[14]

In addition to passenger plane parts, Boeing Australia makes parts for military aircraft, including for the Super Hornet jet fighter and the Chinook helicopter. Its parent company in the US is a major nuclear weapons contractor, producing key components for the B61-12 gravity bombs, as well as for the Minuteman III ICBMs and other nuclear missile programs. So where is the boundary between what Boeing does in Australia and what it does in the United States?

This is a question not just for Boeing, but for *all* the major nuclear weapons companies, which have offices, plants, suppliers, projects, customers and investors in Australia.

Northrop Grumman, for instance, claims to have contributed more than $1 billion to the Australian economy between 2016-2020. This includes direct employment of about 1,500 people in Australia, purchases from Australian suppliers, investments in plants and infrastructure as well as in research partnerships with Australian universities, sponsorships and donations to charities.[15]

By taking even this seemingly insignificant step of voting in favor of the TPNW at the UN, Australia serves notice that it may not be "business as usual" for much longer.

Voting for the TPNW is an important first step for countries that have not yet done that. Signing the treaty is a logical next step, and yet there are a number of countries who continue to vote for it and still haven't signed it. Which of these will be the next one to sign?

PRESSURE FROM THE WORLD

- [ ] VOTE FOR UN RESOLUTION
- [x] SIGN THE TPNW
- [ ] RATIFY THE TPNW
- [ ] IMPLEMENT LAWS
- [ ] INCLUDE FINANCE
- [ ] COMMIT TO DIVESTMENT
- [ ] BAN CONTRACTS
- [ ] ADD NATO COUNTRIES
- [ ] US BOMBS OUT OF EUROPE

5 From Sierra Leone to Egypt: Transforming votes into signatures

So far, 98 countries out of the 197 that can join international treaties have either signed or ratified the Treaty on the Prohibition of Nuclear Weapons (TPNW). Of the 99 remaining countries, 40 of them have been voting every year at the UN in favor of the resolution that calls on all countries to sign the TPNW. But they haven't yet signed the treaty themselves. This chapter is about getting those countries that vote *for the treaty to actually* sign *it.*

Like a vote in the UN General Assembly, signing a treaty in itself is not such a big deal. It indicates an *intention* to ratify or accede[1]. to the treaty at some point (see next chapter), and carries a rather vague commitment not to do anything that could undermine the ratifying of the treaty in the meantime. It certainly does not mean that a country signing the TPNW suddenly has to comply with all its prohibitions.

None of the countries that have signed the TPNW so far have nuclear weapons of their own. And all of those countries are already signatories to the NPT (see Chapter 2), which forbids them from starting a nuclear weapons program.

So why does this step matter at all? What difference does it make if one or two more countries sign the TPNW at this point?

The real significance of the TPNW

The significance of the TPNW is not that it commits the parties to renouncing the option of ever developing nuclear weapons. The NPT already does that. It is not even that the TPNW outlaws the use or threat of use of nuclear weapons in international law. The Geneva Conventions already (largely) do that.[2]

The real significance of the TPNW lies in the fact that this treaty exists at all, given the intense opposition it faced from the nuclear-armed countries and their nuclear allies.

Any time the idea of abolishing nuclear weapons comes up in the UN Security Council, it is vetoed by one or more of the five Permanent Members (the so-called "P5" – US, Russia, China, UK and France), each of which has the power to veto a decision and each of which just happens to possess nuclear weapons themselves. The P5, vehemently opposed to one another on so many other issues, have one thing in common: they don't want to give up their nuclear weapons.

When it comes to negotiating new treaties, especially ones relating to weapons of any kind, it has generally been the US and other P5 members taking part and ensuring that the language reflects what they want it to say.

But when the countries *without* nuclear weapons initiated the negotiations that led to the TPNW, they were the ones who set the rules. And they chose majority rule, not consensus, so no one country could block the decision of the majority. And *that* meant the US and their friends could not dictate or control the proceedings.

So instead, the US chose to boycott the negotiations and denounce the results. There was the odd spectacle of the US Ambassador to the UN at that time, Nikki Haley, holding her own "demonstration" (along with a few close allies of the US) outside the room where TPNW negotiations were taking place. "We all want a world without nuclear weapons," she claimed, "but we can't let the bad people have nuclear weapons and the good people not have them..."[3]

The United States had previously circulated a memo urging NATO members to oppose any steps that might (and subsequently did) lead to adoption of the TPNW, warning them that a ban on nuclear weapons would be "fundamentally at odds with NATO's basic policies."[4] France and Russia also weighed in at various points to try to stop the TPNW negotiations from going forward, and there were several claims of pressure and even intimidation being used to prevent the adoption of the TPNW.[5]

Once the TPNW was adopted, the nuclear-armed countries, and especially the United States, did not stop their efforts to prevent countries from joining it. In a bizarre, unprecedented move during Trump's first Presidency, the US State Department actually wrote to countries already in the treaty, urging them to rescind their ratification. "We believe that you have made a strategic error and should withdraw your instrument of ratification or accession," the letter said, according to the Associated Press.[6]

Every country that signs, ratifies or takes further steps to implement this treaty does so in the face of this fierce and sometimes unrelenting pressure from one or more nuclear-armed country who has encouraged them not to do it.

It takes enormous bravery for countries to stand up to the United States or another nuclear-armed country and join this treaty.

So while it may seem like a very small step in the grand scheme of things, every new signature that is added to the TPNW really is something to be celebrated. And its true significance will become more apparent as this scenario unfolds.

The example: Sierra Leone

The small West African country of Sierra Leone took part in the TPNW negotiations and voted for its adoption in 2017. In 2018, they voted in favor of the UN resolution calling on all countries to join the treaty. They did so again in 2019. And again in 2020. But still they hadn't signed it themselves.

Finally, after five years, Sierra Leone signed the TPNW in 2022 (and went on to ratify it in 2024). To understand how that happened, we go now to Abdul M. Fatoma, Chief Executive of the Campaign for Human Rights and Development International (CHRDI).

Abdul Fatoma and CHRDI

Abdul is a well-known Sierra Leonean human rights activist who has won several awards and appears regularly on Sierra Leone TV stations. And the CHRDI is a well-respected Sierra Leonean human rights organization that has built its reputation with the public by defending ordinary people and standing up to corrupt judges and politicians.[7]

Once, when over 400 staff from the government statistics office were unfairly dismissed without proper compensation, Abdul and his team organized a public protest, held a press conference, took the government to court and issued them with an ultimatum. In the end, the workers got their rights and CHRDI strengthened its credibility with the people of Sierra Leone.

But Abdul also knows how to take a softer, more diplomatic approach when that's needed, working quietly behind the scenes with politicians and government officials to get commitments and buy-in on important human rights issues.

Members of delegation to ECOWAS with Hon. Chernor Ramadan Maju Bah, chair of Human Rights and Legal Affairs Committee of the ECOWAS parliament (center). PHOTO: CHRDI

Nuclear weapons as a human rights issue

It was at a regional meeting of the Economic Community of West African States (ECOWAS) in Nigeria that Abdul was first introduced to ICAN and the TPNW. He immediately understood the issue of nuclear weapons as a human rights issue.

Even without any nuclear weapons *in* Africa or even *aimed at* Africa, the people of Africa would still suffer terrible consequences from the use of nuclear weapons anywhere.[8] How could it be right that people potentially *affected* by such weapons have no say in whether these weapons are used or whether they are even allowed to exist?

On his return to Sierra Leone, Abdul immediately set about trying to get his own government to sign the new treaty. He quickly discovered that the main reason Sierra Leone had not yet signed was not because they had any real misgivings or doubts about doing so. It was mostly a general lack of knowledge about the treaty and what it would mean for Sierra Leone to join it.

Abdul had already built a relationship with the Foreign Minister of Sierra Leone, as well as with the President and other government ministers. Once he had the opportunity to talk with them personally and explain to them more about the TPNW, they were ready to sign.

Next up: Guinea

Now that Sierra Leone is finally on board, Abdul is able to turn his attention to Guinea. Guinea participated in the negotiations that led to the TPNW, but was not present for the vote. Nevertheless, like Sierra Leone, Guinea has been voting ever since then in favor of the UN resolution calling on all countries to sign the treaty.

Abdul remains confident that he can get Guinea to sign it next, even though it has been more than seven years since they said they would do it and there is still no clear sign that they will. Although, like Sierra Leone, it is mostly a question of capacity, it also comes down to the simple question for the government of Guinea: "what's in it for us?" Why should the government of Guinea prioritize signing a treaty when they have so many urgent and important daily matters to attend to?

Abdul's strategy for winning over Guinea requires some support from his own government in Sierra Leone. He is able to call on the (new) Foreign Minister to reach out to his counterpart in Guinea. It is the Foreign Minister of Guinea, Dr. Morrisanda Kouyaté, who is the key to getting Guinea to sign the TPNW.

Although the current President of Guinea came to power through a *coup d'etat* in 2021, Guinea has a functioning parliament, with a Prime Minister and other Ministers who do not come from a military background. Dr. Kouyaté is, in fact, a highly respected medical doctor, who has led an international campaign against female genital mutilation (FGM) for over 40 years.[9]

At a meeting arranged by the Foreign Minister of Sierra Leone, Abdul easily convinces Dr. Kouyaté, in this scenario, that, like FGM, nuclear weapons are also a human rights issue. And just as FGM is often justified by suggesting that it somehow benefits and "protects" the girls that are subjected to it, so nuclear weapons are also justified on similarly spurious grounds.

Dr. Kouyaté must now convince his President to sign the treaty. President Doumbouya is not a human rights activist or a medical doctor. He is a military man. And he is under intense

pressure, from both inside Guinea and from outside the country, to return that country to civilian rule as soon as possible.

So Dr. Kouyaté urges President Doumbouya to sign the TPNW for political reasons. By signing the TPNW now, Mr. Doumbouya loses nothing and potentially gains an easy win. He can earn some favor with his neighbors who are pushing him to join the treaty. And since Guinea had a civilian government when it first supported the TPNW back in 2017, this is a way of indicating to the rest of the world that he is moving in the right direction towards civilian rule.

As the TPNW has been framed as a human rights treaty in the West African neighborhood, President Doumbouya will also be congratulated for joining another human rights initiative. It will show his commitment to the rule of law and to the international community of nations that conduct their affairs through treaties. He will be showing his solidarity with the other West African countries who are already in the treaty. And he will be showing his own people in Guinea that he is willing to take steps to protect *their* interests and concerns about the overall world situation.

With President Doumbouya's signature now added to the TPNW, the clock in our scenario moves back a further 5 seconds from midnight.

The clock in this scenario moves back five seconds to 11:58:20pm when President Doumbouya of Guinea adds his signature to the Treaty on the Prohibition of Nuclear Weapons (TPNW).

Why is this significant?

On its own, adding one more country to the 98 who have already signed the TPNW does not sound like much of a step forward. And moving the scenario clock by just a few more seconds when it is so dangerously close to midnight seems even less so.

But the cumulative effect of more and more countries signing up to the TPNW *is* significant. With every single country, large or small, that joins the TPNW, its status grows. The global norm that it represents is strengthened in customary international law. And every country that takes this step adds to the pressure on the nuclear weapons companies.

Furthermore, with this new signature, Guinea becomes the 99th country to sign, ratify or accede to the treaty. This means that over half of the world's countries are now committed to the TPNW in some form. The total abolition of nuclear weapons can no longer be ignored as a "minority concern."

Maybe Guinea will be the 99th signature, or maybe that signature will come from one of the other 39 countries that continue to vote in favor of the TPNW but have not yet signed it themselves.[10] By the time you're reading this, one or more of them may have already signed. Then there will be another, and another, and another. With each new country that signs the TPNW, the pressure increases on others to join them.

Figure 4.1 The countries of ECOWAS in West Africa

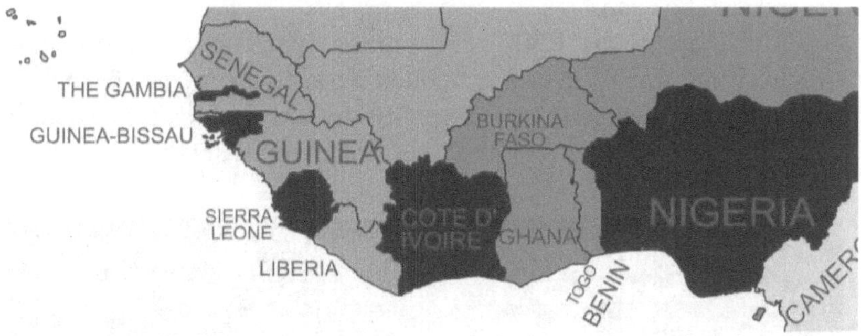

Countries in black have ratified the TPNW as of March, 2025. Countries in dark grey have so far signed it, and countries in light grey have consistently voted for it.

More signatures follow

In this scenario, Guinea's signature opens the floodgates to a number of other African countries who are also supporting the TPNW but have not yet signed it. Abdul's ongoing efforts in the ECOWAS space mean that Liberia, Mali and Senegal are the next to sign. Now all 15 ECOWAS countries are on board with the treaty, with 8 signatures and 7 ratifications.

With these additional 3 signatures added to the TPNW, the clock is now pushed back a further fifteen seconds to 11:58:05pm.

Outside of ECOWAS, in other parts of Africa, **Burundi, Chad, Ethiopia, Gabon, Kenya, Mauritania, Mauritius, Morocco**, **Somalia** and **Tunisia** are all parties to the Treaty of Pelindaba and the NPT. They all voted for, and continue to vote for, the UN resolution calling on *all* countries to join the TPNW. But they all suffer from the same lack of capacity. They just haven't been able to get to the TPNW yet, but sooner or later, they will.

Meanwhile, religious leaders across Africa are speaking up on the issue of nuclear weapons, doing their best to get more countries on board. The African Council of Religious Leaders - Religions for Peace, based in Nairobi, is a multifaith organization of priests, ministers, imams, and other leaders. They run workshops for parliamentarians and communities about the danger of nuclear weapons and the urgency of abolition.

Together with ICAN and other pan-African anti-nuclear organizations, their mission is to build persistent pressure from every possible constituency to get one politician, one diplomat, one country at a time to support nuclear abolition, until eventually the whole world is on board.

These additional 10 signatures from Africa push our **clock back a further 50 seconds to 11:57:15pm**: still far too close to midnight, but at least moving in the right direction.

The Prize: Egypt

Another country in Africa that has voted consistently for all countries to join the TPNW (and also played an active role in the most recent TPNW meeting, the 3MSP) in March, 2025, is **Egypt**.

Although Egypt toyed with the idea of developing its own nuclear weapons in the 1950s and 60s, it quickly abandoned those efforts and has been a champion for nuclear abolition ever since.[11]

When it became clear in the early 1970s that Israel had acquired the Bomb, Egypt grew even more opposed to nuclear weapons. Israel is a neighboring country with which Egypt has fought numerous wars, so Israel's possession of nuclear weapons is considered an existential threat to Egypt.

Figure 4.2 Status of the TPNW across Africa

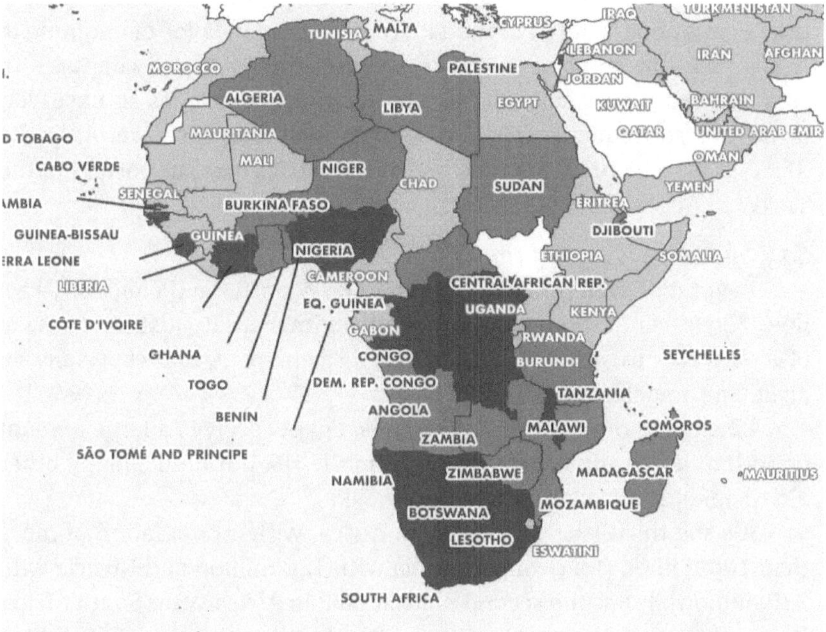

Countries in black have ratified the TPNW, dark grey countries have signed, and light grey countries have voted for it.

Egypt joined the NPT in 1981, but when that treaty came up for indefinite extension in 1995, Egypt was its most vocal opponent. The reason? Egypt and the vast majority of other countries in the NPT had kept their side of the bargain and renounced pursuing any nuclear weapons development. But the five existing nuclear-armed countries had failed to fulfill their end of the bargain, which was to negotiate the elimination of *their* nuclear weapons (see Chapter 2).

Egypt's Foreign Minister at the time, Amr Moussa, fought against US efforts to extend the NPT indefinitely, arguing that the NPT "has not lived up to the expectations of its original forefathers."[12]

In the end, Egypt agreed to the extension, on condition that the P5 countries would commit to ensuring the creation of a nuclear-free zone in the Middle East that included Israel. (That hasn't happened yet.) The P5 countries were also forced to give the rest of the world their "unequivocal undertaking" that they would fulfill their obligation to negotiate complete disarmament. (30 years later, that hasn't happened either.)

Egypt then pushed for a total ban to be negotiated. It took part in the negotiations that led to the TPNW and voted in favor of adopting it. It has voted in favor of the UN resolution calling for all countries to sign the treaty ever since. It has played an active role, as an observer, in all the subsequent TPNW meetings, including most recently the 3MSP in March, 2025. Egypt is one of the most vocal supporters of the TPNW in Africa.

So why hasn't it signed the TPNW yet?

Egypt may well refuse to sign the TPNW until the US and/or Israel does. Egypt is not interested in signing another treaty just for the sake of it. It wants to see real progress on disarmament, and especially on achieving a nuclear-free Middle East.

Like many other African countries, Egypt receives a large amount of both military and economic aid from the US. But unlike many other aid recipients, it is neither poor nor weak.

It's the third largest country in Africa, with a population of more than 100 million (following Ethiopia with 130 million and Nigeria with 230 million). It has the second highest GDP in Africa, after South Africa. It has the most powerful military, thanks to more than $50 billion worth of military aid received from the US since 1978.

Egypt's goals are a nuclear-free Middle East and a nuclear-free world. Neither of those can be achieved at this point without significant pressure being brought to bear on the United States, and through the United States on Israel. If Egypt determines that the TPNW can be effectively used as a tool to exert that pressure, it makes sense for Egypt to join it.

And in this scenario, they do.

Egypt's signature moves the scenario clock back another 5 seconds. **It now stands at 11:57:10pm** as we move onto the next level of commitment to the TPNW: ratification.

Why is Egypt's signature so significant?

Egypt is particularly important to the TPNW because, while it is a country in North Africa, it is also very much a part of the Arab world.

Its influence extends well beyond Africa to key countries in the Middle East.

Bahrain, Iraq, Jordan, Kuwait, Lebanon, Qatar, Oman, Saudi Arabia, and the United Arab Emirates (UAE) are all in the same situation as Egypt was – they all took part in the negotiations for the TPNW and they all voted in favor of it. With the exception of Saudi Arabia,[13] all these countries have continued to vote consistently in favor of the US resolution calling on all countries to sign the treaty.

And yet they themselves have not signed. Why? Maybe because they all have major business connections with US nuclear weapons contractors and close ties to the US military.

The US still has troops stationed (permanently) in Iraq, as well as a military presence in Bahrain, Djibouti, Jordan, Kuwait, Qatar and the UAE. Bahrain, Saudi Arabia and the UAE host some very large investors in US nuclear weapons corporations, and a number of those corporations have operations, projects, and contracts worth billions of dollars in those countries.

Northrop Grumman, for example, one of the largest military contractors in the world, operates in a number of countries outside the United States. So far, none of those countries are party to the TPNW.[14] But two of them are Saudi Arabia and the UAE.

Northrop Grumman – Global presence

Boeing operates all over the world, except it seems to have no direct operations in any TPNW countries. But Boeing has a sizeable presence in Saudi Arabia, the UAE, and Qatar.

Boeing – global presence

RTX, formerly Raytheon, is also present in Saudi Arabia, the UAE, Qatar and Oman (as well as in TPNW parties Brazil and Mexico). And many of the other nuclear weapons companies have business dealings with countries across the Middle East.

RTX – Global reach

So as Egypt joins the TPNW, the pressure mounts on the other countries of the Middle East to also join. And that creates a direct threat to these major nuclear weapons corporations embedded in those countries.

Bechtel in Egypt

Meanwhile, in Egypt itself is the giant US corporation, **Bechtel**. Bechtel has been a major contractor for a number of fossil fuel projects in Egypt since 1976, including a liquid natural gas terminal, a gas processing terminal, an oil refinery, several gas- and oil-fired power plants, a pipeline, a major petrochemical installation, and a coking plant.[15]

Bechtel is now bidding to be a partner in Egypt's transition to a green energy future. New projects on the horizon include capping gas flares at existing fossil fuel facilities, experimental carbon capture and storage projects, and green hydrogen fuel production. These are currently at the feasibility study phase, but could be worth billions of dollars to Bechtel over the coming years.

Like Northrop Grumman, Boeing and RTX, Bechtel is also a major nuclear weapons producer, responsible for designing and building the launch system for the new Sentinel ICBM. It is also part of the team that manages Lawrence Livermore Labs in California, where the actual nuclear warheads are designed, and the Y-12 plant in Tennessee, where the fissile materials for all US nuclear weapons are prepared. From 2013 to 2024, Bechtel was also involved in managing the Pantex plant in Texas, where the final assembly of the nuclear warheads takes place.[16]

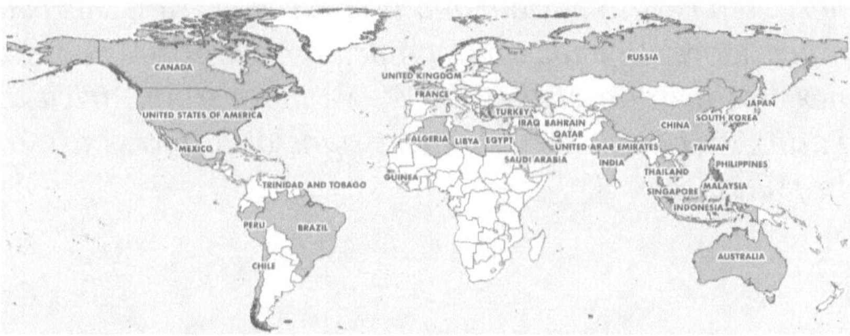

Bechtel has major engineering projects in at least 30 countries...

In our scenario, Egypt signs the TPNW – and this has a negligible impact on Bechtel in the immediate term. But, as with Boeing in Australia, these small steps can lead to bigger steps that sooner or later *will* have an impact on Bechtel and its operations, not just in Egypt but in many other countries.

Bechtel is a well-established and trusted corporation that can implement very large-scale infrastructure projects, but it's not the only one. It competes with major European contractors like Balfour Beatty (British) and Vinci (French). It also competes with large Chinese companies that are moving more and more into Africa, like the China Communications Construction Company and China State Construction Engineering Corporation.

As Egypt and other countries decide the time has come to sign the TPNW, they are setting the stage for the possibility down

the road that companies involved in the nuclear weapons business, like Bechtel, will no longer be favored for big, multi-billion dollar contracts over these other companies that are *not* involved in the nuclear weapons business.

With Egypt's signature on the TPNW, two things happen: The pressure is on for other Middle Eastern countries to follow suit. And the nuclear weapons companies are getting a little message that "business as usual" is just starting to crack. When more countries that host their operations join the TPNW and get to the next steps of "building it out," that crack will grow. And when those countries start ratifying the TPNW, and enforcing it with the steps coming in later chapters, the companies are going to find themselves in real legal, economic, and reputational danger!

Signing is just the first step in joining the TPNW. The next step is ratification, and in most countries, this is a much more difficult and cumbersome process. For the next ratification of the TPNW, we move from Africa to Latin America, where the next signs of progress are to be found.

PRESSURE FROM THE WORLD

- [ ] VOTE FOR UN RESOLUTION
- [ ] SIGN THE TPNW
- [x] RATIFY THE TPNW
- [ ] IMPLEMENT LAWS
- [ ] INCLUDE FINANCE
- [ ] COMMIT TO DIVESTMENT
- [ ] BAN CONTRACTS
- [ ] ADD NATO COUNTRIES
- [ ] US BOMBS OUT OF EUROPE

6 From Guatemala to Brazil: Turning signatures into ratifications

At least 138 countries currently support the TPNW and so far 98 of them have signed it.[1] *And of those 98 who have signed, 73 have so far ratified this treaty. So the next step in this scenario is about getting the other 25 signers to finally ratify it.*

Signing a treaty, in most cases, just takes a single signature by a President or Prime Minister, which as we've seen can nonetheless be difficult to get, even when the country clearly *wants* to join the treaty. Ratification is a much more lengthy and cumbersome process in most countries. It normally requires a vote in at least one legislative chamber, sometimes two. It might also require not just a simple majority vote but a two-thirds or other super-majority vote to be considered valid.

In the United States, for instance, treaties require a two-thirds majority vote in the Senate to be ratified. This can take years, and in some cases, it never happens at all. The US signed the Genocide Convention in 1948, and it took 40 years for it to be finally ratified by the Senate. The Convention on the Elimination of all forms of Discrimination Against Women (CEDAW) was signed by the US in 1979 and still has not been ratified by the Senate. Same with the Convention on the Rights of the Child, signed in 1989 but still not ratified.

Countries and the TPNW

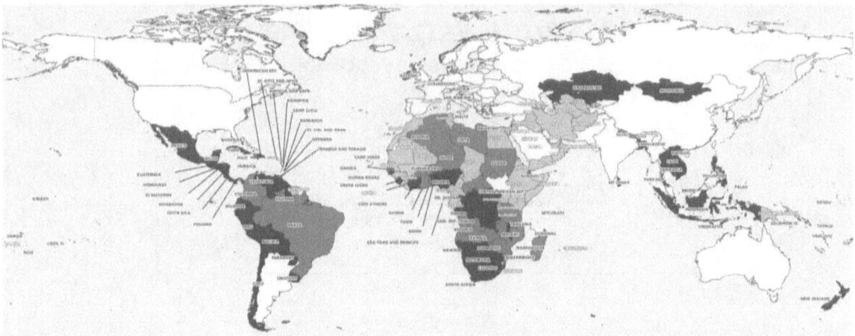

Countries in black have so far ratified the TPNW. Countries in dark grey have signed but not yet ratified. Countries in light grey have voted for the most recent TPNW resolution at the UN.

So when it comes to ratification of the TPNW, the process can seem glacially slow. This is especially the case when governments change hands and the political party in control of the ratification process is not the same party that agreed to sign it.

Nevertheless, as of May 2025, 73 countries have so far managed to ratify the TPNW, and more are coming.

Ratification brings with it legally-binding commitments and responsibilities for that country. As a State Party, that country is now an equal partner with all the other States Parties (yes, the plural is weird) in terms of further development of the TPNW such as proposing and/or deciding about any changes, amendments, or protocols to the treaty, definitions and interpretations of what the treaty means, etc.

The example: Guatemala

Guatemala, along with the other six countries in Central America (Belize, Costa Rica, El Salvador, Honduras, Nicaragua and Panama)[2] signed the TPNW as soon as it was opened for signatures in September 2017. Most of those other countries went on to quickly ratify it over the next two to three years.

Honduras became the sixth in the region to ratify in 2020. It was also the 50th country to ratify worldwide, triggering the treaty's entry into force as a legal international instrument.[3] That was a matter of great pride for Hondurans and others in Central America. But still, Guatemala had not ratified.

Finally, in June, 2022, Guatemala's instrument of ratification was deposited with the UN Secretary-General. This was another major milestone for the treaty as a whole, because it made Central America the first recognizable region of the world to be fully on board with the TPNW. That set a challenge for other regions of the world to follow (like West Africa, as we saw in the previous chapter). Nevertheless, the whole process took almost five years.

Why did Guatemala's ratification take so long, and how did it finally come about? To answer those questions, we need to meet our next ICAN campaigner: María Eugenia Villareal, co-founder of the Human Security Network in Latin America and the Caribbean (SEHLAC).[4]

María Eugenia Villarreal and SEHLAC

María Eugenia is a Mexican sociologist specializing in the impact of armed conflict on children. She did research on child soldiers fighting in the Guatemalan civil war during the 1990s, and she was appalled by the number of children being killed and maimed by the landmines and unexploded cluster bombs that were scattered all over the Guatemalan countryside.

María Eugenia went on to co-found SEHLAC as a network for promoting "humanitarian disarmament" within Latin America. SEHLAC's initial focus was on landmines and cluster munitions.[5] But once those were officially banned by international treaties, SEHLAC and the broader humanitarian disarmament movement turned their attention to nuclear weapons - the only indiscriminate and inhumane weapons *not* yet officially banned by an international treaty.

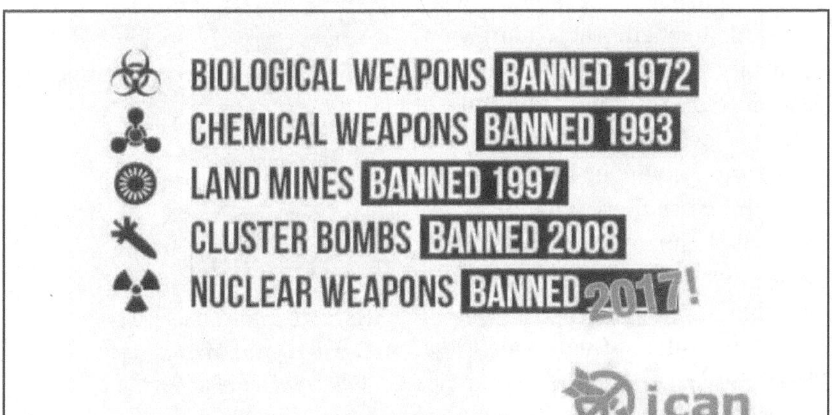

SEHLAC has been an important partner of ICAN ever since. It urged Latin American and Caribbean countries to take an active part in the original negotiations that created the TPNW, and then it urged them all to sign and ratify it.

Like Abdul in West Africa, María Eugenia met with high-level officials across Latin America, building relationships and educating them about the TPNW. But rather than viewing the TPNW through a human rights lens, as in Africa, most of the TPNW work in Latin America has been through the lens of humanitarian disarmament.

Nuclear weapons as a humanitarian issue

On humanitarian grounds, María Eugenia could easily link banning nuclear weapons with the existing bans on landmines and cluster munitions. Most of the countries in Latin America and the Caribbean were already against nuclear weapons since the close call with global nuclear war during the 1962 Cuban Missile Crisis.

After the trauma of that crisis, those countries got together and agreed to make the whole area a nuclear-free zone. They created the Treaty of Tlatelolco, which prohibited the "testing, use, manufacture, production or acquisition by any means whatsoever of any nuclear weapons" as well as the "receipt, storage, installation, deployment and any form of possession of any nuclear weapons" anywhere within the entire Latin America/Caribbean region. (Later, the Pelindaba Treaty similarly made all of Africa a NFZ.)

SEHLAC campaigners (l to r): Camilo Serna, María Eugenia Villarreal and Pia Devota

Unlike in West Africa, where countries needed to be convinced that nuclear weapons were relevant to them, the countries of Central America were already committed to the abolition of nuclear weapons. They did not need any convincing about that.

But since these weapons were already banned from the region, what was the rush to ratify another treaty? Why should a country like Guatemala get involved in what other countries were doing with nuclear weapons

– especially their big and powerful neighbor to the North? Why poke the bear for no good reason?

María Eugenia had to find another reason to persuade Guatemala to ratify the TPNW. She compared the humanitarian impact of landmines and cluster munitions to the humanitarian impact of any potential use of nuclear weapons, which would clearly be so much worse. Surely it would be better for the world to prohibit and eliminate these weapons *before* that happens. And since it had already ratified the landmines treaty and the cluster munitions treaty, surely Guatemala would now want to ratify the TPNW at the earliest possibility.

Central American diplomacy

As in West Africa, there is a regional body for cooperation among the Central American countries. The Central American Integration System (*Sistema de la Integración Centroamericana*, or SICA) was founded in 1993. It includes a Central American bank, a Central American court, and a Central American parliament called the *Parlacen*.

The status of the Parlacen is somewhat disputed among the governments of Central America. Nevertheless, it brings together directly elected representatives from those different countries and provides a venue to discuss and debate, among other things, the importance of joining the TPNW.

In the lead-up to the TPNW negotiations in 2017, María Eugenia held briefings, workshops and one-on-one meetings with members of the Parlacen, as well as with government ministers in each country, to secure their support for a nuclear ban treaty. Thanks, at least in part, to María Eugenia's efforts, Central America played a leading role in those negotiations.

El Salvador was a co-sponsor of the UN resolution that directly led to the negotiations becoming legally possible. Elayne Whyte Gomez, then Ambassador to the UN from Costa Rica, presided over the whole process as President of the negotiations. Guatemala played a very active role in steering some of the key discussions in those negotiations.

Once the treaty was adopted, and all the Central American countries apart from Guatemala had ratified it, María Eugenia continued meeting with the Guatemalan Foreign Minister and negotiating with political parties in Guatemala's Congress to encourage ratification. But as in the case of West Africa, peer pressure from neighboring countries also helped.

At the *Parlacen,* there was discussion about Guatemala being the only Central American country not yet in the TPNW - and the race underway to be the first region fully on board the treaty. With that little extra incentive, Guatemala's congress finally ratified the TPNW, and Central America won the race.

Figure 5.1: The status of the TPNW in Central America and the Caribbean

Up next: Colombia

Successes in Central America, as well as in the Caribbean and much of South America (apart from Argentina) encourage SEHLAC to believe that the next country to ratify the TPNW will be Colombia. SEHLAC is represented in Colombia by the Colombian Campaign to Ban Landmines (CCBL), and Camilo Serna and Carolina Barrios Martinez are campaigners from CCBL with a special focus on the TPNW. Camilo, Carolina and their colleagues in CCBL have worked closely with the Colombian government and also with civil society in Colombia. They have used videos, public events, and political debates that are mainly focused on the problem of landmines to bring up the issue of nuclear weapons.

As in Guatemala, landmines are a very real and present threat to the people of Colombia. After 50 years of civil war, the Colombian countryside remains riddled with anti-personnel landmines, which have killed over 2,300 people and injured over 10,000 since 1990. Demining has been the main focus of CCBL. Until the cancellation of

USAID funding in January 2025, the CCBL had as many as 500 staff engaged in demining activities across the country.

Like Guatemala, Colombia has been supportive of the TPNW from the very beginning. And beyond being a party to the Treaty of Tlatelolco, Colombia even included a prohibition of nuclear weapons in its 1991 constitution.[6] Colombia took part in the TPNW negotiations and voted in favor of its adoption. Next, it signed the TPNW in September, 2018. And yet Colombia has still not ratified it.

In August 2024 a bill for the ratification of the treaty was finally submitted to the Colombian Congress. The bill must be debated and voted on four times in the Senate and four more times in the Chamber of Representatives. It goes to the President for his signature, and then there is a final review by the Constitutional Court. In December 2024, the bill passed its first test in the Senate. As of March 2025, there are still seven more to go.

This whole process normally takes from one to one and a half years, but now that it has begun, there is nothing in the political situation of Colombia that is likely to get in the way of it being successfully concluded. The President of Colombia supports the TPNW. So do the political parties in the Congress, and so do the citizens of Colombia.

So is there anything that could push Colombia to finish this process sooner rather than later? Admirably, Colombia is also leading the way on a new treaty to ban lethal autonomous weapons, as well as a proposed new treaty to phase out the burning of fossil fuels.[7] Perhaps Colombia can be encouraged to get the TPNW out of the way so it can focus on these other treaty proposals.

Colombia and the US

In our scenario, the key to Colombia's speedy ratification has to do with a whole new issue: Colombian President Gustavo Petro and his relationship with US President Donald Trump.

President Petro picked a fight with Trump during the first week of Trump's return to the White House in January 2025. He was appalled that Colombians being deported from the US to Colombia were shown to be shackled and loaded onto military planes.

President Petro demanded that Colombian citizens be treated with respect and dignity. Trump responded by threatening punitive tariffs on Colombian imports to the US. Both sides backed down after behind-the-scenes compromises were reached, but (as of this writing)

Trump is still going ahead with his trade wars on countries all over the world, including Colombia.

In this scenario, President Petro doesn't want to court more trouble with Trump, but he also wants to show the world that he is willing and able to stand up to him. He needs an easy win that Trump won't like but is unlikely to do anything about. And there's another race on to see which world leader is going to push back first against some of Trump's more outrageous policies.

So, in our scenario, Petro steps up, and Colombia is the next country to complete the TPNW ratification process. (In any case, Colombia will certainly ratify sooner or later.)

There are 24 other countries that have signed but not ratified the TPNW. By the time you're reading this book, maybe Colombia, or maybe one of the others, will be next.

The increased significance of ratification moves our scenario clock ten seconds further away from doomsday instead of just one or five. It's still a relatively small step to take compared to how close we still are to doomsday. But ratification also lays a crucially important foundation for further steps to come that will be progressively more significant as this scenario unfolds.

Our scenario clock moves back 10 seconds to 11:57:00 when President Gustavo Francisco Petro Urrego deposits Colombia's instrument of ratification with the United Nations, bringing the total number of States Parties to this treaty to 74.

Why is this significant?

Colombia is already a party to the Nuclear Non-Proliferation Treaty (see previous chapter) and the Treaty of Tlatelolco. These treaties forbid Colombia from developing nuclear weapons, and they forbid countries that already have nuclear weapons from assisting Colombia in any attempt to develop nuclear weapons.

However, the language of both of these other treaties talks only about Colombia's commitment not to *receive* any assistance in building a nuclear weapon from an existing nuclear-armed country. Neither one prohibits Colombia from assisting an existing nuclear-armed country to develop *its* nuclear weapons.

Only by signing and ratifying the TPNW is Colombia, along with the other States Parties to the TPNW, prohibited from assisting other countries in developing their nuclear weapons. This is a crucial point, since it gets to the heart of the strategy described in this scenario. By prohibiting assistance of any kind with the development, manufacture or stockpiling of nuclear weapons, the TPNW provides countries with a very powerful tool with which to pressure the companies.

The "Assistance Clause" appears in a number of disarmament and other related treaties. The NPT, as noted earlier, prohibits *nuclear-weapons states* "in any way to assist, encourage, or induce any non-nuclear-weapon State to manufacture or otherwise acquire nuclear weapons or other nuclear explosive devices, or control over such weapons or explosive devices." But it does not mention anything about *non-nuclear-weapon states* assisting nuclear-weapon states.

The Chemical Weapons Convention (CWC), the Anti-Personnel Mine Ban Convention (APMBC) and Convention on Cluster Munitions (CCM) have all explicitly banned any form of assistance with the prohibited activities, no matter who is assisting whom. The TPNW takes its language directly from these other treaties.

Helpfully, the International Committee of the Red Cross has compiled a list of activities which it would regard as "assistance," based on the discussions that took place during the negotiations for the TPNW:

- planning or training with others for the use of nuclear weapons
- agreeing operational plans or instructions permitting the use of nuclear weapons in multinational operations
- requesting another country to use or threaten to use nuclear weapons
- providing security or transport for nuclear weapons
- exporting or otherwise transferring nuclear material or technology to a recipient that will use it to develop nuclear weapons
- financing prohibited activities such as the development, production or manufacture of nuclear weapons or other nuclear explosive devices

The "assistance clause" in the TPNW (Article 1e), which is identical to similar wording in other treaties, states that "*each State Party undertakes never under any circumstances to assist, encourage or induce, in any way, anyone to engage in any activity prohibited to a*

State Party under this Treaty." And the activities that are prohibited in Article 1a of the treaty are to "develop, test, produce, manufacture, otherwise acquire, possess or stockpile nuclear weapons or other nuclear explosive devices."[8]

Note that this clause does not prohibit assistance only to another state possessing nuclear weapons, but to *anyone* who may be engaged in the prohibited activities. This is a door that opens up opportunities for countries all over the world to put real *pressure on the nuclear weapons companies who operate on their soil.*

At least five of the top two dozen corporations involved in the development, manufacture or maintenance of nuclear weapons are present in Colombia: **Leidos** and **Honeywell**, both heavily involved in US nuclear weapons production, **BAE Systems**, which is involved in UK as well as US nuclear weapons production, **Walchandnagar Industries**, which is involved in the Indian nuclear weapons program, and **Airbus**, which is involved in the French nuclear weapons program.

Location of projects executed by Walchandnagar Industries Ltd.

Whether, and to what extent, Colombia is willing to constrain the activities of these corporations will depend on further steps they may or may not take. (These are described in subsequent chapters.)

Who will ratify the treaty next?

The prize: Brazil

Brazil is a very likely candidate. It gave up its own nuclear weapons program over three decades ago, and it has been a leader in the global effort to eliminate all nuclear weapons, It played a key role in negotiating the TPNW.

The President of Brazil at the time, Michel Temer, was the first world leader to sign the treaty when it opened for signatures at the UN on September 20, 2017. He sent the treaty to the National Congress for ratification, but under the subsequent Presidency of Jair Bolsonaro, it got nowhere.

With the (re-)election of Luiz Inacio Lula da Silva as President in January 2023, Brazil was poised to finally ratify the TPNW - and to play a leading role in working for its universalization. During the 2023 G7 meeting in Hiroshima, at which Brazil was an invited guest, President Lula da Silva made an impassioned speech in support of the total elimination of nuclear weapons.[9] He claimed that ratifying the TPNW is one of his priorities.[10]

However, there are still influential *Bolsonaristas* in the Brazilian Congress, including Luiz Philippe de Orléans e Bragança, a Federal Deputy representing São Paulo and claimant to the throne of the Brazilian monarchy that ruled Brazil from 1815 to 1889.

Luiz Philippe, also known as "the Prince," was the rapporteur on the Congressional Commission for External Relations and National Defense, leading the consultation on the TPNW ratification bill when it first came to the Congress in 2019. That Commission has to approve the ratification, but Phillipe recommended that the Congress vote No on the ratification, giving very confused and garbled reasoning for it.[11] Luckily a vote never took place, but Phillipe is still a major stumbling block to getting the ratification through Congress.

Of the 38 Deputies on the Commission, only about a third of them currently support ratification, even though the President, the government, the churches, the unions, most of the political parties and the people of Brazil overwhelming support it. It is opposed by a few *Bolsonaristas* and that is enough to hold up the process.

Cristian Wittman, SEHLAC's main TPNW campaigner in Brazil, is confident that Brazil will ratify the treaty sooner or later. But he doesn't want to push it to a vote while there is a chance that it would be voted down. Elections in Brazil are coming up in October, 2026. Bolsonaro could get back in, as Trump did, even if he ends up in prison for an attempted coup attempt in 2023. And even if the left-wing gets back in, Phillipe may still be able to prevent passage of the ratification bill.

But with Trump causing so much chaos and making enemies of former allies every day, the political situation could be very different by October, 2026. As Brazilians increasingly reject everything that Trump and the US are doing, so they may also reject the Trump-like party and Trump-like personalities in

Brazil. Time will tell, but in this scenario, the left sweeps the board in 2026, and Brazil ratifies the TPNW shortly thereafter.

The clock goes back a further 10 seconds to 11:56:50 when the Brazilian National Congress, or *Congresso Nacional*, votes overwhelming to ratify the Treaty on the Prohibition of Nuclear Weapons, bringing the total number of States Parties to this treaty to 75.

What does this mean?

Brazil is a big deal. It's the largest country in Latin America and the seventh largest in the world by population. **With the addition of Brazil, half of the 10 largest countries in the world are now parties to the TPNW (Indonesia, Brazil, Mexico, Bangladesh and Nigeria). The other half all have nuclear weapons (China, India, US, Russia and Pakistan).**

Brazil is an important player in the BRICS bloc[1] (Brazil, Russia, India, China, South Africa), which, importantly, includes three nuclear-armed countries (Russia, India and China) as well as South Africa, a formerly nuclear-armed country that voluntarily dismantled its bombs in the 1990s and ratified the TPNW in 2019,

As the BRICS bloc expands to include other countries, the balance of nuclear-armed to non-nuclear-armed states is rapidly shifting. That could play a role in convincing some of the remaining nuclear-armed countries to give up their nuclear weapons. BRICS now includes Indonesia, the fourth largest country in the world by population, which ratified and joined the TPNW in 2024.

Egypt, Ethiopia, Iran and the UAE have also recently joined the BRICS bloc. All four of these countries took part in the negotiations, voted for the TPNW, and are expected at some point to join it.

L3Harris and Embraer

Embraer is a large Brazilian aircraft company with over 20,000 employees working at five locations across Brazil and in seven other countries. It is the third largest producer of civilian aircraft in the world, after Boeing and Airbus. It is a major producer of military aircraft, including the C-390 military transport plane that is capable of re-fueling other aircraft mid-air.

Embraer is important, not only to the Brazilian economy, but to the Brazilian psyche. It is a source of great pride that Brazil is a major player in the global aerospace industry. When Boeing attempted a corporate take-over of Embraer in 2017, the Brazilian government stepped in and said it was "out of the question." A strategic partnership was then proposed, but eventually fell through, keeping Embraer firmly in Brazilian hands.

In 2022, Embraer announced a new partnership, this time with L3Harris, another major US military contractor and nuclear weapons producer. This was to build a new aerial re-fueling tanker for the US military called the KC-390, based on the Embraer C-390.

The US military has relied mainly on the KC-135 Boeing "Stratotanker" to refuel its fleet of B-52 strategic bombers since the 1950s. The KC-135 is now old and outdated; a second tanker, the KC-10, is fully retired; and a third tanker in the USAF inventory, the KC-46, has been grounded after cracks were discovered in 11 planes.

The next generation of tanker aircraft is under development, but it's still a long way off. So the US is scrambling around for an interim replacement for the aging Stratotanker – *specifically to re-fuel B-52 bombers designed to carry nuclear weapons.*[12] The Embraer KC-390 is one option under consideration.

Just prior to Trump's return to the White House, it appeared that L3Harris had lost interest in the partnership with Embraer,[13] but if the Trump administration follows through with its Project 2025 agenda, the KC-390 option may end up back on the table. **This time, it will be Brazil's government who again will say it is "out of the question" that a major Brazilian company should be directly involved in "assisting" the United States with its nuclear weapons program.**

Brazil's ratification would likely inspire many of the 25 countries who have signed but not yet ratified the treaty. Some are medium-sized countries like Myanmar, Sudan, Ghana, and Algeria. Some are smaller but geopolitically significant countries like Nepal, Djibouti and Liechtenstein.

But, in our scenario, Barbados, the Bahamas, and Haiti are the next to ratify - and that brings the whole of the Caribbean into the TPNW family, marking the second complete "region" to fully join the treaty. They are swiftly followed by Sudan and Djibouti, adding to the pressure on the other countries of the Middle East...

Our clock goes back a further 50 seconds to 11:56:00 when these additional five countries ratify the Treaty on the Prohibition of Nuclear Weapons, bringing the total number of States Parties to this treaty to 80.

With Brazil now a State Party to the TPNW, and many more countries on their way, our attention turns to the next logical step in treaty implementation: enforcing the treaty's prohibitions inside each of those countries. Most of them already have at least some laws in place that do this, with Ireland setting the most serious example. Which will be the next country to pass a law like that, and what will it mean for the corporations that develop, manufacture and maintain nuclear weapons?

PRESSURE FROM THE WORLD

- [ ] VOTE FOR UN RESOLUTION
- [ ] SIGN THE TPNW
- [ ] RATIFY THE TPNW
- [x] IMPLEMENT LAWS
- [ ] INCLUDE FINANCE
- [ ] COMMIT TO DIVESTMENT
- [ ] BAN CONTRACTS
- [ ] ADD NATO COUNTRIES
- [ ] US BOMBS OUT OF EUROPE

7 From Ireland to Mexico: Moving on to implementation

How can individuals or corporations be held accountable for violating the TPNW? That responsibility falls to the States Parties. After they ratify, countries are expected to implement Article 5 of the TPNW[1] by passing enforcement legislation. These laws enable a country to prosecute "persons" (both human and corporate) and to set penalties for violations.

Countries that ratify the TPNW are committed to abiding by all of its prohibitions and obligations,[2] but those commitments don't automatically apply to individuals or corporations ("legal persons")[3] within that country. So it's up to each government to create domestic laws to implement the TPNW, and to enforce those laws with their police, courts and prison systems.

The TPNW doesn't spell out what those laws should look like, but it does prohibit *assistance* with nuclear weapons activities. As we saw in the last chapter, this can raise serious questions about the activities of entities (investors, suppliers, offices, subsidiaries, etc. connected with the nuclear weapons business) who are operating within the jurisdiction of a State Party. The assistance prohibition opens the door to more powerful tools (covered in later chapters).

States Parties can choose to enforce the TPNW with harsh laws, *directly* threatening serious legal consequences for individuals and corporations involved in nuclear weapons inside that country's jurisdiction. Such laws strengthen the global norm against everything to do with nuclear weapons, and thereby serve as an *indirect* threat to the industry as a whole. That puts pressure on the industry to find other ways to stay profitable. And that, in turn, may help speed abolition.

But most States Parties are reluctant to take this step *because* it threatens powerful corporations that may provide jobs and income. Stuck in this position, some simply delay crafting enforcement legislation.

Delays are common anyway, because drafting and passing any kind of national legislation can take considerable time and resources that many countries do not have at hand. Almost all parties to the TPNW have *some* laws already in place that align with its purpose, but it can be a difficult process for countries to untangle exactly how many of the TPNW requirements are already covered by existing laws and what gaps may still exist. That work is just getting underway in some of the parties to the TPNW.

So, convincing countries that have signed and ratified the TPNW to go ahead and take this next step is not easy. And the countries that are most willing to do it are the ones least likely to have much impact on the nuclear weapons companies. But every one that *does* take this step is an incentive for others to follow.

The example: Ireland

So far, only two countries, Ireland and Niue, have passed laws specifically to implement the TPNW.

Ireland passed its Prohibition of Nuclear Weapons Act in 2019, prior to ratifying the treaty. (It had to do things in that order: under Irish law, they can't ratify an international treaty *until* it has cleared all the legal hurdles of how the treaty would be applied.)

Ireland's Act is a prime example of what States Parties to the TPNW can do (see the full text of this law in Appendix II). It specifies that any person (natural or legal) within the boundaries of Ireland, or on an Irish ship or Irish plane, is subject to penalties for violating any of the prohibitions in the TPNW. A person who "assists, encourages or induces" the commission of an offense under this Act is also guilty of that offense, and that can include "a director, manager, secretary or other officer" of a corporation.

The penalties include a fine of unlimited amount and/or a custodial sentence of up to life in prison.[4]

The island of Niue is a "self-governing" state in "free association" with New Zealand, which means it is *not* an independent member state of the UN, but it *can* sign international treaties and pass its own laws. In relation to the TPNW, it has done both.

Niue's Prohibition of Nuclear Weapons Act of 2021 is very similar to Ireland's. It applies the TPNW's prohibitions to both natural and legal persons within Niue, and sets a penalty of up to 10 years imprisonment and/or a fine for any violations. As in Ireland, the penalties also apply to corporate officers.

That leaves 71 countries who have ratified the treaty and could now take the next step of national implementation.

Next up: Malta

In our scenario, Malta is the next State Party to the TPNW to pass national implementation legislation. After all, they have a history of taking this step after ratifying the Landmines Convention,[5] the Comprehensive Test Ban Treaty,[6] and other treaties. They don't have connections with the nuclear weapons industry, and thus they don't have to worry about consequences on their economy, jobs, trade, or relations with the United States.

Malta also has a number of nuclear weapons-related laws already on the books – including ones relating to nuclear weapons as terrorism.

Nuclear weapons as terrorism

When Malta was required by Security Council Resolution 1540 (see box below) to implement comprehensive legislation to prevent terrorists from obtaining or using nuclear weapons (or other WMDs), Malta updated their anti-terrorist legislation in the Criminal Code with very comprehensive prohibitions relating to nuclear weapons.[7]

Malta's Criminal Code now prohibits "*the manufacture, possession, acquisition, transport, supply, or use of... nuclear, biological, radiological or chemical weapons; research into or development of... nuclear and chemical weapons; and promoting, constituting, organising, or financing*" any of those activities.

These prohibitions refer specifically to "terrorists" and to "terrorist activities." It's interesting to consider what Malta includes within its definition of terrorism:

> *"threatening to...cause extensive destruction...with the aim of unduly compelling a Government...to perform or abstain from performing any act..."*

That is an almost perfect definition of "nuclear deterrence." It qualifies every country that claims to rely on nuclear deterrence for their defense as a "terrorist" entity. Nevertheless, it is doubtful that a country like Malta would want to go so far as to label the US or UK as terrorist entities, so additional laws are undoubtedly needed for Malta to fully comply with Article 5 of the TPNW.

UN Security Council Resolution 1540 of 2004 requires all countries to adopt "appropriate effective laws which prohibit any non-State actor to manufacture, acquire, possess, develop, transport, transfer or use nuclear, chemical or biological weapons and their means of delivery, in particular for terrorist purposes, as well as attempts to engage in any of the foregoing activities, participate in them as an accomplice, assist or finance them."

This language covers many of the same prohibitions that are in the TPNW, except that they apply only to "non-state actors" (meaning, in this case, non-governmental paramilitary organizations). And even then, the goal is to prevent these activities if they are "for terrorist purposes." Non-state actors are defined in the Resolution as "individuals or entities, not acting under the lawful authority of any State in conducting activities which come within the scope of this resolution."

There is also a more general obligation to prevent nuclear weapons "proliferation" in the Resolution. Although proliferation actors are not defined in the Resolution, the assumption is that they are only countries that do not already possess nuclear weapons, or as in the case of North Korea, are considered to possess nuclear weapons illegitimately.

It is therefore not the intention of UNSCR 1540 to prohibit countries from being involved in the development or manufacture of nuclear weapons for countries that already have nuclear weapons, nor to prohibit assistance or financing of those activities by anyone who is acting under the "lawful authority" of that country.

And as one of only eight States Parties that is not in a nuclear free zone, Malta lacks the laws these other countries have. So they're actively studying what other States Parties are doing so far. They hosted a meeting during the 3MSP in March, 2025, to discuss the results of an initial "mapping exercise" exploring this question. **And in this scenario, Malta is the next to pass national legislation to implement the TPNW into their domestic law.**

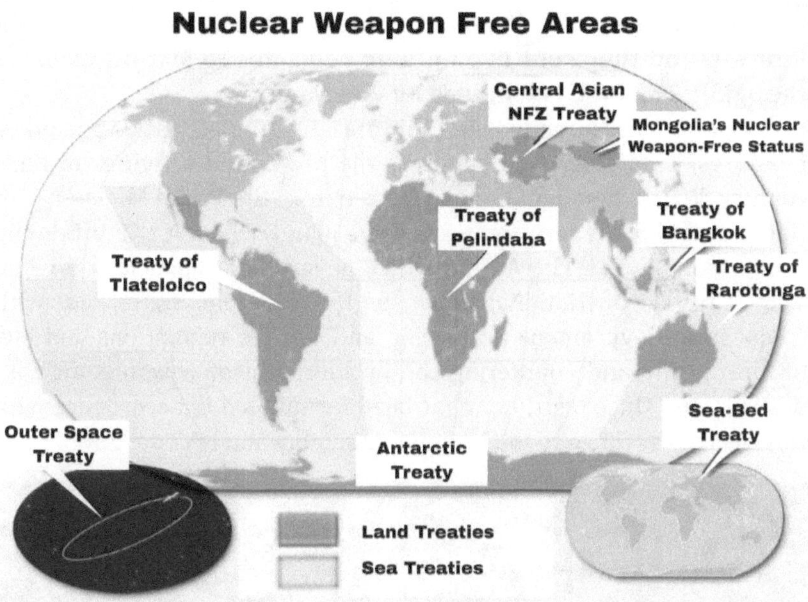

There are four main treaties creating nuclear weapon-free zones covering the whole of Latin America (Treaty of Tlatelolco), the whole of Africa (Pelindaba), Southeast Asia (Bangkok Treaty) and much of the Pacific (Treaty of Rarotonga). Additionally, there are treaties prohibiting nuclear weapons in the Antarctic, on the sea-bed and in outer space.

Whether it's Malta or another one of the 71 States Parties that joins Ireland and Niue in passing national legislation specific to the TPNW, there can be no doubt that national implementation is a very significant step. Abolition is still a long way off, but this development is worth 15 seconds on our scenario clock.

The scenario clock is now 15 seconds further away from midnight, at 11:55:45, after lawmakers in the parliament of Malta pass the "Nuclear Weapons Prohibition Act" that applies the TPNW to persons *in* Malta, and defines the penalties for violations.

In our scenario, Thailand is next. They've shown a keen interest, and they sent five of their delegates to Malta's event at the 3MSP. Thailand is followed by Viet Nam.

Viet Nam has already taken appropriate "administrative and other measures" to prevent and suppress the prohibited activities in their country. With a detailed 23-page Decree from the Prime Minister, Viet Nam has laid out a very comprehensive plan for how it will tackle the prohibitions in the TPNW, and which government agencies do what. The Ministry of National Defense, for example, is tasked with "requesting Government to develop and finalize regulations and law on preventing and countering the proliferation of weapons of mass destruction." Once legislation has been formulated in accordance with this Decree, it will go to the National Assembly and become law.

Our clock is now 30 seconds further away from midnight, at 11:55:15, after Thailand and Viet Nam pass national legislation to implement the TPNW.

Unlike Malta, Thailand and Viet Nam have more to lose in terms of trade and business with the multinational nuclear weapons corporations that have operations on their soil. Their implementation of Article 5 of the TPNW is a brave step.

Can they inspire countries with an even greater stake in these companies? This is where we'll see the real impact of national implementation. Mexico is one of those countries.

The prize: Mexico

Once these other countries in the TPNW start passing national legislation to implement the TPNW, the pressure is on Mexico and the other countries in the TPNW "core group"[8] to follow suit.

Mexico has played a key role in the TPNW from the very beginning. It hosted one of the three conferences on the humanitarian consequences of nuclear weapons in 2014. It was these conferences that led directly to the treaty negotiations. Mexico was one of the more active participants in those negotiations and it subsequently signed and ratified the TPNW.

Mexico has remained in the TPNW coordination group, working with New Zealand to advance work on Article 4 of the treaty, relating to the steps and a timetable for countries that have nuclear weapons and want to join the treaty. Mexico also presided over the Second Meeting of States Parties to the TPNW at the UN in New York in 2023.

Notably, Mexico has been committed to nuclear abolition since long before the TPNW. After the Cuban Missile Crisis of 1962, Mexico led the way in establishing the Treaty of Tlatelolco (see chapter 6), named after the district in Mexico City where it was negotiated.

After it signed and ratified the NPT, the CTBT, the Treaty of Tlatelolco, [9] and various other treaties and Security Council resolutions, Mexico has passed implementation legislation that codifies those treaties in Mexican law. This means that Mexico now has at least two dozen laws on its books that relate to nuclear weapons.[10]

Having done so much already, Mexico is a bit reluctant to have to go through the process of passing yet another law. At the same time, it cannot be left behind as a champion of the TPNW if other countries are moving in this direction.

Dr. Jans Fromow Guerra and AMMPGN

Dr. Jans Fromow Guerra is a professor of ophthalmology at the National Autonomous University of Mexico (UNAM) and a world specialist on retina care. Jans is also a member of *Asociación de Médicos Mexicanos para la Prevención de la Guerra Nuclear* (AMMPGN), the Mexican branch of International Physicians for the Prevention of Nuclear War (IPPNW).

Jans and AMMPGN represent an important category of campaigners for nuclear abolition – the medical profession. Doctors, medical students, public health workers and other medical professionals the world over have long been at the forefront of campaigns to reduce the risk of nuclear war and to abolish nuclear weapons.

Doctors are acutely aware of the effects of radiation on the human body, and they've led the research on the effects of nuclear war on the climate, and thus on global food supplies. But most importantly, doctors are aware of the limitations of modern medicine and the inability to "cure" even a tiny proportion of the people who would be affected by a single nuclear blast, let alone a full-scale nuclear war. "We must prevent what we cannot cure" has been a IPPNW's mantra since it was founded in 1980.

IPPNW was awarded the Nobel Peace Prize in 1985 for its efforts to raise awareness about the dangers of nuclear weapons with the public and with political leaders in both the US and the USSR. In 2007, IPPNW launched ICAN, which then went on to win *another* Nobel Peace Prize for its work on the TPNW in 2017 (see Chapter 4).

Since Mexico itself is already so committed to the TPNW, AMMPGN's work there has been largely focused on educating other medical professionals and the general public about nuclear weapons and their medical effects. Together with Soka Gokkai International (SGI) in Mexico, AMMPGN also promotes the international work of ICAN throughout Mexico.

Jans himself has maintained good relations with Mexico's Ministry of Foreign Affairs, and especially with the department responsible for nuclear disarmament. Mexico's current Foreign Secretary, Juan Ramon de la Fuente Ramirez, has been supportive of Jans' work since 1991. Prior to his appointment as Foreign Secretary in 2024, de la Fuente was ambassador of Mexico to the United Nations and very involved in TPNW matters. On leaving that post, he was elected to preside over the Second Meeting of States Parties to the TPNW in November, 2023.

National implementation in Mexico

De la Fuente needs convincing that passing a new law is really necessary for meeting Mexico's treaty obligations under Article 5 of the TPNW. He needs to be convinced that the prohibitions of the TPNW do not already apply to *individuals and corporations in Mexico*, given that, under Article 133 of the Mexican Constitution, the TPNW is already the law of the land in Mexico.

As a professional diplomat, de la Fuente does not want to provoke the US unnecessarily, nor to put jobs and income at risk by upsetting some of the powerful US corporations operating in Mexico. These corporations contribute millions in corporate taxes to the Mexican treasury and help maintain a healthy balance of trade.

Mexico shares a 2,000-mile border with its powerful neighbor to the north, and it works hard to maintain friendly relations. Mexico has been at pains to help the US curb the flow of refugees crossing the border illegally from Mexico into the US and to stop the illegal production and export of fentanyl.

But with President Trump back in Washington, imposing crippling tariffs and making enemies of his closest allies, everything has now changed in that relationship. Even before tariffs went into effect, it was clear that the Trump administration wanted to force US corporations to move jobs and factories back to the US. This is having a direct effect on US auto manufacturers, for example, who have spent decades setting up plants in Mexico to exploit its cheaper labor market and more relaxed environmental regulations.

Presidents Sheirbaum and Trump

In this scenario, it is actually the President who takes the lead in getting Mexico to take this next step.

Claudia Sheirbaum became the first woman to be elected President of Mexico in 2024. She is a climate scientist who shared the 2007 Nobel Peace Prize with Al Gore for her work on climate change. President Sheirbaum has called herself an "idealist." She has committed herself to continuing the widely popular efforts of the former Mexican President, Andrés Manuel López Obrador, to reduce poverty and tackle gang violence. And, like her fellow Mexicans, she's very much committed to abolishing nuclear weapons.

At the G-20 Summit held in Brazil in November, 2024, President Sheirbaum proposed that 1% of global military spending be redirected to finance projects addressing climate change and promoting sustainable development. She described this proposal as being based on the "new Mexican humanist model, which prioritizes community-based development, shared prosperity, inclusion, equality, and social justice."

In response to Trump's threat to impose 25% tariffs on Mexico, President Sheirbaum rushed Mexican troops to the border to tackle illegal crossings into the US. This was something she was already committed to doing for Biden, however, so while it looked like a "success" for Trump, it was in fact a victory for Mexico that the tariffs were abandoned, at least for the moment.

Mexico is under no illusions, however, that President Trump is going to do anything other than continue to push for more and more concessions from Mexico in order to bolster the US economy, no matter the cost to the Mexican economy.

Given that relations with the US are already at an all-time low, President Sheirbaum decides that the time has come to

incorporate the TPNW's prohibitions into domestic law, regardless of the impact it will have on US corporations operating in Mexico.

> The scenario clock is now a further 15 seconds away from midnight, at 11:55:00, after lawmakers in the Mexican Chamber of Deputies, *La Cámara de Diputados*, pass a "Nuclear Abolition" bill that potentially has big implications for some of the largest US nuclear weapons contractors.

Mexico passes a law with language taken directly from the TPNW. It makes it an offense within Mexico, punishable by up to life in prison, for any person to "assist, encourage or induce, in any way, anyone to engage in any activity relating to the development, testing, production, manufacture, possession or stockpiling of nuclear weapons."

Honeywell in Mexico

Honeywell does exactly those things at the Kansas City National Security Campus (KCNSC) in Kansas City, Missouri. Honeywell directly oversees the development, production, procurement and delivery of 80% of the non-nuclear components of all US nuclear weapons.[11]

Honeywell also has 12,000 employees working in 11 manufacturing plants across Mexico.

What exactly is produced by these plants in Mexico? Does any of it have any direct connection to the work of the KCNSC in Kansas City? This isn't publicly known. But if Honeywell is anything like the US auto manufacturers operating in Mexico, it's almost impossible to imagine that they don't use their plants in Mexico to produce whatever components can be produced more cheaply there - then shipping those components to the US for final assembly, just as the auto manufacturers do (to ensure compliance with the "Buy American" laws that were introduced long before Trump came along[12]).

Honeywell International

Unlike Boeing, RTX and other nuclear weapons companies that operate in only a few other countries, Honeywell claims to operate in 110 countries, many of which are already States Parties to the TPNW.

There's nothing in the TPNW that explicitly forbids US companies involved in the nuclear weapons business from operating in Mexico. But the TPNW states that assisting, *in any way*, with the development or production of nuclear weapons is a violation.

By incorporating that language into their national legislation, Mexico is putting US corporations like Honeywell operating in Mexico on notice that they are potentially risking prosecution if they are assisting in any way with the development or production of nuclear weapons.

How does that impact Honeywell? The additional costs of moving back to the US, building new factories, and paying better wages would make the company less profitable. They'd also be less competitive, so they could lose contracts and business that they were able to secure with their lower costs in Mexico. For a company like Honeywell, this might just be a temporary annoyance for them to deal with, but it could also affect their entire business model and require a major restructuring of the business.

At least six other US nuclear weapons contractors have operations or facilities in Mexico.[13] Many other States Parties to the TPNW are also host to nuclear weapons companies and/or have contractual relations with these companies. To what extent those companies are directly involved in "assisting" the development, production or maintenance of nuclear weapons is still unknown. But the *legislative risk* that these companies will face is real.

When Mexico passes this law, it sets off a domino effect with other States Parties that have been hesitating. It's only a matter of time before many more countries have made it a criminal offense to assist in the development, manufacture, possession or stockpiling of nuclear weapons.

And meanwhile, other countries are moving on to the *next* level of pressure that can be put on these US corporations – defining investment as a form of prohibited assistance.

With laws in Mexico directly threatening US corporations like Honeywell, the pressure is building on the nuclear weapons industry. But there are still more pressures available to the States Parties to the TPNW. As the TPNW continues to expand, so does the level of commitment from each country. A next step they can take is to explicitly define the financing of these corporations as a form of "assistance" that is prohibited under the treaty. Only Cuba has so far made such a declaration. Which country will be next?

PRESSURE FROM THE WORLD

- [ ] VOTE FOR UN RESOLUTION
- [ ] SIGN THE TPNW
- [ ] RATIFY THE TPNW
- [ ] IMPLEMENT LAWS
- [x] INCLUDE FINANCE
- [ ] COMMIT TO DIVESTMENT
- [ ] BAN CONTRACTS
- [ ] ADD NATO COUNTRIES
- [ ] US BOMBS OUT OF EUROPE

8 From Cuba to the Holy See: Defining financing as "assistance"

The TPNW does not explicitly prohibit financing of nuclear weapons activities, but it does prohibit "assistance" of any kind. Does that include loaning money to the companies that make nuclear weapons – or buying shares in those companies? It falls to each State Party to make a statement defining whether it understands "assistance" to include "financial assistance." They can even pass enforcement laws that make financial assistance a crime.

When States Parties to the TPNW pass their own national implementation laws, it's a crucial step toward putting pressure on the corporations that develop, manufacture and maintain nuclear weapons. This is especially the case if the legislation applies to "legal" persons (i.e. corporations) as well as to "natural" persons (i.e. human beings). When directors and other officers of a corporation can also be held liable for any violations of the law by that corporation, the pressure of the law is complete.

However, there's still some ambiguity that begs to be clarified when it comes to the TPNW's prohibition on assistance. During the treaty negotiations, the idea of explicitly prohibiting financial assistance was debated, but the delegates chose to follow the precedent (and even to use the same wording) as several previous treaties. Following that norm, they left it up to each State Party to make a statement and/or pass a law about whether – for that country – assistance includes financing.

The example: Cuba

So far, only Cuba has defined financing of nuclear weapons as a form of assistance prohibited by the TPNW. Cuba's official declaration states that they are joining the TPNW with the understanding that:

> *"1. The prohibition on the testing of nuclear weapons contained in Article 1(a) encompasses all forms of testing, including those performed using non-explosive methods such as subcritical testing and computer simulation.*
>
> *2. The transit of nuclear weapons and other nuclear explosive devices through territory under the jurisdiction of the States Parties to this Treaty is also a prohibited activity according to the provisions of Article 1(e).*
>
> *3. The financing of any activity prohibited to a State Party under this Treaty is also a prohibited activity according to the provisions of Article 1(e).*

Cuba has a long history of opposition to US imperialism and to global domination by US corporations. So it is not surprising that they might be willing to prohibit the financing of nuclear weapons companies and to see this as a means of putting pressure on the United States. Other countries in the TPNW have been more hesitant to challenge US dominance and risk potential damage to their own economies.

It is not necessary, however, for *all* the countries in the TPNW to explicitly prohibit financial assistance for the impact to be felt by the nuclear weapons industry. After all, action by only 40 States Parties to the CCM had a significant effect on the cluster munitions industry (see box below). And the action itself can be as simple as a statement in an email or a speech at the UN for the impact to be felt.

The TPNW used identical language to the **Convention on Cluster Munitions**' Article 1(1)(c), which commits States Parties never to "assist, encourage or induce anyone to engage in any activity prohibited to a State Party under this Convention."

So far, 38 States Parties to the CCM have made statements defining financing as part of assistance. At least 20 of these are also parties to the TPNW.

And 11 States Parties to the CCM have enacted legislation explicitly criminalizing investments in cluster munitions. Three of them are currently in the TPNW: Ireland, New Zealand and Mexico.

Although other factors were involved, it made a huge impact on cluster munitions companies when *whole countries stopped investing* in them. Even though the United States has never joined the CCM, six US companies that were producing cluster munitions have subsequently stopped production: Northrop Grumman, Textron, General Dynamics, Lockheed Martin, L3 (now part of L3Harris) and Orbital ATK (since acquired by Northrop Grumman). Textron cited declining demand and "the current political climate" as their reasons for pulling out of the cluster munitions business.

Ireland defined financing as part of assistance in the case of the CCM. It has not yet made such a statement or law regarding the TPNW, but it has already begun some national divestment. The Irish Sovereign Fund (ISIF, which is already divested by law from cluster munitions, landmines, and even and fossil fuels) took immediate steps to divest from nuclear weapons when they joined the TPNW. But ISIF was not guided by any clear Irish law or instructions, and there is not yet public information about exactly what ISIF has divested from and what criteria they applied. (We'll be coming back to Ireland to pick up on this in the next chapter.)

Up next: Costa Rica

As noted in Chapter 6, Costa Rica has been a strong supporter of the TPNW from the beginning, along with its neighbors in Central America. It was one of the first 11 CCM States Parties to pass legislation to outlaw "financing" as a form of "assisting" the cluster munitions industry.[1] Will it follow Cuba in making such a declaration or law about the TPNW?

In our scenario, Costa Rica does indeed take that step at the first review conference of the TPNW, which will take place in New York at the end of 2026. That empowers Ecuador, Guatemala, Peru and Chile to follow suit.

As momentum builds, panicked meetings in the boardrooms of several nuclear weapons corporations ensue.

The clock in our scenario goes back 30 seconds to 11:54:30 when Costa Rica announces its interpretation of the assistance clause in the TPNW to include a prohibition on all forms of financing. This sets in motion further moves by other States Parties to the TPNW, encouraged to follow Costa Rica's example.

Nuclear weapons as "controversial weapons"

Already, as countries in the TPNW step up the pressure on the nuclear weapons companies, so too have private banks and other financial institutions, especially in Europe.

Several companies provide global indices that help investors identify which companies match certain criteria. One index is for socially responsible investment (SRI) criteria. A subset of SRI is an index that identifies companies that meet certain environmental, social and governance (ESG) criteria. And a subset of ESG identifies companies that are not involved in "controversial weapons" production.

Are nuclear weapons listed as "controversial?" That depends on the source. Yes, according to **Standard and Poor (S&P)**, **Institutional Shareholder Services (ISS)**, **Solactive,** and **MorningStar** (incorporating **Sustainalytics**).

But **Bloomberg** does *not* include nuclear weapons in their screening of controversial weapons, and neither does the most influential index, which is from **Morgan Stanley Capital International (MSCI).**

MSCI defines controversial weapons as those that have been "subject to widespread bans or restrictions by international treaties or conventions, [as long as] such treaties or conventions are deemed 'material' to international investors..."[2] In other words, they're banned by an international treaty AND a sufficient number of investors think that that particular treaty is important enough to pay attention to. In the case of nuclear weapons, clearly MSCI does not think *as yet* that the

TPNW has the same status as the CCM or the Landmines Treaty, for instance.

Other criteria used by MSCI to define controversial weapons include:

- The weapon is indiscriminate, i.e., there is an increased risk of civilian casualties
- The weapon can be classified as a weapon of mass destruction with a single incident resulting in a large number of deaths
- The weapon is considered to be excessively injurious, i.e., it causes an inordinate amount of pain and suffering
- The weapon may have long term health impacts on the populations in areas where they are used

Clearly, all these criteria apply to nuclear weapons. And yet, MCSI's current list of controversial weapons includes cluster bombs, landmines, depleted uranium, chemical and biological weapons, blinding laser weapons, non-detectable fragments and incendiary weapons (white phosphorus) – but *not* nuclear weapons.

In 2019, an open letter from over 100 institutional investors representing assets worth $6.8 trillion urged the global index providers to standardize their definitions of controversial weapons – and to include nuclear weapons in that definition.[3] But so far, the results are still mixed.

MSCI, for its part, has indicated that its definition of controversial weapons "may evolve over time to reflect changes in international treaties or conventions, national regulations and market perspectives." Those changes depend, above all else, on *feedback they get from the investment community.*

So the more countries prohibit nuclear weapons investments, and the more investors insist on excluding nuclear weapons companies from their portfolios, the more it will become the global norm that nuclear weapons *are* controversial weapons and should not be included in *any* ESG or SRI investment portfolio.

The clock goes back a further 2 minutes to 11:52:30 when Ecuador, Guatemala, Peru, and Chile also announce their interpretation of the assistance clause in the TPNW to include a prohibition on all forms of financing.

The prize: Holy See

The Holy See is the smallest country in the world, covering a territory of just 100 acres. But with 1.4 billion Catholics in the world, its global influence is vastly greater than the space it occupies.

The Roman Catholic Church has assets globally of at least $73 billion, according to one estimate.[4] Catholic orders and institutions have great influence over the investment policies and decisions of other entities, even whole countries, that are nominally or partially Catholic.[5]

Pope Francis and divestment

The late Pope Francis, in his *Laudato Si'* encyclical, encouraged every Catholic institution to "align its investment policy with the Vatican guidelines" and to divest, specifically, from fossil fuels. This has led to over $500 billion being divested from fossil fuels so far from those institutions.

The Pope declared the mere possession of nuclear weapons to be "immoral" and denounced the concept of nuclear "deterrence." Unfortunately, before he died, he had not yet called on Catholics to divest from nuclear weapons with the same moral force as he had called for divestment from fossil fuels.

The US Conference of Catholic Bishops, which in the 1980s was more outspoken than the then Pope in their denunciation of nuclear weapons, is now less so. Nevertheless, in their 2021 socially responsible investment guidelines, the US bishops declare they "will not invest in firms that derive any revenue from the production of weapons inconsistent with Catholic teaching on war (e.g., biological and chemical weapons, landmines, nuclear weapons, weapons of mass destruction, etc.).[6]

The potential is certainly there for mass divestment of Catholic institutions from nuclear weapons companies on a scale similar to their divestment from fossil fuels.

In our scenario, the Holy See issues a written statement to the first Review Conference of the TPNW, clarifying their interpretation of the prohibition on assistance (article 1e) to include a prohibition on investments. This simple statement by the Holy See in relation to the TPNW could be what sets off a wave of divestment by Catholics.

Much like their prior statement about cluster munitions, their statement reads:

> ***"In a world ever more globalized and interdependent, some countries may have investments in companies that are involved in the development, production or stockpiling of nuclear weapons outside their national borders. It is important for the integrity of the TPNW and for its application to include these investments in the list of prohibitions."***

More momentum, and from an influential moral voice. Another 30 seconds on our clock.

> `The clock goes back another 30 seconds to 11:52:00` when the Holy See announces its interpretation of the assistance clause in the TPNW to include a prohibition on all forms of financing. This sets off a further flurry of divestment from Catholic institutions around the world.

Catholic Church divestment

The Vatican itself announced in 2022 that it was divesting from all arms manufacturers. But what about other Catholic investors? They still seem to be exploring where else to put their money.

At a meeting of asset managers in London in November 2024, Jean-Baptiste de Franssu, President of the Institute for the Works of Religion (the "Vatican Bank,") claimed that Catholics around the world had the potential to invest as much as $1.75 trillion in line with the Church's teaching. The problem, he explained, was that there were only a handful of funds available to them that met the Church's criteria (about armaments, among many other things.).

Ave Maria Mutual Fund is the largest Catholic investment firm in the US. They don't invest in abortion clinics or producers of pornography, but they *do* invest in arms manufacturers.[7] Knights of Columbus, a large Catholic charity, likewise has millions invested in arms companies, including nuclear weapons producers. Will that change?

In our scenario, with leadership from the Vatican Bank, the new Pope, and some key bishops, cardinals and archbishops, there's a seismic shift inside the Catholic Church. Suddenly it's becoming unacceptable to call oneself or one's organization Catholic while holding investments in companies that threaten

the whole planet – whether with fossil fuels or nuclear weapons. That excuse is gone.

All across Europe, Catholic institutions are divesting from all armament companies, even conventional (non-nuclear) weapons. And in the US, Catholic funds like Ave Maria decide to keep conventional weapons but remove the nuclear companies from their portfolios. Catholic charities, like Knights of Columbus, do likewise.

In 2024, the Diocese of San Diego was the first in the US to divest from fossil fuels, and **now they're divesting from nuclear weapons too. So is the Archdiocese of Chicago,** which was the first to commit to powering all their churches with renewable energy.

Archbishop Wester of Santa Fe, already an outspoken opponent of nuclear weapons, has joined with Archbishop Etienne of Seattle in committing to divest their own diocesan funds from nuclear weapons companies. They issue a statement calling on all US Catholics to do the same.

Rolls-Royce feels the heat

The first company to be directly affected by a surge in divestment from Catholics around the world is the British manufacturer of luxury cars – and nuclear submarines. Rolls-Royce is relatively new to the nuclear weapons business, but it now has several multi-year contracts with the UK Ministry of Defence for work on the new Dreadnought submarines that are due to carry the UK's nuclear missiles starting in the mid-2030s.

Rolls-Royce is a well-established name brand, having started in the luxury car business in 1904. It's been a favorite "safe stock" for investors over many decades. As of April, 2025, Rolls Royce's overall value (their market capitalization, or "market cap") is almost $80 billion.

Market cap has very little to do with the actual profits of the company. Rather, it's an overall reflection of how the world "values" that company. At least 50% of the market cap of most companies comes from "intangibles," like the value of their brand name, their public reputation, their relationship with their competitors, and how they fit into the market. When a company's reputation is tarnished, its not just bad for morale. It's bad for the bank balance, because the company loses value.

In our scenario, Rolls-Royce's reputation takes a beating from the Holy See's statement at the TPNW Review Conference.

Its involvement in the nuclear weapons business gets Rolls-Royce added to the list of investments banned by Catholic institutions. After frenzied divestment by Catholic individuals and institutions, especially in Europe, the value of Rolls-Royce starts to drop drastically.

Of course, stock prices go up and down all the time. What one investor sells, another will buy up – as long as it's safe and popular. **But now, Rolls Royce's remaining investors are suffering what's known as "investor anxiety." They're more ready to sell off their shares at the slightest provocation. The board of Rolls-Royce announces they are pulling out of the nuclear submarine business. They are going to stick to luxury cars.**

That's the kind of impact a divestment movement can have. And we know because it already happened to Serco.

Serco is a multinational corporation based in the UK. It provides a wide range of services to the UK government, including management of pensions, prisons, hospitals, garbage collection, train services – and until 2021, the UK's nuclear weapons program.

Serco had the job, together with Lockheed Martin and Jacobs, of running the UK's Atomic Weapons Establishment (AWE) at Aldermaston. When that contract came up for renewal, Serco put in a bid for it. But according to "City sources," Serco shareholders objected to Serco's continued involvement with nuclear weapons and their bid was subsequently withdrawn.

"The decision," according to *The Sunday Telegraph*, "follows warnings from fund managers that working with nuclear weapons might force them to dump Serco shares due to non-compliance with Environmental, Social and Governance (ESG) standards."

At least 28 European financial institutions had already divested from Serco as a result of their involvement in the nuclear weapons industry. After announcing they would not have any future involvement in the UK's nuclear weapons program, Serco was removed from divestment lists and returned to the good graces of ethical investors (even as some of those investors have relaxed their opposition to nuclear weapons work in the wake of Russia's invasion of Ukraine).

The clock goes back another minute to 11:51:00 when Rolls-Royce announces it is pulling out of the nuclear weapons business to concentrate on its luxury cars.

As more and more countries define financing of nuclear weapons corporations as a form of assistance, the pressure on these corporations grows. But there's an even more powerful tool: States Parties can explicitly prohibit those investments by law.

PRESSURE FROM THE WORLD

- [ ] VOTE FOR UN RESOLUTION
- [ ] SIGN THE TPNW
- [ ] RATIFY THE TPNW
- [ ] IMPLEMENT LAWS
- [ ] INCLUDE FINANCE
- [x] COMMIT TO DIVESTMENT
- [ ] BAN CONTRACTS
- [ ] ADD NATO COUNTRIES
- [ ] US BOMBS OUT OF EUROPE

9 From Switzerland to South Africa: The commitment to divest

Once States Parties have defined investing in nuclear weapons companies as prohibited under the Assistance Clause of the TPNW, the next step is to pass that prohibition into law. This can be a powerful tool indeed.

So far, Ireland is the only State Party to the TPNW that is actively divesting from nuclear weapons companies, but it hasn't yet passed a law enforcing that. Ironically, the one country that *has* a law banning such investments is Switzerland – which has not yet joined the TPNW.

Divestment laws are sure to have an impact on the corporations, and the more countries pass investment ban laws, the sooner the companies will have to take a hard look at whether their involvement in the nuclear weapons industry is worth the legislative, reputational, and economic risks.

The example: Switzerland

Switzerland took part in the negotiations for the TPNW and voted in favor of its adoption. Both houses of the Swiss Federal Parliament then passed a resolution calling on the Swiss government to sign the treaty and submit it to the parliament for ratification "without delay."[1]

But so far, the Swiss government has refused. In 2018 it published a report concluding that "at this stage, the reasons against an accession of Switzerland outweigh the potential opportunities..." It has officially abstained on UN resolutions in support of the TPNW ever since then. And in March, 2024, the Swiss government again announced that Switzerland will not join the TPNW "for the time being."

The Swiss War Materiel Act was adopted by the Federal Assembly of the Swiss Confederation in 1996 and has been updated several times since then (see partial text at Appendix III). The Act defines "prohibited war materiel" to include nuclear weapons, and prohibits both direct and indirect financing of any activities relating to prohibited war materiel.

Article 8b of the Act defines **direct financing** as "the direct granting of credits, loans or gifts or comparable financial advantages in order to pay or advance costs and expenditures that are associated with the development, manufacture or acquisition of prohibited war materiel."

This has been interpreted so far to mean that credits, loans or gifts to a company that makes nuclear weapons are acceptable as long as these are for "other" activities of the company and not "associated with" their nuclear weapons activities.

Article 8c of the Act also prohibits **indirect financing**, "where the prohibition of direct financing is circumvented thereby..." Indirect financing is defined as:

a. *participation* in companies that develop, manufacture or acquire prohibited war materiel;
b. the *acquisition of debt securities or other investment products* (i.e. shares) issued by such companies.

This would appear to rule out owning shares in companies that develop, manufacture or acquire nuclear weapons, but only if this is considered to be an attempt to "circumvent" the prohibition of direct financing.

Despite these apparent loopholes and lack of enforcement at this time, it remains the most comprehensive national prohibition of nuclear weapons financing to date.

Not accepting that for an answer, campaigners in Switzerland launched an initiative in July 2024 to collect 100,000 signatures needed from the Swiss public to trigger a popular vote on joining the TPNW. If Switzerland votes in favor of joining the treaty, the government would be forced under Swiss law to oblige.

In the meantime, Switzerland, a country that is *not* yet party to the TPNW, already bans investments in nuclear weapons companies as part of the Swiss War Materiel Act. This Act strictly controls all arms production and exports from Switzerland, and defines prohibited war materiel that cannot be produced or exported at all.

The Swiss War Materiel Act is an important model for other countries. It's the only current example of national legislation that bans private as well as public investments in nuclear weapons companies. The Act appears to prohibit holding shares in a nuclear weapons company as a form of indirect financing.

Article 35b of the Act specifies a penalty of up to five years in prison or a fine for "any person who wilfully fails to comply with the prohibition of financing." But so far, there has been no legal enforcement of this Act in Switzerland.

And Swiss banks, including the largest one, UBS, seem to have found a loophole. Why do they still hold shares in nuclear weapons companies? It's not clear how they get away with it, but it may not be for much longer.[2]

Next up: Ireland

There are other precedents for passing treaty-related laws prohibiting investment in the relevant corporations. For example, after joining the Cluster Munitions Treaty (see box in Chapter 8), eleven countries (including Ireland) passed laws prohibiting investments in cluster munitions.[3]

Ireland has even passed the world's first laws against investing in fossil fuels, even though there is not yet a fossil fuels treaty.[4]

During the TPNW negotiations, Ireland was open to the treaty explicitly banning financing as a form of prohibited "assistance," but in the end, as we saw in Chapter 8, it was left up to each country to define for themselves what was meant by "assistance."

Thus, when Ireland joined the TPNW, the national legislation implementing the treaty into Irish law did *not* include such a commitment (see Chapter 7 and Appendix II). But because of Ireland's history with other treaties, Ireland's Strategic Investment Fund (ISIF) assumed the TPNW would be the same, so ISIF announced it was divesting its holdings from nuclear weapons companies even before Ireland had ratified the treaty (see Chapter 8).[5] Ireland's two largest banks, Bank of Ireland and Allied Irish, did the same. Both of those banks at the time had part public ownership, so they were expecting to have to follow government decisions on investment.

It's a bit of an anomaly that Ireland doesn't have a law *mandating* Ireland to divest from nuclear weapons, even though it *is* divesting. It could be argued that the legal precedent has now been established, so a distinct law is no longer needed. However, the absence of a law has several consequences: ISIF is not required to publicly disclose how its divestment is being defined or which companies are being targeted; if ISIF or the other banks wanted to reverse their decision, there would be nothing to stop them; and other international banks operating in Ireland remain invested in numerous nuclear weapons companies.[6]

A bill mandating nuclear weapons divestment was already drafted and presented to the Irish Parliament in 2012, before the TPNW was even a pipe dream. It's still there, waiting to be revived and passed into law. Here is the story of that bill...

David Hutchinson Edgar and the Irish Campaign for Nuclear Disarmament

David Hutchinson Edgar is the chair of the Irish Campaign for Nuclear Disarmament (Irish CND). As a peace campaigner, he has long been urging the Irish government to do more to get the nuclear-armed countries to fulfill their disarmament commitments under Article VI of the NPT.

David worked closely with a Dublin City Councillor named Eoghan (pronounced "Owen") Murphy, who was one of the keynote speakers at Irish CND's Hiroshima commemoration ceremony in 2010. Eoghan had previously worked in the Ministry of Foreign Affairs on matters relating to the NPT. Then Eoghan was elected to the Irish Parliament as a member of the Fine Gael center-right party.

This gave David and Irish CND the opportunity they had been looking for to get a bill passed with cross-party support. All the political parties in Ireland support nuclear disarmament, though at this time Irish CND was more used to active engagement on disarmament issues from the Labour Party and Greens than from Fine Gael.

David drafted a bill to ban investments in nuclear weapons, based on the bill that Ireland had just passed prohibiting investments in land mines and cluster munitions. David and Eoghan agreed that it seemed highly incongruous to ban investments in certain categories of indiscriminate and inhumane weapons and *not* to ban investments in the most indiscriminate and inhumane weapon of them all – nuclear weapons.

So Eoghan polished up the language and presented the bill to his colleagues in the Parliament and various ministries. The Ministry of Foreign Affairs was fine with it, but officials in the Ministry of Finance raised concerns about its possible impact on a major project being planned for Shannon Airport involving a hub for a major nuclear weapons producer, Boeing.

As a junior backbencher in the Parliament, Eoghan didn't have the clout to get his bill onto the floor for a vote. So it sat there for several years, while momentum was building for a new treaty that might make his bill obsolete.

Ireland as a global leader on nuclear abolition

Ireland's leadership role in promoting nuclear abolition already gives it credence and international recognition that far exceed its "weight" as a relatively small island on the outskirts of Europe. Ireland works very closely with Mexico and New Zealand on all global matters relating to nuclear weapons. Together with Thailand, it co-chairs a TPNW informal working group on "complementarity," focused especially on addressing the claim brought up by some countries that the TPNW somehow undermines, rather than strengthens, the NPT.

Ireland has so far seen no need to pass an actual law to divest public funds from nuclear weapons companies, because in practice they're already doing it. But divestment legislation would make its existing practices more structured, more accountable, more airtight. More importantly, it would set an example for other States Parties: this is the next step.

In our scenario, Ireland passes the law first proposed by Eoghan Murphy in 2012. It doesn't actually change much *in* Ireland, since the national fund and the major banks have already divested. And since Ireland wasn't a player in the industry anyway, it doesn't have a major impact on the nuclear weapons companies.

But then, other States Parties sit up and see Ireland's clear marker of where they need to be heading if they're serious about nuclear abolition. As more and more countries take the same bold step, it's scaring corporate investors and damaging their precious corporate reputations. Which country will be next?

The clock in our scenario goes back a full minute to 11:50:00 when lawmakers in the Irish Parliament, or *Oireachtas,* overwhelmingly pass a "Nuclear Weapons Divestment" bill that outlaws both direct and indirect investments in companies engaged in the development and manufacture of nuclear weapons.

On its way: Austria

Austria is one of the core TPNW countries, along with Brazil, Ireland, Mexico, New Zealand, and South Africa. It was Austria who threw down the gauntlet that set the world on course for negotiating the TPNW.

Instead of focusing on nuclear weapons as a "security" issue, the bedrock of the TPNW is a sharp focus on what these weapons actually do to people. In 2014, Austria hosted the third conference on the humanitarian impacts of nuclear weapons.

The US reportedly agreed to attend this Vienna conference on the condition that there would be no discussion of a new treaty. Deputy Foreign Minister of Austria Michael Linhart neatly sidestepped that restriction by unexpectedly announcing, in his closing remarks of the conference, what came to be known as the "Austrian Pledge." This read in part:

> *Austria calls on all states parties to the NPT to renew their commitment to the urgent and full implementation of existing obligations under Article VI, and to this end, to identify and pursue effective measures to fill the legal gap for the prohibition and elimination of nuclear weapons and Austria pledges to cooperate with all stakeholders to achieve this goal.*[7]

What was the "legal gap" that Austria was pledging to fill? The NPT commits the nuclear-armed countries to negotiate the elimination of nuclear weapons. *But it does not define these weapons as "illegal."* Other weapons of mass destruction - chemical and biological weapons - were already comprehensively outlawed by international treaty. Other inhumane and indiscriminate weapons having a disproportional impact on civilians - like landmines and cluster munitions - were also made illegal by international treaty. And yet the most inhumane, indiscriminate, mass destruction weapon of them all was still "legal" in terms of international law. The Austrian Pledge was about fixing that. And it did.

Alexander Kmentt, Director for Disarmament, Arms Control and Non-proliferation in the Austrian Ministry of Foreign Affairs, was one of the architects of the Austrian pledge. He was a key player in the numerous discussions and negotiations that took place afterwards, leading up to the final adoption of the TPNW. He describes in his book[8] all the many different influences and forces that converged to make the TPNW possible. Austria played a key role throughout that whole process.

But at the same time, Austria is an important hub for US corporations operating in Central Europe. It has a very pro-business government that does not want to disturb those relationships. And although Austria has also joined all the other disarmament treaties that incorporate the prohibition to "assist," it has so far avoided making any kind of commitment to divest from any of these weapons.

In our scenario, Austria sees that its extraordinary leadership in the nuclear disarmament sphere is at odds with some of its business relationships. Inspired by Ireland, Austria takes up the challenge. It makes a very big stretch. It passes a law to divest public funds from the nuclear weapons companies.

There may be another scenario in which Austria isn't ready, and other States Parties follow Ireland's lead. But someone will do it. And others will join. Even just a handful may be sufficient. The fact that more countries *could* decide to take this step is enough to scare the companies.

> **The clock in our scenario goes back another minute to 11:49:00** when Austria outlaws investments in companies engaged in the development and manufacture of nuclear weapons.

The Prize: South Africa

South Africa holds a special place in the story of nuclear abolition. It once had a fully developed (very small) arsenal of nuclear weapons, and then it completely dismantled them. No other country has ever done that! It's the prime showcase for how nuclear disarmament *has* taken place and *can* take place around the world.

Along with Ireland, Austria, Brazil, Mexico, and New Zealand, South Africa was one of the core group of countries that shepherded the TPNW through all the stages of development from an initial idea to the final result. South Africa has remained a key player in the TPNW ever since, and was chosen to be the President of the first Review Conference of the TPNW to be held at the end of 2026.

On top of all that, South Africa knows, from its experience with apartheid, how powerful large-scale boycotts and divestment can be. Inside South Africa, the apartheid struggle took an enormous amount of resistance and sacrifice. And the boycotts and divestment from *outside* definitely helped. South Africans know that, and appreciate it.

But despite South Africa's leadership in nuclear disarmament efforts, it is the only State Party to the TPNW that hosts some of the financial institutions identified as being most heavily invested in the nuclear weapons business.

South African investors

Of the 260 financial institutions identified by Don't Bank on the Bomb[9] as major investors in the nuclear weapons business in 2024, three are based in South Africa. **Ninety One Limited** is a South Africa-based investment firm that has $220 million invested in Jacobs Solutions, a nuclear weapons company.[10]

PSG Konsult is a financial services provider with $29 million dollars invested in Babcock,[11] and **Truffle** is an investment firm with $24 million invested. Notably, Truffle claims to focus on "responsible investing," but only through corporate engagement, not divestment.[12]

Standard Bank of South Africa has an outstanding $74 million loan to another US-based nuclear weapons company, Fluor.

Figure 9.1 Countries hosting major investors in the top nuclear weapons companies[13]

South Africa is the only country currently in the TPNW that hosts nuclear weapons investors, according to the latest Don't Bank on the Bomb report.

Joseph Dube and South Africa Disarmament and Arms Control

Joseph Dube, Director of the South African NGO, Disarmament and Arms Control, has felt a strong commitment to peace and social justice from an early age. He wants his country to live up to its highest ideals.

Joseph witnessed history in 1994, when he worked as an elections officer during South Africa's momentous, first fully democratic election that ended apartheid rule. He went on to do human rights work for a local Catholic Justice and Peace Commission in Johannesburg, before joining Gun Free South Africa in 1998.

Joseph became an internationally recognized campaigner on small arms. He has worked on this issue for Amnesty International and the International Action Network on Small Arms (IANSA). As well as working on small arms, Joseph now works on "big" arms – including nuclear weapons.

Nuclear weapons and gun violence

Gun violence in South Africa is of epidemic proportions, with an average of 33 people murdered with guns every day. That is much less than the 125 gun deaths per day in the United States. But *per capita,* the rate of gun deaths in South Africa is actually much higher.

Every South African is aware of the danger and of the seriousness of this problem. The reasons for so much gun violence in South Africa are complex, but the solution is simple. Joseph and his colleagues want to get guns off the streets – and out of the hands of those who are only too willing to use them.

Nuclear weapons are, in one sense, just very big guns. And to prevent the whole world from blowing up, Joseph wants to remove these weapons from national arsenals – and out of the hands of political and military leaders who appear only too willing to use them.

So when the government of South Africa needed more civil society involvement in the development and implementation of a new treaty to ban nuclear weapons, they came to Joseph for help. They invited him to attend a training on nuclear disarmament facilitated by international experts, including the International Committee of the Red Cross.

Joseph came home and got to work, connecting with other civil society organizations and churches to build support within South Africa for the TPNW. He continues to work on the problem of gun violence in South Africa and on many other arms control issues, including the emerging threats from killer robots, autonomous weapons, and the use of AI in warfare.

Joseph remains very much committed to nuclear abolition, and to supporting the South African government in their efforts to strengthen and universalize the TPNW. He meets once a month with staff in the Ministry of Foreign Affairs (MFA) who handle disarmament issues. Sometimes it is a Desk Officer and sometimes it is the Director, but they always listen to him and take note of his concerns.

Will South Africa be brave enough to take the next logical step in their commitment to nuclear abolition, and ban investments in nuclear weapons companies?

In our scenario, Joseph talks to his counterparts at the MFA about the additional steps that other countries are taking to put real pressure on the nuclear weapons companies who are blocking progress towards nuclear abolition. He convinces them that prohibiting investments in those companies would not immediately or directly affect their existing projects in South Africa or hurt employment and jobs in South Africa – a key concern of the government. But divestment *would* send a powerful signal to these companies: if you want to stay profitable and remain in countries like South Africa, it's time to get out of the nuclear weapons business.

And to support his case, Joseph has gathered signatures from church leaders and other dignitaries from all across the country. They have all signed an Op-Ed appearing in three of the largest newspapers in South Africa. There have been interviews on national TV news programs, and suddenly the whole country is calling on the government to take this next step.

The South African government decides to follow the example of Ireland and Austria and pass a law prohibiting investments in the nuclear weapons companies. This is for the sake of South Africa's standing in the world and among the leaders in nuclear abolition.

The clock moves back another minute, to 11:48:00pm, after South Africa passes national legislation to prohibit investments in nuclear weapons companies.

South Africa's new law raises the stakes. The South Africa-based investors pull out of Jacobs, Fluor and Babcock. These companies can find other investors to fill the gap. But investor anxiety continues to grow. These companies are getting the message.[14]

There is still one more powerful tool available to the countries that have joined the TPNW. Historically, divestment campaigns have been most effective when they're combined with boycotts *of the same corporations. Countries that are already divested from nuclear weapons corporations may still be signing contracts with them to purchase airplanes, IT services, roads, bridges, tunnels, etc. If countries begin to refuse contracts with those corporations, it's a potentially fatal blow to their business models.*

PRESSURE FROM THE WORLD

- [ ] VOTE FOR UN RESOLUTION
- [ ] SIGN THE TPNW
- [ ] RATIFY THE TPNW
- [ ] IMPLEMENT LAWS
- [ ] INCLUDE FINANCE
- [ ] COMMIT TO DIVESTMENT
- [x] BAN CONTRACTS
- [ ] ADD NATO COUNTRIES
- [ ] US BOMBS OUT OF EUROPE

10 From Venezuela to the Philippines: Banning nuclear contracts

Imagine a country that wants to take every possible step to help eliminate nuclear weapons. It has signed the Treaty on the Prohibition of Nuclear Weapons. It has ratified the treaty. It has passed national laws to hold anyone inside their borders, including corporate executives, accountable for having anything to do with nuclear weapons. It has explicitly prohibited the financing of nuclear weapons and has divested public funds from the companies involved in that industry. There's still one more tool it can use to put maximum pressure on the companies that are responsible for the continued existence of nuclear weapons: our imaginary country can prohibit doing business with these companies altogether.

For every step in this scenario so far, there's an example of a country that has done it. Precedents have been established. But now we're moving into uncharted territory. No country has so far passed a law that bans entering into a contract with a nuclear weapons company (although such laws do exist in relation to other types of companies – see below).

No one pretends that this would be an easy step for any country to take, given the complex economic and financial relationships involved. Which countries would be willing to exert that kind of pressure, and face the wrath of the US and other nuclear-armed countries?

All of the countries that are currently party to the TPNW are, at least in theory, committed to the goal of abolishing nuclear weapons. But they are not all *equally* committed to that goal.

There can be many reasons for a country to throw in its lot with the TPNW. For some, it's a domestic issue. For others, it's geopolitical – a move to align more closely with certain countries rather than with others.

Whatever their different reasons for joining the TPNW, not many of the States Parties are going to be willing to take this final step of banning business with the nuclear weapons companies, and that's okay. It only takes a few to have a big impact.

Some historical examples

One of the laws passed in the US to try to end apartheid in South Africa was the Comprehensive Anti-Apartheid Act of 1986. This was passed by Congress despite enormous opposition, and even a veto, from President Reagan. The Act included a huge number of measures to stop trade of all kinds with South Africa. It also specifically prohibited doing business with "parastatal" companies[1] (those that were directly connected with the South African government and thus considered complicit in apartheid).

Here's another example: In response to the full-scale Russian invasion of Ukraine in 2022, the US, the EU and some other countries imposed comprehensive sets of economic sanctions against Russia. These sanctions include prohibitions against doing business with specific companies and individuals.

So it's not far-fetched that countries might pass laws prohibiting all business dealings with nuclear weapons companies. Using the "parastatal" definition from the US Anti-Apartheid Act, corporations that are directly assisting governments (like the US) in maintaining their nuclear weapons arsenals could be considered "parastatal" and complicit with activities prohibited by the TPNW. Should these companies be banned from the global marketplace?

Almost all countries now have laws designed to stop terrorists from obtaining a nuclear weapon (see Chapter 7), and many of those laws include prohibitions against having any dealings with companies or other entities that may be complicit with such activities. As we saw in the case of Malta, for example, only a small change of wording or of interpretation could make those laws applicable to companies involved in the nuclear weapons programs of the US and the other nuclear-armed countries.

President Trump may have inadvertently spurred the first countries into action with his sweeping tariffs and various penalties targeting other countries. He had even handed them a tool: his raft of Executive Orders requiring government agencies to boycott specific law firms he's angry with could be their inspiration for their own form of boycotts and sanctions – in this case against US companies making nuclear weapons.

Any one of the 73 States Parties could make this next big move to ban contracts with nuclear weapons countries. It could be a long time before any of them are ready to do it. But sooner or later, those countries that really do care about the future of the planet as much as they claim they do are going to step up the pressure. They have the power to do this, and it may be the only tool they have left.

The first to ban: Venezuela

Venezuela's commitment to nuclear abolition is resolute. They have nothing to lose by taking a strong stand against the (predominantly US-based) nuclear weapons companies – they were already facing crippling sanctions even before Donald Trump's global trade wars got underway. They have little or no connection to any of the major nuclear weapons companies, and even less after Trump's additional second-term sanctions on Venezuela. The Maduro government has already fought back against US sanctions and tariffs with a number of laws and pronouncements.[2]

But Venezuela has yet to respond to US tariffs and sanctions with tariffs or sanctions of their own, targeting the US. In this scenario, that's about to change.

The President of the Republic issues a proclamation:

Decree Updating Public Contracting Law and Regulations in Place Regarding Public Procurement of the Bolivarian Republic of Venezuela

All contracting parties must be registered with the National Registry of Contractors* (Registro Nacional de Contratistas, or RNC) *in order to contract with the State and with the grassroots organizations of the Popular Power, when they handle public funds, in the terms and conditions established by the RNC to that

end. In order to enter into contracts with the State, natural and legal persons with no domicile in the country must have the registration required, which will be processed by them or by the contracting parties.

Companies determined to have more than a* de minimus *involvement in any of the following activities prohibited by law in the Bolivarian Republic of Venezuela or by international treaties entered into by the Bolivarian Republic of Venezuela shall be hereby suspended from the RNC:

> ***(i) Production or distribution of narcotics***
> ***(ii) Production or distribution of pornography***
> ***(iii) Production or distribution of illegal drugs***
> ***(iv) Production of palm tree products***
> ***(v) Explosive material***
> ***(vi) Development, production or maintenance of nuclear, chemical or biological weapons, landmines or cluster munitions***

Companies thus suspended from the RNC are disqualified from participating in public bids. This disqualification extends to individuals who participate as partners, members or managers in the structure and organization of the disqualified company.

> With this Decree in place, Venezuela sends our **scenario clock back a further 2 minutes to 11:46:00pm**

The impact of this particular Decree on the affairs of Venezuela is negligible, as is its impact on the nuclear weapons companies. Nevertheless, Venezuela's brave step shames some of the other TPNW countries into action. The next to prohibit contracts with nuclear weapons companies is Cuba.

Cuba follows

As we saw in Chapter 8, Cuba took the lead among States Parties to the TPNW when it came to defining financing as a banned form of assistance under the treaty. It is only a matter of time before it takes this next step.

> Our **scenario clock goes back a further 2 minutes to 11:44:00pm** when Cuba passes a law banning all business dealings with the nuclear weapons companies.

Now it is not just Venezuela taking this next step. There is forward momentum. As with Venezuela, the impact on the companies - and on Cuba itself - is negligible. Cuba does not have dealings with the companies. But the impact on other parties to the TPNW is more significant.

Next up: Aotearoa/New Zealand

After the Second World War, the US and its closest allies in Europe and North America established the NATO military alliance to counter the Soviet Union in the North Atlantic (in 1949). Shortly thereafter (in 1952), the US and its closest allies in the South Pacific established the ANZUS military alliance as NATO's counterpart in the Pacific.

Aotearoa/New Zealand remained a member of ANZUS and a close military ally of the United States until 1984, when a left-wing Labour government swept into power, largely on the back of a very strong anti-nuclear movement. The new Prime Minister, David Lange, pledged to pass legislation to make New Zealand nuclear-free, and to refuse entry into New Zealand of any ship, submarine or aircraft carrying nuclear weapons.

The US maintained (and still does) a policy of "neither confirming nor denying" the presence of nuclear weapons on their ships. But at that time, many US warships carried nuclear weapons as a normal practice, as did all the submarines specifically fitted for submarine-launched ballistic missiles.

Immediately after Lange announced this new policy, the Reagan administration sent the warship *USS Buchanan* on a mission to New Zealand "to test the new government's resolve."[3] On February 4th, 1985, the *USS Buchanan* arrived in New Zealand waters and was denied permission to enter the port of Auckland. This was unheard of. The US military was not accustomed to being turned away by anyone, let alone by a key military ally.

The reaction from the Reagan administration was swift and comprehensive. The US Navy immediately banned all US ships from visiting New Zealand and banned all New Zealand ships from docking at US naval facilities anywhere in the world. President Reagan reduced intelligence cooperation with New Zealand and effectively froze New Zealand out of the ANZUS alliance. New Zealand's status was downgraded from "ally" to "friend" of the US.

Although the US unilaterally removed nuclear weapons from all its surface ships in 1992, the first US navy vessel did not enter New Zealand waters until 2016. This was more than 30 years after the original ban took effect. No other country in the world has held out for so long enforcing a policy so bitterly opposed by the United States, under so much diplomatic pressure to reverse it.

Lockheed Martin and Rocket Lab

In this scenario, Aotearoa/New Zealand is once again on the frontlines of the global effort to eliminate nuclear weapons. The spark? Satellite launches.

New Zealand's own satellite launching company, Rocket Lab, was founded in 2006. It later moved its headquarters to the US, but it retains a rocket launching site on the Mahia Peninsula on New Zealand's North Island. Local residents, including the Maori community on whose land the site was built, were told it would be used for launching commercial and scientific satellites. There was no mention of it being used for military purposes.

But by 2016, Rocket Lab was supplying rocket fuel to Lockheed Martin for their Patriot Missile – a decidedly military activity. Lockheed Martin soon became a major investor in Rocket Lab.

Lockheed Martin is not just a bit player in the world of warfighting. It's the world's largest arms manufacturer, with over $60 billion in military sales, both nuclear and conventional.

Mark Rocket (his real name), co-founder of Rocket Lab, left his namesake company shortly thereafter, saying, "We're about science. We're not about killing people."[4]

Local Maori elder Pauline Tangiora was a veteran of the 1980s anti-nuclear campaigns. She was not happy seeing the Lockheed Martin logo at the entrance to the launch site just down the road from her house. "Everyone knows they make nuclear weapons," she says. "I went around the world to protest against them. To see that company at my back door..."[5]

Pauline has been fighting Rocket Lab ever since, gathering more and more protesters to the launch site on the Mahia Peninsula. The locals were informed that a launch in 2018 was on behalf of NASA for "educational" purposes, but it turned out to be a military launch for the Defense Advanced Research Agency (DARPA), the Pentagon agency responsible for developing new weapons systems for the US military.[6]

The locals responded with protests outside Rocket Lab's main production facility in Auckland, as well as at the launch site.[7] A New Zealand Space Agency spokesperson issued protesters with a warning not to try to disrupt any of the launches: "Even a single protester could have a disproportionate effect, potentially undermining the commercial viability of this growing industry."[8]

Of course, that just let the campaigners know that they were on the right track. In September 2023, they threatened to disrupt the launches if military payloads were allowed to continue. They also started demonstrating regularly at a new launch site under development at an airfield outside Christchurch.

New Zealand has recently joined the so-called "Olympic Defender" agreement, which gives the US Space Force access to military resources in New Zealand (as well as in several other countries). It involves closer integration of anti-satellite technologies and military communication systems between the two countries.[9]

In response to this growing military cooperation with the US, our scenario envisions a growing peace movement, determined to stop it. Aotearoa/New Zealand is once again becoming a scene of nonviolent demonstrations that are growing beyond all expectations. Protesters are making good on their threats to disrupt rocket launches. The demonstrations in Auckland are drawing bigger and bigger crowds. There's a whole new set of protests focused on the Olympic Defender and New Zealand's deepening ties with the Pentagon.

The New Zealand government has been trying to quell the resistance. They are claiming, on the one hand, that "no one, from a commercial outfit to a government agency, could ever gain permission to launch nuclear, chemical or biological weapons from New Zealand."[10] On the other hand, they are trying to emphasize the social and economic benefits of increased military cooperation with the United States, claiming that "space-based systems like GPS, which is operated by the military, are vital for enabling things like commercial air travel, international shipping and freight, agriculture, Google maps, and even bank transactions."[11]

Kevin Clements and PACDAC

Kevin Clements is a member of New Zealand's Public Advisory Committee on Disarmament and Arms Control (PACDAC). PACDAC was set up as part of the 1987 Act that made New Zealand a nuclear-free zone. Over the decades, members of PACDAC have advised Prime Ministers and briefed the Ministry of Foreign Affairs about matters relating to disarmament and arms control treaties. They've published papers and reports, held public hearings, and given out government grants to universities and NGOs engaged in relevant research and education initiatives.

Kevin is also a Professor Emeritus of Peace and Conflict Studies, having taught at a number of universities and institutes around the world. He has directed several international NGOs and written a number of books on peacebuilding and conflict resolution.

So it's appropriate that Kevin and his colleagues at PACDAC are now tasked, in our scenario, with squaring the circle that has upended the country. How to ensure Aotearoa/New Zealand remains true to its nuclear-free heritage and at the same time moves forward with its world-class leadership in satellite launches?

Banning business ties with the nuclear weapons industry

Due to the general revulsion against Trump and the rise of anti-nuclear activism across New Zealand, a more progressive Labour government gets elected. They come to PACDAC for help with the deepening divide in the country over the satellite launches and the potential connections to nuclear weapons companies. PACDAC advises the new government on ways to beef up its existing nuclear-free law by banning all business ties with nuclear weapons producers. They recommend that Rocket Lab must dissociate itself from Lockheed Martin, a known nuclear weapons producer.

But in a compromise befitting the conflict resolution community, they don't suggest requiring New Zealand to cease military-related launches, as long as these have nothing to do with nuclear weapons or nuclear weapons companies.

In this scenario, that compromise works – at least for the time being. It reaffirms New Zealand's unswerving commitment to nuclear abolition. It respects their longstanding willingness to stand up to the US and the other nuclear-armed countries. Most importantly, it sets an important precedent that other TPNW States Parties can follow.

> With this new law in place, New Zealand sends our **scenario clock back a further 2 minutes to 11:42:00pm**

The Prize: The Philippines

The Philippines is also an important ally of the United States. Subic Bay hosted one of the largest overseas naval bases for the US

Navy for 90 years, until it was handed over to the Philippine government in 1992. Under new defense agreements between the US and the Philippines, Subic Bay will once again be a staging post for US troops and equipment heading toward Taiwan and other Asian ports.

As the US continues its relentless, unnecessary and dangerous build-up to war with China, the Philippines plays a crucial role as a first line of defense for US forces. In addition to Subic Bay, the US has now been given access to two other naval bases, five air bases, and two army camps in the Philippines.

The Trump administration is currently developing more defense cooperation between the US and the Philippines. Defense Secretary Pete Hegseth was in Manila at the end of March 2025, announcing plans to provide more ships and equipment to the Philippine Navy and more funds to train and "modernize" their armed forces.

President BongBong Marcos, son of the former Philippine dictator, has promised to strengthen the partnership with the US. He has also committed to buying a large amount of weaponry from US military contractors, including a deal worth $5.5 billion to buy a squadron of F-16 fighter jets from Lockheed Martin.

So why would the Philippines risk this cozy relationship with the US and its military-industrial complex?

Weapons of war vs. weapons of mass destruction

The Philippines, under President Marcos, is not going to back down any time soon on its plans to invest much more in its military and to strengthen its defense ties with the US military. But that's about being ready and able to fight an actual war with China. It's not about being part of the US nuclear "umbrella."

The Philippines is a member of the Bangkok Treaty, which is the Nuclear Weapons-Free Zone of Southeast Asia, so it has already renounced being part of the umbrella. In any case, the presence of nuclear weapons in the country is forbidden by Article II Section 8 of the Philippine constitution, and that is unlikely to be changed.

The Philippines is also an important player in the TPNW. It was among the first group of countries to sign the treaty, and the Philippine Senate ratified it in 2021. The Philippines has taken its commitments to the TPNW very seriously, and in March, 2025, agreed to co-chair, with Malaysia, the Informal Working Group on Article 4 of the treaty. This concerns plans and processes to verify disarmament by nuclear-armed countries when those countries eventually join the treaty.

New Zealand had previously been doing this work, together with Malaysia, but withdrew in favor of joining the working group on universalization (Article 12). That left a gap, which the Philippines gladly filled, bringing them for the first time into the core group of countries most active in the TPNW.

So, although there are many forces in the Philippines working against any deeper commitment to putting real pressure on the nuclear weapons companies, there are also forces working in its favor. There is already a total rejection of nuclear weapons by civil society, all political parties and the current government in the Philippines. And there is a renewed commitment to play a bigger role within the TPNW.

Trump's tariff wars

On April 10, 2025, just ten days after Pete Hegseth was in Manila touting the "iron-clad" military agreements between the US and the Philippines, the Philippine ambassador to the US announced that the Philippines might *not* buy the F-16 planes from the US after all.[12] Trump's threatened tariffs on the Philippines, as on every other country, would make it difficult for them to afford the new planes, he said.

The Philippines has earmarked a total of $35 billion for major upgrades to its armed forces, from fighter jets and submarines to advanced missile systems and other military hardware. There are plenty of military contractors from Israel, Sweden, India, Russia, etc. to choose from, so they don't *have* to buy F-16s from Lockheed Martin – which also makes the re-entry vehicles designed to carry all US nuclear warheads to their targets.

The previous President of the Philippines, currently behind bars and awaiting trial by the International Criminal Court in the Hague, had a decidedly "cool" relationship with the US, and was willing to accept military equipment even from China. President Marcos has not yet gone that far, but he has claimed that his policy is to maintain a "balance" between the US and China, despite all the military ties he is developing with the US.[13]

One of the ways he can demonstrate "balance," in this scenario, is to buy from some of these other countries rather than from the US. And given his country's steadfast commitment to nuclear abolition, coupled with the economic warfare that Trump is unleashing on his country, this is an opportunity for President Marcos to swerve away from some of these US corporations – without swerving away from the US as such.

In our scenario, the Philippine National Assembly passes the Nuclear Weapons Procurement Prohibition Act, which disqualifies companies involved in the development, production or maintenance of nuclear weapons from bidding for government contracts in the Philippines.

The new law in the Philippines moves the hands of our scenario clock 2 minutes further away from Doomsday. It now reads 11:40:00pm

This comes as a shock to Lockheed Martin. They just lost the $5.5 billion for fighter jets that they thought they had a lock on.

They were already on alert after Colombia and Brazil ratified the TPNW (Chapter 6): Colombia buys their Black Hawk helicopters, Brazil buys their Sikorsky helicopters, and they have training, maintenance and repair facilities in both of those countries.

They were impacted again when Mexico passed its TPNW national implementation law (Chapter 7). And although Rolls Royce had it worse from European divestment, Lockheed Martin certainly felt the heat of investor anxiety as more and more institutions kept pulling their money out of controversial weapons (Chapter 8).

As divestment and boycotts gather steam (Chapter 9), executives and board members of Lockheed Martin have started losing sleep over their nuclear weapons work. They can still count on billions more in contracts coming from the Pentagon, but now that they've started to lose actual contracts in the Philippines, a hefty chunk of their business model has just collapsed.

They switch into panic mode. A shiver runs through the other nuclear weapons companies, because unlike Venezuela or even New Zealand, the Philippines is a major player. If *they* can pass legislation like this, where will it stop?

And even that is small potatoes compared to what is to come next...

By now, the TPNW is gathering enormous strength among the majority of countries in the world. They are

using the treaty to exert as much pressure as they can on the US and on the corporations that dominate US policy. But nothing these many countries can do compares with the impact of just a few key countries who still remain outside of the treaty. Once these other countries, who are all close military (and nuclear) allies of the United States, start to come on board, the game is over for US corporations still trying to cling to the nuclear weapons business. First to topple is Norway...

PRESSURE FROM THE WORLD

- [ ] VOTE FOR UN RESOLUTION
- [ ] SIGN THE TPNW
- [ ] RATIFY THE TPNW
- [ ] IMPLEMENT LAWS
- [ ] INCLUDE FINANCE
- [ ] COMMIT TO DIVESTMENT
- [ ] BAN CONTRACTS
- [x] ADD NATO COUNTRIES
- [ ] US BOMBS OUT OF EUROPE

11 From Norway to Spain: The non-supporters start to sign

So far, we have been following the steps that countries already committed to the TPNW can take to put increasing pressure on the corporations, and ultimately on the US, to abolish nuclear weapons. But the strongest pressure will come from its closest allies in NATO and the other "nuclear umbrella" countries. Once these countries start joining the TPNW, all the pressures described in the previous chapters will be multiplied.

Apart from the nine nuclear-armed countries themselves, opposition to the TPNW has so far come largely from the remaining members of the North Atlantic Treaty Organization. NATO was formed in 1949 as a military alliance to counter the Soviet Union. It started out with just 12 countries, and increased to 16 during the Cold War period.[1]

After the collapse of the Soviet Union, instead of disbanding as the Warsaw Pact did, NATO doubled in size to 32 countries. Three of these countries have nuclear weapons (US, UK and France). The other 29 are considered "umbrella states" (along with Australia, South Korea and Japan) because they consider themselves to be protected by the US nuclear arsenal.

There is nothing in the NATO founding documents about nuclear weapons, and nothing inherent in NATO itself that makes it reliant on nuclear weapons. However, the NATO "strategic concept," approved by all 32 Heads of Government on June 29, 2022, reaffirms that "as long as nuclear weapons exist, NATO will remain a nuclear alliance."[2]

Spain and Lithuania prohibit hosting of nuclear weapons at any time. Iceland, Norway, Denmark, Finland prohibit nuclear weapons in peacetime. Greece, Canada and the UK ended US nuclear hosting arrangements. France is not in the NATO nuclear planning group.

All members of NATO, apart from France,[3] take part in NATO's nuclear war preparations through participation in the Nuclear Planning Group. Only 13 of those countries, however, took part in the most recent NATO exercises involving nuclear weapons. And only five NATO countries actually host US nuclear weapons on their soil (Germany, Italy, Belgium, Netherlands and Türkiye (Turkey)).

The majority of countries within NATO have chosen *not* to host US nuclear weapons, and a number have explicitly rejected hosting them in peacetime or even in wartime. Iceland, Finland, Denmark and Norway have all passed laws that prohibit them from hosting. Spain and Lithuania both have clauses written into their constitutions that prohibit the stationing of nuclear weapons. The UK, Greece and Canada all hosted US nuclear weapons at one time, and later withdrew from that arrangement.[4]

So the cracks within NATO over the nuclear weapons issue are already there. And in this scenario, those cracks become ravines.

First in NATO to sign the TPNW: Norway

For 75 years, Norway has performed a delicate balancing act between active participation in NATO and opposition to nuclear weapons. Norway has been a loyal member of NATO since the alliance was founded in 1949. It shares a 200-km border with Russia and is strategically positioned to monitor and potentially control access to and from the Barents Sea, where Russia keeps its largest fleet of warships and submarines. This makes Norway a valuable asset for NATO, but also puts the country in a uniquely vulnerable position with Russia.

Norway has the recent history of being invaded and occupied by Nazi Germany, so Norwegians are especially nervous about being left defenseless against Russia. Since Norway cannot be described as a major military power itself, many Norwegians see this as a reason to remain closely allied with the United States.

Nevertheless, Norway has never (publicly at least)[5] allowed US nuclear weapons to be stationed on its soil,[6] and Norwegians have been largely opposed to nuclear weapons the whole time they have been in NATO.[7]

In the 1980s, Norway took an interest in the idea of creating a Nordic Nuclear-Free Zone, first proposed by Finland, although that idea never came to fruition. And in 2013, under a previous Labor government, Norway hosted the first of three conferences on the humanitarian impact of nuclear weapons – a conference which ultimately led to the negotiations and adoption of the TPNW.

Before the TPNW was adopted in 2017, however, Norway had elections and a change of government. The new center-right government chose to have nothing to do with the TPNW and voted consistently against it.

Then, in 2021, parliamentary elections brought the Labor Party back into power. Espen Barth Eide, who presided over the humanitarian impacts conference on behalf of the Norwegian government in 2013, was back in the government as Foreign Minister. There was hope that as a progressive and constructive politician, Eide would bring Norway into the TPNW.

But the new Prime Minister, Jonas Gahr Støre, is under a great deal of pressure *not* to sign the treaty, from more conservative elements inside his own party, from other political parties, from much of the Norwegian media, and from practically all of the Norwegian civil servants and military officers currently dealing with Norway's relations with the US.

So despite opinion polls showing as much as 78% of the Norwegian public want their country to join the TPNW; despite the Norwegian Confederation of Trade Unions calling for Norway to join the TPNW; and despite the Labor Party's position since 2021 that it should be a "goal" for Norway to sign the TPNW, the government has held back until now, largely in deference to the United States.

NATO in the time of Trump

At this writing, in early 2025, Trump is demanding that NATO governments across Europe start spending 3-5% of their GDP on building up their militaries (after demanding they spend 2% during his previous term in office – a goal which few were able to meet). NATO governments are so far falling all over themselves to meet his demands.

At the same time, Trump's return to power has also encouraged European governments to talk openly about a "Eurobomb." This would supposedly involve French (and possibly UK) nuclear weapons replacing the US "nuclear umbrella" over Western Europe (see Chapter 22). This, too, would involve huge costs to European taxpayers.

But these planned huge increases in military spending across Europe will mean deep cuts to social programs that large numbers of people depend on. Western Europeans are already fearful of an impending war with Russia. But to justify all this increased military expenditure to their populations, governments will need to make them even more afraid.

With extreme right-wing parties on the ascendency all across Europe, many of these governments are already passing draconian measures to deter protests against these measures. And they're preparing to throw thousands of people in jail if protests start getting too big.

A few of the more left-leaning governments still in power are trying to take a more diplomatic approach to the emerging civil unrest. Chief among these is Norway, which still has a popular, Labor-led government – with a long history of *being* a protest movement. It has no intention of criminalizing dissent.

In our scenario, a protest movement in Norway continues to grow, and among its many demands is a call for Norway to join the TPNW. A new resolution is introduced at the Labor Party annual conference: "We call on the Norwegian government to sign the TPNW without delay..."

The government of Jonas Støre must choose between the growing demands for a world without nuclear weapons versus the demands of an autocratic administration in the White House. Støre makes his choice: Norway will sign the TPNW.

Norway becomes the first NATO country to sign the TPNW. Now the door is open for the rest of NATO to do the same.

Our scenario clock goes back a full 5 minutes to 11:35:00pm when the first country in NATO signs the Treaty on the Prohibition of Nuclear Weapons, sending shockwaves across the Alliance.

Next up: Iceland

The recent Prime Minister of Iceland, Katrin Jakobsdottir, along with two of her Cabinet Ministers and a third of the entire Icelandic Parliament (21 of 63 members), have already signed the ICAN Pledge[8] calling on Iceland to sign the TPNW. Iceland also has some of the strongest public support for the TPNW of any NATO country, with a recent opinion poll showing 86% in support of Iceland joining the treaty.[9]

Iceland has been ready to sign the TPNW for some time. But Iceland, like Norway, is heavily dependent on the United States for its security. It doesn't want to be the first NATO country to go against the US and its doctrine of "extended nuclear deterrence."

Iceland does not have a standing army of its own. For a time, the US based as many as 4,000 troops at Keflavik air base, but these were withdrawn in 2006. The US also had secret plans to deploy nuclear weapons to Iceland in the event of a war with the Soviet Union, but these were never implemented.[10] Iceland is a self-declared nuclear-free zone, but this is couched as being "subject to international commitments."[11]

In its statement to the NPT Review Conference in August 2022, Iceland affirmed that it is "strongly committed to work towards the objective of eliminating nuclear weapons,"[12] but this was not translated into joining the TPNW. Privately, Icelandic parliamentarians have said that they would join the TPNW – only if and when another NATO country joined.

So, in our scenario, once Norway is in, Iceland is determined to be next. And then it's only a matter of time before Denmark, Finland and Sweden also sign, bringing the Nordic states en masse into the treaty.

Our scenario clock goes back another 5 minutes to 11:30:00pm when Iceland signs the Treaty on the Prohibition of Nuclear Weapons.

Finland and Denmark

Unlike Norway, Finland has much stronger reasons to be fearful of Russia. Norway's shared border with Russia is 200 km, while Finland's is 1,340 km. Norway was invaded during World War II by Nazi Germany, whereas Finland was invaded, initially, by the Soviet Union.

After the war, Finland stayed out of NATO and remained neutral in order to maintain peace with both the Soviets and the West.

Finns have prided themselves as a peace-loving country all this time, and 84% of Finns in a recent poll wanted their country to join the TPNW.[13] Thirty Finnish Parliamentarians, including a former Foreign Minister,[14] have signed the ICAN Pledge.

But the Russian invasion of Ukraine has greatly complicated the situation for Finland, and after 78 years as a neutral country, Finland joined NATO in 2023. The controversial move included a decision not to allow nuclear weapons to be stationed on Finnish territory, although Finland now takes part in NATO nuclear war planning.[15]

A majority of Finns now support Finland's membership in NATO, but still oppose Finland having anything to do with nuclear weapons. Like other NATO governments, the Finnish government has been led to believe that NATO membership requires acceptance of nuclear weapons and involvement in nuclear war planning. **But now that both Norway and Iceland have signed the TPNW in this scenario, the cat is out of the bag! Finland can remain in NATO and still sign the TPNW. So it does.**

Like their counterparts in the other Nordic countries, Danes are generally opposed to nuclear weapons and want Denmark to join the TPNW. **Once Norway, Iceland and Finland have signed the treaty, there is no hesitation. Denmark also signs.**

Our scenario clock goes back another 10 minutes to 11:20:00pm when Finland and Denmark sign the Treaty on the Prohibition of Nuclear Weapons.

Sweden

It's been a bit of a roller coaster ride in Sweden. It was the only Nordic country that took part in the negotiations for the TPNW, and it voted in favor of its adoption at the UN on July 7, 2017.

But in 2019, the Swedish government published a report recommending against joining the TPNW. However, the door was left open to reconsider that decision. Margot Wallström, Sweden's Foreign Minister at the time, later said she had regretted not being able to convince her colleagues to join the Treaty.[16]

Then in 2021, Sweden's largest political party, the Social Democrats, stated unequivocally in their party platform, for the first time, that "the goal is that Sweden will join" the treaty.[17]

But in 2024, like Finland, Sweden broke its long tradition of neutrality by joining NATO, and it was expected to declare that its membership in NATO would not include the option of hosting US nuclear weapons on its soil.[18] This declaration never materialized.

In our scenario, all this vacillation ends. It may take elections and a change of government, but there is little doubt that sooner or later, Sweden will join the rest of the Nordic countries in signing the TPNW.

> Our scenario clock is another 5 minutes further away from midnight, at 11:15:00pm, after Sweden joins the TPNW.

Before becoming a member of the NATO alliance, Sweden joining the TPNW would not have caused much of a stir. But now, with both Sweden and Finland inside NATO, the internal discussions, and the balance of positions for and against nuclear weapons, are beginning to shift.

The prize: Spain

Spain is another member of NATO that prohibits the stationing of US nuclear weapons on its soil. Spain also has the highest popular support in Europe for joining the TPNW: a whopping 89% according to a recent poll.[19]

The coalition agreement that brought the left-wing parties into power in 2018 included a commitment by both parties, PSOE and Podemos, to join the TPNW. The Prime Minister himself announced that he would sign.

Then he retracted.[20] No further action was taken before that coalition collapsed and a more centrist coalition came to power in Spain.

Since then, the focus of campaigners in Spain has been to build support for signing the TPNW one city and one parliamentarian at a time, through the ICAN Cities Appeal and the ICAN Parliamentary Pledge (see Chapter 4).

Carlos Umaña and the Alliance for Nuclear Disarmament

Carlos Umaña is Costa Rican doctor who has dedicated his life to nuclear abolition. He's a Co-President of IPPNW. He worked to get Costa Rica and other Latin American countries on board the TPNW (see Chapter 6) before moving to Spain to do the same thing there.

Since 2018, Carlos has been working to promote the TPNW with other ICAN partners in Spain. In 2020, he organized a national tour for Hiroshima survivor Setsuko Thurlow, a remarkable witness to history. Setsuko crawled out of the atomic bomb rubble as a child, and has been working all her long life toward making sure that nobody else ever has to endure what she did. She met with Spanish city mayors, regional governments, parliamentarians and members of the public in different parts of the country.

The response to Setsuko's tour, and to Carlos' ongoing efforts, has been overwhelming. Over 100 cities have joined the ICAN Cities Appeal. Some 36 elected officials have signed the ICAN Pledge, and 64 organizations joined together to form the Alliance for Nuclear Disarmament.

The Alliance was able to hire a part-time staff person and organize national events, with regular meetings, a popular website and a regular output of blogs and news articles. Just before COVID hit, it looked like they might succeed in getting Spain to attend the first meeting of TPNW States Parties as an observer.

Since then, as in so many other countries, the Alliance has lost a bit of its momentum - as well as its funding. **But in our scenario, a revitalized Alliance takes full advantage of the rapidly changing landscape across NATO and pushes hard for Spain to join the TPNW. Mayors from across the country descend on Madrid to lobby the parliament in support of signing the TPNW. Regional parliaments in Cataluna and Asturias send delegations to meet with their counterparts in the Parliament.**

With new elections coming and the Sumar bloc of parties poised to do very well, the socialist party, PSOE, gives way and agrees to sign the TPNW.

Our scenario clock is another 5 minutes further away from midnight, at 11:10:00pm, after Spain signs the Treaty on the Prohibition of Nuclear Weapons.

The impact of Spain joining the TPNW is considerable. Spain's entry into the treaty opens the door even wider for the rest of NATO. But it also has a direct effect on a nuclear weapons company, Airbus.

Airbus

Spain has a 4% stake in Airbus.[21] That may not sound like much, but it's enough to force Airbus out of the nuclear weapons business. Here's how.

Airbus is directly involved in the development, production and maintenance of France's nuclear arsenal, through its participation in two industrial consortiums – the ArianeGroup and MDBA France.[22] But only 5% of its income is nuclear weapons related income from those two ventures. (In 2023, that came to roughly $3.2 billion out of $70 billion in total revenues.) The other 95% of Airbus revenues come from the production of commercial aircraft and other military, but non-nuclear, products.

Investors across Europe are *already* divesting from Airbus because of its nuclear weapons involvement. If this trickle starts to become a raging stream, the company is not going to risk 95% of its business for the sake of just 5%.

In 2021, Airbus was almost excluded from Germany's updated stock market index (equivalent to the UK's Financial Times Stock Exchange or the US's Dow Jones index) because of its involvement with "controversial weapons" – meaning, in this case, the French nuclear weapons.[23]

The board of Airbus subsequently discussed the possibility of pulling back from nuclear weapons work. "We have the first financial institutions that say we don't want to invest in such companies any more," Airbus Defence & Space CEO Michael Schoellhorn told journalists in 2022.[24]

In this scenario, both Bloomberg and MSCI have decided to define nuclear weapons as controversial weapons. This leads to more and more banks and financial institutions in Europe divesting from this companies (see Chapter 8).[25]

Crédit Agricole is one of Airbus's top five private investors and one of their largest lenders. It's the second largest bank in France and the third largest in Europe. When it finally joins other major European banks in defining nuclear weapons as controversial weapons, it sends shockwaves through the entire nuclear weapons industry, but especially Airbus.

Another major lender to Airbus is Deutche Bank. They already consider nuclear weapons to be controversial weapons and claim to base their policy on International Humanitarian Law (IHL) principles. Deutche Bank's justification for continuing to lend to Airbus is that their loans are purportedly for the financing of non-nuclear weapons related projects, and thus they're not counted as "direct financing" of nuclear weapons work.

In this scenario, Deutche Bank decides to amend their lending policy to exclude all companies involved in nuclear weapons work. With this change at Deutche Bank, other large financial institutions across Europe are also reconsidering their policies.

The Airbus board feels they must now choose: either shift the company to focus their remaining resources on the 95% of their (non-nuclear-related) work that is *uncontroversial,* or risk losing public support and investor confidence over the remaining 5% of their (nuclear weapons-related) work that *is* controversial.

As Spain is looking like it will soon divest its 4% of Airbus, it's an easy decision. Guillaume Faury, CEO of Airbus, announces his intention to focus the company on commercial aircraft production, and to withdraw from ArianeGroup, MBDA France, and the production of nuclear missiles for France.

With the Nordic countries, and now Spain, committed to the TPNW, the nuclear question in Europe is thrown wide open. Countries that have had US nuclear weapons on their soil for decades are now in political turmoil as demands grow for the removal of these weapons and the creation of a European nuclear-free zone.

PRESSURE FROM THE WORLD

- [ ] VOTE FOR UN RESOLUTION
- [ ] SIGN THE TPNW
- [ ] RATIFY THE TPNW
- [ ] IMPLEMENT LAWS
- [ ] INCLUDE FINANCE
- [ ] COMMIT TO DIVESTMENT
- [ ] BAN CONTRACTS
- [ ] ADD NATO COUNTRIES
- [x] US BOMBS OUT OF EUROPE

12 From Italy to Germany: Sending back US nuclear weapons

Currently just five countries - Germany, Italy, Belgium, Netherlands and Türkiye (Turkey) - have US nuclear weapons on their soil as part of NATO "nuclear sharing" arrangements. Four of these countries are already under enormous pressure to join the TPNW.

For Germany, Italy, Belgium and the Netherlands, joining the TPNW is difficult, since they would have to remove US nuclear weapons that they have hosted all this time – along with the logic that has justified their presence.

But as Western European governments alienate their voters by trying to meet Trump's demands to expand their militaries (see previous chapter) and cut social programs, a new European anti-nuclear movement is on its way. How long will it still be acceptable to deploy US nuclear weapons in Europe?

The European anti-nuclear movement of the 1980s

The European anti-nuclear movement sprung up almost overnight in response to the NATO decision in 1979 to put a new generation of intermediate-range nuclear missiles in five European countries. There were several reasons that this decision made people jump out of their beds and swarm out onto the streets in protest.

The first reason: these missiles were part of a general drift toward the US and NATO going to war with the Soviet Union. Nobody in Europe wanted to be caught in the middle of such a war, and *especially* not a nuclear war.

And it looked alarmingly like the US was preparing to fight that war *in* Europe to avoid it reaching the United States. Putting missiles in Europe was seen as a willingness to "sacrifice" Europe in a war aimed at destroying the Soviet Union. And a nuclear war in Europe would mean the end of Europe.

An additional motivation for opposing these new nuclear cruise missiles involved their mode of deployment. The missiles were due to be periodically driven out of their bases and driven around in giant military convoys on the winding village lanes of Europe. Supposedly, they would thus "melt into the countryside" so that the Soviets would not be able to target them.

The mere thought of this plan was deeply disturbing to the villagers who happened to live along those little winding lanes all across Europe. (When the military started taking these convoys out on trial runs, they became a focal point for moveable protests all across Europe.)

The protests across Europe in the 1980s ended up with millions of people marching on the streets, hundreds of thousands blocking roads with sit-ins and blockades, and many thousands being arrested in almost every Western European country. And the conditions for that happening again are rapidly building up now.

Protests against nuclear weapons in the 1980s were common

Is a new anti-nuclear movement brewing in Europe, like it did in the 1980s? PHOTO: Wikimedia Commons

European Anti-Nuclear Movement 2.0?

Now, a combination of slightly different factors are at play in Western Europe. Trump's damaging trade war between the US and the EU is expected to put millions of people in Europe out of work and to drive millions more to poverty levels not seen for many years. And governments are increasing military spending to appease Trump.

Those governments are already on a collision course with their citizens. And many of their citizens harbor growing revulsion for everything Trump stands for – and that includes the far-right parties that have been on the ascendency in Europe as well as everywhere else.

Recession, cuts to social programs, a new anti-Americanism: this combination will likely mean a return to more left-of-center governments and policies in Europe. With that may come much stronger support for nuclear abolition and getting rid of US nuclear weapons.

On top of all that, there is increasing fear of a nuclear war with Russia that would turn Western Europe into a radioactive desert. Is conscription next?

Most European countries maintained universal conscription into the armed forces well into the 1990s, and most have since done away with it. But as European governments prepare themselves and their citizens for war with Russia, conscription is very much back on the table.

But conscription has always been the best recruitment tool for peace movements, because a lot of young men (and women) do not want to die on some distant battlefield for a cause they may not even agree with. And when young people grow up in a society that does *not* have conscription, they are even *less* willing to give up that freedom if the government comes calling for them.

European governments try to claim that yet more nuclear weapons would prevent conscription. But the prospect of a nuclear war in Europe just fuels the anti-nuclear component of the new peace movement even more. Where will it have its next big success?

Next up: Italy

Italy hosts US nuclear weapons at two air bases (Aviano and Ghedi). The mainstream media, as in the rest of Europe and North America, is heavily biased in favor of the government position that nuclear weapons are somehow "essential" for Italy's defense and that without them, Russia would "almost certainly" overrun Italy and the rest of Europe.

Italy's current Prime Minister, Giorgia Meloni, is leader of the right-wing *Fratelli d'Italia*, (Brothers of Italy) and the only world leader to attend Donald Trump's inauguration in Washington, DC, in 2025. As a fellow right-wing populist, she's close to Trump on many issues, though she has called his tariff wars "wrong"[1] and his demand that Italy increase its military spending has put her in an awkward political situation.[2]

Disarmament support in Italy

Meanwhile, Italy has huge popular support for nuclear disarmament and the TPNW. Over 100 cities and towns have joined the ICAN Cities Appeal, calling for the government to sign the TPNW. And although they are not all still in parliament, nearly 250 members of the Italian Parliament have signed the ICAN Pledge, promising to work toward that end. The Italian Parliament has passed a number of resolutions since 2017 that call on the government to continue evaluating the merits of joining the TPNW.[3]

Italy's peace movement has historical roots in two very disparate traditions – the Catholic Church and the Communist Party. These may have diametrically opposing views on many social issues, but when it comes to peace and nuclear disarmament, they're on the same page.

For decades now, tens of thousands – sometimes even hundreds of thousands - of Catholics and Communists have walked hand in hand the 25 kilometers from Perugia to Assisi on peace marches every other year.

Polls show 80% of Italians in favor of nuclear abolition. Some 60% want to reduce military spending, not increase it as Trump is demanding. And only 6% are in favor of sending troops to fight in Ukraine. This is all despite electing the most right-wing government in Italy for some time.

Francesco Vignarca and Rete Italiana Pace e Disarmo

Francesco Vignarca is the Campaigns Coordinator for the Italian Peace and Disarmament Network, *Rete Italiana Pace e Disarmo*. He has written books on nuclear disarmament[4] and has worked hard to ensure that the Network has accurate and reliable data to share in reports, papers, and briefings for politicians, and in educational materials for the general public.

For example, when the Italian government was publicly denying that the US was deploying a new type of nuclear weapon in Italy,

Francesco found a photo on Facebook of US soldiers showing off their new weapon *at an Italian airbase*!

The Network joins together more than 65 organizations, including the largest trade union in Italy, CGIL, with over 5 million members. A steering group meets every month to plan national activities, and as many as 150 people from the different groups attend a National Assembly once a year. In addition to the overall campaign of the Network, there are numerous local networks organizing their own campaigns and days of action at the city level.

Nuclear weapons as a municipal issue

There's a long history of Italian cities undertaking their own foreign policy initiatives. In the 1960s, the Mayor of Florence took it upon himself to try to negotiate peace between the US and the Soviet Union by traveling to both Washington and Moscow.

Since the TPNW was adopted, over 100 cities in Italy have joined the ICAN cities appeal, focusing on cities as the targets of a nuclear war. The basic message, as with the Mayors for Peace initiative (see chapter 13), is "Look what happened to Hiroshima and Nagasaki. This must never happen again, not to *our* city, or *any* city."

80 years after Hiroshima and Nagasaki, we are losing the remaining *hibakusha* (survivors) who can describe their lived experience. Since nuclear war has faded from living memory and become abstract, Soka Gokkai International (SGI) Italy is using new technology to help people comprehend the reality.

Their virtual reality experience of Hiroshima, created as part of their "Senzatomica" exhibition, is one of the most successful educational tools in recent years. Visitors can put on VR goggles and look around the city of Hiroshima to see first-hand the devastation that befell the city on August 6, 1945. As many as 30,000 people viewed the exhibition in Florence in early 2025.

Overall, the exhibition has been viewed by as many as 420,000 visitors in 80 other Italian cities, including Rome.[5] According to Francesco, this kind of educational work is crucial to the effort of building support for the TPNW inside the Parliament.

Italia Ripensaci – Italy, think again!

In 2016, in a UN Committee, Italy voted against the proposal to open negotiations for a new treaty – and in response, the campaign to get Italy to support the TPNW was born. The campaign had its first "success" when, two months later, Italy voted again on same proposal, and this time voted *in favor* of the TPNW negotiations.

The Italian government later confirmed that they had made a mistake – they had meant to vote No again. But by then it was too late. The negotiations went ahead and the rest is history.

Italian peace campaigners have not forgotten the "victory" of Italy's Yes vote at the UN in 2016. They say it's not too late for Italy to "think again" about the TPNW.

Italy signs the TPNW

By the time the treaty was adopted in 2017, there were 240 members of the Italian Parliament publicly calling for Italy to join the treaty. The Parliament passed a resolution instructing the government "to explore the possibility" of becoming a state party to the TPNW "in a way compatible with [Italy's] NATO obligations and with the positioning of allied states."

In 2020, the former Italian Prime Minister Enrico Letta signed an open letter calling on his successor to "show courage and boldness – and join the [TPNW]." And in 2023, the Parliamentary Foreign Affairs Committee called on the government to consider attending the Second Meeting of States Parties to the TPNW at UN as an observer (they didn't).

A recent opinion poll in 2020 suggests that as many as 87% of the Italian public wants Italy to join the TPNW.[6] And only 5% support the government's position of remaining outside it.

In our scenario, far-right leadership has fallen out of favor. US influence is no match for massive support for the TPNW from Italian citizens, cities, Parliament, labor unions, and NGOs. And since Spain took that decisive step and signed the TPNW (see Chapter 11), Italy has no more arguments for staying out of the TPNW.

Our scenario clock moves back a full 10 minutes, to 11:00:00pm, after Italy signs the TPNW.

Italy's signature would not instantly mean that US nuclear weapons have to be removed from Italian soil. The TPNW sets out a timeline for that to happen once the treaty has been ratified and the instrument of ratification has been deposited with the UN.

A country hosting nuclear weapons then has 90 days after depositing their ratification before the treaty enters into force in that country. And then they have another 90 days to remove the nuclear weapons. So in total, Italy will be expected to remove US nuclear weapons from Aviano and Ghedi within 6 months after ratifying the treaty.

This isn't the first time that US nuclear weapons have been removed from another country. We mentioned Greece and Canada above. South Korea had as many as 1,000 US nuclear weapons before those were withdrawn. Spain, under General Franco, hosted US nuclear weapons before it became a member of NATO and renounced any possibility of hosting them again. The UK also once had US nuclear weapons, as well as their own. (Unfortunately, US nuclear weapons are now set to return to the UK).

Nevertheless, the removal of US nuclear weapons from Italy at this point in our scenario undermines everything the United States says about nuclear weapons as an "umbrella" for its allies – and it's a major setback for the nuclear weapons industry.

Belgium

Belgium hosts US nuclear weapons at the Kleine Brogel air base, despite strong public opposition. After parliamentary elections in 2020, a coalition agreement among seven political parties included a commitment to explore "how the UN Treaty on the Prohibition of Nuclear Weapons can give new impetus to multilateral nuclear disarmament." That was followed by a parliamentary motion to direct the government to withdraw US nuclear weapons from Belgian territory and to join the TPNW. That motion was only narrowly defeated by 74 votes to 66.[7]

In 2022, Belgium sent an official delegation to observe the First Meeting of States Parties to the TPNW in Vienna, along with a number of other countries who had not previously engaged with the Treaty.

In 2023, Belgium again sent an official observer to the Second Meeting (2MSP). Domestic pressures in favor of joining the TPNW have continued.

In our scenario, after Italy signs the TPNW, it is impossible for Belgians to imagine that they would not. Belgium becomes the 8th NATO member to sign the TPNW, and the second to commit to removing its US nuclear weapons from their country.

> `The clock goes back 10 minutes to 10:50:00` when Belgium signs the TPNW.

Netherlands

In the 1980s, the US planned to deploy nuclear-tipped cruise missiles to the Netherlands as well as to several other European countries. After the signing of the INF Treaty, deployment to the Netherlands was canceled. Since then, however, US gravity bombs have been stored at Volkel airbase, primed and ready to be loaded onto Dutch planes and flown by Dutch pilots to targets in Russia.

Of all the European governments that were threatened by the popular uprising against nuclear weapons in the 1980s, the Dutch government (with the Christian Democrats in coalition with the Liberal Party) came closest to collapsing over the issue. It managed to delay the Cruise deployment three times in order to avoid a defeat in the Dutch Parliament that would have brought down the governing coalition.[8]

At that time, there was overwhelming opposition to nuclear weapons coming from all the main churches and all the main trade unions in the country, as well as from a majority in the Parliament itself.

Opposition to nuclear weapons is not as strong in the Netherlands today as it was in the 1980s. However, a national letter-writing campaign coordinated by PAX in 2016 called on the Dutch Parliament make nuclear weapons illegal. The resulting parliamentary decision was to engage in all international efforts to do so.

That, in turn, led to the Netherlands being the only NATO country participating in the TPNW negotiations – and the only delegation in the room that opposed the whole process. When it came to the final session of the negotiations and it was clear that there was overwhelming support for adoption of the treaty, the Netherlands insisted on calling for a recorded vote. They were the only country to vote against it (there was also one abstention).

Since the TPNW was adopted, the Dutch Parliament has on more than one occasion demanded that the government sign the TPNW. Up to now, the government has refused.

But in our scenario, with so much momentum growing, including NATO countries signing the treaty, the Dutch government finally decides the time has come. The Netherlands joins the TPNW – and does so with pride at having been at the negotiations and committed "as it has always been" to upholding the primacy of international law and multilateral diplomacy.

The clock goes back another 10 minutes to 10:40:00 when the Netherlands signs the TPNW.

The prize: Germany

Germany is the largest country in Europe by population and an extremely important military ally of the United States. As a legacy of the Second World War, it is host to more than 35,000 US troops stationed at military bases around the country.

Germany is also host to around 20 B-61 nuclear bombs that are deployed at the US base in Buchel, near the city of Koblenz. These bombs are technically under the control of the US military, but as in Italy, the Netherlands and Belgium, they're certified to be dropped by German planes flown by German pilots.[9]

The B-61 bombs based in Europe currently have a yield of up to 170 Kilotons (KT) each – more than ten times the size of the bomb that destroyed the city of Hiroshima. They can allegedly be "dialed down" to a yield of "only" 0.3 KT, which is still roughly thirty times the size of the largest conventional bomb in the US arsenal today (the GBU-43, which has a destructive force equivalent to 11 tons of TNT).[10]

After elections in early 2025, the new government of Chancellor Merz is poised to move in a strongly rightward direction in the coming years. Already the previous government had pledged to vastly increase military spending and to introduce a form of "voluntary conscription" whereby all Germans will get a letter "inviting" them to join the military when they turn 18.[11]

The German peace movement grows

Recent polls suggest that as many as 83% of Germans want the US nuclear weapons removed.[12] There's also strong support for Germany to sign the TPNW: more than 180 parliamentarians in the German Bundestag have signed the ICAN pledge, and more than 100,000 Germans have signed a petition calling on Germany to join the TPNW.[13]

Two of the main political parties in Germany, the Greens and the Social Democrats (SPD), had also committed to change German policy on nuclear weapons when they formed the previous coalition government in 2021.[14]

And as we've seen elsewhere, increasing militarization leads to increasing support for peace movements. This may be especially true in Germany, where every child still grows up learning about the horror and shame of war, rather than reveling in the glories of it. And as other European countries rebel against Trump and everything he stands for, so too is protest growing in Germany.

Germany joins the TPNW

In our scenario, nine NATO countries have already joined the TPNW by this point. Three of them, Italy, the Netherlands, and Belgium, are removing US nuclear weapons from their soil, drastically curtailing the "nuclear sharing" arrangement. When Germany also signs the TPNW, this has a seismic effect on US foreign policy, and also on some of the key corporations involved. For one thing, with no nuclear weapons, there's no need for countries like Germany to buy the specialized aircraft that deliver them.

> **The clock goes back 10 minutes to 10:30:00pm** when Germany signs the TPNW and announces plans for the removal of the last US nuclear weapons from German soil.

The F-35s

The F-35 jet fighter is already the most expensive military project in US history, estimated to cost US taxpayers $1.7 trillion over the full life cycle of the planes.[15] But it's also a huge overseas sales opportunity for US military contractors, with eight other countries set to buy over 3,000 of them (UK, Italy, Denmark, Germany, Canada, Australia, Türkiye (Turkey) and Norway), and more countries lining up.

The unit cost of each F-35 sold to the Pentagon in 2022 was $78 million per plane.[16] That's a bargain price available to the US taxpayer, subsidized by foreign partners who are paying much more than that. For example, Germany is due to pay the equivalent of $288 million per plane,[17] and Canada as much as $450 million.[18]

Most of the F-35s are designed to carry conventional weapons, but a certain number are being upgraded to "dual capable aircraft" (DCA) status, which means they can handle nuclear weapons too.[19] Each DCA is capable of carrying two B61-12 nuclear bombs.[20] The cost of this upgrade alone was estimated to be $16.5 billion.[21]

These non-US countries are helping to cover the enormous research and development costs that have already been incurred. The more planes get sold, the cheaper the unit cost per plane. So the whole business model that convinced Congress to bankroll this enormously expensive megadeath machine is heavily dependent on exports.

In our scenario, Germany cancels the plan to purchase nuclear-capable F-35s, and other European countries follow suit.

The prime contractor for the F-35 program is Lockheed Martin. They are already set to lose a major contract for F-16 fighter jets with the Philippines (Chapter 10). But that's nothing compared to losing billions of dollars worth of sales that are needed to justify the entire F-35 program.

Lockheed Martin is not the only corporation to lose out from the loss of F-35 sales to Europe. Northrop Grumman, normally the main competitor to Lockheed Martin for major defense contracts, is a sub-contractor to Lockheed on the F-35 program.

Northrop Grumman produces the central fuselage of every plane. Those are currently made at their Integrated Assembly Line (IAL) facility in Palmdale, California. But they've just partnered with German arms manufacturer Rheinmetall to build a new $100 million IAL facility in Weeze, Germany.[22]

With the cancellation of F-35s to Germany, that new IAL is now $100 million of wasted investment, a "stranded asset."

Other US and UK military contractors will also be affected by cancelled orders for F-35s. These include BAE Systems (who build the tail and other electronics), Pratt & Whitney (the engines), Rolls-Royce (vertical-takeoff ability), Raytheon/RTX (electro-optical parts), Collins and Elbit (helmet display), and L3Harris (computer core processor). [23]

And as the unit price of the remaining F-35s being purchased by the US Department of Defense begins to skyrocket with the loss of sales to other countries, the whole enormous program is brought into question. Relying on nuclear weapons production as a core product is starting to be very bad for business.

With the US's closest allies now party to the TPNW, the US is under maximum external pressure to disarm. But the external pressures need to be combined with internal pressures to be successful. So our scenario now switches to activities going on inside *the United States to pressure it to abolish nuclear weapons. As with the external pressures, these start small, with towns and cities, calling for nuclear abolition (as they did in the 1980s), and build as the scenario unfolds.*

PART III: US PRESSURES

Pressures from other countries will certainly have an impact on the companies that develop, manufacture and maintain nuclear weapons. But for those companies to *really* feel squeezed, there must *also* be campaigns inside the United States. These will come from individuals, faith communities, civic organizations, and universities, stigmatizing, divesting, boycotting, and refusing to do business with these companies – and most of all from towns, cities and ultimately states doing this.

PRESSURE FROM THE US

- [x] CITIES COMMIT TO ABOLITION
- [ ] CITIES URGE US TO SIGN TPNW
- [ ] CITIES PASS NFZ RESOLUTONS
- [ ] CITIES PASS NFZ ORDINANCES
- [ ] CITIES DIVEST
- [ ] CITIES BAN CONTRACTS
- [ ] STATES TAKE ACTION
- [ ] GOING NATIONAL

13 From Syracuse to Phoenix: Committing to nuclear abolition

In our scenario, the first step that US cities can take toward abolishing nuclear weapons is to commit to it. One way they can do that is for their mayor to join Mayors for Peace. So far, 53 of the 200 largest cities in the US have joined (plus another 176 smaller cities and towns).

Who supports nuclear abolition?

We know that the vast majority of countries in the world support nuclear abolition, because they consistently vote in favor of resolutions at the UN calling for it. We also know from opinion polls that even in countries that still vote *against* those resolutions, a large majority of the *people* support nuclear abolition.

That includes the United States. Public opinion polls have consistently shown that a very large number of US-Americans support getting rid of all nuclear weapons, despite the unwillingness of the US government to take the necessary steps to get there.

In 1982, in what was claimed at the time to be the "largest public referendum in US history,"[1] referendums on a Nuclear Freeze appeared in nine states and 38 cities and counties, giving over one third of the American electorate the opportunity to vote directly on the question. Only one state (Arizona), one city (Fairbanks, Alaska) and one county (Stone County, Arkansas) rejected the Freeze. All the others passed it by wide margins. In Massachusetts and New Jersey, the Freeze won over 75% of the vote. Across the country, 11 million

US-Americans voted in favor of the Nuclear Freeze, and overall it passed 60% to 40%.

This level of support was reflected in the US House of Representatives the following year, when the House voted 278 to 149 in favor of the Freeze resolution (although it then failed in the Senate – see Chapter 2). National opinion polls were showing 70% to 80% of the American public favoring the Freeze by that point.[2]

Since the 1980s, there have been only sporadic attempts to gauge US public opinion on nuclear weapons, and these have largely focused on specific policy questions, such as whether the US should adopt a policy of "no first use" of nuclear weapons. Nevertheless, these polls have continued to show widespread public concern about nuclear weapons even as public attention to the issue has all but disappeared.[3]

In 2019, a national opinion poll conducted by YouGov on behalf of NuclearBan.US revealed that 49% of US-Americans thought that "the US should work with the other nuclear-armed countries to eliminate all nuclear weapons from all countries, in line with the TPNW."[4] Only 32% thought that the US should ignore the new treaty and hold on to its nuclear weapons regardless of what other countries think or do, while a further 19% said they "don't know."

Among Democrats, the figures were 70% in favor of working to eliminate all nuclear weapons versus 17% for holding onto them no matter what. Among Republicans, the figures were reversed, with 57% for holding onto nuclear weapons and only 30% wanting to eliminate them all.

Overall, strongest support for the elimination of all nuclear weapons came from women (52%), those aged 55 or over (53%), those on the West Coast (54%), Hispanics (56%), those with a four year college degree (61%) and those who voted for Hillary Clinton in 2016 (74%).

A more recent poll conducted in Massachusetts in 2022 found only a slightly higher percentage (51% of MA adults, and 76% of MA Democrats) supporting the identical language of "working with the other nuclear-armed countries to eliminate all nuclear weapons from all countries, in line with the TPNW."[5]

With just over 50% support for nuclear abolition in a progressive state like Massachusetts, and just under 50% support nationally, the US public is clearly not as concerned about the nuclear issue as they were in the 1980s. Nevertheless, there is much more support for nuclear abolition in the United States than one might think, given the overwhelming lack of support for it in the US Congress, and especially in the Senate.[6]

Largest US cities

As noted above, there is widespread support across the US for nuclear abolition, but it's especially strong among Democratic voters. A majority of Democrats live in a few large "blue" states, like California, New York and Illinois. But even in "red" and "purple" states, the larger cities tend to be heavily Democratic.

The US has 10 cities with a population of over one million (an 11th, Fort Worth, TX, is estimated to have reached one million by 2025). Of these, half (New York, Los Angeles, Chicago, Houston and Philadelphia) have so far committed themselves to nuclear abolition in one form or another.

An additional 30 cities in the US have populations over half a million. So far, 16 of these have committed to nuclear abolition.[7] There is therefore considerable potential for more of these heavily Democratic major cities to commit to nuclear abolition – especially in Blue states.

Mayors for Peace

Mayors for Peace is a movement of cities around the world standing in solidarity with Hiroshima and Nagasaki and supporting nuclear abolition so that no other city will ever suffer the same fate. As of April 1, 2025, nearly 8,500 cities in 166 countries have joined Mayors for Peace, including a total of 229 in the US.

In response to advocacy from members around the world, including in the global south, Mayors for Peace in recent years has added "realization of safe and resilient cities" and "promotion of a culture of peace" to its objective of "realization of a world without nuclear weapons." These three objectives are mutually reinforcing goals. Together, they aim to cultivate a shared sense of belonging to a single human family, regardless of our cultural, religious, or ethnic differences, and provide additional entry points for U.S. mayors who are contending with immediate local concerns.[8]

The text for joining merely asks the Mayor or other municipal leader to sign:

> *"I hereby express my city/municipality's support for the abolition of nuclear weapons and desire to join Mayors for Peace."*

This is not a huge ask, but it comes with activities and expectations, and it requires payment of a small annual fee (the equivalent of $13.86 per year). Importantly, it denotes that city or town as one committed to the abolition of nuclear weapons.

The example: Syracuse, NY

Ben Walsh, the popular Mayor of Syracuse, New York, joined Mayors for Peace in 2024. Ben has a long history of supporting progressive causes. When the Black Lives Matter protests broke out across the country in 2020 in response to the police murder of George Floyd in Minneapolis, protests also broke out in Syracuse.

As Mayor, Ben did not send the riot police to quash the demonstrators. He *joined* the demonstrators. And in an effort to reduce gang violence on the streets of Syracuse, Ben set up a pilot program to actually *pay* gang members not to fight – and to attend trainings and therapy sessions instead.

Syracuse itself has a long history of peace activism. The Syracuse Peace Council, which was founded by local Quakers in 1936, claims to be "the oldest local, autonomous, grassroots peace and social justice organization in the United States." The Council played a major role in opposing the Vietnam War, the wars in Central America, Iraq and elsewhere. It was also very active in opposing nuclear weapons, but somewhat surprisingly, Syracuse itself never became a nuclear-free zone.

In 2024, Syracuse moved a step forward by joining Mayors for Peace, and setting an example for more to follow. Ben Walsh will be stepping down as Mayor of Syracuse at the end of 2025, as he is not allowed to run for a third term. But Syracuse will remain a proud member of Mayors for Peace no matter who is the next Mayor.

Up next: South Fulton, Georgia

South Fulton is a city of 100,000 on the outskirts of Atlanta. Its population is 92% Black. And its mayor is a Black Lives Matter (BLM) activist, khalid kamau (spelled with no capital letters).

Khalid is a member of Democratic Socialists of America and he is supported by the Working Families Party. He's passionate about improving the lives of African Americans in his community. And he's deeply committed to a wide range of progressive issues, from worker rights to affordable housing to paying a living wage.

Because of his politics, and especially his history with BLM, khalid has been the subject of countless attacks in the right-wing media, and he has faced a number of allegations during his time as Mayor of South Fulton. At one point, he was accused of misusing city funds and suspended from his post, but he was reinstated shortly thereafter.

In April, 2025, khalid announced he would not be seeking re-election at the end of his term as Mayor.

But, in our scenario, before he leaves office, khalid receives an email from Abdul Fatoma in Sierra Leone (see Chapter 5).

Abdul urges khalid to support nuclear abolition by joining Mayors for Peace, and khalid agrees. Even though he will no longer be Mayor of South Fulton by January 2026, khalid will be leaving a legacy for his successor, like Ben Walsh is doing in Syracuse.

In South Fulton, being part of this global movement quickly becomes a source of pride.

[A note on our scenario clock: the steps taking place in the US are happening *simultaneously* with the steps taking place around the world in previous chapters. The effect is cumulative. But to make the math easier to follow, our clock continues to run backwards *consecutively* from the previous chapter. As we start over in this section with small initial steps worth only one second on our clock, we're adding these to the bigger multi-minute steps that have already taken place in the previous section.]

The clock in our scenario goes back 1 second to 10:29:59 when the Mayor of South Fulton, Georgia becomes the 230th Mayor in the US to join Mayors for Peace.

More cities join

In our scenario, more cities and towns keep joining Mayors for Peace. These include cities in blue states that for whatever reason have never gotten around to it, like Colorado Springs, Colorado and Brattleboro, Vermont.

There are also some bigger cities in the blue states that require a bit more effort to get on board, like San Jose and San Diego, both in California. And there are some surprises from deep red states, like Jacksonville, Florida, Forth Worth, Texas, Charlotte, North Carolina and Indianapolis, Indiana.

The clock goes back a further 8 seconds to 10:29:51 when the Mayors of Colorado Springs, Brattleboro, San Jose, San Diego, Jacksonville, Fort Worth, Charlotte and Indianapolis all join Mayors for Peace.

The prize: Phoenix, AZ

With 1.65 million inhabitants. Phoenix is the fifth largest city in the US, and the fastest growing. It's a fairly "purple" city in a fairly purple state. Trump won Arizona in 2016 by a small margin. Biden won the state by just 11,000 votes in 2020. Trump won it back in 2024 with a larger margin. The Phoenix City Council consists of 5 Democrats, 3 Republicans and 1 independent.

Phoenix's Mayor Kate Gallego, a Democrat, is one of the youngest big city mayors in the country. She studied environmental science and public policy at Harvard. As Mayor, she has focused her climate mitigation efforts on trying to reduce the extreme temperatures in Phoenix through a program of urban tree planting.

In our scenario, Kate is willing to take the small step of joining Mayors for Peace in order to address climate's twin existential threat: nuclear weapons.

The clock goes back 1 second to 10:29:50 when the Mayor of Phoenix, Arizona joins Mayors for Peace.

As mayors continue to join their colleagues in calling for a peaceful world without the Bomb, cities still need to take many more steps to start putting serious pressure on the companies that profit from nuclear weapons. The next step is for cities to call on the US government to abolish them.

PRESSURE FROM THE US

- [ ] CITIES COMMIT TO ABOLITION
- [x] CITIES URGE US TO SIGN TPNW
- [ ] CITIES PASS NFZ RESOLUTONS
- [ ] CITIES PASS NFZ ORDINANCES
- [ ] CITIES DIVEST
- [ ] CITIES BAN CONTRACTS
- [ ] STATES TAKE ACTION
- [ ] GOING NATIONAL

14 From Milwaukee to Kansas City: Cities calling on the US to act

Cities and towns in the US that already support nuclear abolition can take the next step to actually pass a (recommendatory) resolution *calling on the US to abolish nuclear weapons. Of the 229 US Mayors for Peace, so far 79 of them have passed a Back from the Brink resolution.*[1]

Resolutions as recommendations

As we saw in Chapter 4, the TPNW resolution in the UN General Assembly is a "recommendatory" resolution, calling on countries *other* than the resolution signer to sign the TPNW. This is the simplest, easiest and most common type of resolution, because it calls on somebody else to do something and doesn't necessarily have any effect at all on those who vote for it.

Likewise, it's recommendatory when cities, counties, states and other institutions within the United States pass resolutions that call on the US President to sign the TPNW (or call on the federal government to take other actions). These resolutions are also non-binding: they carry no legal authority to compel anyone to do anything.

The **ICAN Cities Appeal** is an example of a non-binding recommendatory resolution. Hundreds of towns and cities around the world have signed the appeal, including at least 75 in the US. The text of the appeal is a very short and to the point:

> *"Our city/town is deeply concerned about the grave threat that nuclear weapons pose to communities*

> *throughout the world. We firmly believe that our residents have the right to live in a world free from this threat. Any use of nuclear weapons, whether deliberate or accidental, would have catastrophic, far-reaching and long-lasting consequences for people and the environment. Therefore, we support the Treaty on the Prohibition of Nuclear Weapons and* ***call on our governments to sign and ratify it****."*

Back from the Brink

A major focus for nuclear-related city resolutions in the United States at the present time is the **Back from the Brink** platform, consisting of five common sense policy proposals that aim to bring the US and the world back from the brink of nuclear war.[2] The campaign calls on the federal government to lead a global effort to prevent nuclear war by:

- Actively pursuing a verifiable agreement among nuclear-armed states to eliminate their nuclear arsenals
- Renouncing the option of using nuclear weapons first
- Ending the sole, unchecked authority of any U.S. President to launch a nuclear attack
- Taking U.S. nuclear weapons off hair-trigger alert
- Cancelling the plan to replace the entire U.S. nuclear arsenal with enhanced weapons

These are all steps that only the President (or possibly Congress) can take, so most Back from the Brink resolutions, including the one in Congress (currently H.Res. 317), are non-binding and recommendatory. (Some Back from the Brink groups around the country have taken liberties with the text of the model resolution, adapting it to local situations and also sometimes adding decisional elements. We'll look at some of those in the next chapter.)

As of April, 2025, 170 faith communities, 324 civil society organizations, 79 municipalities and counties and 8 state legislative bodies have passed some form of Back from the Brink resolution. This chapter focuses on municipalities (and counties), where elected representatives vote on behalf of their constituents.

Physicians for Social Responsibility

Physicians for Social Responsibility (PSR) is a network of medical professionals in the US who are committed, among other things, to nuclear abolition. PSR is affiliated with IPPNW, the global network of medical professionals (see Chapter 7). PSR has played a key role in US anti-nuclear movements for many decades, and remains committed to the total abolition of nuclear weapons.[3]

Together with the Union of Concerned Scientists, PSR has been a lead sponsor of the Back from the Brink initiative, launched by former PSR President Dr. Ira Helfand and others in 2017. Ira is also a past President of IPPNW and serves on the International Steering Group of ICAN.

The example: Milwaukee

Milwaukee, Wisconsin is among the 40 largest cities in the US, with a population of just over 500,000. Wisconsin is a "purple" state that voted for Biden in 2020 and for Trump in 2024. The rural parts of Wisconsin are strongly Republican, but this is counter-balanced by cities like Milwaukee that are strongly Democratic.

Milwaukee has an interesting history. It was a major center of a US brand of socialism in the late 19th and early 20th centuries that focused on new sanitation systems, city-owned water and power systems and improved education. These "sewer socialists" ran the city council for a number of years. The people of Milwaukee still remember this legacy and are proud of their socialist heritage. The city today is overwhelmingly Democratic (even though the Republican National Convention took place here in 2024, where Trump was anointed as their nominee for President).[4]

Milwaukee also has a history of anti-nuclear activism. In 1982, voters passed a Nuclear Freeze referendum by a 3 to 1 margin. It became a Mayors for Peace city in 2006. In 2022, a Madison City Council member was among the speakers at a rally to celebrate the one-year anniversary of the entry into force of the TPNW, held at the Wisconsin State Capitol.

And in August 2023, Milwaukee's Mayor Cavalier Johnson hosted the Golden Rule sailboat which had sailed US waters for eight years educating the public about the need for the US to join the TPNW.[5]

Milwaukee Back from the Brink Campaign – Core Group

Thanks to the efforts of County Commissioner Steven Shea, the Milwaukee County Board of Supervisors had adopted a resolution endorsing Back from the Brink in 2021. This was followed by a resolution passed in Madison in 2023 that included a commitment not to buy from or invest in nuclear weapons companies.

A core group was formed in late summer of 2024 to get the *city* of Milwaukee to follow the examples of the County (and Madison) and pass a similar Back from the Brink resolution. Pam Richard from Peace Action Wisconsin, Keith Brumley from Milwaukee Veterans for Peace, Steve Watrous from the Milwaukee United Nations Association and Dr. Paula Rogge from PSR Wisconsin had been working on nuclear disarmament for years. They met through the fall and early spring of 2025.

Two experienced nuclear disarmament activists joined them: Bill Christofferson of Veterans For Peace and Julie Enslow of 350 Milwaukee. Bill was a former journalist and chief of staff to the mayor of Milwaukee, so was very helpful in publicizing the campaign and helping the core group understand Common Council procedures.

PSR WI provided a sample Back from the Brink resolution and background info sheet for Alders[6] and their constituents. Both documents were edited to include highlights of Milwaukee's nuclear disarmament history, the effects of a single modern nuclear bomb attack on the City, and the costs to Milwaukee of the US nuclear weapons program.

Getting the word out

Each member of the core group took on the responsibility of contacting the members of their organizations about the campaign and asking them to reach out to their elected representatives on the Common Council.

On November 11, 2024, the Milwaukee Veterans For Peace chapter put on an Armistice Day event at the City Hall. Ann Wright, a retired US Army Colonel and former State Department official, attracted a lot of attention speaking to the crowd in favor of the Resolution.

Milwaukee members of the core group also spoke at several meetings of peace and justice groups throughout the city about the campaign. Several articles were printed in the local press that mentioned the campaign. Copies of Annie Jacobsen's *Nuclear War: A Scenario* were distributed to members of the Common Council.

Building a coalition

The six core group members began collecting endorsements from other groups including local climate groups (350, Sierra Club, Green Party), faith communities (Quakers, Methodists, Catholics and the Muslim Women's Coalition) and other local organizations (the Marquette University Center for Peacemaking, Women's International League for Peace and Freedom and a Cuba solidarity group). Several statewide groups (the Interfaith Peace Working Group, Building Unity, and Our Wisconsin Revolution) had already endorsed Back from the Brink, so were included in the list of endorsers.

Once the core group had collected these organizational endorsements, Bill approached his Alder, Marina Dimitrijevic, about sponsoring a Back from the Brink resolution, as he knew she was supportive of nuclear disarmament. She introduced the resolution to the Common Council in February 2025.

Help from County Supervisor Shea

The resolution was then referred by the Council to the Judiciary Committee which met in March. Initially, the Committee Chair announced that he did not support the resolution, and he allowed only one member of the public to speak to it. Fortunately, that person was Steven Shea from the Milwaukee County Board of Supervisors. He drew the committee's attention to the fact that the Milwaukee County Board had passed a Back from the Brink resolution in 2019, and convinced the Committee's members to support the City version.

When the resolution came before the Common Council for a vote on April 1, 2025, it had the support of the Judiciary Committee as well as four Alder co-sponsors. The vote in favor was unanimous. Milwaukee was now on record in support of nuclear weapons abolition.

Next up: Seattle

Seattle is considerably larger than Milwaukee, with over 750,000 people. Unlike Wisconsin, however, Washington is a deep blue state, with a strong anti-nuclear movement.

More than 200 activists gathered in Seattle in April 2025 for a two-day conference called "Re-Building the Anti-Nuclear Weapons Movement Together." It was hosted by Washington Against Nuclear Weapons, a coalition that already consists of more than 40 organizations working together on the nuclear issue in Washington, under the umbrella of Washington Physicians for Social Responsibility (PSR).

The conference discussed the growing danger of nuclear warfare at any one of the numerous "flashpoints" around the world. Participants heard from communities who are already affected by nuclear weapons testing and production. And at the end of the two days, the gathering discussed strategies for nuclear abolition and specific steps to be taken in the coming months.

One of those steps was to coordinate efforts to pass a Back from the Brink resolution in the Seattle City Council.

It's an easy ask. Seattle is a blue city in a blue state. Plus, residents are uncomfortably aware that they live next to a potential target or accident site: it's just 83 miles from downtown Seattle to Kitsap Naval base, home to one of the biggest stockpiles of nuclear weapons in the country. **In our scenario, the resolution passes quickly.**

The clock goes back by 5 seconds to 10:29:45 when Seattle becomes the 80th city, town or county in the US to pass a Back from the Brink resolution.

More cities join

Of the other major, Democrat-dominated cities in the US that have so far *not* passed a resolution in support of nuclear abolition, the two most likely to come next are Denver, in the blue state of Colorado, and San Jose, in the blue state of California.

In our scenario, Denver and San Jose pass resolutions, and so do many other smaller cities, towns, and counties, again mostly in blue states – soon bringing the total up to 100 municipalities in the US calling for the US to abolish nuclear weapons.

The clock goes back by a further 100 seconds to 10:28:05 when yet another 20 cities and towns around the country pass resolutions calling for nuclear abolition, for a total of 100.

The Prize: Kansas City

As Back from the Brink resolutions pick up steam around the US, it would be significant to add Kansas City, Missouri. It's in the top 40 population-wise, with just over half a million residents. Missouri is a deep red state, but Kansas City, its largest city, is a Democratic Party stronghold. Donald Trump won the state with about 60% of the vote in 2024. But in Jackson County, which includes most of Kansas City, Kamala Harris won with about 60%.

Kansas City also hosts a major nuclear weapons plant, the Kansas City National Security Campus (KCNSC).

Ann Suellentrop and the broad coalition

Ann Suellentrop is a retired nurse – and a leader in two anti-nuclear organizations. She's the Vice Chair of PeaceWorks Kansas City and Program Director for Kansas City PSR. She has also been very active with the Back from the Brink campaign and is on the national board of PSR.

Ann's goal is to raise the city's awareness of the nuclear weapons plant in their midst. She has published op-eds in the local papers and run workshops and seminars to educate the public, but many residents still have no idea that their neighbors play such a big role in omnicidal technology.

In this scenario, Ann organizes her networks to get a Back from the Brink resolution passed by the Kansas City Council. She draws on lots of local groups for support, like local churches, the Interfaith Peace Council, Veterans For Peace, CodePink, and United for Peace and Justice. She can also count on help from groups like climate activists from the Sunrise Movement, prison abolitionists from Decarcerate Kansas City, housing activists from KC Tenants Union, and even some new groups that are already springing up in response to Trump's agenda, including Boots on the Ground.

All these groups are willing to lobby for this resolution to pass, even if it's not their main focus. It's important, it's a winnable campaign, and it's relatively easy because it's non-binding and purely symbolic.

It does pass, and it has a significant impact. Kansas City is home to the 7,000 people who work at the KCNSC, plus their families, friends, and neighbors. Many were proud to have jobs they believed were keeping the USA safe and secure. But with this resolution, they can't escape finding out that they're working in an industry that does *not* have the wholehearted support of the wider community – or the rest of the world. In fact, their products are deeply controversial, and they're strongly opposed by a growing number of people – including the people *in their city.*

The clock goes back by 5 seconds to 10:28:00 when the City Council of Kansas City passes a Back from the Brink resolution.

Honeywell and the National Security Campus

KCNSC is a sprawling industrial site where 80% of the non-nuclear components that go into every US nuclear weapon are manufactured. These include electronic guidance systems, arming systems, parts that hold and carry the plutonium, uranium, and tritium, and fuses that set off the bomb.

PHOTO: Peter Metz

KCNSC is in the process of doubling in size as it gears up for its role in "modernizing" every nuclear weapon in the US arsenal.

The KCNSC itself is a federal facility of the National Nuclear Security Administration (NNSA). And the NNSA is the government agency responsible for all US nuclear weapons under the Department of Energy. A private company, however, is the sole manager and operator of the plant. And that company is Honeywell.

The Honeywell brand is on everything from home thermostats to safety goggles to nuclear missile parts. But the Honeywell corporation has been splitting off various parts of its business into separate companies since 2018.[7] And by 2026, the corporation that runs KCNSC will be **Honeywell Aerospace**, which will be legally separate from all the other Honeywell companies.

Honeywell has to recruit on a regular basis to fill the vacancies at the KCNSC. Recruiters go to the local colleges, high schools, and even grade schools[8] suggesting to young would-be engineers that they could be "working to make the world a better place today and for the future." **That kind of claim is now being met with a sneer more than with an offer to sign up. It's suddenly getting a lot harder to find employees. The workers at the plant are also facing morale issues as they watch their city commit itself to nuclear abolition.**

One third of Kansas City residents identify as Catholic. Their Archbishop is James V. Johnson, who has recently agreed to sign on to John Wester's pastoral letter (see box below) as a "second tier" supporter.

In our scenario, Archbishop Johnson is inspired to go the next step and directly challenge his parishioners who work at the National Security Campus.

Archbishop John Wester presides over the archdiocese of Santa Fe, New Mexico. In 2022, he published a 50-page pastoral letter entitled "Living in the Light of Christ's Peace: A Conversation Toward Nuclear Disarmament." It reflects on the horrors of Hiroshima and Nagasaki and the moral imperative of eliminating these weapons before they are used again.

> *"We [in the US] are the people who designed and built these weapons of mass destruction. We were the first to use them. We must be the people to dismantle them and make sure they are never used again."*

He quotes Pope Francis talking about the immorality of even *possessing* such weapons. And he follows his own faith to its logical conclusion:

> *"If we listen, we can hear Jesus' voice crying out today: Stop building nuclear weapons, do not prepare for nuclear war, dismantle your nuclear weapons, and welcome God's reign of universal love and peace."*

Archbishop Wester's archdiocese includes Los Alamos, where the first nuclear weapon was built and tested, Kirtland Air Force Base, where up to 2,500 nuclear weapons are in storage (the largest repository of nuclear weapons in the country), and Sandia National Laboratory, which, together with Los Alamos and Lawrence Livermore Lab in California, is responsible for the ongoing design and development of nuclear weapons today.

So when Archbishop Wester says, "Stop building nuclear weapons," he is not talking into a void. He is talking to his Catholic parishioners who work at these facilities.

(For link to the full text of Archbishop Wester's pastoral letter, see footnote[1])

It's a good step when cities across the US pass non-binding recommendatory resolutions calling for the US to sign the TPNW. But much more is needed to really put pressure on the corporations that are calling the shots in Washington. Decisional resolutions are next.

PRESSURE FROM THE US

- [ ] CITIES COMMIT TO ABOLITION
- [ ] CITIES URGE US TO SIGN TPNW
- [x] CITIES PASS NFZ RESOLUTONS
- [ ] CITIES PASS NFZ ORDINANCES
- [ ] CITIES DIVEST
- [ ] CITIES BAN CONTRACTS
- [ ] STATES TAKE ACTION
- [ ] GOING NATIONAL

15 From Evanston, IL to Washington, DC: Cities taking action

When cities pass resolutions that commit the city itself *to taking action, it's a step up from* calling on the federal government *to take action. These resolutions are still non-binding and unenforceable. But at least they can be acted upon by the body that votes for them, and that makes these resolutions more likely to be implemented. Of the 79 cities and towns that have passed a Back from the Brink resolution, 29 of them have also declared themselves to be Nuclear Free Zones.*

A country that signs the TPNW is announcing its unqualified commitment to the goal of nuclear abolition. That country still has to ratify the treaty before it is *legally* committed to that goal. But signing is certainly a much stronger commitment than voting for a resolution calling on *other* countries to sign the TPNW.

A city that passes a *decisional* resolution, committing itself to taking some action towards the goal of nuclear abolition, is taking a similar step. It is not yet a legal commitment, but it is, again, much stronger than calling on the federal government to do something (like sign the TPNW) over which the city has no control.

By 1985, over 400 cities, towns and counties across the US had passed *recommendatory* resolutions calling on the federal government to "freeze" the nuclear arms race (see Chapter 2). But then along came the "nuclear free zone" (NFZ) movement, with the goal of passing *decisional* resolutions that committed cities and towns to taking a bolder stance *themselves* to abolish nuclear weapons. These were still non-binding resolutions with no power to be legally enforced. But they were a step forward, and even without carrying any legal force, many were nonetheless implemented.

The example: Evanston, Illinois

On October 28, 1985, the City Council of Evanston, Illinois, passed Resolution 79-R-85, declaring Evanston to be an NFZ. The resolution prohibited producing, researching, supplying, or transporting materials for the production of nuclear weapons within the city

Like all such resolutions, it was non-binding. But unlike the Back from the Brink resolutions in the previous chapter, requesting the federal government to take action, this was a *decisional* resolution, committing the City of Evanston to take some concrete actions itself.

Municipal NFZs

Altogether, in the 1980s and 90s, over 200 US cities, towns, counties and Native American nations declared themselves to be NFZs. Many of these were legally-binding ordinances and by-laws (which we'll look at in the next chapter). But most were just resolutions or other forms of non-binding declarations.

Nevertheless, the NFZ resolutions represented a significant portion of the US population who were declaring to their federal government - and the world - that they wanted nothing to do with anything nuclear. In almost all cases, this meant nuclear weapons. But many NFZs also declared opposition to nuclear power plants in their cities, as well as to stationing or transporting nuclear waste.

NFZ resolutions were passed in numerous towns and cities in predominantly blue states: 30 in California, 11 in Connecticut, 29 in Massachusetts, 14 in New Jersey, 19 in Oregon. There were also a good number passed in what are now purple states, like Wisconsin with 18.

But NFZ resolutions were also getting passed in unlikely places, like Homer, Alaska; Palm Beach Gardens, Florida; Blaine County, Idaho; Miller, Indiana; North Newton, Kansas; Reno, Nevada; and Louisville, Kentucky.

The industry wasn't particularly alarmed by these largely symbolic resolutions, even in deep red states. But they were definitely threatened as more and more cities were turning these non-binding resolutions into *legally binding ordinances and bylaws* - and then starting to divest from and ban city contracts with nuclear weapons companies.

So just as with the votes in favor of the TPNW at the UN, even symbolic resolutions become a threat to the nuclear weapons companies *because they can see that this could lead to stronger actions in the future* (see the following chapters).

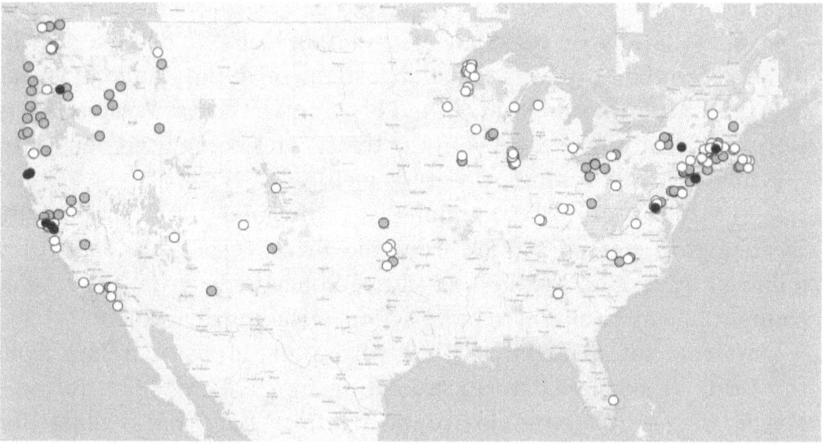

Cities and towns with white dot have passed a NFZ resolution since 1980. Those with grey dots passed a NFZ ordinance, and those with black dots have passed ordinances including divestment and banning of contracts.

Aligning with the TPNW

Cities cannot join an international treaty. But they *can* ban things that are under their own jurisdiction or control.

After the adoption of the TPNW in 2017, a few towns in Western Massachusetts passed resolutions declaring themselves to be "aligned" with the new treaty. This was an updated version of being a Nuclear Free Zone, since the TPNW bans the development, testing, production, stockpiling or stationing of nuclear weapons at any place "under the jurisdiction or control" of the parties to the treaty.

The town of Chesterfield, Mass, for instance, passed a Back from the Brink resolution in 2019. It included calling on the federal government to take the five steps called for in the campaign. But it went further, committing the town "to take all necessary steps to align the Town of Chesterfield with the UN Treaty on the Prohibition of Nuclear Weapons."

Because it was a resolution rather than a legally-binding ordinance, no further steps were taken to do the actual "aligning." Nevertheless, this set a precedent for several other towns, and at least one city (Northampton) did follow through with several more steps (still to come in later chapters).

Up next: Holyoke, Mass.

Holyoke is a small city in Western Massachusetts. Just over 50% of the population identifies as Hispanic, and it has the largest Puerto Rican population, per capita, of any city in the US. Many are low income.

In 2012, Holyoke residents elected Alex Morse to be their Mayor. At 22 years of age, he was the youngest Mayor in the United States at that time. After the adoption of the TPNW, towns across Western Mass were "aligning" themselves with the treaty. Alex committed himself to "aligning" Holyoke with the Treaty as well.

In 2019, Holyoke's immediate neighbor to the north, Easthampton, passed a Back from the Brink resolution. Then they followed up in 2021 with an Executive Policy Order from the Mayor, committing Easthampton to more action, including divestment.

Holyoke is catching up with Easthampton. It passed a Back from the Brink (recommendatory) resolution in 2022. In 2024, its new Mayor signed a letter in support of a state bill calling for Massachusetts to look into ways it could align the whole state with the TPNW. But until now, Holyoke has yet to take further steps to align *itself* with the treaty.

In our scenario, local organizers in Holyoke convince the new Mayor and members of the City Council to pass a decisional resolution committing Holyoke to remain nuclear-free and align itself with the TPNW.

> **The clock goes back by 10 seconds to 10:27:50** when the City Council of Holyoke, MA, passes a resolution declaring the city to be a nuclear-free zone and aligned with the TPNW.

More cities become nuclear-free

Campaigners in cities and towns that have passed Back from the Brink resolutions are now looking for what they can do next. Many are now picking up the nuclear-free zone idea from the 1980s and/or linking it to the TPNW to create "treaty aligned" cities.

When the city of **Oakland, California**, passed a very strong city ordinance in 1988 banning everything to do with nuclear weapons, it ran into trouble with the federal government because nuclear weapons components were being regularly transported in and out of the Port of Oakland by ship.

The federal government took the city of Oakland to court over their NFZ statute, and won. Oakland's nuclear-free ordinance was struck down. But Oakland simply turned around and re-wrote their law to exclude the Port Authority of Oakland, since that was not under the city's jurisdiction but controlled by the federal government.

The new NFZ law in Oakland was not challenged further and has remained on the books ever since 1992 (see Appendix IV). A few attempts were made to throw out other NFZ laws in court, but none of them succeeded. Oakland thus set a legal precedent for any city in the US to prohibit nuclear weapons (or any other) activities within the area that is legally under their jurisdiction.

A NFZ ordinance approved by the Town Meeting in Amherst, Massachusetts in 1984 was also struck down. The state's Attorney General sent it back to the town as "disapproved."

But had Amherst contested that decision in court, it almost certainly would have won, since at least two other towns in Massachusetts had also passed NFZ ordinances very similar to Amherst's by then, and those were never challenged and remain in place today.

These cities and towns are not only calling on the federal government to support the TPNW. They are committing themselves to ban nuclear weapons activities – to the extent that they are able – within their own locale.

Amherst, which tried to pass a NFZ ordinance in the 1980s, is trying again – this time with just a resolution. It passes, and it holds up in court. Brookline, Massachusetts, is next.

On the other side of the country, Salem, Oregon, passes a NFZ ordinance to top off its earlier Back from the Brink resolution. Salem is followed by Eureka, California.

The clock goes back by 40 seconds to 10:27:10 when the cities of Amherst, Brookline, Salem and Eureka pass nuclear-free zone resolutions.

The Prize: Washington, DC

DC is of course the center of the US federal government, where all the wrong decisions are made, where all the corruption takes place, and where all the lobbyists keep the nuclear weapons programs going.

Just outside the DC city boundary, in Arlington, Virgina, the Pentagon directs all the nuclear war preparations. Most of the nuclear weapons companies have big buildings and a very visible presence nearby.

The people who actually live *in* DC are mostly not the people running the government or the nuclear weapons companies. DC has the largest percentage of Black Americans of any major city in the US. It also has a very high percentage of people living at or below the poverty line.

And DC is one of the most heavily Democratic cities in the US. Donald Trump got just 6.6% of DC's total vote in the last election, compared to 92.5% for Kamala Harris.

Ellen Thomas and Proposition One

A 24-hour anti-nuclear vigil outside the White House began in 1981 and has been maintained ever since – now in its 44th year.[1] Ellen Thomas was one of the activists who joined that vigil back in the 1980s. She and her then-husband William Thomas, the founder of the vigil, launched a campaign in 1990 called Proposition One, to get an initiative on the DC ballot calling for nuclear abolition.

In 1993, DC residents voted overwhelmingly for nuclear abolition. The Delegate to Congress from DC, Eleanor Holmes Norton, introduced a bill in Congress the following year, calling on the US to negotiate a treaty eliminating all nuclear weapons from the planet.[2]

Norton has re-introduced her bill in every session of Congress since then (see Chapter 20). In 2017, when the treaty she hoped for was adopted, the Norton bill was updated to call on the US to *sign the TPNW.*

In 2019, the City Council of Washington, DC passed a Back from the Brink resolution. The next step is to pass a *decisional* resolution committing DC to being nuclear-free in line with the TPNW.

Nuclear-Free DC

A bill introduced in the US House of Representatives by Rep. Byron Donalds of Florida in 2023 would have instructed the Architects of the US Capitol to investigate the option of powering the congressional buildings in DC with nuclear energy. This idea was utterly unacceptable to Eleanor Holmes Norton and the residents of DC.

In our scenario, this alarming proposal is the catalyst for the City Council of Washington, DC, to pass the resolution declaring the city to be a nuclear-free zone – not only free of nuclear weapons but also free of nuclear power.

The clock goes back by 10 seconds to 10:27:00 when the City Council of Washington, DC, passes a resolution declaring the city to be a nuclear-free zone and aligned with the TPNW.

The city controls everything within the District of Colombia *except* the buildings and areas that are under the control of the federal government. So there's no conflict about whose jurisdiction is whose, and the new NFZ doesn't set up a direct confrontation with the federal government. In any case, it's only a non-binding resolution – but the impact is nonetheless significant.

Boeing

Boeing began in Seattle, and most of its major facilities are still in that area. But in 2022, Boeing moved its headquarters to the DC area in order to be, in their words, "in proximity to our customers and stakeholders."[3] Their new headquarters are not in DC proper, but in Arlington, Virginia, across the river from the Jefferson Memorial, but literally *next door to the Pentagon.*

In our scenario, the DC Council puts "Welcome to Nuclear-Free DC" signs up on all the bridges coming into DC. At least two of these signs are clearly visible from the Boeing headquarters on the other side of the Potomac.

Boeing starts to get very nervous about drawing attention to their headquarters in Arlington. They don't like the public knowing that their most important clients are not airlines but the Pentagon. And their products are not just airplanes designed to get people where they need to go but missiles designed to kill millions of people all at once.

DC's NFZ resolution will not put an end to Boeing's nuclear weapons work. But it's another blow to morale and to the company's public image and reputation. It's another nail in the

corporate coffin, not just for Boeing, but for all the companies involved in this barbaric business.

The next logical step for cities is to pass legally-binding city ordinances banning nuclear weapons-related activities within their jurisdiction, as many did in the 1980s. What city will be the next to tackle the nuclear industry head-on?

PRESSURE FROM THE US

- [ ] CITIES COMMIT TO ABOLITION
- [ ] CITIES URGE US TO SIGN TPNW
- [ ] CITIES PASS NFZ RESOLUTONS
- [x] CITIES PASS NFZ ORDINANCES
- [ ] CITIES DIVEST
- [ ] CITIES BAN CONTRACTS
- [ ] STATES TAKE ACTION
- [ ] GOING NATIONAL

16 From Spokane to Providence: Turning resolutions into city ordinances

Passing a decisional resolution is a step up from passing a recommendatory resolution. But passing a legally-binding ordinance that commits a city to take concrete actions in support of nuclear abolition is even stronger. This is when the companies that develop, manufacture and maintain nuclear weapons begin to feel the real pressure. Of the 29 currently active Nuclear Free Zone municipalities in the US, 12 of them have passed legally-binding ordinances to that effect.

A country that *ratifies* the TPNW is making a legally-binding commitment to abide by the terms of the treaty. In most countries of the world, cities do not have the authority to make legally-binding commitments that have anything to do with nuclear weapons. But in the United States, they do.

Towns, cities and counties across the United States have gone beyond resolutions to pass legally-binding statutes, bylaws and ordinances that prohibit nuclear weapons-related activities within their jurisdiction. As we saw in Oakland and DC, federal facilities within their geographical boundary may not be within the jurisdiction of a given municipality. Nevertheless, prohibiting certain activities that *are* within their jurisdiction is an immensely powerful step for a city to take. And in this scenario, more and more cities are willing to take that step.

The example: Spokane, Washington

Spokane is a medium-sized city of about 230,000 people. It is among the top 100 cities in the US by population. It's also a deep blue city in a deep blue state. So it's the ideal sort of place to take this next step and pass a city ordinance that goes on the statute books and has legal consequences if it is violated.

Tom Charles and Veterans For Peace

After the adoption of the TPNW in 2017, the Spokane chapter of Veterans For Peace approached members of the City Council with a resolution calling on the US to sign and ratify the TPNW. It also called on Spokane to declare itself a nuclear-weapons-free community. The resolution was duly passed by the City Council, but Vietnam veteran Tom Charles, for one, was not satisfied.

Tom joined VFP to work toward a more peaceful world. He cares deeply about children in the United States who go to bed hungry every night (15 million of them). He cares about his fellow Americans who live in tents, under bridges and on the streets (half a million of them). He cares about all the people going bankrupt because they can't pay their medical bills (550,000 every year). And he cares about the trillions of dollars that are being spent on nuclear weapons instead of on these people.

Tom is passionate about nuclear abolition, and not only because of the misspent money. "We live in a world that is one computer glitch, one human error, or one deliberate malevolent act away from nuclear destruction," he says.

For Tom and others in his VFP group, a city resolution was just "wishful thinking." They wanted more. They wanted a city ordinance because it would be an actual law that could be enforced.

So Tom and his colleagues worked for three years on getting a city ordinance passed. They had an ally in the President of the City Council, a lawyer who helped them draft a legally watertight ordinance.

They made their case individually with each of the City Councillors (all but one were willing to meet). They needed a veto-proof majority on the Council, because they were sure the Mayor would veto it.

They had the support of Pax Christi and one Episcopal Bishop, but it was still a pretty small group that diligently chipped away on the ordinance until it was finally passed in late 2022 by a vote of 5-2 – enough to preclude a veto by the Mayor.

The Spokane ordinance (full text in Appendix V) is an ideal model law for US cities that are ready to take this step. It prohibits all persons, corporations, universities, laboratories, institutions or other entities from being "knowingly and intentionally engaged in the production of nuclear weapons" in the city. And "no facility, equipment, components, supplies or substance used to produce nuclear weapons shall be allowed" in the city.

The ordinance further calls for city funds to be divested from the nuclear weapons industry. It boycotts nuclear weapons producers by disqualifying them from "any award, contract or purchase order" with the city. It sets a mechanism for waivers in exceptional circumstances, and defines penalties for violations.

As a modern-day version of the 20th century NFZ ordinances, this comes close to some of the most comprehensive ordinances, like Oakland's, that had the biggest impact on the nuclear weapons industry.

It's still too early to say how this two-year-old ordinance may turn out to affect any of the nuclear weapons companies. But in October, 2024, it was confirmed that a shipment of nuclear waste from the Hanford nuclear site[1] passed through the city of Spokane, so there are still challenges to making Spokane truly nuclear-free.

Next up: Santa Barbara, CA

Santa Barbara is a relatively small city of 100,000. It hosts facilities of at least three nuclear weapons companies: RTX, Lockheed Martin and Northrop Grumman. It also hosts the national headquarters of the Nuclear Age Peace Foundation (NAPF), one of the nation's foremost organizations committed to nuclear abolition.

Ivana Hughes and the Nuclear Age Peace Foundation

NAPF was founded in the 1980s by the legendary peace campaigner David Krieger. Over the decades, NAPF has played a major role in articulating the dangers of nuclear weapons and the imperative of abolishing them. To reinforce his message to reach a wider public, David brought an impressive number of international luminaries to the NAPF offices in Santa Barbara for lectures and artistic events, including the Dalai Lama, Yehudi Menuhin, Carl Sagan, Jacques Cousteau, and Desmond Tutu.

In 2018, after the nearby town of Ojai passed a resolution making itself a nuclear-free zone, NAPF drafted a city resolution to get Santa Barbara to do likewise. They collected signatures and met with City

Councillors. The resolution would have banned nuclear reactors and/or nuclear weapons work (including developing, testing, producing, manufacturing, otherwise acquiring, possessing or stockpiling) within the city of Santa Barbara. But it did not get through.

Then in 2019, NAPF presented a revised proposal to the City Council, asking for language to be included in the city's "legislative program" calling for the US to join the TPNW (and to take other steps from the Back from the Brink platform). This was agreed and added to Santa Barbara's Federal Legislative Platform for 2019.

What that meant in practice, however, was simply that the wording was included in a document published by the City that year. The City itself was not even put on record as supporting those goals, as it would have been in the case of passing a city resolution. And when the next year's Federal Legislative Platform document was published, the wording about the TPNW was already gone.

In 2022, Dr. Ivana Nikolić Hughes took the helm of the Foundation. Ivana brings fresh new energy for nuclear abolition to the NAPF, and has been an outspoken supporter of the TPNW.

With Ivana's help, NAPF is now ready to try again with the city of Santa Barbara. This time, they want a permanent, legally-binding commitment from the city.

In this scenario, thanks to what Ivana has built on David's legacy, it passes. Third time's the charm! Or, as it says in the I Ching, "Persistence furthers."

The clock goes back by 15 seconds to 10:26:45 when the City Council of Santa Barbara creates a city ordinance declaring the city to be a nuclear-free zone and aligned with the TPNW.

The prize: Providence, Rhode Island

Providence, the capital city of Rhode Island, is a small city in a small state. But it's also where Textron, of one of the top nuclear weapons companies, has their global headquarters. Also, RTX, another major nuclear weapons company, has a major plant nearby.

For such a small state, Rhode Island has an abundance of organizations working to address poverty, immigrant rights, militarism, racial justice, gun violence and many other issues. These groups were all willing to work together to get a Back from the Brink resolution into the RI State House.[2]

With the support of this coalition, the Rhode Island State Senate passed a Back from the Brink resolution in 2022. Then the Rhode Island House of Representatives passed one in 2024. The Rhode Island version of the Back from the Brink resolution is one of the few that *specifically calls on the US to sign and ratify the TPNW.*

Some towns in Rhode Island have also passed similar resolutions, including East Providence, Little Compton and Jamestown. But so far, not the city of Providence itself.

In our scenario, all the same groups are ready and willing to tackle the Providence City Council and mobilize support around the city for passing a nuclear-free ordinance, and they succeed.

> **The clock goes back by another 15 seconds to 10:26:30** when the City Council of Providence, RI, passes an ordinance making the city a nuclear-free zone and aligned with the TPNW.

Textron and nuclear weapons

Textron is one of the companies that stopped manufacturing cluster munitions after the international treaty banning those weapons went into effect and public pressure began to mount (see Chapter 8). Textron no longer makes cluster munitions, but they do still make nuclear weapons.

Textron has two multi-million-dollar contracts for work on the existing Minuteman III nuclear missiles, and a third contract for work on the new Sentinel missile. These are highly specialized projects that are sub-contracted to Textron because they're the only ones who know how to do them. If Textron were to pull out of those projects, it would potentially leave a gaping hole in the US ICBM program.

And in this scenario, Textron *is* about to pull out of those projects. It has already shown its vulnerability to public pressure over cluster munitions. And as more and more investors internationally classify nuclear weapons as "controversial weapons" (see Chapter 8), and more and more cities in the US make it clear they don't want anything to do with nuclear weapons, Textron feels the pressure mounting.

This is not a financial pressure being put on the company – it's a social pressure. Textron board members, executives, and employees are facing their neighbors who are saying "no" to nuclear weapons, just as they said "no" to cluster munitions.

City ordinances that prohibit nuclear weapons activities within the city's jurisdiction are a serious blow to corporations involved in the nuclear weapons business. But as we saw in the case of countries, an even more powerful step for cities to take is to divest public funds from these companies.

PRESSURE FROM THE US

- [ ] CITIES COMMIT TO ABOLITION
- [ ] CITIES URGE US TO SIGN TPNW
- [ ] CITIES PASS NFZ RESOLUTONS
- [ ] CITIES PASS NFZ ORDINANCES
- [x] CITIES DIVEST
- [ ] CITIES BAN CONTRACTS
- [ ] STATES TAKE ACTION
- [ ] GOING NATIONAL

17 From New York to Philadelphia: The commitment to divest

Divestment is a powerful tool with which to pressure the nuclear weapons companies, as we have seen in previous chapters. Cities and other institutions in the US that commit to divesting from these companies are taking a very important step in this scenario.

Divestment was a major tool in the global campaign against apartheid in South Africa. It has been an important component of many campaigns since then, including campaigns against tobacco companies,[1] gambling, private prisons, handguns, in support of farm workers, and many other issues. Most recently, divestment from fossil fuels has been a key tool in the struggle to address climate change.

According to the Global Fossil Fuel Divestment Database,[2] roughly 1,600 institutions with responsibility for more than $40.5 trillion in total assets have so far committed to divesting from fossil fuels worldwide. These include roughly 570 faith-based organizations, 250 educational institutions, 185 pension funds, 190 philanthropic institutions, and 175 municipal, state, provincial and national governments.[3]

Cities have played an important role in divestment to the extent that they have any responsibility for funds being invested, such as public pension funds. While many cities do not control pension funds directly, they may still have important influence over how those funds are invested.

City divestment from nuclear weapons companies began with the nuclear-free zone movement in the 1980s. Several cities, including Oakland, California (see Chapter 15), committed to divest from companies involved in the development or production of nuclear weapons. Berkeley, Hayward, and Marin County in California, Takoma Park in Maryland, Oneonta, New York and several other cities across the US divested from nuclear weapons in the 1980s.[4]

More recently, the cities of Northampton and Easthampton, Massachusetts have committed to divestment from nuclear weapons, as have Spokane, Washington and Corvallis, Oregon. The City Council of Cambridge, Mass, voted to divest its pension fund from nuclear weapons in 2016 but was blocked by the state.[5]

Not all of these divestment commitments have been fully carried out in practice. But many have. The strongest commitments have been grounded in legally-binding statutes rather than in non-binding resolutions or executive orders, as discussed in previous chapters.

But even with a legal requirement to divest, if no one is watching, it can be quietly forgotten about. That is why the best practice in the divestment world more generally has included setting up reporting mechanisms and assigning a body to monitor the divestment process.

Best practice has also included clauses that define which companies are to be divested from and how those are chosen; what threshold of involvement in the prohibited activities is considered acceptable; how long it will take to complete the divestment process; and how any exceptions to the rule will be handled.

In the case of nuclear weapons divestment, few of these additional considerations have been included. Nevertheless there are some important examples to draw from in going forward with our scenario.

The example: New York City

New York City has a long history of opposition to nuclear weapons, ever since its initial involvement in the Manhattan Project (part of which did in fact take place in Manhattan). During the 1950s, nuclear missiles were actually stationed at 19 sites in and around the city. Nuclear-armed ships and submarines almost certainly came into New York Harbor (although this was "neither confirmed nor denied" as per the standard US policy).[6]

In 1983, a year after a million people demonstrated for nuclear abolition in Central Park, the City Council passed a resolution proclaiming New York City a nuclear-free zone. But this did not include a commitment to divest.

After a successful effort by campaigners in New York City, the City Council finally voted to divest its $250 billion pension fund from nuclear weapons in 2021.[7] Only about $480 million of this is invested in nuclear weapons companies, but it could have a powerful impact on the companies because of the example it sets for other cities.[8]

New York's pension fund is actually five separate funds, controlled by five separate pension boards. Each one must now sign off on implementation plans. Four years and one pandemic later, the process is proceeding slower than some campaigners would like, but the commitment is still there to finish the job.

Campaigners outside New York City Hall, preparing to testify in favor of the nuclear weapons divestment resolution, July 27, 2020.

Up next: Boulder, Colorado

Boulder is a very progressive town in a very progressive state. It is the home of the Rocky Mountain Peace and Justice Center, which led the campaign to shut down a major nuclear weapons facility located nearby at Rocky Flats. The plant was finally shut down in 1992 after the owners, Rockwell, were fined $18.5 million for illegal dumping of radioactive waste products.

Even before that, in 1985, Boulder City Council passed an ordinance declaring Boulder a Nuclear Free Zone. The Boulder ordinance prohibits research on nuclear weapons as well as "production, storage, processing or disposal of a nuclear weapon or component of a nuclear weapon." But, as with New York's NFZ, it does not prohibit investments in nuclear weapons companies.

The Rocky Mountain Peace and Justice Center is still going strong. There's also an active PSR Colorado group, a Boulder branch of Democratic Socialists of America, an immigrant rights coalition, Palestinian support groups and others.

The Mayor, the City Council, the local newspaper and the local residents of Boulder are all proud of Boulder's NFZ and the steps the city has taken since then to maintain its commitment to nuclear abolition.[9]

In our scenario, Boulder is inspired by NYC's divestment. It's not a big stretch for Boulder to take the next step and divest from nuclear weapons, and it only takes a handful of campaigners working with the City Council to get it done.

The clock goes back by 30 seconds to 10:26:00pm when the City Council of Boulder, CO, passes an ordinance to divest the city from nuclear weapons.

Missoula, MT

Missoula County, Montana, was the first district in the United States to be declared a Nuclear Free Zone. The people of Missoula County voted overwhelming in favor of a ballot initiative in 1978 that banned all nuclear facilities from the county, except for medical purposes.

The original zoning ordinance said nothing about divestment or banning of contracts. So, not to be outdone, the voters of Missoula County have come back to the issue almost 50 years later with a new ballot initiative calling for Missoula County to divest any funds it holds from the nuclear weapons companies. **Again, it passes overwhelmingly.**

The clock goes back by 30 seconds to 10:25:30pm when the County of Missoula, MT, passes an ordinance to divest the county from nuclear weapons.

The prize: Philadelphia

Philadelphia joined Mayors for Peace in 1985. It passed a resolution in 2018 urging Congress to prohibit a nuclear "first strike" without authorization from Congress. It then passed a resolution in 2019 calling for the President to "enter" the Treaty on the Prohibition of Nuclear Weapons. Its next step is to pass a resolution calling on the city's pension board to divest from nuclear weapons.

David Gibson and the Divest Philly coalition

David Gibson is on the staff of national Peace Action and co-coordinator of a Peace Action associate group called Peace, Justice and Sustainability Now. David also coordinates the nuclear weapons divestment campaign in Philadelphia.

The Philadelphia Board of Pensions and Retirement (PBPR) agreed to divest from guns in 2013, and from private prisons in 2021. So the precedent is there for them to divest from nuclear weapons as well.

At the start of 2025, the PBPR had almost $13 billion invested via several financial institutions, including **Lord Abbett** and **Northern Trust** (see below). Both of these were found to have major investments in the top nuclear weapons companies.

The City Council has already urged the PBPR to use the latest ESG criteria for investing its funds in socially responsible companies. The staff of the PBPR, however, have so far been unwilling to bring this to their board. So another resolution has been drafted for the City Council, calling on the PBPR to divest from nuclear weapons.

A coalition of 28 groups across the Philadelphia area was formed to get the divestment resolution passed. They built an online tool for people to send letters to the pension board. They organized public meetings and online events to raise awareness about nuclear weapons and the fact that Philadelphians are paying for these weapons through their taxes and pension contributions.

As of May 2025, 9 out of 12 City Councilmembers are in support of the divestment resolution – enough to overturn a possible veto by the Mayor. All they need now is for it to be put to a vote. And for that, the group is pulling out all the stops to get people to write and call their representatives on the City Council.

In our scenario, the coalition succeeds in getting a resolution passed by the Philadelphia City Council calling on the Pension Board to divest from nuclear weapons. That's still just the first step in getting the Pension Board to actually implement the

divestment. The Pension Board ultimately agrees to do it, and over a period of months, Philadelphia divests from the nuclear weapons companies, mainly by withdrawing their money from Northern Trust.

> **The clock goes back by 30 seconds to 10:25:00pm** when the Philadelphia City Council passes a resolution to divest the city pension fund from nuclear weapons companies.

Northern Trust and BAE

Northern Trust claims to be one of the world's largest asset managers, with approximately $1 trillion in assets under management. Large public pension funds, like Philadelphia's, use Northern Trust and other asset managers to ensure their money is wisely invested to reap the best possible returns.

And, like many other asset managers, Northern invests a lot of that money in arms manufacturers. In total, Northern has almost $5 billion invested in 11 of the top 24 nuclear weapons companies, including both loans and shares.

This is a drop in the bucket compared to Vanguard, which had a total of $78.5 billion invested in nuclear weapons companies in 2024.[10] Nevertheless, Northern Trust is a major player in the nuclear weapons investment world, and the Philadelphia pension fund is a major client.

BAE Systems is a UK company that contributes to UK, French, *and* US nuclear weapons programs (see Chapter 6). BAE owes $12 billion in outstanding loans to just five companies, one of them being Northern Trust.

In our scenario, BAE is already facing difficulties with all three programs because other companies are pulling out of joint contracts. Rolls-Royce has by this point withdrawn from the UK nuclear submarine program, leaving BAE high and dry as the lead contractor for that project. Airbus has pulled out of the French MDBA joint venture because of shareholder pressures. That leaves BAE and Leonardo without the specialist input from Airbus.

And the US Sentinel program, which BAE is also part of, is facing its biggest hurdle yet, as the main contractor for that project, Northrop Grumman, is reeling from the financial shock of F-35 cancellations from across Europe.

In this evolving situation, BAE could soon be unable to service the debt it owes to Northern Trust and its other lenders. With Philadelphia now moving its money out of Northern Trust, that puts Northern Trust in a double bind. Even with a trillion dollars at their disposal, Northern Trust cannot afford to lose Philadelphia as a client worth $5 billion to them.

Both BAE and Northern Trust are suddenly in serious financial difficulty.

As we noted in relation to countries in the TPNW putting external pressure on the US nuclear weapons companies, divestment is a powerful tool – but even more powerful when it is combined with boycotting those same companies. As with countries, cities can refuse contracts with these companies to create serious difficulties for them.

PRESSURE FROM THE US

- [ ] CITIES COMMIT TO ABOLITION
- [ ] CITIES URGE US TO SIGN TPNW
- [ ] CITIES PASS NFZ RESOLUTONS
- [ ] CITIES PASS NFZ ORDINANCES
- [ ] CITIES DIVEST
- [x] CITIES BAN CONTRACTS
- [ ] STATES TAKE ACTION
- [ ] GOING NATIONAL

18 From Northampton to Boston: Refusing city contracts

As we saw in relation to countries, divestment is a very powerful tool for putting pressure on the nuclear weapons companies. But an even more powerful tool, for countries, is to deny them contracts and refuse to do business with them. This also applies to cities within the United States.

Cities award municipal contracts worth millions of dollars for IT services, police radios, computers for public libraries, school equipment and other products and services. Many of the nuclear weapons companies rely on these contracts not just to balance their books, but burnish their reputations as good citizens.

We've seen cities apply pressure on the nuclear weapons industry by denying them access to city contracts in the 1980s (Chapter 3). Did it work? There's no direct proof, but companies were filing lawsuits, publicly denying involvement, publishing disclaimers, and pulling out of the nuclear weapons business. Clearly, they took it seriously.

Many of the Nuclear Free Zones from the 1980s still continue to refuse contracts with nuclear weapons companies. Today, it's back in fashion, and more cities are joining in.

The example: Northampton, MA

Northampton is a college town in Western Massachusetts. It's a progressive city in a progressive state, so it comes as no surprise that it's a hotbed of campaigning for nuclear abolition. In fact, two currently active national nuclear abolition campaigns were founded there: the Back from the Brink campaign and NuclearBan.US are both products of a single event organized shortly after the adoption of the TPNW in 2017.

Western Massachusetts also happens to be where the Nuclear Freeze movement in the 1980s had its first foothold, before it spread across the whole country. (It ending up being based in St. Louis, Missouri.)

Northampton Home Rule Petition

Northampton has divested from the nuclear weapons companies *and* banned them from city contracts. Here's the story, starting in 2018.

The city passed the Back from the Brink resolution. Then, with guidance from NuclearBan.US, the mayor of Northampton issued an Executive Policy Order,[1] committing the city to divest from and to refuse to enter into city contracts with nuclear weapons companies.

But first, they had to bypass state laws requiring contracts to go to the lowest bidder, so their State Representative Lindsay Sabadosa and their State Senator Jo Comerford took a "home rule petition" to the Massachusetts State House.[2] The petition passed both houses of the state legislature, the governor signed it into law, and now Northampton has the right to disqualify bidders from city contracts if they are involved in nuclear weapons production. That set a precedent for 350 other towns and cities in Massachusetts to follow their example.[3]

It's complicated to implement Northampton's disqualification of bidders policy. The City Procurement Officer is doing his best. He has written up the procedures and informed all 17 city departments that buy products and services for the city. He has produced paperwork that must be signed by companies bidding for city contracts, certifying that they are not involved in any nuclear weapons work.

But the reality is that 17 different city departments each do their own procurement. While they're theoretically regulated by city policies, procurement officers don't have the capacity to monitor where every single paper clip or computer comes from if it's purchased by a school, or a library, or the public works department.

Furthermore, a state agency allows schools and other city facilities to purchase supplies and equipment directly from the state, bypassing the city procurement process altogether. So implementing a ban on purchasing from nuclear weapons companies can be difficult, but that doesn't mean it has no effect.

The Mayor wrote to each and every nuclear weapons company to inform them of the City's divestment policy. When similar letters are written informing these companies that they cannot bid for city contracts, even when it cannot easily be enforced, this sends a clear and powerful message to the companies: as long as you make nuclear weapons, you are *persona non grata* in this city.

Next up: Cambridge

Several other towns and cities in Massachusetts have toyed with the idea of following Northampton's example, but so far none have followed through. Will Cambridge be next?

The Mayor of Cambridge is a former board member of Massachusetts Peace Action (MAPA). And in 2016, before the TPNW even existed, the Cambridge City Council passed a resolution calling for the city pension fund to divest from nuclear weapons. This, however, was never implemented (see Chapter 19).

Massachusetts Peace Action

MAPA is based in Cambridge, although it works on state-level peace issues and has become an important player in the anti-nuclear movement nationally. Students from Harvard, MIT, Tufts, Northeastern University and Boston College have all been involved in MAPA activities, including the successful effort to get the Cambridge divestment resolution through.

In our scenario, MAPA draws in additional groups in the Boston area to support an effort to get a new ordinance passed in Cambridge that will ban city contracts with nuclear weapons companies. They remind Cambridge that its existing divestment is part of a bigger commitment to abolish nuclear weapons, and they urge the city to take the next logical step, banning city contracts.

They succeed, and since Northampton blazed the trail with its home rule petition, Cambridge's petition sails through the state legislature and they don't have to worry about hiring the lowest bidder for city contracts. The city writes to all the nuclear weapons companies, adding one more piece to the stigmatization of the industry. But no company is more embarrassed by this than Draper Labs.

The clock goes back by 1 minute to 10:24:00pm when the Cambridge City Council passes an ordinance banning nuclear weapons companies from bidding for city contracts.

Draper Labs

The Charles Stark Draper Laboratory is a nuclear weapons research facility in the heart of Cambridge, Massachusetts. It is responsible for designing and developing the guidance systems on the Trident submarine-launched nuclear missiles used by both the US and the UK.

Draper Labs also makes artificial heart valves and other medical devices, which it promotes to the public as the benevolent face of the research it does. But this cannot disguise the fact that without Draper Labs, the US nuclear weapons program would soon grind to a halt.

The City of Cambridge is unlikely to purchase goods or services from Draper Labs directly. But a ban on contracts with nuclear weapons companies would be a major blow to such a key institution in the center of Cambridge. As with other steps being taken against these companies, it is not only the direct effects on their balance sheet and stock price that matter.

In the case of Draper Labs, the morale of its workers and the reputation of the institution is highly dependent on the support it gets from the people of Cambridge. When people are forced to choose between their allegiance to friends, family and neighbors or allegiance to their workplace, for most people it's a very easy choice. They will keep their friends and find another job.

More cities ban contracts

As opposition to the MAGA agenda gathers pace in the United States, campaigners are searching for things they can do at the local level to push back. The movement is not focused only on nuclear weapons. It is a movement for *survival*. But the targets are the same: billionaire investors and giant corporations that are threatening people's lives and the entire planet.

And when cities up and down the country start passing local ordinances that ban contracts or doing business with some of these giant corporations, the idea catches on fast.

After Cambridge, more cities and towns in Massachusetts follow, like Brookline (which came close to passing a ban in 2024), Williamsburg and Somerville. But there will soon be many more on the West Coast.

The clock goes back by 3 minute to 10:21:00pm after Brookline, Williamsburg and Somerville pass ordinances banning nuclear weapons companies from bidding for city contracts.

The prize: Boston

Boston awards over $1 billion in contracts to private companies each year. A study in 2020 showed that only a small percentage of those contracts were going to minority-owned or woman-owned businesses.[4] The Mayor of Boston, Michelle Wu, wants to fix that.

And now she has an opportunity to do so, by excluding from the bidding process some very large multinational corporations who happen to make nuclear weapons. Instead of Boston taxpayers' money going to Leidos, for instance, it could be going to small, local, Black-owned businesses instead.

The clock goes back by 1 minute to 10:20:00pm when the Boston City Council passes an ordinance banning nuclear weapons companies from bidding for city contracts.

Leidos

Leidos is a major nuclear weapons contractor, directly involved in recycling and refurbishing nuclear warheads at the Y-12 National Security Complex in Oak Ridge, Tennessee.

It's also a major producer of metal detectors, luggage scanners and other security systems used in airports and other public buildings. You can't swing a carry-on at Boston's Logan Airport without hitting a Leidos machine.

In our scenario, the airport's Leidos presence remains (for now), since Logan is owned and operated by the state rather than by the city. But now that Boston has cancelled contracts, the brand will soon disappear from the rest of the city.

No more Leidos metal detectors for public schools, libraries, museums and government buildings, no more Leidos security equipment for police and fire services, no more Leidos scanners used on city buses and the subway system, and no more specialized Leidos equipment and IT services for construction projects and public works -- unless Leidos gets out of the nuclear weapons business, and by now they're certainly thinking about it.

Cities divesting and boycotting. What's next? States also have contracts with these companies, and these may run into the billions of dollars.

PRESSURE FROM THE US

- [ ] CITIES COMMIT TO ABOLITION
- [ ] CITIES URGE US TO SIGN TPNW
- [ ] CITIES PASS NFZ RESOLUTONS
- [ ] CITIES PASS NFZ ORDINANCES
- [ ] CITIES DIVEST
- [ ] CITIES BAN CONTRACTS
- [x] STATES TAKE ACTION
- [ ] GOING NATIONAL

19 From Oregon to California: The states step in

It's powerful when cities pass resolutions and then enact legally-binding ordinances banning relations with nuclear weapons companies. What if whole states start to pass legislation that impacts the nuclear weapons companies?

The example: Oregon

In 1986, voters in Oregon were given the opportunity to pass a ballot initiative that would have, in effect, created the first state level nuclear-free zone in the US. The Act Relating to Nuclear Weapons (see Appendix VI) would have provided tax relief for businesses in Oregon that converted from making nuclear weapons or nuclear weapons components to making consumer products instead.

It would have set up a Governor's Task Force to identify the businesses in Oregon that were involved in the nuclear weapons industry and would thus qualify for the tax relief. Then, after three years, it would have prohibited anyone in Oregon from "knowingly engag[ing] in the manufacture of nuclear weapons or nuclear weapon components after January 1, 1990."

Just over 400,000 Oregonians voted in favor, but 591,000 voted against it. It did not become law, and it was never tried again.

In our scenario, the Oregon Act Relating to Nuclear Weapons is reborn as a useful model of what *could* be passed in any state. But there are other models out there. And a bill already pending in Massachusetts.

Next up: Massachusetts

Massachusetts was the first state in the country to divest from South Africa in 1982. The next year, it divested from companies selling weapons for use in Northern Ireland. In 1998, it became the first state to divest from tobacco companies. And in response to the genocide in Darfur, it subsequently divested from companies doing business in Sudan.

So apart from being one of the bluest of blue states in the country, Massachusetts has a long history of divesting its state pension fund from companies that do not reflect the values of its people.

Efforts to divest the state from nuclear weapons began in 2019, after the city of Cambridge passed a divestment resolution but was told that only the state could divest the pension money belonging to the people of Cambridge (see Chapter 18).

Each state has its own complicated system for managing the pensions of its public employees (teachers, police, firefighters, etc.). In Massachusetts, most cities collect and distribute those funds themselves, but they can choose to invest that money in the meantime through the state Pension Reserves Investment Management (PRIM) board.

So for Cambridge to divest from nuclear weapons, they need to get PRIM to divest. MA State Representative Mike Connolly has been faithfully submitting a bill to each session of the state legislature ever since, calling for PRIM to divest from nuclear weapons. And in 2025, a new group of activists took on this challenge.

Walae Hayek and Malika Sud, CFRI

Walae and Malika represent a new generation of peace activists in the US. They are both young health professionals, and they are both first generation Americans.

Malika's family is from India. Malika grew up spending summers in India with extended family, where she learned values of collectivism and community care - in stark contrast to the hyper-independence, separateness, and power hoarding that she saw in the US.

Walae's family is from Syria. Walae spent some of her teenage years in Syria and has seen first-hand the ravages of war and the effects of US foreign policy in ways that most US-Americans have not.

Walae, Malika and their colleagues in the Coalition for Responsible Investment (CFRI) are focused on helping people make connections between issues - and demonstrating that divestment from weapons (including nuclear weapons) is a tool that benefits many other causes, from Palestine to climate justice to reproductive justice. They are concerned about *all* weapons that are used to control people – and if they can't be controlled, to kill them.

The immediate inspiration for CFRI came from watching activists in Cambridge successfully shut down the local office of Elbit, an Israeli arms company. After a year of weekly protests outside Elbit, sometimes involving nonviolent direct action and mass arrests, the company gave up and moved out.[1] That demonstration of people power gave Walae and Malika the idea to take their efforts up a notch and work on making a tangible difference at the state level. They founded CFRI in late 2024 and began drafting a divestment bill for the State House.

Warheads to Windmills campaigners at the Massachusetts State House to testify for a bill that would create a Citizens Commission on Nuclear Weapons and Climate, July 2024. PHOTO: MA Warheads to Windmills

CFRI already has deep connections in the grassroots groups around Massachusetts who have been organizing on college campuses and in local towns and cities, mostly focused on trying to stop the genocide in Gaza. They recruited Jeff, an anti-Zionist Jew who had been organizing a city divestment campaign in Jamaica Plain with Jewish Voice for Peace. They recruited other activists working on fossil fuel divestment and divestment from private prisons.

Instead of focusing exclusively on weapons going to Israel, the group decided to go broad. They put together a bill that would divest the state pension fund from all weapons of mass destruction. Walae found from her research that the US Criminal Code defines WMDs to include not only nuclear, chemical and biological weapons, but also any type of explosive above a certain size - bombs, grenades, missiles, rockets, mines – pretty much any weapon that is not a firearm.[2]

The Act Promoting Responsible Investment requires the Massachusetts state pension fund to identify any holdings it may have in companies that manufacture, produce, promote, sell or distribute WMDs (as defined above), and to sell, redeem, divest or withdraw all investments from those companies within an agreed timeframe. It also requires all state agencies to terminate any contracts they may have with those companies (as far as it is possible) and to refrain from entering into any new contracts with them.

CFRI and their coalition partners across the state of Massachusetts are confident that after seven years of efforts to get a state divestment bill passed, this time will be different. The coalition is much broader and deeper than ever before. There is a heightened awareness of the issues with Trump back in the White House and international tensions rising.

In our scenario, they succeed. It might not be right away, but at some point Massachusetts *will* divest its pension funds from nuclear weapons companies. And that will set the ball rolling for other states to join them.

> The clock goes back by 5 minutes to 10:15pm when the Massachusetts state legislature passes the Responsible Investment Act that commits the state pension fund to divest from nuclear weapons companies..

More states on the way

Maine has already passed legislation divesting the state pension fund from fossil fuels. Maine's largest city, Portland, has already committed to divesting from weapons going to Israel.

As more and more towns and cities in Maine also pass nuclear weapons resolutions and ordinances, campaigners are ready to push for a comprehensive divestment bill that includes nuclear weapons. And it passes.

As we saw in Chapter 16, both Houses of the Rhode Island State Legislature passed resolutions calling for nuclear abolition. In our scenario, the city of Providence turns their resolution into a legally-binding ordinance, and campaigners are ready to get the State to do the same. **So they do.**

After three northeastern states take the lead, the West Coast is next. Campaigners in Oregon revive the 1986 bill that failed as a ballot initiative. This time, they take it straight to the legislature. And this time it passes.

This is the first of the more comprehensive bills to get passed at the state level. And it is followed by similar legislation in Washington State. By this point in our scenario, the nuclear weapons companies are facing the prospect of billions of dollars worth of lost contracts as well as crashing stock prices as investors start to flee *en masse*. And then we come to California.

> `The clock goes back by 20 minutes to 9:55pm` when state legislation is passed in Rhode Island, Maine, Oregon and Washington.

The prize: California

California is not only the largest state in the US by population. It is also the largest economy within the US, and has recently surpassed Japan to become the fourth largest economy *in the world.* Only the US as a whole, China and Germany have a higher GDP than California.

A false alarm

California is not only big, powerful and wealthy. It is also very progressive. California has led the nation in tackling the climate crisis, protecting reproductive rights, reforming the criminal justice system, legislating gun control, and many other issues. It also passed the first state resolution in support of the TPNW, back in 2018.[3]

And in addition to all that has been happening in this scenario so far - both domestically and internationally - California is now facing an additional incentive to join the growing movement for nuclear abolition. In this scenario, due to heightened tensions with North Korea (again), there is a growing fear that California could be the target of a nuclear missile.

And then, one sunny day, that fear explodes across the state. Just as in 2018, when residents in Hawai'i received a text message warning of an imminent missile attack (see box), the residents of California suddenly receive a message on their mobile phones,

warning of an incoming missile. This time, instead of one million people being affected, nearly 20 million Californians receive this message. Like in Hawai'i, it quickly turns out to be a false alarm. But not before millions of panicked parents rush to collect their children from school, office buildings empty out, traffic jams clog all the major freeways, and numerous cases of heart attack and stroke are recorded.

The false alarm in Hawai'i

At 8:08am on January 13, 2018, over one million people in Hawaii received a text message on their phone: "BALLISTIC MISSILE THREAT INBOUND TO HAWAII. SEEK IMMEDIATE SHELTER. THIS IS NOT A DRILL." Local television stations also interrupted their programs to broadcast a more detailed message, announcing that "a missile may impact on land or sea within minutes..."

38 minutes later, the message was rescinded. It was a false alarm. But during those 38 minutes, fear and panic spread rapidly across Hawaii. People said good-bye to their loved ones, assuming they would never see them again. Others rushed to find shelter. Many broke down in sobs, knowing there was no shelter from a nuclear attack.

Three days later, a similar false alarm was sent out erroneously to 300,000 people in Japan. That one was rescinded within 5 minutes, and caused less panic.

In both cases, heightened tensions over North Korea's nuclear weapons program made the alarm believable. But the reality is that we are all living every single day with the possibility of an incoming nuclear missile.

The false alarm in Hawaii led to the creation of the Nuclear Wake-Up Call campaign, alerting people that "this moment right now is the most dangerous time in human history." With a virtual reality exhibit that allows people to experience the false alarm for themselves, along with other tools and resources, this campaign has helped raise awareness of just how vulnerable we are.

The false alarm in this scenario is a wake-up call that changes everything for Californians. It's only a matter of time before the state drafts legislation to follow up on its earlier resolution in support of nuclear abolition. And the question is not whether it

will pass both houses of the state legislature. The only question is how strong the legislation will be.

States like California have very significant purchasing power. They have contracts to build highways, airports, hospitals, ports and other infrastructure projects that can be worth billions of dollars to corporations who bid on them. California has contracts with nuclear weapons companies – and it can choose to cancel them.

State pension funds can be worth billions of dollars. In many cases, these include direct investments in the nuclear weapons industry. The California Public Employees Retirement System, CalPERS, is the largest public pension fund in the US, with over $500 billion in assets as of 2024. It has investments in nuclear weapons companies – and it can choose to remove them.

The University of California system and the National Labs

In addition to divestment and refusing contracts, California also has a third avenue for pressuring the nuclear weapons companies. It has direct control over the University of California (UC) system. And the UC system is integral to two of the three national laboratories responsible for nuclear weapons research and development.

Lawrence Livermore National Laboratory (LLNL) is responsible for designing nuclear weapons to be manufactured by other parts of the industry. LLNL is run by a partnership consisting of Bechtel, BWX, Amentum, Battelle – and UC.

The **Los Alamos National Laboratory** (LANL), is run by a consortium called "Triad National Security," consisting of Battelle, Texas A&M University – and UC. They subcontract work to two other major nuclear weapons companies, Fluor and Huntington Ingalls Industries (HII).

In our scenario, it's a crushing blow to the nuclear weapons industry in the US when the state of California passes the Nuclear Weapons Abolition Act, banning state contracts with nuclear weapons companies, committing the state pension fund to divest from those companies, and calling on the University of California Board of Regents (most of whom are appointed by the Governor and confirmed by the Senate) to withdraw their involvement from nuclear weapons research and development.

The clock goes back by 5 minutes to 9:50pm when California passes the Nuclear Weapons Abolition Act.

UC subsequently pulls out of *both* consortiums it's part of. For LLNL and its partners, that's a major blow. And at LANL, it's a disaster. Since UC represents one-third of the management and oversight of LANL, that consortium is unlikely to survive without it. LANL will have to re-negotiate their entire management structure. The entire nuclear weapons complex in the US is going to feel the pain.

> The clock goes back by another 5 minutes to **9:45pm** when the University of California pulls out of consortiums running LLNL and LANL.

Meanwhile, when UC pulls out of LANL, things start to unravel for Fluor and HII. Up till now, they've been the only two major nuclear weapons companies that have remained relatively untouched by the TPNW. Fluor operates in parts of Africa and Latin America, and it has not yet lost contracts nor been directly affected by divestment efforts. HII has no operations outside the United States and almost no work that is not directly paid for by the Pentagon.

Neither Fluor nor HII needs nuclear weapons work to stay in business, however. And they don't need the hassle either, as the TPNW gains ground. Fluor has a much larger stake in other engineering projects, mainly related to fossil fuels and nuclear power (which have their own challenges and uncertain futures). HII has huge multi-billion dollar contracts with the Department of Defense for building conventional aircraft carriers and other very large warships.

Both companies are ready to jump ship, and in this scenario, they do.

HII's departure from the nuclear weapons industry has further repercussions. Besides LANL, it drops out of another consortium it's part of. That one runs the Savanna River Site and the Nevada National Security Site (formerly called the Nevada Test Site), both of which play critical roles in the production of plutonium and tritium for US nuclear weapons.

Now that whole states are applying maximum pressure to the nuclear weapons companies, we're one step beyond anything achieved in the 1980s. But building more pressure within the US means making nuclear abolition a mainstream issue for a large and mobilized section of the population. Progressives and their peace, justice, and environmental agendas are currently marginalized in US politics, but progressive organizations have a strong base across large parts of the country. One person who can galvanize the progressive movement to take on nuclear abolition is AOC.

PRESSURE FROM THE US

- [ ] CITIES COMMIT TO ABOLITION
- [ ] CITIES URGE US TO SIGN TPNW
- [ ] CITIES PASS NFZ RESOLUTONS
- [ ] CITIES PASS NFZ ORDINANCES
- [ ] CITIES DIVEST
- [ ] CITIES BAN CONTRACTS
- [ ] STATES TAKE ACTION
- [x] GOING NATIONAL

20 From AOC to the DNC: Nuclear abolition goes national

What will it take for the President of the United States to sign the TPNW? At least one of the two major US political parties needs to make nuclear abolition a major plank of their platform (and it's not likely to be MAGA Republicans). Some prominent progressive Democrats are already on board, and more are needed so that all progressives are moved to align with nuclear abolition. From there, the rest of the Democratic Party can follow.

At this point in our scenario, US cities and even states are divesting from the nuclear weapons companies and refusing to give them city contracts. Around the world, whole countries are piling on the pressure. Some of the companies have already fallen by the wayside.

And a mass movement is rising up to oppose authoritarian rule in the US and in many other countries. Elections are bringing more left-wing governments into power in many countries as a result.

This broad-based, intergenerational global movement is not focused solely on nuclear abolition by any means. It is focused primarily on protecting and upholding democracy, human rights and the rule of law in those countries, including the US, where these basic principles are under threat.

But it is also focused on human survival – on trying to secure the basic needs of people who are struggling to survive. And that includes vulnerable communities in every country, but especially the Palestinians facing genocide in Gaza and the civilians in Ukraine and so many other countries who are caught up in the carnage of armed conflict.

Ultimately, this mass movement is about human survival in the broadest sense. There is a growing awareness that humanity is under threat, not just from global warming but also from nuclear weapons.

Once that connection is made, it is only a small step to add nuclear abolition to the overall survival agenda of that wider movement. And that's what happens now.

The catalyst: Representative Alexandria Ocasio-Cortez

Alexandria Ocasio-Cortez (AOC) was working as a waitress and struggling to make ends meet when she felt the call to do something about the state of the world. She was just 29 years old when she was elected to Congress in 2018, unseating a more conservative Democrat who had been in Congress for 20 years. AOC has continued to get re-elected in her home district of Queens in New York City, despite the millions of dollars that have been spent trying to oust her.

And she is even more popular outside Queens, with an almost rock-star status among young progressives across the US. She has 9 million followers on Instagram and in December, 2024, became the first person to reach one million followers on Bluesky, the new social media site that is seeking to replace X (formerly known as Twitter).

While many of her colleagues in the Democratic Party consider AOC's politics to be on the "extreme" end of the spectrum, the humane and sensible policies that she supports have been hugely popular among voters, according to most opinion polls. These include her passion for a Green New Deal, for Medicare for All, for cancelling student debt, and many other progressive causes.

AOC and the Norton bill

Eleanor Holmes Norton is the only person *in* Congress who is not a Member *of* Congress (see Chapter 14). Her priority since entering Congress in 1991 has been to achieve DC statehood, a goal that finally passed the first hurdle of a vote in the House of Representatives in 2023, but fell far short of getting any further in the Senate.

Norton's other priority – for more than thirty years – has been her Nuclear Weapons Abolition and Conversion Act, described in Chapter 14. Since the TPNW was adopted, the "Norton Bill" (currently H.R. 1888) has been updated to call on the US to sign the TPNW and to work toward eliminating all nuclear weapons from all countries. Importantly (and logically), it also calls for all the human and financial resources wasted on nuclear weapons to be *converted* to addressing the climate crisis and other pressing human needs.

So far, all of the Congressional support for the Norton Bill has come from the Congressional Progressive Caucus (CPC). A small but admirable 13% of the CPC's 100 members have been bold enough to oppose the dangerous but powerful nuclear weapons industry.

Including Norton herself, there are currently only nine co-sponsors of the Norton Bill: Greg Casar, Jim McGovern, Ilhan Omar, Chellie Pingree, Delia Ramirez, Jan Schakowsky, and Rashida Tlaib. (Raul Grijalva still counts: he co-sponsored before he died in office. His daughter Adelita is running for his seat in a special election.) In the recent past, Mark Pocan, Sri Thanedar, Yvette Clarke, Ayanna Pressley, and Pramila Jayapal have co-sponsored it, and they may again.

That's also true of AOC, who co-sponsored the Norton Bill in the 2021-2022 session of Congress, albeit without any fanfare. [1] But she hasn't co-sponsored it since then, for reasons unknown. It seems like it should be in character for AOC to oppose the most exorbitantly expensive weapons system in the world when there is not enough in the federal budget to address homelessness, hunger, poverty, inequality or climate justice.

But maybe she's picking her battles, considering the pressure she's under as the most progressive of the progressives. Or maybe, like other Democrats and a lot of Republicans, she's simply flooded with other issues since Trump returned to the White House in January 2025 and MAGA loyalists took control of Congress and the Cabinet. Her constituents are surely seeking her help, support, and protection.

In our scenario, two things happen in Queens that ignite AOC's commitment to nuclear abolition. The first relates to a Superfund site in a nearby neighborhood.

Cleaning up Queens

The Wolff-Alport site, dubbed by the *New Yorker* magazine as "most radioactive place in New York,"[2] is not directly in AOC's congressional district, but it's close by. It's in a Spanish-speaking neighborhood of Queens with close ties to the Spanish-speaking communities in AOC's district.

The ¾ acre site is contaminated with radioactive waste left over from activities connected to the original Manhattan Project. It was declared a federal "Superfund" site and decontamination began in 2017. Now, 80 years after it was polluted, it still hasn't been fully cleaned up.

When Trump was in the White House the first time around (2021-2024), he slashed EPA funding and closed down 82 Superfund sites before cleanup was finished. When he returned to the White House in 2025, he immediately cut funding again and pulled the plug on clean-up operations all over the country.

It's likely that this time around, the Wolff-Alport cleanup will be on the chopping block. Like so many contaminated sites around the country, it's in the middle of a low-income, marginalized community, and Trump has historically de-prioritized cleanup in such places.

In our scenario, the half-completed Wolff-Alport site in Queens is one of the Superfund sites abandoned by the Trump Administration. Residents who were shocked to learn in 2017 that they were living and working on top of a radioactive waste dump are shocked again when they learn that the government won't finish decontaminating it.

There is immediate outrage throughout Queens. Local groups spring up to protest and demand that the cleanup be reinstated. Residents organize and hold public meetings. And they complain to AOC.

In the event of a nuclear war, get inside

Since 2021, subways and buses have been plastered with public service announcements telling New Yorkers that in the case of a nuclear attack they should "get inside, stay inside and stay tuned."[3] This is such absurd and useless advice that passengers have been heard to mutter, "WTF? This can't be serious." And yet it comes directly from the New York City Emergency Management Department.

Despite Trump's repeated promises of "peace" and "denuclearization" (see Epilogue), he is now embarking on the biggest nuclear weapons program ever seen. This involves further slashing of federal agencies and cuts to social programs in order to fund an enormous multi-trillion dollar build-up of both conventional and nuclear forces. The Pentagon is openly talking about war with both Russia *and* China, as well as the "possible" use of nuclear weapons.

In our scenario, Queens residents are enraged about the radioactive environmental damage that nuclear weapons have caused in their neighborhood. And they're appalled that their most basic needs for survival are being sacrificed to make ever more machinery that has no purpose but to kill people.

When the predominantly Black and Brown people of Queens make nuclear abolition *their* issue, AOC makes it *her* issue. And she doesn't just quietly go along with their concern. She *embraces* it. She takes it on as her own, and she *fights* for it.

As Trump is busy dismantling every regulation and piece of legislation that had any chance of reducing global carbon emissions, AOC becomes the leading voice for the Warheads to Windmills Campaign – calling for all the money and brainpower currently being wasted on nuclear weapons to be used instead to address the climate crisis.[4]

This is the essence of the Norton Bill, and by adding her name back on to this bill, AOC brings it national attention for the first time.

> `The clock goes back 1 second to 9:44:59pm` when AOC announces her decision to co-sponsor the Nuclear Weapons Abolition and Climate Conversion Act.

In one fell swoop, AOC increases by several million the number of people who know about the Norton Bill. She educates and encourages young people to reject the "deterrence" propaganda and take action toward abolition, not just in her own constituency, but across the country.

Next up: More Members of Congress

In our scenario, getting AOC herself on board the nuclear abolition train is just a tiny step forward in the grand scheme of things, moving our clock back by only 1 second. But it opens the door to other progressives in Congress, who come on board next.

Next up are Mark Pocan, Sri Thanedar, Yvette Clarke, Ayanna Pressley, and Pramila Jayapal. They have all co-sponsored the Norton bill in the past, and are now motivated by AOC to do it again.

The **Warheads to Windmills Campaign** calls on the US to join the TPNW, work with the other nuclear-armed countries to eliminate all nuclear weapons from all countries, and use all those wasted human and financial resources to fully address the climate crisis. The campaign was launched in the summer of 2023 by the Warheads to Windmills Coalition. By 2025, this coalition consisted of 70 national, state and local organizations wanting to work together on these two existential threats to the planet.

In the US, the coalition lobbies in support of the Norton Bill (currently H.R.1888) and provides support to cities, colleges, faith communities and other institutions wanting to divest from and/or boycott both the nuclear weapons and the fossil fuel industries. Internationally, the coalition supports both the TPNW and the proposal for a Fossil Fuel Treaty.

There is also a statewide W2W coalition in Massachusetts and others in development. The state coalitions focus on similar legislation at the state level and also support local divestment and boycott campaigns.

See the list of participating organizations at: warheadstowindmills.org/coalition-partners

Other progressives in Congress who have not yet committed themselves to nuclear abolition or the Norton Bill include AOC's colleagues Adriano Espaillat and Nydia Valezquez. They represent nearby New York districts and often join her in cosponsoring bills. Another is "squad" member Summer Lee of Pennsylvania, who has been outspoken on a number of other issues. Another young progressive ready to come on board with the others is Maxwell Frost of Florida.

In this scenario, they all sign on to cosponsor the Norton Bill right after AOC does. The momentum is building.

The clock goes back another 9 seconds to 9:44:50pm when another 9 Members of Congress sign onto the Nuclear Weapons Abolition and Climate Conversion Act.

On the Senate side, **Bernie Sanders** is currently the lone member of the Congressional Progressive Caucus. To date, no Senator will openly support the TPNW or nuclear abolition, but he could be the first.[5]

AOC is of course very closely aligned with Bernie on the climate issue as well as on many other social issues. Since Trump's second inauguration, AOC and Bernie have been touring the country together and speaking to huge crowds who are angry and terrified about what is happening under Trump.

In our scenario, AOC helps to get Bernie on board with nuclear abolition. It's a major achievement that wins popular support for the TPNW across the country. When Bernie agrees to file a companion bill to the Nuclear Weapons Abolition and Climate Conversion bill in the Senate, it secures a foothold in the Senate – and our clock moves back another 5 seconds.

> **The clock goes back another 5 seconds to 9:44:45pm** when Bernie Sanders introduces a Nuclear Weapons Abolition and Climate Conversion Act in the Senate.

The Congressional Progressive Caucus

The handful of Representatives who currently support the Norton Bill are all in the CPC, but they're a minority in that Caucus. The CPC's 100 members make up about half the Democrats in the House, and Democrats make up just less than half of the entire House. If the entire CPC were to support the Norton Bill, that would be about half the Democrats, and a quarter of the House – a seismic change.

In our scenario, with AOC and CPC Chair Greg Casar taking the lead, a critical mass of CPC members commits to nuclear abolition. Now it's up to Casar to move it up the agenda. As a caucus, the CPC supports a number of priority bills that need to be agreed by the whole CPC, and there are still many members who are not yet on board with nuclear abolition.

With all that has gone on in the proceeding chapters of this scenario, the nuclear issue is by now very much front and center (again) among progressives. It's up there with the climate crisis as an issue that affects everyone, even though its effects aren't immediately felt.

There is more nuclear saber-rattling in the news, and more protesting in the streets. This is now the opening for AOC, Bernie, and other progressive leaders (with help from doctors, veterans and disarmament campaigners all over the country) to successfully make the case for nuclear abolition – and win over the CPC.

Our clock goes back by a full 10 seconds when the CPC votes to add the Norton Bill to its list of endorsed bills, and also to include nuclear abolition as one of its goals. Although the CPC's own rules allow for quite a bit of flexibility, in theory, the Caucus is committed to voting as a bloc. So when half the Democratic Party stands for nuclear abolition, the other half starts to take notice.

> `The clock goes back 10 seconds to 9:44:35pm` when the CPC officially endorses the Nuclear Weapons Abolition and Climate Conversion Act and urges all its members to support it.

Up next: Progressive Democrats of America

Progressive Democrats of America (PDA) is an independent entity outside the Democratic Party with chapters in 38 states and 17 local branches in California alone. It's already in favor of nuclear abolition, at least in theory. "Windmills not Weapons" is even one of their more popular slogans for bumper stickers and signs.

PDA has key influencers within the Democratic Party and the ability to mobilize its members around the country. Nuclear abolition will never be their only (or even their top) priority, but if they add it to the list of issues they stand for, they can begin to influence the rank and file of the Democratic Party.

In our scenario, PDA chapters across the country vote to support nuclear abolition and add it to their list of issues. It's on the agenda for "Progressive Central," the big national gathering that takes place once every four years, prior to the Democratic National Convention. Progressives vote overwhelmingly to push for the Democratic Party to take it on.

> `The clock goes back 15 seconds to 9:44:20pm` when PDA agrees to add nuclear abolition to their list of issues and starts campaigning for it through all its branches.

Local and State Democratic Committees

With Trump and the MAGA Republicans in control of the country, it's unlikely that the moment is ripe for nuclear abolition. (But who knows? See the Epilogue.) It's more likely that *steps taken now can lay the groundwork* for when there's a new administration.

New federal leadership may come sooner rather than later. Trump's deep and widespread damage - to ethnic minorities, LGBTQ people, immigrants (documented or not), women, students, poor people, public health, the environment, the climate, the economy, health care, international relations, government systems, free speech, the rule of law, due process, even democracy itself - is sudden and universal, and it affects Trump's own voters at least as much as everyone else. So it's easy to imagine that it's only a matter of time before Democrats are again in power.

But what sort of Democrats? It's certainly possible that centrist Democrats could regain the upper hand, and that a return to Democratic control would simply mean a return to the status quo, including business as usual for the nuclear weapons industry.

In our scenario, Trump has pushed the whole country to the left, including the Democratic Party. US-Americans are no longer willing to settle for centrist Democratic policies when these have clearly led the country directly to Trump. People are demanding radical changes to the way the US is governed. And that includes being ready to dump nuclear weapons along with a lot of other wasteful, stupid and self-annihilating policies that mainstream Democrats have supported for far too long.

Progressives were once seen within the Democratic Party establishment as "too radical," but that was before MAGA showed everyone what radical really looks like. Progressives are now seen as pragmatic, responsible, and *necessary.* They gain the upper hand inside the Democratic Party. Local and state Democratic bodies take on the campaign for nuclear abolition and other measures that protect the world as well as their own citizens. From Precinct and Ward party meetings to city, county and congressional district committees, Democrats pass resolutions calling for more progressive positions - including nuclear abolition.

Our clock is having trouble keeping up with all these resolutions, so let's say precinct level resolutions get 1 second each, ward resolutions get 5 seconds, city committees get 10 seconds, counties 15, and congressional districts 30. With

hundreds of precinct and ward resolutions and dozens of city and district resolutions, our clock has moved back more than 30 minutes by now.

> `The clock goes back 33 minutes and 20 seconds to 9:11:00pm` after more than 250 precinct, 100 ward, 50 city, 25 county and 10 CD Democratic Committees pass resolutions calling for nuclear abolition.

As resolutions in support of nuclear abolition (along with a host of other progressive positions) make their way up the party ladder, cross-cutting groups of Democratic voters also weigh in: Democratic Women, LGBTQ+ Democrats, Black Caucus, Young Democrats, and Democrats Abroad.

These are all moving strongly to the progressive end of the spectrum. They *all* support nuclear abolition, and each group is worth 1 minute on the clock.

> `The clock goes back a further 6 minutes to 9:05:00pm` after 6 cross-cutting party caucus groups pass resolutions calling for nuclear abolition.

Now it's up to the State Democratic Committees to vote on these resolutions. They're worth 5 minutes each on our clock. There are majorities of Democrats already on board in states like Massachusetts and California, but many more State Committees are still needed to turn the Party itself around. The progressive Members of Congress, PDA, and the many nuclear abolitionist groups around the country all make a major effort.

By the time nuclear abolition makes it to the Democratic National Committee (DNC), there is solid support from a majority of state committees, moving our clock back a further 2 hours and 5 minutes.

The clock goes back a further 2 hours and 5 minutes to 7:00:00pm after 25 state Democratic Committees pass resolutions calling for nuclear abolition.

The Prize: The Democratic National Committee

The DNC[6] consists of two representatives (normally the Chair and Vice Chair) from the state-level Democratic Committee of each state, another 200 delegates chosen by state committees, 75 delegates elected by the DNC itself, and various representatives of other Democratic Party and related bodies, for a total of 452 members.

In our scenario, 25 states already support nuclear abolition, including most of the biggest states (CA, NY, IL, TX, FL, PA, NJ, OH, MI), so already close to half of the DNC members are on board. Together with representatives from the various caucuses and other related groups, a clear majority favors nuclear abolition. But what tips the balance is the election of David Hogg to be the chair of the DNC.

David Hogg was a student at Stoneman Douglas High School in Parkland, Florida, when a gunman shot and killed 17 of his classmates. He found himself in the national spotlight when he co-founded the March For Our Lives national campaign for gun control. He went on to co-found Leaders We Deserve, a grassroots organization to help get young progressives elected to Congress and to local government positions.

In 2025, David was elected a Vice Chair of the DNC. But the newly-elected Chair, Ken Martin, gave David an ultimatum: either be Vice Chair of the DNC or be a campaigner who is trying to unseat sitting Democrats – you can't be both.

In our scenario, David gives up his Vice Chairmanship of the DNC to continue his battle with mainstream Democrats. But he then gets elected as Chair of the DNC to succeed Ken Martin.

With David Hogg as Chair and overwhelming grassroots support for nuclear abolition from Democrats across the country, the DNC adds nuclear abolition to their national platform. And our clock goes back a full 15 minutes.

The clock goes back 15 minutes to 6:45pm when the Democratic National Committee votes to include nuclear abolition in their next national platform.

The DNC's national platform is not something many people pay attention to. But for the nuclear weapons companies, this is the final straw. It's clear that the United States is on its way to nuclear abolition, along with the rest of the world. Their only hope now, to save their businesses, is to use all their power and influence in Washington to get the best possible deal out of the transition away from nuclear weapons and into other work that will keep them profitable.

PART IV: ENDGAME

It may or may not take all the steps in the preceding two parts of this scenario for the nuclear weapons companies to feel sufficient pressure to demand an end to the nuclear era in order to save their businesses. It may take many more steps, or ones quite outside this scenario. But sooner or later, and preferably sooner, the pressure will be great enough that the US administration feels it has no other choice but to sign the TPNW and move to the total elimination of nuclear weapons. From there, the other nuclear-armed countries all need to come on board, and the weapons need to actually be dismantled.

21 The US signs the TPNW

This is it. Between pressures from abroad and pressures from within the US, the nuclear weapons companies have been squeezed into a corner. To save their profits and their businesses, they need to extract themselves from the nuclear enterprise. They ask their "clients" in the White House and Congress to help them transition to other work for the government. An obvious choice is addressing the climate crisis.

In our scenario, the US nuclear weapons industry is facing insurmountable pressures both domestic and international. In order to save their companies and safeguard their profits, they're turning to the federal government for a rescue plan.

As trillions of dollars' worth of nuclear weapons contracts are canceled, the companies want trillions of dollars in taxpayer subsidies to re-tool factories, re-train workers and re-orient an entire industry toward innovations in clean energy, battery storage, and electric technologies for aviation and other uses. (It might seem obvious that companies with nuclear-oriented expertise and infrastructure could transition most directly into nuclear power, but that's a problematic climate "solution.")[1]

The deterrence summit

Hidden away in the basement of a big Crystal City hotel just one mile from the Pentagon, there's an annual three-day gathering of the "military-industrial complex" that President Eisenhower warned us about. Among the 500-ish attendees: the nuclear weapons corporations, their suppliers, their sub-contractors, their customers from the Pentagon, DOE, and the National Nuclear Security Administration (NNSA), some White House officials, and some Members of Congress.

For years, these meetings have been self-congratulatory celebrations of the continual and seemingly bottomless bipartisan support for the industry that single-handedly makes doomsday possible. The agenda: keep tax dollars flowing because there's a desperate need to keep building an ever more terrifying "deterrent."

On occasion, there have been mumblings about safety regulations getting in the way of their "mission," about young people preferring to work on wind turbine designs than on warhead designs, or about too many of the older generation retiring from the scene, and taking their crucial, irreplaceable, and arcane expertise with them. [2] But there has never been any question that this industry would continue to reap enormous financial rewards on top of the warm glow they regularly receive for their "patriotic" service to the country.

In our scenario, the warm glow is turning to cold panic. Unlike previous years, no press passes have been issued for this year's Summit. The few critical voices, like Greg Mello of the Los Alamos Study Group, who have been allowed to attend this event many times in the past, have been denied registration. This is a closed meeting: no phones, no photography, no recording.

But Google is there. And so is Amazon. So are researchers from prestigious universities like MIT, John Hopkins, Texas A&M, and University of Nebraska.[3]

Summit participants find themselves running a gauntlet of noisy but nonviolent protesters as they make their way toward the hotel. Arlington County police are on hand to keep the protesters off of hotel property. Arrests just bring more protesters to the scene.

Protesters outside the Deterrence Summit, January 2024 PHOTO: Vicki Elson

Across the street, where in previous years a few lonely protesters would gather with their signs, a large crowd is chanting and singing so boisterously that their voices can be

heard inside the hotel. The participants settle into their seats and try to pretend that this is just their normal annual gathering.

The keynote speaker is introduced at the podium: former US Congressman Brandon Williams, Administrator of the National Nuclear Security Administration (NNSA) and Under-Secretary of Energy for Nuclear Security. "I know you're all as concerned as I am about, um, issues with our nuclear weapons mission," he begins. "But I want to assure you that this government will do everything possible to ensure at *least* as good a return on investment and as much long-term job security as you've been enjoying up until now."

There is muted applause in the room. Everyone there had suspected that the government might shift its stance in some way. They just weren't expecting anything so bleak to come out of the mouth of a government spokesperson as the very first words in the very first speech of the entire 3-day event.

Inside the Deterrence Summit, 2023. PHOTO: Vicki Elson

A litany of problems

The next speaker is Honeywell Board Chair and former CEO Darius Adamcyzk. He goes into some details about the recruitment problems facing Honeywell at the National Security Campus in Kansas City. It's been becoming impossible to fill vacancies. Young people in particular, fresh out of engineering schools, are queuing up to work on green energy projects instead of on nuclear weapons. One person in the audience starts clapping, before looking around the room and realizing this is not a clapping matter.

Kathy Warden, Chair, CEO and President of Northrop Grumman Corporation, is up next. She speaks about supply chain issues with the delivery of parts needed for the new Sentinel ICBM system. "While our rocket motors continue to test successfully, we cannot proceed to construction phase without

the core processors being produced by our sub-contractor L3Harris, who has notified us that they can no longer produce these because of issues further down the supply chain," she says.

"There are also supply chain issues from Rolls-Royce, which has pulled out of this mission, and from Boeing, which is facing bankruptcy as we speak. Without further intervention, we cannot meet our deadlines and we cannot see a way around this problem in the foreseeable future. I don't need to tell anyone here what you already know. But our board is deeply concerned about our viability going forward."

RTX President and Chief Executive Officer Christopher T. Calio takes the floor: "RTX is fully committed to delivering the Long-Range Standoff system and the Sentinel secondary-launch platform as per requirement. But we are also facing serious challenges with our plants in New England. Students have been sitting in front of our gates for days at a time and harassing our workforce. This is causing serious morale issues."

Darlene Costello, Acting Assistant Secretary of the Air Force for Acquisition, Technology & Logistics, explains to the audience the process the Pentagon is now going through to re-evaluate all nuclear weapons programs in the light of recent developments.

Someone in the audience bursts out, "What you mean is, these programs are being scrapped, is that correct?"

The room goes silent for a moment. "Yes," says Costello. The room erupts in chatter and raised voices. Deodorants fail.

"Relax, folks," says Senator Roger Wicker of Mississippi, Chair of the Senate Arms Services Committee and former Air Force pilot, walking up to the podium. "We've got you covered."

Senator Wicker explains how Congress and the Administration plan to keep all these companies in business. "I know you all think I'm here to tell you to tighten your belts and stop acting like a bunch of wimps. But that's not how we're going to treat the companies that have been at the cutting edge of technology and have so much to offer this country and the world."

The room goes silent again as he continues, "The President has agreed, and we in the Congress will now implement, a bill to fund a national economic recovery plan the likes of which has never been seen before. This plan is going to include issuing contracts worth over $3 trillion over the next ten years to design, develop and build out the new technologies we are going to need to save this country and the planet from a climate catastrophe."

This time, several people dare to clap.

The presidential golf club

Have you ever wondered why US Presidents play so much golf? Ever since Nixon wrecked his own legacy by insisting that everything he did at the White House be recorded, no President wants to discuss the most sensitive issues, even with their own staff or advisors, inside the White House – or indeed at Camp David or any other venue that had previously been used for confidential meetings.

Instead, they choose a golf course, miles away from the nearest journalist or bugging device, as the venue for having the most confidential conversations with advisors – and businessmen.

President Ronald Reagan rarely played golf. But on October 22nd, 1983, when the Able Archer nuclear war exercise that almost led to World War III (see Chapter 1) was about to start, he wanted a private conversation with his top advisors. He took them on a two-day golfing trip to Augusta, Georgia.[2]

That day, over a million people were on the streets of West Germany, protesting the deployment of nuclear missiles that were due to arrive in that country at any moment. Hundreds of thousands were also marching in Paris, Rome, London, Stockholm and Vienna.[3]

One of the business executives that Reagan played golf with regularly was Chase Morsey, CEO of Ford Motor Company.[4] Ford was being targeted with boycotts and divestment campaigns for its involvement with the nuclear weapons industry at the time (see Chapter 3). Could Morsey have influenced Reagan to help Ford find an alternative revenue stream? If so, the golf course would have been a likely venue, but we'll never know.

General Electric Chair John F. "Jack" Welch, Jr. was a huge fan of Reagan's economic policies – and also very concerned about the heavy losses GE was facing from the anti-nuclear boycotts. There's no public information about Reagan playing golf with Welch, but it's likely that they discussed both of these issues on a golf course at some point.

In our scenario, whatever happens behind the scenes to facilitate converting corporate resources to peaceful uses, it's likely that squirrels and sparrows will be the only witnesses.

For references inside the box, see [4,5,6]

"That means, for all of you folks, contracts to re-train all your workers, re-tool all your factories, re-structure your business models, and transition all your infrastructure, including the labs, to be able to deliver these new technologies." More clapping.

"There's also another $300 billion in there to safely dismantle and dispose of our existing nuclear weapon stockpile, once the process gets fully underway."

In the chatter over lunch, there's a bit of outrage and alarm, but mostly there two flavors of relief. Some are glad that their incomes are not suddenly going to dry up. And some feel their muscles releasing as their private fears and their gnawing guilt ease up a notch.

Getting the President on board

In this scenario, it has taken an enormous amount of pressure *on the nuclear weapons companies* to get the US to the point where it's ready to sign the TPNW and abolish nuclear weapons. As long as the companies were doing very nicely from Pentagon and DOE contracts and had no reason to change that arrangement, they used their power and influence over the White House and Congress to keep it that way.

But once the companies start to feel the pain – financially but also personally – of boycotts, divestment, and stigmatization of nuclear weapons coming from all over the United States and from all over the world, they no longer want to be part of this business.

These companies exist for one reason only, and that is to make a profit for their shareholders. Now that it's no longer profitable for them to be in the nuclear weapons business, they want out, and they want the government to help them.

Getting the President on board is the easy part. Having a nuclear arsenal was never about "deterrence" or "national security." It was always about profits.

The President calls a special meeting in Congress and says, "In all honesty, we've decided that nuclear weapons are too expensive and too out of date for the needs of our modern military forces. We need that money to address the urgency of climate change, and we need our best scientists, engineers and technicians fully dedicated to that task."

He or she looks directly into the camera and continues, "So I've decided to lead the world into the post-nuclear age. I will sign the Treaty on the Prohibition of Nuclear Weapons and invite

Russia, China and the other nuclear-armed countries to do the same. We will not give up our nuclear weapons until they too have signed this treaty. *Together* we will eliminate all nuclear weapons from this planet."

Our scenario clock goes back by a full hour, to 5:45pm when the President of the United States of America, sitting behind the desk in the Oval Office of the White House, signs the TPNW in front of the world's media.

Signing the TPNW

The US President is empowered by the Constitution to sign treaties on behalf of the United States. No Act of Congress is required, no vote needs to take place, and no one other than the President needs to agree to it.

Signing a treaty in and of itself also has no immediate legal ramifications. It does not mean the United States is suddenly bound by the terms of the treaty. *It does not mean that the US is unilaterally disarming itself.* It does not even guarantee that the US will ever *ratify* the treaty and thereby take on the treaty's commitments. The US has signed numerous treaties and never ratified them. Other countries have done the same.

It is, of course, the *intention* of international law that by signing a treaty, a country commits itself to the goals of the treaty and to the goal of getting the treaty ratified. In the meantime, a treaty signatory is also supposed to refrain from doing anything that goes against the treaty, although there is nothing other countries can do to enforce that.

In any case, signing the TPNW would mean committing the US to the goal of eliminating nuclear weapons, a goal it is – at least in theory – *already committed to* under the Nuclear Non-Proliferation Treaty.

While seeking ratification in the Senate (see Chapter 26), the US could be expected to stop any further development of new weapons, or even to remove existing weapons from operational status. Can the US be forced to take such steps? No, but it seems highly unlikely that any other party to the TPNW would kick the US out of the treaty.

In fact, the whole point of the TPNW is to get the US and the other nuclear-armed states to eventually come on board. If and when the US is ready to sign, the whole world will celebrate.

Will Russia, China and North Korea give up their nuclear weapons if the US does? There is no guarantee that they will, but they are certainly more likely to do so if the US does.[7] And even if they don't, the US still has the most powerful military on the planet, even *without* nuclear weapons.

For the US to sign the TPNW would be momentous. But that still leaves another 8 nuclear-armed countries who will also need to join the TPNW if nuclear weapons are to be abolished. What will it take to get those countries on board? Who would be the next after the US, and how might that happen?

22 The UK, France and Israel sign

Once the US signs the TPNW, there will be enormous pressure for the other nuclear-armed countries to sign as well. This is immediately true for the UK, whose nuclear weapons are heavily dependent on the US. Once the UK signs, France will also sign, not least because of their *nuclear weapons cooperation with the UK. That leaves Israel as the only remaining US ally having nuclear weapons. Getting Israel to give them up will require other steps to happen in the Middle East.*

The United Kingdom

British scientists were involved, along with US scientists, in the development of the atom bomb during World War II. But when the war ended, they were shut out of the US nuclear weapons program, so they built their own. By 1952, they had conducted their first nuclear test.[1]

Then, very soon, the UK found itself integrated back into the US program through the US-UK Mutual Defense Agreement (MDA) of 1958. The MDA gave the UK access to US technology and resources, including quantities of highly-enriched uranium (HEU), plutonium, and tritium necessary for the UK's own nuclear weapons, as well as for its growing fleet of nuclear submarines.

The UK "independent" deterrent

The US and UK nuclear programs have been intertwined ever since. In 1963, the UK decided to deploy US-made Polaris missiles on their ballistic missile submarines instead of producing their own. This began the bizarre arrangement that continues to this day, whereby UK-made nuclear warheads are loaded onto US-made missiles which are then deployed on (mostly) UK-built submarines.

The missiles themselves remain the property of the United States and are "leased" to the UK for use in their submarines. But the whole arrangement begs many questions. For one thing, the guidance system that takes the warhead to its target is part of the missile, not part of the warhead. It is dependent on US satellites which remain under the control of the US military, and on software that must be regularly updated by the US for the whole system to work.[2] So could the UK launch its missiles without active acquiescence and technical assistance from the United States? It seems doubtful.

Furthermore, the MDA commits the UK to assign its nuclear weapons to NATO, which places them under the control of the Supreme Allied Commander of NATO, which is a position reserved for a top US military official.[3]

Given all this, to what extent is Britain's so-called independent nuclear deterrent actually "independent?" The answer is almost certainly "not very." If the US were to give up its nuclear weapons, it's hard to imagine that the UK could remain a nuclear-armed country.

The Scotland dilemma

All of the UK's nuclear weapons are currently stored and based in Scotland.[4] The need for a deep water port to house the nuclear submarines rules out most of the UK coastline outside Scotland. And current safety and security regulations rule out locating nuclear weapons storage and handling facilities anywhere near dense population centers.[5]

But Scotland doesn't want these weapons. "Nae nukes!" say the Scottish people, the Scottish parliament, and the Scottish government. And if Scotland were an independent country today, it would almost certainly demand that the UK's nuclear weapons be removed from Scotland.

The UK would then have difficulty holding on to its nuclear weapons, since it doesn't seem to have anywhere else to put them.[6] That could happen even before the US gets to the point of joining the TPNW in this scenario.

Scotland has had its own parliament and domestic policies since devolution[7] in 1999, but the UK parliament in London still controls defense and foreign policy decisions. Without full independence, Scotland's democratic deficit means that it cannot make decisions about nuclear weapons currently stationed on its own soil (or, in this case, in its lochs).

But that may change. According to recent polls,[8] a narrow majority of Scots support holding another referendum on full independence. The UK government, unsurprisingly, is opposed to it.

Internecine fighting within the Scottish National Party (SNP), along with charges of corruption and bad management, have hampered the independence movement in recent years. But as Brexit slowly destroys the UK economy, and the British grow weary of their current government, support for an independent Scotland could increase to the point where it becomes unstoppable. That would be the short route to the elimination of UK's nuclear weapons.

The UK Labour Party

Meanwhile, just like the US Republican and Democratic Parties, the UK's two largest political parties (the Conservative and Labour Parties) *both* support continued possession of nuclear weapons.

It was a Labour government that initiated the UK's nuclear weapons policy in 1947, and a Labour government decided in 2006 to modernize the UK's nuclear weapons. The current Labour Prime Minister, Keir Starmer, is an avid supporter of the UK's nuclear weapons.

But many Labour Party members disagree. Jeremy Corbyn, former leader of the Labour Party, has long been a strong nuclear abolitionist and supporter of the TPNW.

Some consider it only a matter of time before a Labour Prime Minister emerges who *will* end the UK's nuclear weapons program. The only question is whether it will happen before or after a vote for Scottish independence.

In our scenario, it's not Scottish independence *or* a change of leadership in the UK Labour Party that puts an end to the UK's ambitions to remain a nuclear power. Instead, it is the combination of factors that have been taking place throughout this scenario that make it impossible for the UK to continue holding onto its nuclear weapons. This includes more and more NATO countries joining the TPNW, the removal of US nuclear weapons from Europe, and most importantly, all the pressures leading up to the US finally signing the TPNW.

The UK Prime Minister dutifully signs the TPNW soon after the US President does. The Scots are happy to be getting their lochs back.

The clock goes back one hour to 4:45pm when the UK Prime Minister signs the TPNW.

France

Both the UK and France had their own reasons for developing nuclear weapons in the first place, but those reasons make little sense today.[9] At the time, both countries were clinging to the international status they had enjoyed before their overseas empires began to disappear after WWII.[10]

Now, since the UK "brexited" the European Union, France is the EU's only remaining nuclear-armed country. As the EU moves toward closer and closer integration of defense and security matters, France would like to see a fully integrated EU military force. That would be in contrast to the current NATO arrangement which is strictly under the control of the United States.[11]

The problem for France is that having nuclear weapons makes it rather complicated to just "hand over" the French military to the EU, not least because of the NPT, which forbids it.

In 2020, President Macron of France tried to offer France's nuclear arsenal to the EU.[12] This was met with a muted response, especially in the European Parliament, which supports the TPNW and has urged all EU members to join it.

Following the re-election of Donald Trump, and especially after his harsh treatment of Ukrainian President Volodymyr Zelenskyy, there has been renewed discussion of a "Eurobomb" to replace the US nuclear "umbrella." The new German Chancellor has shown some interest in the French proposal to use their nuclear forces as an umbrella to other European countries.

But in this scenario, Germany has forgone that option and already signed the TPNW, along with several other NATO countries. Public opinion in most other European countries is strongly opposed to nuclear weapons. So by now there is no possibility at all of France offering their nuclear weapons to the rest of Europe.

If France wants to integrate its armed forces into an EU military structure, and if the EU doesn't want France's nuclear weapons, what will France do with them? At some point, it will make no sense at all for France to hold onto its nuclear weapons, especially if the UK is pushed into giving up theirs.

The Teutates Treaty

Like the US-UK Mutual Defence Agreement, the UK and France also have an agreement on sharing nuclear weapons technologies and information. The Teutates Treaty was signed by the two countries in

2010 and gives them unprecedented access to each other's nuclear secrets.

In particular, the Teutates Treaty created a research center for "sub-critical" testing of both countries' nuclear warhead designs. Sharing research and development avoids duplication of effort and saves both countries a great deal of money.

Can France continue its nuclear weapons program if the UK ends theirs? It's certainly possible, since France does not rely on US technology and it managed just fine for many decades without any cooperation with the UK.

But *would* France continue its nuclear weapons program if the UK ended theirs? Almost certainly not.

Jean-Marie Collin and ICAN France

Jean-Marie Collin is a researcher on peace and security issues and Director of ICAN France. He and his colleagues have been promoting nuclear disarmament and building support for the TPNW in France, even as the government – and much of the French population – appears to be moving in the opposite direction.

In 2018, a national poll showed that 76% of the people in France wanted the government to commit to an international process for the total elimination of nuclear weapons. And 67% already wanted France to join the TPNW.[13]

Within a few years, ICAN France had convinced 90 cities and towns and four departments (provinces) in France to sign the ICAN Cities Appeal, including Paris, Lyon, and Bordeaux. But the constant stream of pro-nuclear propaganda from politicians and the mass media has hampered further progress.

Just 23 French parliamentarians have so far signed ICAN's Parliamentary Pledge (compared to 200 in the UK and over 500 in Germany). Nevertheless, in 2022, 56 French parliamentarians called on the government to attend the first meeting of the TPNW as an observer. And in 2023, a similar appeal was supported by 69 parliamentarians.

And in this scenario, resistance to conscription and to the threat of a nuclear war with Russia has been spreading across Europe (see Chapters 11 and 12). This movement is also growing in France. More and more mayors, parliamentarians, academics and leading figures of French culture speak out against the imminent threat of nuclear war. With US nuclear weapons already removed from Germany, Italy, Belgium and the

Netherlands, and the UK and the US already committed to joining the TPNW, the French government finally capitulates and signs the treaty.

The clock goes back another hour to 3:45pm when the Prime Minister of France signs the TPNW.

Israel

Israel doesn't publicly admit to having nuclear weapons, which makes it harder to discuss getting rid of them. It has been fully substantiated by now that Israel *does* in fact have nuclear weapons, and yet Israel chooses to maintain the ambiguity.[14] Every other country with nuclear weapons wants their adversaries to know about it and to be "deterred" by it, so Israel's secrecy seems baffling – until you consider the Glenn Amendment.[15]

Israel is a very small and compact country. It's only 6 miles across at its narrowest point, meaning that even the smallest nuclear weapon launched at a neighboring country would potentially irradiate the whole of Israel itself. Still, the Israeli government sees nuclear weapons as the ultimate safeguard against their country being destroyed by the hostile countries that surround it.[16]

As with the remaining nuclear-armed countries (especially Russia, India, Pakistan and North Korea), Israel isn't likely to part with its nuclear weapons until there is a wider security agreement across the whole region, backed by a reliable means of enforcing it. An effective security agreement would guarantee peace not just between Israel and a few isolated Arab kingdoms, but peace between all the countries of the region. The US has a crucially important role to play in this, not only as Israel's military ally and multi-billion-dollar benefactor, but as a potential peacemaker.

Sharon Dolev and the Middle East Treaty Organization

Sharon Dolev is an Israeli campaigner working to eliminate all nuclear weapons – and other weapons of mass destruction – from the Middle East. She is Executive Director of the Middle East Treaty Organization (METO), established in 2016 to achieve that goal.

When Sharon began working on this in 2007, she was able to get people *in* Israel to talk about Israel's own nuclear weapons by focusing first on the nuclear weapons of *other* countries – specifically those of

India and Pakistan. This enabled her to raise awareness about the dangers of nuclear weapons in *any* context. And she talked about regional security in terms of *all* WMDs, not just nuclear weapons.

The Middle East Treaty Organization (METO) is a coalition of civil society activists and practitioners seeking to rid the Middle East from all weapons of mass destruction as a gateway toward regional security and peace. The coalition engages in policy, advocacy and educational programs to advance a peaceful, integrated and thriving Middle East built on human and environmental security.

And their Mission is to eradicate WMDs, broker peace and build security in the Middle East through the establishment of a Weapons of Mass Destruction Free Zone in the Middle East. The zone would include all countries in the Arab League (Algeria, Bahrain, Comoros, Djibouti, Egypt, Iraq, Jordan, Kuwait, Lebanon, Libya, Mauritania, Morocco, Oman, Palestine, Qatar, Saudi Arabia, Somalia, Sudan, Syria, Tunisia, the United Arab Emirates, and Yemen) plus Iran and Israel.

Of these, five are already signatories to the TPNW as of May, 2025 (Algeria, Djibouti, Libya, Palestine, and Sudan). All the others, apart from Israel and Saudi Arabia, have been voting for the TPNW. And several of these are likely to join it soon. **In this scenario, many already have.**

The WMD-Free Zone would include countries in the Middle East and North Africa that are in the Arab League plus Israel and Iran.

Once a year, since 2019, the United Nations has been convening a conference to move this Middle East treaty forward. Twenty-three out of the 24 countries that would be part of this zone attend (all except Israel). So Sharon's goal is to make it possible for Israel to attend.

This is unlikely with the current government of Benjamin Netanyahu. He is only able to remain in power with the support of two extreme right-wing parties that do not accept any form of peace settlement with Israel's enemies. But his government will not last forever.

So Sharon is working towards getting the *next* government of Israel to the negotiating table. It is not at all an impossibility. Since at least 1986, Israel has said it would join a WMD-free zone under the right circumstances. And the UN Conferences to discuss this matter are held under conditions of consensus, so if Israel attends, nothing can be decided without their agreement. It is in Israel's interests to attend – and to reach an agreement on the creation of this zone.

In this scenario, Sharon and her colleagues are working hard to get the new government of Israel on board with the WMD-free zone. The US, UK and France have already agreed to sign the TPNW, so the world is moving rapidly away from nuclear weapons. And a secure and stable Middle East is in everyone's interest. It is about to happen.

Once Israel and 23 Arab states sign up to the WMD-free Zone Treaty, Israel is ready to get rid of its nuclear weapons. It signs the TPNW, along with Iran and Saudi Arabia.

The clock goes back again another hour to 2:45pm when Israel signs the TPNW, along with Iran and Saudi Arabia.

The UK, France and Israel are the US's closest allies, so if the US renounces nuclear weapons, it makes sense that they eventually will, too. But what about India and Pakistan, whose weapons are aimed at each other and who have a long history of animosity and open hostilities against each other? It may take more than persuasion to get these two countries on board.

23 India and Pakistan join

Once the UK decides to relinquish its nuclear weapons, it is suddenly in a stronger position to help India and Pakistan to relinquish theirs. This won't be possible without additional negotiations to settle the issue of Kashmir. But as the Western world begins to turn its back on nuclear weapons, it's only a matter of time before India and Pakistan do the same.

India and Pakistan are currently the most volatile of the nuclear-armed countries. They're in a near-constant state of war readiness that could be sparked at any moment. Since they both acquired nuclear weapons capability, they've already had one major war and several smaller conflicts.[1]

The two countries share a very bloody history and a 2,000-mile border. When the British Empire withdrew from the sub-continent in 1947, their parting gift was to partition India and Pakistan. Between 12 and 20 million people were forced from their homes – Hindus fled from Pakistan to India, and Muslims fled from India to Pakistan. As many as 2 million people were killed in the violence that accompanied the mass migration.

Kashmir

There has been tension between the two countries ever since, but especially over Kashmir, a region which is claimed by both. After several wars over several decades, there is a de facto border, or "line of control," that runs through Kashmir. On the east is Indian-administered Kashmir and on the west is Pakistani-administered Kashmir.

UN mediation attempts after partition were unsuccessful, so it set up the United Nations Military Observer Group in India and Pakistan (UNMOGIP) to monitor the Line of Control between India and Pakistan in Kashmir. UNMOGIP troops from ten countries have remained in Kashmir since the peacekeeping force was first established in 1951.

But UNMOGIP is not equipped to prevent violent incursions from either side of the conflict. In 2019, India unilaterally absorbed its claimed part of Kashmir, and it has been impossible for UNMOGIP to monitor in that area.

In 2022, in the course of a routine maintenance operation, India accidentally fired an unarmed nuclear-capable BrahMos missile into Pakistani territory. Miraculously, the missile did not cause any death or injury, and even more miraculously, Pakistan did not immediately retaliate.[2] But this is the kind of incident that could very quickly escalate out of control.

On April 22, 2025, a terrorist attack killed 26 Indian tourists in Kashmir. India responded by threatening to cut off the water supply to 16 million hectares of farmland in Pakistan, which would have a devastating impact on a country of 240 million people.[3]

After several nights of shooting at each other across the border, Pakistan's Defence Minister Khawaja Muhammad Asif warned that it would only use its arsenal of nuclear weapons if "there is a direct threat to our existence."[4]

Despite more bombing from both sides, a fragile ceasefire appears to be holding. But as of this writing, the situation in Kashmir remains dangerously precarious.

India

India overtook China as the most populous country on the planet in 2023. It is a country with extreme levels of poverty and social deprivation, and yet it has no problem spending enormous sums of money on maintaining an arsenal of nuclear weapons.

Most Indians see nuclear weapons as symbols of national pride, and have little understanding of what it would mean to use them. (The same can be said of the US and the other nuclear-armed countries, too, of course.)

Girish Menon and the NADAM Foundation

One of the groups working to correct this misperception is the NADAM Foundation in Kerala State, India. NADAM means "voice of humanity." It takes the idea of "think globally, act locally" very seriously. It is committed to supporting everything that the United Nations supports – and that includes treaties like the TPNW.

Girish Menon and Dr. Viswanathan of the NADAM Foundation hand a memento to Mr. Satyapal, President of the Kollengode Grama Panchayat and other staff of the Panchayat after Kollengode signed the ICAN Cities Appeal on Hiroshima Day, 2024. PHOTO: NADAM Foundation

Founder and Chairman Girish Menon has been committed to many charitable causes, including efforts to eradicate poverty, child labor, blindness and heart disease. Although NADAM is working only in one small part of a very big country, it has a network of more than 20,000 people to call on for its various projects.

Most recently, NADAM has been educating people about Covid and encouraging vaccinations. "But nuclear weapons are more dangerous than the coronavirus," says Girish.

Since the TPNW entered into force in 2021, NADAM has been promoting it and offering educational seminars and workshops. When Girish saw that cities all over the world were joining the ICAN Cities Appeal, he decided it was time to get his local village council, or "panchayat," to join it, too.

Now he's working to get more panchayats to join the Cities Appeal – first in Kerala state, next in Tamil Nadu. Beyond that, there are potential supporters of nuclear abolition on the Delhi Municipal Council.

But Girish is under no illusions about India as a whole, as it's still heavily dominated by Prime Minister Narendra Modi and the BJP

Hindu nationalist party, who remain determined to hold onto India's nuclear weapons.

Pakistan

Pakistan could theoretically target its nuclear weapons at Iran or even Israel, but its main adversary is India. Now that India is more than four times the size of Pakistan, with a much larger and more powerful conventional military force, Pakistan sees its nuclear arsenal as its only "defense" against a possible attack by India.

But it's a flawed idea (as explained in Chapter 1): For Pakistan to ever *use* its nuclear weapons against India would be national suicide, since India would almost certainly fire back with *its* nuclear weapons. And even if India didn't retaliate, radioactive fallout from any attack on India would almost certainly affect large portions of Pakistan.

There are two more absurdities in the notion of nuclear war between these countries. First, prevailing winds blow toward Pakistan in the winter months and toward India in the summer months. So either side would have to wait six months to retaliate if they didn't want radioactive fallout blowing directly back in their faces.

But in any season, even a so-called "limited" nuclear war between India and Pakistan could blast enough soot into the upper atmosphere to cause widespread famine across the whole world, (see Chapter 1), but especially in those two countries.

Nevertheless, both countries take great pride in the status they believe they get from having nuclear weapons, and neither is likely to give up its nuclear weapons unless the other one does.

A stable peace in Kashmir is an absolute pre-condition for the elimination of nuclear weapons on the sub-continent. And that will require a mediated peace agreement and a much larger contingent of peacekeeping troops to maintain it. That's all entirely possible, and the UK can help.

Help from the UK

Both India and Pakistan have strong ties to the UK, both because of their colonial past and because large numbers of Indians and Pakistanis subsequently emigrated to the UK. So the UK government and its Indian and Pakistani citizens could play a role in finally convincing these two countries to eliminate their nuclear weapons.

That's been impossible while the UK retains its own nuclear weapons. The UK is surrounded by sea and has no enemies within a thousand miles, but it justifies its nukes as essential for "defending the realm." It's in no position to challenge India and Pakistan on their nuclear arsenals.

But in our scenario, the UK is entering its post-Bomb era. It has large Pakistani and Indian populations that don't want to see their homelands destroyed by war, pollution, or poverty. There are many reasons for the UK to find ways to help India and Pakistan move past their own nuclear era and into a stable peace and prosperity that benefits everyone.

Now that the British are saving a fortune on nuclear weapons, there is even a movement calling for reparations for all the wealth stolen from the Indian sub-continent over the centuries. A more progressive Labour government in the UK is also taking some responsibility for creating the gaping wound of partition that has left Pakistan and India in a state of war with each other ever since.

The UK is also opening its eyes to the danger that *any* nuclear weapons present to the whole planet, themselves included. By now, the UK, US, France, and Israel have already signed the TPNW. Nuclear weapons are starting to be seen less as symbols of status or power, and more as wasteful and dangerous liabilities.

Moreover, it's becoming obvious that even if nobody fights a nuclear war, the Bomb is a huge impediment to the level of global cooperation necessary to address the climate crisis, the mass migrations of climate refugees, new pandemics, and other manmade problems. And both India and Pakistan need to be part of that global cooperation.

So the UK supports an aid package to speed both India and Pakistan into the green economy, with large-scale wind farms and massive solar projects. And, in the interest of helping both countries to sign the TPNW, the UK commits to helping fund a much larger peacekeeping force along the Line of Control in Kashmir. The UN also ramps up diplomatic efforts to define a permanent border with no further bloodshed, and to ensure Pakistan's security into the future.

With all this additional support, Pakistan and India are ready to eliminate their nuclear weapons – as long as it happens in both countries simultaneously.

`The clock goes back 2 hours to 12:45pm` when India and Pakistan both sign the TPNW in a joint ceremony at the United Nations.

With India and Pakistan on board, all that remains now are the hard-core "adversaries" of the United States: China, North Korea and Russia. What will it take to get them on board with nuclear abolition? In the case of China, it probably won't take much.

24 China and North Korea are next

China maintains a nuclear arsenal mainly as "protection" against a possible US attack. So does North Korea. Once the US commits itself to eliminating its nuclear weapons, China no reason to keep its own. There are, of course, many other issues at play between the US and China that need to be resolved to ensure China joins the treaty. And there are different issues for North Korea.

China

With almost 1.5 billion people, China is more than four times the size of the US. The Chinese military doesn't need to worry about the balance of conventional forces, despite the fact that its forces may be technologically inferior to those of the United States.

But China *does* have reason to be increasingly worried about a nuclear attack from the US. Both Republicans and Democrats in the US seem hell-bent on war with China,[1] and talk openly about building up both nuclear and conventional forces to prepare for it.

So it's not surprising that China is reputedly building a large number of nuclear missile sites, and it has reportedly added about 60 nuclear warheads to its arsenal in the last year.[2]

Even if all the new missile sites are fitted with new nuclear missiles, however (and so far, there's no evidence for that), China's nuclear arsenal would still be a fraction of the size of the US's or Russia's. As far as we know, China has only around 500 nuclear warheads compared to more than 5,400 in the US and almost 6,000 in Russia.[3]

China's nuclear weapons are also kept in storage. They are not deployed like US or Russian nuclear weapons. They are not on hair-trigger alert. And China has a "No First Use" policy, meaning that it won't be the first to use them.

What about Taiwan?

Can the future of Taiwan be resolved without recourse to war? Of course it can. Taiwan is claimed by mainland China, but has maintained its *de facto* independence since 1949. Unlike the dispute over Kashmir, there have been no armed clashes over Taiwan in almost 60 years.[4]

Ambiguity is a virtue in that part of the world. China and Taiwan do not need to agree about the official status of the island in order to continue the peaceful coexistence they have enjoyed, more or less, for the past 60 years.

It is the United States that continues to provoke a conflict over Taiwan when there is no need for one. Democrats and Republicans alike have taken it upon themselves to be the "defenders" of Taiwan against the imminent threat they perceive from Communist China.

The irony is that the "solution" to the Taiwan problem is not to have a solution, but to allow diplomacy and strategic ambiguity to rule the day. What is really at stake here is not Taiwan, but the US relationship with China more generally.

If the US were to sign the TPNW, China would almost certainly respond positively. Chinese President Xi Jinping has said on many occasions that he supports the complete elimination of nuclear weapons.[5]

But we'll never know unless the US *does* sign the TPNW. China is unlikely to go first.

In our scenario, China is relieved when the US joins the TPNW. They do the same, and now both countries can free up vast amounts of money to address the needs of their citizens. Both are major carbon emitters, and nuclear disarmament removes a major obstacle to deeper cooperation on climate issues.

The clock goes back 1 hour to 11:45am when China joins the TPNW.

North Korea follows[6]

At an early stage of the discussions that ultimately led to the TPNW, only one nuclear-armed country voted in favor. Can you guess which one? North Korea.[7] But that was shortly before President Trump threatened them with "fire and fury," and their position changed.

If the United States and China were on the path to abolishing their nuclear weapons, it would pave the way for North Korea to follow suit.

But North Korea will not give up its nuclear weapons without a peace agreement that officially ends the Korean War[8] and guarantees their security from any attack by the US, whether nuclear or conventional. Further negotiations will be needed to enable North Korea to sign the TPNW.

Kim Jong-un became "supreme leader" of North Korea after the death of his father, Kim Jong-il, in 2011. He rules a very secretive state, and is considered by many in the West to be the most dangerous of the nine men in the world with their fingers on the nuclear button.[9]

The contrast between North and South Korea, in terms of economic development and prosperity, could not be greater. South Korea is a very advanced, highly industrialized and thriving "Asian Tiger," trading with the rest of the world and closely tied to Japan, Australia, the USA and even China.

North Korea, on the other hand, is poor, isolated, and technologically less developed. It suffered massive carpet-bombing by the US during the Korean War, including 32,000 tons of napalm. Whole cities were destroyed. During the 1990s, North Korea suffered a famine that killed hundreds of thousands, possibly even millions, of its people. It also suffered major floods and drought, and the failure of 85 per cent of its electricity.

With the collapse of the Soviet Union around that time, North Korea was left with China as its only ally and benefactor. Today, even China is tiring of the situation in North Korea, as UN sanctions bite even further into an already bleak and desperate situation there.

Kim Jong-un has one overriding priority, and that is the survival of his country.[10] Shortly after 9/11, George W. Bush labeled Iraq, Iran and North Korea the "axis of evil," and later added Cuba, Libya and Syria to that list. Within a few years, Iraq's leader Saddam Hussein was dead and his country in ruins. The same fate befell Libya and Colonel Gaddafi. The US tried unsuccessfully to topple Bashar al-Assad of Syria, but in 2024 he too was overthrown. Iran is certainly very high on the US hit-list, and to a lesser extent so is Cuba. That's five out of the six. Is it surprising that North Korea might fear for its existence?

At one point, the US had over 1,000 nuclear weapons stationed in South Korea. These were all removed by 1991, but the US continues to conduct massive war games with South Korea, and US nuclear missile submarines still patrol the waters around North Korea.

Many Western diplomats and commentators claim that Kim Jong-un is building a nuclear arsenal with long-range missiles in order to be able to launch a pre-emptive nuclear attack on the United States. That is the scenario which forms the basis for Annie Jacobsen's book.

But given all the credit that the US and other countries continually give to "deterrence," it would be surprising for Kim Jong-un not to believe the same – that North Korea's possession of nuclear weapons is, in fact, successfully "deterring" a possible US attack.

There is every reason, as with China, to think that North Korea would respond favorably to the US signing the TPNW. But for North Korea to reciprocate would require further confidence-building measures, since the US has already bombed that country into the ground once, and could easily do so again, with purely conventional weapons.

In our scenario, an agreement is reached to make the whole of the Korean peninsula nuclear-free, along with the Sea of Japan to the east and the Yellow Sea to the west. That means keeping US nuclear submarines out of those waters as well as keeping nuclear weapons out of both South Korea and North Korea.

And crucially, since the Korean War still technically continues to this day, a long-awaited peace treaty officially ends the war and provides security guarantees against any future hostilities. Since nuclear weapons have eaten up a huge chunk of North Korea's economy, the quality of life improves and the people find other sources of national pride. Then, it's up to the people of both Koreas to decide about opening borders or even reuniting their country as one.

The clock goes back 1 hour to 10:45am when North Korea signs the TPNW.

Arms control agreements have historically been between the US and Russia. The assumption has been that other nuclear-armed countries would join if and when US and Russian arsenals have been reduced to their levels. But in this scenario, the other countries come first and it is only at the very end that Russia agrees to disarm. That's because a lot of other issues about European and global security will need to be negotiated before Russia is likely to give up its nuclear weapons.

25 Russia closes the circle

With all the other nuclear-armed countries on board with the TPNW and the abolition of nuclear weapons, that leaves only Russia. Like North Korea and China, the Soviet Union built a nuclear arsenal specifically to protect itself from possible nuclear attack by the US and NATO. With the dissolution of the Soviet Union and their Warsaw Pact allies, Russia now has much smaller and less powerful conventional forces at its disposal. It is unlikely, therefore, to give up its nuclear weapons until it feels protected from a conventional *attack by the US and/or NATO. That's likely to require a major restructuring of European and global security arrangements.*

Many US-Americans and Western Europeans are appalled that Russia invaded Ukraine, a sovereign nation and a member of the United Nations, in direct violation of the UN Charter. President Putin has threatened the use of nuclear weapons. He has built his argument for war on lies and euphemistically called it merely a "military operation." The Russian Army has undoubtedly committed atrocities and war crimes in Ukraine. Large numbers of civilians have been killed. Civilian infrastructure has been targeted. Russia unilaterally recognized Donbass provinces as independent states, and then, by popular plebiscite, incorporated them into the Russian Federation.

And, just 20 years previously, the US invaded Iraq, a sovereign nation and member of the United Nations, also in direct violation of the UN Charter.[1] And on numerous occasions a US President has threatened the use of nuclear weapons, most recently against North Korea in 2018.[2] President George W. Bush built his argument for war with Iraq on lies, and also euphemistically called it a "military operation."[3] The US Army committed atrocities and war crimes in Iraq as well as in numerous other wars.[4] Large numbers of civilians have been killed in all these wars. Civilian infrastructure has been targeted.[5]

The US unilaterally recognized Kosovo as an independent country when it was still claimed as part of Serbia.[6] Not as recently, but certainly with greater frequency, the US has used popular plebiscites to incorporate territories into the United States, including Hawaii,[7] and more recently to determine the status of Puerto Rico.

Two wrongs don't make a right, and nothing that the US has done in Iraq or elsewhere justifies or excuses what Russia has been doing in Ukraine. *Nevertheless, it's a breathtaking double standard.* President Putin is, if anything, a copycat. He may well be autocratic and extremely socially conservative, but he is also immensely popular in his own country, and he has been elected again and again in what observers have generally considered to be democratic elections.[8]

Russia and Ukraine

As this book goes to print, in May 2025, the war in Ukraine is still no closer to ending than ever. Although the position of the Trump administration appears to be different, the US and its NATO allies in Europe have been viewing Russia throughout this war as an implacable enemy who cannot be negotiated with but must be defeated on the battlefields of Ukraine.

This was, of course, also how Soviet Russia was viewed during decades of the Cold War, when it was the number one "enemy" of the US, even when the US was fighting in Korea or Viet Nam, or supporting government forces or guerrilla fighters in Mozambique, Angola, Nicaragua, El Salvador and Cuba.

And yet, even at the height of the Cold War, the US was willing to sit down with the Soviets and negotiate at a time when a misunderstanding or miscommunication could have led to World War III. President Kennedy negotiated his way out of the Cuban Missile Crisis in 1962, with the help of his brother, Bobby Kennedy.[9] Then he successfully negotiated an end to above-ground nuclear testing with Premier Khrushchev himself.

President Johnson negotiated the Non-Proliferation Treaty (NPT) together with the Soviets. President Nixon negotiated the Anti-Ballistic Missile Treaty (ABM) with General Secretary Brezhnev. President Reagan famously negotiated with President Gorbachev, *almost to the point of eliminating all nuclear weapons.*[10] All of this took place at a time when Soviet Russia was considered the number one enemy of the

United States, and there were hot wars raging in many parts of the world that both the US and the Soviets were fighting by proxy.

In 1968, just a few weeks after the US and the USSR signed the NPT, the Soviet-led Warsaw Pact invaded Czechoslovakia. They quickly withdrew, but the invasion put an end to the liberal reforms that were underway in Czechoslovakia and created a major jolt to the post-war "peace" in Europe.

Nevertheless, the US Senate went on to ratify the NPT. The US and the Soviets continued to dialogue with each other, leading to the period of "détente" between the two countries in the 1970s.

The point is, even when tensions were running high, even when wars and invasions were going on – even when these were going on *in Europe* (i.e. Czechoslovakia) – the US and the Soviets still found a way to sit down and negotiate about nuclear weapons. So there's nothing inherently preventing them from doing so now, despite the 2022 Russian invasion of Ukraine (which is also in Europe).

Possible outcomes to the Ukraine War

There are four possible outcomes to the Ukraine War:

(1) An ongoing military stalemate, like the one that existed between the Ukrainian government and Ukrainian separatists in the Donbass region from 2014-2022. This is not so much an outcome as a non-outcome. In other words, the war just drags on indefinitely with no clear winner or loser, but also no agreement to stop fighting. There are many on-going, "low-level" wars[11] in the world today that fit into this category, including wars between Armenia and Azerbaijan over Nagorno-Karabakh,[12] between Georgia and South Ossetia, the war in the Western Sahara, and so on.

(2) A ceasefire or armistice agreement that stops the fighting but does not resolve the underlying issues. At least with a ceasefire, the killing stops, but with no long-term settlement of the issues it can, of course, start up again at any time.

For a ceasefire to stick, there would almost certainly have to be a peacekeeping force put in place between the two armies. This could be an Organization for Security and Cooperation in Europe (OSCE) operation, since both Russia and Ukraine are OSCE members.[13] However, almost all member states of the OSCE are siding with Ukraine over this war, so it would be difficult for Russia to accept such a force as being neutral.

Instead, it could be a UN operation involving peacekeeping troops from neutral countries in, say, Africa and Latin America. This would have the advantage of being perceived by all sides as truly neutral and fair, but might be too much for the Ukrainians *or* the Russians to swallow.

(3) A peace agreement in which both/all sides agree that their fight with each other is over and not just temporarily halted. Peace agreements often begin with a ceasefire, followed by peace negotiations and a final settlement. But complex conflicts can take a long time to resolve at the negotiating table. And this one is complex – but entirely resolvable.

(4) One side prevails and the other capitulates. This is by far the least likely of the four options, because the US and NATO are too invested in Ukraine now to let it be defeated on the battlefield,[14] and Russia is too invested to withdraw. If Ukraine loses too many soldiers to be able to keep up the fight, neighboring countries could start sending personnel along with the tanks and fighter jets they are already sending.

Ukrainian Territory Occupied by Russian Forces: November 13, 2022

After more than two and half years of fierce fighting in Ukraine, the battle lines have not changed significantly since November 2022.

Even with all the money and modern weaponry pouring into Ukraine from the US and other NATO countries, and even with additional boots on the ground, Ukraine is unlikely to be able to defeat a former superpower with three times the size of its army and with vastly greater resources.[15] The idea that Ukraine will ever push Russia back to its internationally recognized borders, including out of Crimea, is fanciful at best.

Option 4 might not mean the defeat of one side or the other, but potentially the defeat of the *entire world* in a nuclear conflagration. If Russia were to press ahead and try to conquer the whole of Ukraine or even to destroy Kiev and decapitate the regime, would the US and the rest of NATO stand idly by? And if Ukraine were to push Russia out of eastern Ukraine and try to take back the whole of Crimea, would Russia stand idly by?

These are the nightmare scenarios that are still possible with Ukraine unless people come to their senses. There are numerous other scenarios that could lead to a major disaster of unknown proportions, including a meltdown at the Zaporizhzhia nuclear power complex or indeed at one of the many other nuclear power plants in Ukraine.[16] There are other potentially dangerous unknowns, for example if neighboring countries like Belarus are drawn in.

And of course there are other possible scenarios, but in terms of Russia, the most important takeaways from the Ukraine war are that (1) Russia values its own nuclear weapons very highly, has used them to try to "deter" the US and other countries from intervening, and clearly sees how dangerously precarious its own conventional forces are in relation to NATO's. On the other hand, (2) Russia has not been able to use its nuclear weapons to gain advantage on the battlefield. And despite all the talk about Russia's possible use of "tactical" nuclear weapons, that is unlikely to change.[17]

This second point is important, because ultimately the best way to eliminate nuclear weapons is for the countries possessing them to realize that *they are actually useless as weapons.* Nuclear weapons can destroy whole cities, but wars are not won by destroying whole cities. They are won by destroying enemy forces that are spread out over large areas in tanks and trenches and bunkers and encampments. Nuclear weapons cannot destroy those things effectively without also destroying one's own forces in the process.

Russia's sense of security

The United States has not yet learned the important lesson that no country can be secure unless its potential adversaries are also secure. *As long as the US – and many other countries – insist on building their own sense of security by creating a sense of insecurity in other countries, they cannot themselves be secure.* Russia needs to feel secure from possible attack or invasion from the US or NATO just as much as NATO countries and the US need to feel secure from possible attack or invasion from Russia.

This is not about being "pro-Russian" or "soft" on President Putin. This is just the reality of the world we live in. Russia is a country of 150 million people. In terms of land mass, it is by far the largest country in the world, stretching from the Pacific to the Baltic across 11 time zones. There are 26 official languages spoken in Russia and another 100 or more so-called "minority" languages.[18]

And however much we may disagree with, disapprove of, or even loathe Vladimir Putin, what he does, or what he stands for, the reality is that he is hugely popular in his own country. He's far more popular than previous Russian leaders, and, by all accounts, he's more popular in Russia than Presidents Biden or Trump have ever been in the United States.[19] And although many in the West have criticized Russian elections as "undemocratic" or a "sham," numerous opinion polls, including those conducted by skeptical western academics, show that Putin's electoral victories are closely aligned with his polling popularity.[20]

What would it take for Russia to feel secure without its nuclear weapons? Nothing less than a new security architecture that protects them from the US/NATO.

Historical positions

During the Cold War, if the US had decided to abolish its nuclear weapons, the Soviets would likely have done the same.

At that time, the Soviet Union, together with its Warsaw Pact allies, had a *conventional* military advantage over NATO and the US, in terms of numbers of troops and tanks, etc.[21] But they were at a considerable *nuclear* disadvantage. Even with their growing nuclear arsenal, they were vulnerable to the superior US nuclear weapons, so they had every reason to favor the elimination of nuclear weapons.

Meanwhile, NATO feared that it could easily be overwhelmed in a surprise Soviet attack with conventional weapons, so they felt justified in stationing US nuclear weapons in Europe.

Now the tables have turned. Russia has half the population it once had,[22] and the Warsaw Pact has dissolved. NATO is much larger and has vastly more conventional forces than Russia does.[23] Now Russia fears that without its nuclear weapons, *it* could be easily overwhelmed by a surprise attack from NATO.

What about the Organization for Security and Cooperation in Europe?

The OSCE grew out of the Helsinki Final Act, which officially ended World War II.[24] It is recognized by the UN as a "regional arrangement" for collective security under Article VIII of the UN Charter. Unlike NATO, the OSCE includes *all* the countries of Europe and North America, including Russia and many neutral countries that are not part of NATO (including Ireland, Austria, Switzerland, etc.). Unlike NATO, the OSCE is not primarily a military organization, although it has access to military personnel of its member states for some of its peacekeeping operations. And unlike NATO, the OSCE's primary goal is to ensure the security of Europe by all available means—not just military means.

The OSCE is therefore involved in election monitoring and human rights monitoring in all its member states. And it's involved in ceasefire monitoring to ensure peace agreements are upheld by all the parties.

The OSCE had a ceasefire mission monitoring the situation in eastern Ukraine for eight years until the Russian invasion meant they had to evacuate. The OSCE had similarly been monitoring the situation in Kosovo prior to the US bombing and NATO military intervention there, which forced them to evacuate back in 1999. So the OSCE is accustomed to being pushed out in favor of military intervention. This time, however, it has led to a deep crisis within the OSCE, as many of its members are now actively supporting Ukraine in its war against the Russian invaders.

It's in doubt, therefore, whether the OSCE can play a constructive role in ending the war in Ukraine at this point, but it's not impossible. The real question is whether the OSCE can again play a collective security role for the whole of Europe. Clearly it was not effective enough to prevent the Russian invasion of Ukraine nor to prevent the NATO intervention in Kosovo. Something much stronger than the OSCE, as it is presently constituted, seems to be needed to keep the peace in Europe.

A new NATO including Russia?

The entire UN system enshrines the concept of "collective security," meaning that the whole world is collectively responsible for maintaining peace and security of all countries, and for restoring it should any breach of the peace occur.

By contrast, NATO is defined as a "collective defense" organization, meaning that its members agree to come to the defense of another country in the alliance if it is attacked. In UN parlance, collective defense is an extension of the national right to self-defense, which is itself strictly limited under the UN charter.[25]

Here is one alternative that could form the basis for a new security architecture for Europe: a NATO that *incorporates* Russia rather than being a military alliance *against* Russia.

The deep-seated suspicion and hostility by existing NATO members toward Russia would make such a transformation difficult, but not impossible. After all, it was only ten years after the Second World War that the US, UK, France, and others who had fought not one but two world wars against Germany invited their former enemy to be part of NATO in 1955.

It would require NATO becoming a true collective *security* organization as opposed to a collective *defense* organization. That could mean taking on many if not all of the many important roles played by the OSCE up to now. It could also mean re-defining NATO's concept of security as well as its concept of self-defense, which in any case is not in line with the UN's concept as defined in Article 51 of the UN Charter, as noted above.[26]

Whatever the future security architecture of Europe becomes, what it *cannot* be is a large military alliance lined up against a single country, no matter how big that country is. That has been a recipe for trouble that many identified long before 2022.[27] However the war in Ukraine ends, that problem will remain as long as Russia feels threatened by NATO.

Russia signs the TPNW

In this scenario, the US, UK and France have already signed the TPNW (along with India, Pakistan, China, North Korea and Israel). There's intense pressure on Russia to be the final nuclear-armed country to join in the abolition of nuclear weapons.

But pressure is not enough. Russia won't join the TPNW without some major concessions from the United States and its European allies.

These demands are not unreasonable. Russia has been pleading with the United States for years to conclude a treaty banning deployment of weapons in space.[28] It has called for a treaty to prohibit cyberwarfare.[29] It has asked repeatedly for a reinstatement of the Anti-Ballistic Missile Treaty that US President George W. Bush unilaterally pulled out of.

Russia also wants agreements to end all punitive sanctions against it, to restore full diplomatic relations, to invite Russia back into the G8, to treat Russia with dignity and respect in all UN and international fora where Russia is present, and to enter into full negotiations for a European treaty that guarantees peace and security for all parties, including a permanent settlement for Ukraine.

These conditions hardly seem onerous and are nothing more than could be requested of *any* country wanting to be taken seriously as an equal partner on the world stage. But of course, being treated as an equal on the world stage is the one thing that has been lacking from Russia's perspective, since long before its invasion of Ukraine. In our scenario, all these conditions are met and Russia signs.

`The clock goes back a full hour to 9:45am` when Russia signs the TPNW and the process can begin for the final elimination of all nuclear weapons from the face of the earth.

Once all nine nuclear-armed nations have signed the TPNW, the final abolition of nuclear weapons is relatively straightforward. The structure of an agreement for identifying, destroying, and verifying the elimination of nuclear weapons already exists, as do all the mechanisms for making it happen. All that is required is the political will, which now exists. But how will it unfold? The final chapter in this scenario takes us through the steps.

26 Final steps to abolition

Once they have all signed the TPNW, the nine nuclear-armed countries can proceed to ratification and implementation of legally-binding, time-bound plans for the verified and irreversible elimination of their nuclear arsenals.

In Chapter 20 of our scenario. the United States signs the TPNW. But they are not willing to *ratify* it until all the other nuclear-armed countries are also on board. Now the time has come.

There are many ways this can happen. In this particular scenario, the nine nuclear-armed countries are going to negotiate and sign a written agreement that spells out the steps each one will take in concert with the others, and the means by which they can each satisfy themselves that everything is being done in accordance with the agreement. Once they have that agreement worked out, they will all ratify the TPNW together.

This is a separate agreement, outside of the TPNW. But it is not another full-fledged treaty. It is simply a "preview" of what each country will present to the States Parties of the TPNW in accordance with their obligations under Article 4 of the treaty.

An agreement among the nuclear-armed countries

Graduated and Reciprocated Initiatives in Tension-Reduction

Under Article 4 of the TPNW, each country that still has nuclear weapons must produce a plan for how they will eliminate those weapons within an agreed period. That plan must be legally-binding, time-bound, verifiable, and irreversible.

In our scenario, the detailed disarmament plans are worked out ahead of time among the nine nuclear-armed countries and synchronized with each other before being submitted to the TPNW States Parties. This enables each country to time and

coordinate each step in the process to coincide with steps being taken by the other countries, applying an established procedure known as "GRIT."

During the 1960s, conflict resolution experts developed the concept called Graduated and Reciprocated Initiatives in Tension-reduction, or GRIT.[1] The idea was that even in the most hostile environments, two adversaries could reduce tensions by taking small, unilateral steps and waiting to see if these were reciprocated.

If the second party reciprocated, the first party would then take the next step, and wait again for reciprocation. If the second party did *not* reciprocate as expected, the process would be halted until they did.

This approach was implemented very successfully with the 1991-92 Presidential Nuclear Initiatives (see Chapter 2). In that example, the US took the initiative and waited to see if Russia would reciprocate, which they did. The US then took additional steps and these were also reciprocated.

GRIT has also been used successfully in many other contexts, including in labor and family disputes as well as in major international peace processes such as between Egypt and Israel.[2] It has a proven track record and enables a country like the United States, with deep distrust of a country like Russia, to nevertheless engage in meaningful steps to reduce tension without having to rely on lengthy negotiations and a complex verification regime. It's more complicated to apply the GRIT concept to multiple parties rather than just two, but it's perfectly feasible.

The US and Russia have by far the largest nuclear arsenals, with over 5,000 warheads each. The other seven nuclear-armed countries have at most only a few hundred warheads each. It is already generally accepted, therefore, that other nuclear-armed countries would not be directly involved in the disarmament process until those two big arsenals are reduced to a size comparable to theirs.

In our scenario, once the timetables have been worked out among the nine countries, they're ready to agree on means of monitoring and verification.

Figure 26.1 Disarmament by means of GRIT

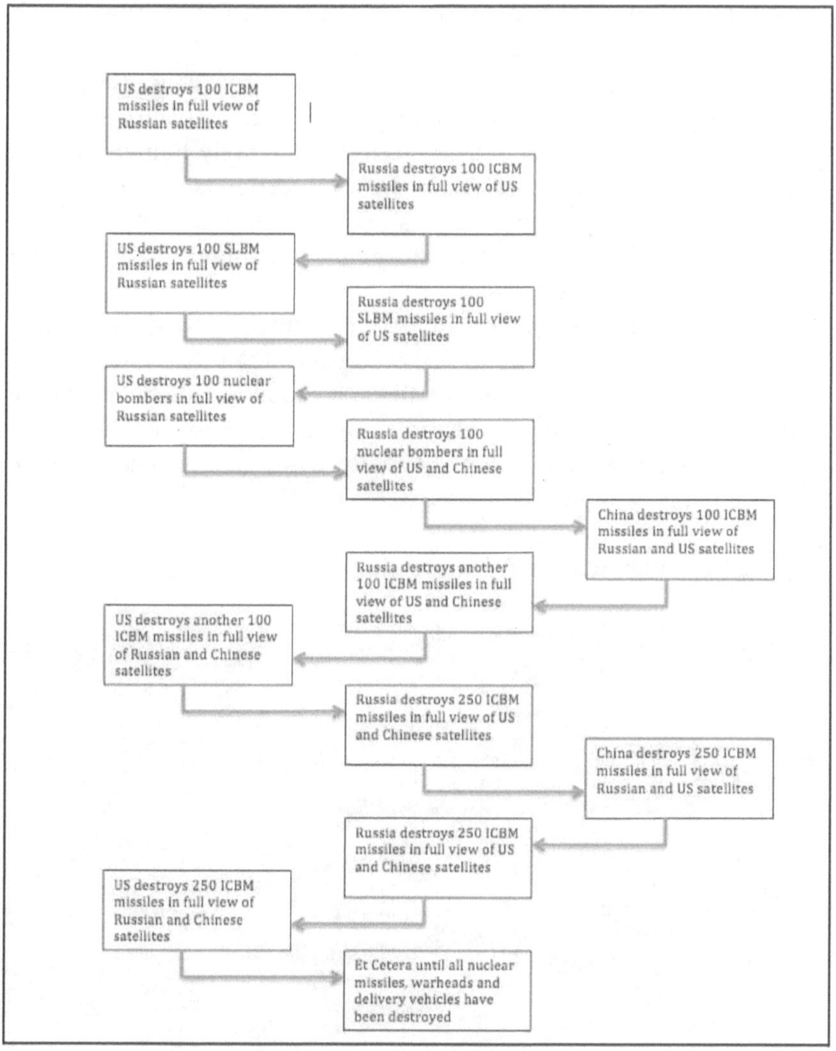

National Technical Means of Verification

Free and unfettered access to military inspectors from each party has been a standard procedure for bilateral treaties between the US and Russia since the INF Treaty. This process has been remarkably successful, given the general level of distrust between these two countries.

Verification can also be achieved through what is known as "national technical means" (NTM). This means relying primarily on satellite and airplane surveillance, rather than on on-site inspections. Seismographic and other data can also be collected without physically inspecting sensitive military sites in another country.

A certain degree of trust is required, no matter what methods of monitoring and verification are used, since even the most intrusive on-site inspections can miss items that are deliberately hidden. (On the other hand, in the case of Iraq's chemical weapons program, mere suspicion about hidden WMDs was used to justify a war, but in the end, after the fall of Saddam Hussein, none were found – just as the UN inspectors had reported all along.)

Ironically, the complete elimination of nuclear weapons may be easier to verify, through non-intrusive means, than the elimination of biological, chemical, or other WMDs. The total numbers of nuclear weapons in both countries is already more or less known. Sites for the development, production, testing and deployment of nuclear weapons are also publicly known.

Figure 26.2 Verification from the air

B-52 nuclear bombers chopped into pieces in accordance with START treaty and laid out for Russian satellites to see. PHOTO: USAF Staff Sgt. Perry Aston

To prove that heavy strategic bombers have been taken out of service in the past, militaries have simply lined them up in a field and literally cut them into pieces, clearly visible from a satellite. Missiles are comparatively smaller, but they could still be laid out and chopped up to prove they have been rendered unusable.

The actual nuclear bombs and warheads that go onto the missiles and planes are much smaller, some of them only the size of a large suitcase. Even these may be clearly visible by today's very advanced satellite imagery. But proving they have been destroyed may be more of a challenge.

The International Atomic Energy Agency

This is where the International Atomic Energy Agency (IAEA) comes in. The IAEA has global responsibility for ensuring that countries with nuclear power plants and research reactors are not diverting any of the nuclear material for use as nuclear weapons. They already carry out intrusive inspections of nuclear facilities that are arranged through an IAEA safeguards agreement that is negotiated bilaterally with each country.

IAEA inspectors represent a neutral third party, rather than the military of a potential adversary. That could be more acceptable to the nuclear-armed countries, who have generally been wary of inspectors from each other's countries visiting their most sensitive military bases.

Almost all non-nuclear-armed countries by now have signed a "comprehensive safeguard agreement" with the IAEA. This gives the IAEA access to their nuclear facilities and allows for various types of inspection. The nuclear-armed countries (apart from North Korea) have more limited agreements with the IAEA that allow for some monitoring but are not *comprehensive*.

Although signing a comprehensive safeguard agreement with the IAEA is a requirement for all countries once they join the TPNW, in this scenario, they all agree to sign such an agreement *prior to ratifying* the treaty, as an extra confidence-building measure and a signal of their intention to fully comply with the treaty after they ratify it.

Our scenario clock goes back a full hour to 8:45am when all nine nuclear-armed countries sign the informal agreement setting out the joint terms for ratifying the TPNW.

Ratification

In our scenario, now that all nine countries have agreed to a post-ratification process, they are ready to ratify the TPNW.

Ratification involves different procedures in each country, and it takes some time.

In the US, a two-thirds majority in the Senate is needed for ratification. This is not politically possible until there is confirmation that the Russian *Duma* has ratified - and vice versa. There are skeptical legislators on both sides. Nobody wants to go first.

So there's a bit of to-ing and fro-ing between these two national bodies before they are both ready to announce their votes on ratification at (more or less) the same time. In this scenario, good sense prevails and both countries ratify the TPNW.

The other seven, having already signed the treaty and committed themselves to this process, also ratify. The world celebrates as our scenario clock goes back *another two hours.* At last, the stage is set for the final step.

Our scenario clock goes back by another 2 hours to 6:45am once all nine nuclear-armed countries finally ratify the TPNW. The world is now approaching the dawn of the post-nuclear age, but further steps are still needed before the weapons are completely eliminated.

Steps to zero

Proposals from organizations like Global Zero describe the steps necessary to get from the current levels of nuclear weapons down to zero through gradual reductions of the number of warheads on all sides.[3] The START treaty process followed that kind of logic.

The draft Nuclear Weapons Convention (NWC),[4] first deposited with the UN in 1997 and then updated in 2007, sets out five phases for implementation. These follow similar patterns to the INF Treaty and START Treaties.

But in this scenario we are well beyond the point of merely *reducing* stockpiles. The five phases in the NWC form a solid basis for the process that will *eliminate* all nuclear weapons as required by the TPNW.

The nine nuclear-armed countries have already agreed to complete the NWC's five phases in concert with each other. This is how it might look:

1. Remove weapons from operational status

Ninety days after ratification, the TPNW enters into force in each of those countries. They must then remove all nuclear weapons from operational status.

Only four countries have nuclear weapons operationally deployed and ready to launch from missile silos, submarines and bombers: US, Russia, UK and France. The others already keep their warheads stored separately from their missiles and bombers.

Additional steps that all nine countries can take in this initial phase include:

a. **Remove targeting coordinates and navigational information**
b. **Disable and de-alert all delivery vehicles**
c. **Cease all further production of components and equipment**
d. **Cease all further funding and research on nuclear weapons, except as may be necessary for their elimination**
e. **Cease production of fissile material (uranium, plutonium, tritium)**

> `Our scenario clock goes back 2 more hours to 4:45am` when all remaining nuclear weapons have been removed from operational status.

2. Declarations

Within 30 days of entry into force, submit a declaration to the Secretary-General of the United Nations. It only needs to say that the country still possesses nuclear weapons, but it could also include, for the purposes of transparency and confidence-building:

a. **A complete inventory of all nuclear weapons held, including locations and quantities**
b. **An inventory of all fissile materials capable of making a nuclear weapon**
c. **A report on any nuclear material that has gone missing and plans for its recovery**
d. **A complete inventory of nuclear weapons facilities**
e. **A complete inventory of all nuclear-capable delivery systems**

3. Legally-binding, time-bounds plans

These plans have already been agreed among the nine nuclear-armed countries, so this step merely involves presenting these to the existing States Parties for their approval. There is some reluctance on the part of nuclear-armed countries to seek the "approval" of their disarmament plans from the non-nuclear-armed countries of the world, but the grumbling dies down to allow the TPNW to reach its goal.

The plans include:

a. Timetable for dismantling and destroying the weapons and delivery systems
b. Timetable for decommissioning or converting testing facilities, research and production facilities
c. Timetable for the safe disposal of all fissile material under IAEA control

4. Negotiate safeguards agreements with the IAEA

These were already agreed prior to ratification, including:

a. Allowing IAEA access to all stages of the nuclear fuel cycle
b. Providing full information to the IAEA on quantities and locations of fissile material
c. Arranging for inspections and testing by IAEA experts
d. Agreeing on final disposal and safe storage of remaining fissile material

5. Dismantle and destroy all nuclear weapons

The final part of this process is the actual elimination of nuclear stockpiles, in the following stages:

e. Separate warheads from delivery vehicles
f. Destroy delivery vehicles
g. Remove fissile material from warheads
h. Destroy warheads
i. Dilute and dispose of fissile material

This total process will take several years. (The TPNW allows up to 10 years, with an option to extend up to 5 years beyond that if necessary.) There will continue to be costs involved throughout that period of time, especially for the security of nuclear materials prior to final disposal.[5]

Our scenario clock goes back a further 4 hours to 00:45:00am when all remaining nuclear weapons have been dismantled and destroyed.

Ongoing monitoring and verification

Many people are worried that somebody might "cheat" on the TPNW. But unlike chemical or biological WMDs, it's pretty hard to hide a nuclear weapons program. The mining and acquisition of uranium is carefully monitored. The enrichment of uranium to the degree needed for a bomb requires very large and expensive facilities that are easy to spot. Without highly sophisticated equipment for virtual testing, nuclear weapons cannot be tested without an explosion that can be detected anywhere in the world. The missiles to carry such weapons likewise cannot be test-fired undetected. At every stage of the process, nuclear weapons are visible to the world. That's why we know that North Korea has them. It's also why we know that so far, at least, Iran does not.

There's nothing new about dismantling and destroying nuclear weapons according to an agreed timetable. The disarmament procedure and the mechanisms for verification are well-established, having been tried and tested through the implementation of previous treaties.[6]

Once nuclear abolition has been achieved, ongoing verification becomes less of an issue or "threat" to national security. **Countries that might have been reluctant to allow on-site inspections while nuclear weapons were still present at those sites are now more relaxed about it. "Surprise" inspections on short notice also become easier to accept.**

Test sites, missile launches, airplane and mobile launcher movements are all closely monitored by a global system of satellites and seismographs. The International Atomic Energy Agency (IAEA) also has sophisticated monitoring equipment and access to important sites along the supply chain required for making nuclear weapons.

Figure 26.3 On-site inspections

Soviet inspectors watch a US Pershing II missile be destroyed under the INF Treaty in 1989. PHOTO: Jose Lopez, Jr. Public Domain

Economic conversion

In our scenario, all the bombs and their delivery systems are gone from the face of the earth. The next step is to decommission or convert all remaining nuclear weapons facilities.

In the US, the military personnel who are connected directly or indirectly with the deployment of nuclear weapons are easily re-deployed to other responsibilities. Another 27,000 civilian employees and contractors working directly with nuclear weapons at two nuclear submarine bases, two air force bases, and three ballistic missile bases will need other work.[7]

There are a further 42,000 people working at the eight sites across the country where nuclear weapons are developed, tested, assembled and dismantled.[8] These are Sandia Labs and Los Alamos National Lab in New Mexico, Lawrence Livermore Lab in California, the Savannah River Site in South Carolina, the Pantex Plant in Texas, the Kansas City Plant in Missouri, the Nevada Test Site in Nevada, and the Y-12 complex in Tennessee.

And finally, there are approximately 70,000 people working for the 20 or so private companies[9] who make the warheads, missiles and components for US nuclear weapons and oversee most of the labs and complexes listed above. Most will need re-training and re-deployment to other tasks.

Figure 26.4 Jobs in the US Nuclear Weapons Industry[10]

Mapping nuclear weapons jobs to a green economy

By far the most common job qualification for nuclear weapons-related work is some kind of engineering degree and/or experience. These people have transferable skills that could be put to use in ways that do not involve the development or production of nuclear weapons. Some nuclear engineers will still be needed to design and carry out the safe dismantling of nuclear weapons and the means of verifying this process in different countries. And even without building more nuclear power plants,[11] the same skills are needed for the dismantling of the existing plants and disposal of all the radioactive waste.

These people are also urgently needed for jobs that have nothing to do with nuclear engineering. The world needs people who have the necessary skills in research, engineering, design, and many other technical areas to be able to meet the climate targets in the timescale required to prevent and/or mitigate global climate catastrophe, and to make the transition to a green economy affordable.

Job requirements for design and development positions in the nuclear weapons complex overlap extensively with the requirements for positions in green energy. Both require advanced degrees and industrial experience in the fields of engineering, nuclear engineering, computer science, systems architecture, mathematics, physics or chemistry. The skills required overlap in information technology, risk analysis. systems assessment, and computer science, modeling and simulation.[12]

A 2014 study in the UK[13] looked at the workforce requirements, job descriptions, transferable skills and locations of 170,000 people currently employed in the UK making weapons and their delivery systems. It mapped these against the 300,000 or more jobs that would be needed to build and maintain enough offshore wind farms and marine energy projects to put the UK on the path to net-zero carbon emissions.

The results were astounding. The study found a direct correlation between many of the existing skills used to build nuclear submarines, for example, and those that would be needed to build wave and tidal energy projects. Even more surprisingly, there was a direct correlation between the locations where these jobs would be based.

The study found, for example, that marine engineers and naval architects currently building a new generation of nuclear ballistic missile submarines for the UK at the Naval Shipyard in Burrow-on-Furness could switch over to designing and building the Morecambe Bay Tidal Barrage without even having to move house.

Similar studies in the US have looked at the massive potential for jobs in different parts of the country that could result from tapping wind, water and solar energy.[14] These have not yet been comprehensively mapped to the equivalent jobs or infrastructure currently absorbed by the military-industrial complex, but similar correlations to those in the UK are already apparent.

In our scenario, talented STEM experts are happy to shift their skills from building killing machines to building a healthy, sustainable future. Governments strive to provide salaries comparable to what these experts were earning making WMDs.

Disposal of fissile material

Prior to a "final" disposal, for which there is not yet an agreed-upon plan, the goal is to achieve the irreversible and highly secure dilution and isolation of the nuclear material inside the nuclear weapons (uranium, plutonium and tritium) so that this material cannot be re-used to make new nuclear weapons. This step is essential for ensuring that nuclear weapons have well and truly been eliminated.

So far, unfortunately, there is no known way to securely isolate these highly radioactive materials for the thousands of years needed to render them harmless. So even after diluting and securing the waste, we're not done with the story.

Our scenario clock goes back to 00:00:01am when the world has finally eliminated all nuclear weapons and all means of making them. Because the possibility will always remain that someone may try to build them again, the clock remains and the world must remain vigilant .

The future of the clock

In our scenario, the existential threat of nuclear war has now been eradicated as far as is humanly possible. The whole world can breathe much easier and move on to solving other crises, knowing that the world's nuclear stockpiles have been eliminated, the radioactive materials for making a weapon have been diluted and stored away, and all countries have committed themselves never to go back to the nuclear nightmare.

But, in addition to the waste problem, there's another danger. There will always remain the possibility, however slight, that one or more countries may renege on their promise, or that rogue forces we can't foresee build nuclear weapons again. Humanity will have to remain vigilant - forever. We leave our Doomsday Clock set at 23 hours 59 minutes and 59 seconds to midnight, as a reminder.

Figure 26.5 Achieving nuclear abolition – in summary

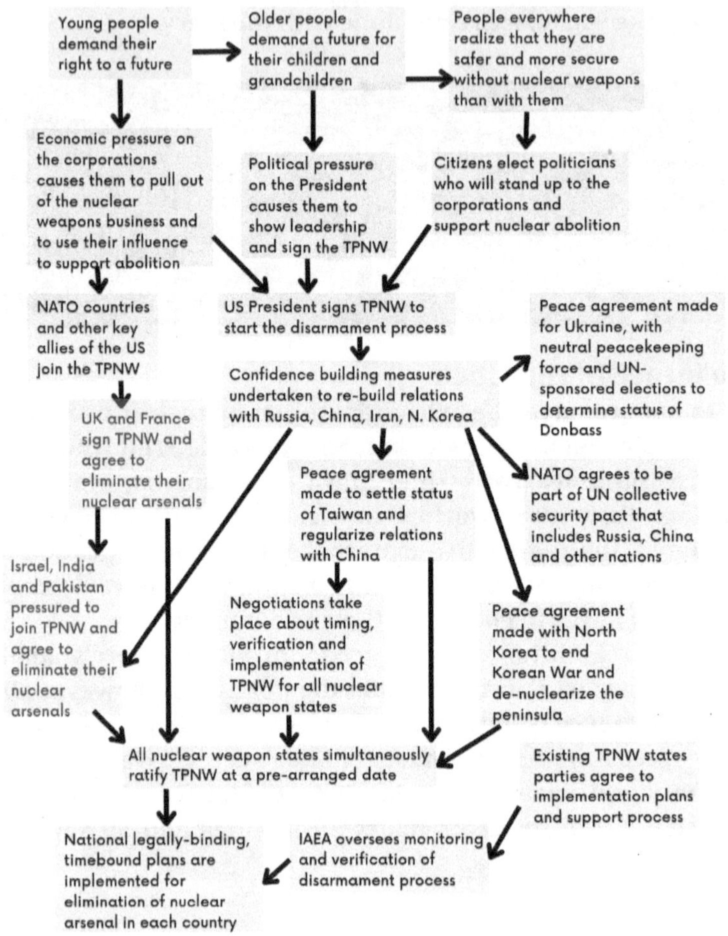

The whole premise of this book has been that it will take a lot of pressure, specifically pressure on the nuclear weapons companies, to reach the point where a US President will be willing to sign the TPNW – and then the other nuclear-armed countries will come on board. Everything described in the scenario is about building enough pressure to make that possible.

But there is an alternative scenario (in an alternative universe) where the President of the United States simply decides to abolish nuclear weapons, and no pressure is involved at all. It is possible, though not likely, that we are in that alternative universe right now, and that Donald Trump is serious about wanting to "denuclearize." That alternative scenario is the premise for the Epilogue that follows.

Epilogue – The Trump card

In the prologue to this scenario, we looked at ways that the Trump presidency is inadvertently helping to mobilize global opposition to nuclear weapons. But there's another possibility - that Trump might just decide to "denuclearize," before that global opposition is mobilized. Here's what it might look like.

The fundamental assumption of the scenario in this book is that significant political change cannot happen without a combination of powerful forces putting *pressure* on those with a vested interest in keeping things as they are (see Chapter 3). That has been the reality facing campaigners for social and political changes of all descriptions over many generations. As Frederick Douglass said more than 150 years ago, "Power concedes nothing without a demand."

The preceding chapters have shown that despite the enormous challenges facing campaigners for nuclear abolition, there *are* pressures that can realistically be brought to bear on the powerful forces that are determined to keep the nuclear enterprise alive - even if it means the rest of us are dead. A combination of international pressures stemming from the TPNW, coupled with domestic pressures on the nuclear weapons companies, especially in the United States, *could* result in the abolition of nuclear weapons.

This is not the only possible scenario for nuclear abolition. There are many other possible pathways, as we have suggested all through the book. However, one possible pathway involves the current US President and does *not* involve the application of any outside pressures. It relies entirely on his personality, his rebellion against following conventions, and his approach to international relations.

In the following "short-cut" scenario, Donald Trump gets the world to disarm, or to use his preferred vocabulary, to "denuclearize." It's a hugely unlikely scenario, for reasons which will become apparent, but it's not an impossibility. If we've learned one thing from Trump, it's that very, very unexpected things *can* happen.

In this new scenario, there's a ceremony in the White House. Presidents Donald Trump, Vladimir Putin and Xi Jinping sign an agreement committing the three countries to denuclearize. It says "A nuclear war cannot be won and must never be fought. So it is in the interest of our three great nations to dismantle our nuclear arsenals and work to ensure that the other six nations still possessing nuclear weapons also denuclearize as soon as possible. The world will be a much safer place for *all* of us when *none* of us have nuclear weapons."

How could this happen?

On January 23rd, 2025, just three days into his second term at the White House, Donald Trump made a surprise announcement in a video address to the annual World Economic Forum meeting in Davos, Switzerland: "We'd like to see denuclearization," he said. He went on to claim that he had been working with Putin during his previous term as President "on the denuclearization of our two countries," adding that "China would have to come along, too."[1]

Trump described Putin as being in favor of "cutting way back on nuclear." And he talked about getting the rest of the world to follow. "I want to see if we can denuclearize, and I think it's very possible... [President Putin] and I wanted to do it... and that would have been an unbelievable thing for the planet... I hope it can be started up again."

What exactly Trump meant by "denuclearizing" was not immediately clear, but he repeated his call for denuclearization talks with Russia and China a few weeks later, at a press briefing in the Oval Office on February 13, 2025. "There's no reason for us to be building brand new nuclear weapons. We already have so many," he said. "You could destroy the world 50 times over, 100 times over. And here we are building new nuclear weapons, and they're building nuclear weapons."[2]

Arms control experts and beltway think-tanks have been quick to suggest that what Trump really means is some kind of arms control agreement to replace the New START Treaty, which is set to expire at the beginning of 2026. That could mean, for instance, agreeing not to *increase* the ceiling set by the New START Treaty, signed by the US and Russia back in 2010.

That treaty limited the total number of deployed strategic nuclear warheads and bombs to 1,550 on each side – a "limit" that is still plenty enough to utterly destroy both countries and potentially the entire planet. The treaty did not limit the total number of "non-deployed" nuclear weapons held by each side, which includes bombs and warheads stored nearby and ready to put back on top of missiles or loaded onto bombers at any point.

The US has another 2,000 or so non-deployed warheads and Russia has an estimated 2,650. On top of these there are also "non-strategic" nuclear warheads and a large number of "retired" warheads supposedly awaiting dismantlement but still usable. That brings the total number of nuclear weapons currently in the combined US and Russian arsenals to around 10,600. The other seven nuclear nuclear-armed countries have an estimated 1,300 or so warheads between them, bringing the current world total to around 12,000 nuclear warheads.

Keeping the lid on any further expansion of the world's nuclear arsenals is the goal of non-proliferation efforts and of agreements like the New START treaty. That's not a bad thing, but it's hardly the same thing as abolishing nuclear weapons, and it's debatable whether it can be considered denuclearization.

The meaning of denuclearization

So which is it? While the arms control community interpreted Trump's "denuclearization" as some kind of arms control agreement, Trump himself has used the word before, and it meant abolition. When he called for the denuclearization of the Korean Peninsula during his first term as President, Trump was very clearly referring to the removal of *all* nuclear weapons from North Korea, as well as keeping US nuclear weapons out of South Korea.[3]

Denuclearization as a term was first used back in the 1950s, when the Foreign Minister of Poland put forward a plan for the denuclearization of Central Europe. In that context, denuclearization very clearly meant the removal of *all* nuclear weapons from the countries that bordered both sides of the so-called Iron Curtain.

Since then, denuclearization has been used synonymously with regional Nuclear-Free Zones that have been established by treaty to prohibit the stationing or use of nuclear weapons in any part of Africa, Latin America, Southeast Asia, Antarctica or the Pacific.

If Trump is proposing the denuclearization of the US and Russia, followed by China and the rest of the world, we should start from the assumption that he is not just talking about freezing nuclear arsenals at the levels they are right now, or negotiating new reductions. Denuclearization is about *deep cuts*, and potentially the complete *elimination* of nuclear arsenals altogether.

Even though there hasn't yet been any real possibility of disarmament talks between Trump and Putin or between Trump and Xi, the nuclear weapons industry has been worried. It has counted on bipartisan support from Congress and from every President in living memory without exception.

Why this may not materialize

Trump is undoubtedly under enormous pressure *not* to follow through with his ideas of denuclearization - pressure from his own military and national security advisors, from influential members of the Republican Party in Congress, and especially from heavyweights in the nuclear weapons industry. These people are determined to keep their nuclear gravy train running smoothly, and, as we have seen, they wield an enormous amount of power in Washington.

Trump's talk of denuclearization since re-entering the Oval Office in January 2025 does not match his approach during his first term. That was anything *but* conducive to nuclear abolition.

During his first administration (2017-2020), Trump undermined a number of existing arms control agreements. One of his first acts as President was to pull the US out of the Iran nuclear deal, or Joint Comprehensive Plan of Action, that had been negotiated together with the European Union, Russia and China to ensure that Iran would not develop its own nuclear weapons capability.

Next, in response to ongoing nuclear weapons testing by North Korea, President Trump threatened that country with "fire and fury like the world has never seen," the most public threat to use nuclear weapons by a President of the United States since President Kennedy threatened Khrushchev during the Cuban Missile Crisis of 1962.

Then, in 2019, Trump pulled the US out of the INF Treaty, a cornerstone of Cold War era arms control that led to the removal of over 2,500 nuclear weapons from the European continent.

In his first budget, President Trump insisted on substantial increases for developing new nuclear weapons, including a new, more "usable" low-yield submarine-launched nuclear weapon, the W-76-1, which went into production in 2018 and was deployed on US Trident submarines in 2019.

In May 2020, President Trump announced that the US would pull out of the Open Skies Treaty that allows countries to fly unarmed surveillance flights over each other in order to verify compliance with other treaties and reduce tensions. And in September 2020, the Trump administration asked the military to assess how quickly it could pull nuclear weapons out of storage and load them onto bombers and submarines if the New START treaty with Russia was allowed to expire.[4]

Given that history from his first term, and the fact that Donald Trump loves "his" military and is above all an extreme nationalist, it seems hard to imagine him negotiating denuclearization with Russia or China. On the other hand...

Why Trump might just do it

Trump's approach to international relations is to bargain with and bully other countries to get what he wants from them, rather than to consider options that might work for, or even benefit, all the parties involved. Nevertheless, those very characteristics could potentially work in favor of getting an agreement with Russia and China for the abolition of nuclear weapons.

Trump would, after all, only be doing this to "make America great again." And because he believes he is uniquely qualified to make decisions on behalf of the United States and does not trust "experts" to advise him, he is unlikely to listen to the national security and arms control experts who tell him that this is not how diplomacy is done.

There are at least four arguments for denuclearization/abolition that Trump might take seriously:

1. Nuclear weapons are too expensive. Trump wants to make drastic cuts to the federal budget, and along with denuclearization, he is talking about cutting the budget of the Pentagon, which is the most expensive government department by far, accounting for more than 60% of the total federal discretionary budget.[5]

As Elon Musk and Vivek Ramaswamy pointed out in the *Wall Street Journal* before Trump took office, the Pentagon is awash with cost overruns, and it has failed numerous audits because billions of dollars cannot be accounted for.[6]

And one of the biggest expenditures *within* the Pentagon budget is for a whole new generation of nuclear weapons. Since these costs are spread across a large number of line items, not only in the DOD budget but also in the DOE budget, it's notoriously difficult to know exactly how much nuclear weapons are costing. According to the

Congressional Budget Office, however, the total cost for nuclear weapons over the next three decades is expected to be at least $1.7 trillion. That includes the cost of upgrading and "modernizing" every element of the US nuclear weapons arsenal.

Given that this cost goes up considerably every time it has been calculated, the true cost is likely to end up significantly higher than that. So it is not at all unreasonable to think that Trump could be looking at the nuclear weapons budget as a place to cut spending – especially if these weapons can't even be used.

2. Nuclear weapons cannot be used to win wars. During his first term as President, Donald Trump was quoted as asking: "*Why do we have nuclear weapons if we can't use them?*"[7] That could be interpreted as "since we have them, we should use them," and at the time, many insiders were afraid that that was what he meant. He must have at least contemplated using nuclear weapons when he was dealing with Kim Jong-un of North Korea.

But it could also be interpreted as "why are we paying for something we can never use?" That would reflect the reality that the US *cannot* use nuclear weapons – certainly not in the same way as it can use conventional weapons to bomb potential missile sites, assassinate military commanders or drive out terrorist cells.

Nuclear weapons are far too big and clumsy to be used on the battlefield. They are designed to destroy entire cities or hardened nuclear missile silos and command bunkers deep underground. And any use of these weapons runs the risk of escalation to an all-out nuclear war in which millions, if not billions, would die, and no one would emerge victorious.

As we've said, even if US nuclear weapons were used as far away as North Korea or China, the continental US would suffer along with the rest of the world from radioactive fallout circling the globe in the upper atmosphere and eventually raining back down, not to mention potential famine from crop failures as soot blocks the sun.

3. Nuclear weapons are a grave threat to national security. A key argument that Trump may well take seriously is that the existence of nuclear weapons actually threatens the national security of the United States far more than the possession of them protects us. The United States has the most advanced, most powerful conventional (non-nuclear) armed forces in the world, by far.

None of the country's potential adversaries can come close to threatening the United States with their conventional forces. It is *only their nuclear weapons* that pose any threat at all to the United States.

With nuclear weapons, even an extremely poor country like North Korea is capable of threatening the United States.

And the longer these weapons exist, the more other countries are going to want them and are going to find a way to acquire them, making the United States increasingly insecure as a result. With no nuclear weapons anywhere in the world, the United States would be *significantly* more secure than it is today.

The whole rationale for maintaining an arsenal of nuclear weapons is supposedly because they are the ultimate deterrent. And yet possession of nuclear weapons by the United States clearly did not deter Russia from invading Ukraine, a close US ally and potential NATO member. Nor has Russia's possession of nuclear weapons deterred the United States and other NATO countries from arming and supporting Ukraine over the past three years.

Since 1945, the US has fought wars in Korea, Viet Nam, Lebanon, Libya, Kosovo, Somalia, Afghanistan, Iraq, Syria and elsewhere. Possession of nuclear weapons did not "deter" any of those wars, nor indeed did possession of nuclear weapons ensure that the US won any of those wars. There are many more examples of nuclear-armed countries suffering attacks from conventional weapons and terrorist attacks, including 9/11.

The trouble with threats is that they're meaningless unless they're carried out. The longer nuclear weapons are *not* used, the less credible they become as a threat. But nuclear threats are never carried out for the very simple reason that to do so would be an act of suicide. What sane political leader would make that choice?

4. Trump wants the Nobel Peace Prize. Other US Presidents (and notoriously, Henry Kissinger) have won it, including Barack Obama. (Obama's prize was clearly for his promise to "seek the peace of a world without nuclear weapons," even though, unfortunately, he failed to deliver on that.)

Donald Trump has made it clear on several occasions that he wants the Nobel. If he can arrange the denuclearization of the world after so many other Presidents have failed to achieve it, he would certainly be considered worthy of it.

Would Trump use the TPNW?

Whether Trump would move to denuclearize *through the TPNW*, however, is more doubtful. The TPNW would require the US to submit a plan for eliminating its nuclear arsenal for approval by the other countries in the treaty. It seems unlikely that any country already party to the TPNW would oppose any plan from the US to actually do what the treaty was set up to achieve. But Trump might not want to subject himself to being dependent on other countries to "approve" his plan.

Nevertheless, as we have stated throughout this book, the TPNW is the only treaty that ensures the complete elimination of nuclear weapons globally, and there is unlikely to be another one. Therefore, what seems most likely in the Trump-led scenario is that instead of signing the TPNW prior to denuclearization, the US and other nuclear-armed nations would sign the TPNW *after* completing the denuclearization process, according to the option described in Article 4 (1) of the treaty.

A possible denuclearization agreement

Why would Russia *or* China agree to denuclearize on Trump's terms? What would a denuclearization agreement with Russia and China potentially look like, and how might it come about? There are, of course, endless possibilities here.

Although Russia and China each have their separate reasons for holding onto nuclear weapons (see Chapters 24 and 25), they are also both subject to the same considerations listed above for Trump. It's enormously costly to continue their nuclear weapons programs just to keep up with the United States. Neither country wants to use up their national resources on an arms race if they can put those opportunity costs into other government programs.

In Chapter 24, we explored how China has little to fear from the US *apart* from their nuclear weapons, so if the US gives them up, China is almost certain to join them. In Chapter 25, we looked at the more complicated calculus for Russia, since their nuclear weapons serve the purpose of keeping the US and other NATO countries in Western Europe at bay.

In this version of the scenario, as a necessary precursor to a denuclearization agreement, there would have to be a negotiated ceasefire in Ukraine that includes security guarantees for both Ukraine and Russia. This could mean a peacekeeping force made up of military units from India and China, for example, or from African and Latin American countries like Nigeria, South Africa, Brazil and/or Argentina, but definitely *not* from NATO.

However the Ukraine ceasefire is agreed, and whoever or whatever is put in place to maintain it, the likelihood is that NATO will be significantly sidelined, and Ukraine will have to give up its

ambitions to join NATO. Other European countries, especially the UK, won't like that at all, but they will likely have to accept it as the new reality.

With a weakened NATO and a more friendly US under Trump, Putin is much more likely to see the pros of nuclear abolition outweighing the cons.

Next possible steps

In this short-cut scenario, the US, Russia and China sign an agreement that slowly but surely reduces each of their nuclear arsenals down to zero. But what about the other six nuclear-armed countries?

Clearly, this is one of the weak links in this short-cut scenario. Trump may be able to get the other strongmen on board with his denuclearization project, but it could also backfire on him.

The UK and France might double down on their resolve to take military matters into their own hands and abandon the US to its own devices. But they will also be under pressure to go along with Trump, for similar reasons already described in chapter 22.

North Korea will still need a final peace agreement ending the Korean War, and other measures in place to guarantee its security. But North Korea will also jump at the opportunity to eliminate its nuclear arsenal when it knows that the US is doing so (Chapter 24).

India and Pakistan will still need an agreement about Kashmir before they are willing to disarm (Chapter 23). But Trump, Putin and Xi together can put a lot of pressure on them and also offer them some incentives.

And finally, there's Israel. Israel is loath to give up its nuclear weapons without a long-term regional security arrangement. But if Trump can arrange deals with Russia and China, maybe he can figure out a way to also arrange a deal with Benjamin Netanyahu. If he can do that, then the abolition of nuclear weapons is complete.

Of the two scenarios, one is more realistic than the other: the one based on *pressure*. But so far, the pressures exerted by voters, peers, influencers, and even foreign governments have not been sufficient to force politicians in the nuclear-armed countries to support nuclear abolition.

The Treaty on the Prohibition of Nuclear Weapons provides the legal tools that can threaten the whole profit-making business model of this industry. It supports efforts by consumers, investors, suppliers, workers, cities, states, and whole countries to stigmatize the complicit corporations and damage their bottom lines.

Is it realistic to think that these pressures, taken together, could tip the balance and force the nuclear weapons industry to use its power over politicians to finally achieve nuclear abolition? What other scenarios might there be?

There's one scenario that is definitely *not* realistic: the one where we continue to tolerate the existence of nuclear weapons on the planet – and expect to survive.

APPENDICES

Appendix I: Treaty on the Prohibition of Nuclear Weapons

The States Parties to this Treaty,

Determined to contribute to the realization of the purposes and principles of the Charter of the United Nations,

Deeply concerned about the catastrophic humanitarian consequences that would result from any use of nuclear weapons, and recognizing the consequent need to completely eliminate such weapons, which remains the only way to guarantee that nuclear weapons are never used again under any circumstances,

Mindful of the risks posed by the continued existence of nuclear weapons, including from any nuclear-weapon detonation by accident, miscalculation or design, and emphasizing that these risks concern the security of all humanity, and that all States share the responsibility to prevent any use of nuclear weapons,

Cognizant that the catastrophic consequences of nuclear weapons cannot be adequately addressed, transcend national borders, pose grave implications for human survival, the environment, socioeconomic development, the global economy, food security and the health of current and future generations, and have a disproportionate impact on women and girls, including as a result of ionizing radiation,

Acknowledging the ethical imperatives for nuclear disarmament and the urgency of achieving and maintaining a nuclear-weapon-free world, which is a global public good of the highest order, serving both national and collective security interests,

Mindful of the unacceptable suffering of and harm caused to the victims of the use of nuclear weapons (hibakusha), as well as of those affected by the testing of nuclear weapons,

Recognizing the disproportionate impact of nuclear-weapon activities on indigenous peoples,

Reaffirming the need for all States at all times to comply with applicable international law, including international humanitarian law and international human rights law,

Basing themselves on the principles and rules of international humanitarian law, in particular the principle that the right of parties to an armed conflict to choose methods or means of warfare is not unlimited, the rule of distinction, the prohibition against indiscriminate attacks, the rules on proportionality and precautions in attack, the prohibition on the use of weapons of a nature to cause superfluous injury or unnecessary suffering, and the rules for the protection of the natural environment,

Considering that any use of nuclear weapons would be contrary to the rules of international law applicable in armed conflict, in particular the principles and rules of international humanitarian law,

Reaffirming that any use of nuclear weapons would also be abhorrent to the principles of humanity and the dictates of public conscience,

Recalling that, in accordance with the Charter of the United Nations, States must refrain in their international relations from the threat or use of force against the territorial integrity or political independence of any State, or in any other manner inconsistent with the Purposes of the United Nations, and that the establishment and maintenance of international peace and security are to be promoted with the least diversion for armaments of the world's human and economic resources,

Recalling also the first resolution of the General Assembly of the United Nations, adopted on 24 January 1946, and subsequent resolutions which call for the elimination of nuclear weapons,

Concerned by the slow pace of nuclear disarmament, the continued reliance on nuclear weapons in military and security concepts, doctrines and policies, and the waste of economic and human resources on programmes for the production, maintenance and modernization of nuclear weapons,

Recognizing that a legally binding prohibition of nuclear weapons constitutes an important contribution towards the achievement and maintenance of a world free of nuclear weapons, including the irreversible, verifiable and transparent elimination of nuclear weapons, and determined to act towards that end,

Determined to act with a view to achieving effective progress towards general and complete disarmament under strict and effective international control,

Reaffirming that there exists an obligation to pursue in good faith and bring to a conclusion negotiations leading to nuclear disarmament in all its aspects under strict and effective international control,

Reaffirming also that the full and effective implementation of the Treaty on the Non-Proliferation of Nuclear Weapons, which serves as the cornerstone of the nuclear disarmament and non-proliferation regime, has a vital role to play in promoting international peace and security,

Recognizing the vital importance of the Comprehensive Nuclear-Test-Ban Treaty and its verification regime as a core element of the nuclear disarmament and non-proliferation regime,

Reaffirming the conviction that the establishment of the internationally recognized nuclear-weapon-free zones on the basis of arrangements freely arrived at among the States of the region concerned enhances global and regional peace and security, strengthens the nuclear non-proliferation regime and contributes towards realizing the objective of nuclear disarmament,

Emphasizing that nothing in this Treaty shall be interpreted as affecting the inalienable right of its States Parties to develop research, production and use of nuclear energy for peaceful purposes without discrimination,

Recognizing that the equal, full and effective participation of both women and men is an essential factor for the promotion and attainment of sustainable peace and security, and committed to supporting and strengthening the effective participation of women in nuclear disarmament,

Recognizing also the importance of peace and disarmament education in all its aspects and of raising awareness of the risks and consequences of nuclear weapons for current and future generations, and committed to the dissemination of the principles and norms of this Treaty,

Stressing the role of public conscience in the furthering of the principles of humanity as evidenced by the call for the total elimination of nuclear weapons, and recognizing the efforts to that end undertaken by the United Nations, the International Red Cross and Red Crescent Movement, other international and regional organizations, non-governmental organizations, religious leaders, parliamentarians, academics and the hibakusha,

Have agreed as follows:

ARTICLE 1

Prohibitions

1. Each State Party undertakes never under any circumstances to:

(a) Develop, test, produce, manufacture, otherwise acquire, possess or stockpile nuclear weapons or other nuclear explosive devices;

(b) Transfer to any recipient whatsoever nuclear weapons or other nuclear explosive devices or control over such weapons or explosive devices directly or indirectly;

(c) Receive the transfer of or control over nuclear weapons or other nuclear explosive devices directly or indirectly;

(d) Use or threaten to use nuclear weapons or other nuclear explosive devices;

(e) Assist, encourage or induce, in any way, anyone to engage in any activity prohibited to a State Party under this Treaty;

(f) Seek or receive any assistance, in any way, from anyone to engage in any activity prohibited to a State Party under this Treaty;

(g) Allow any stationing, installation or deployment of any nuclear weapons or other nuclear explosive devices in its territory or at any place under its jurisdiction or control.

ARTICLE 2

Declarations

1. Each State Party shall submit to the Secretary-General of the United Nations, not later than 30 days after this Treaty enters into force for that State Party, a declaration in which it shall:

(a) Declare whether it owned, possessed or controlled nuclear weapons or nuclear explosive devices and eliminated its nuclear-weapon programme, including the elimination or irreversible conversion of all nuclear-weapons-related facilities, prior to the entry into force of this Treaty for that State Party;

(b) Notwithstanding Article 1 (a), declare whether it owns, possesses or controls any nuclear weapons or other nuclear explosive devices;

(c) Notwithstanding Article 1 (g), declare whether there are any nuclear weapons or other nuclear explosive devices in its territory or in any place under its jurisdiction or control that are owned, possessed or controlled by another State.

2. The Secretary-General of the United Nations shall transmit all such declarations received to the States Parties.

ARTICLE 3

Safeguards

1. Each State Party to which Article 4, paragraph 1 or 2, does not apply shall, at a minimum, maintain its International Atomic Energy Agency safeguards obligations in force at the time of entry into force of this Treaty, without prejudice to any additional relevant instruments that it may adopt in the future.

2. Each State Party to which Article 4, paragraph 1 or 2, does not apply that has not yet done so shall conclude with the International Atomic Energy Agency and bring into force a comprehensive safeguards agreement (INFCIRC/153 (Corrected)). Negotiation of such agreement shall commence within 180 days from the entry into force of this Treaty for that State Party. The agreement shall enter into force no later than 18 months from the

entry into force of this Treaty for that State Party. Each State Party shall thereafter maintain such obligations, without prejudice to any additional relevant instruments that it may adopt in the future.

ARTICLE 4
Towards the total elimination of nuclear weapons

1. Each State Party that after 7 July 2017 owned, possessed or controlled nuclear weapons or other nuclear explosive devices and eliminated its nuclear-weapon programme, including the elimination or irreversible conversion of all nuclear- weapons-related facilities, prior to the entry into force of this Treaty for it, shall cooperate with the competent international authority designated pursuant to paragraph 6 of this Article for the purpose of verifying the irreversible elimination of its nuclear-weapon programme. The competent international authority shall report to the States Parties. Such a State Party shall conclude a safeguards agreement with the International Atomic Energy Agency sufficient to provide credible assurance of the non-diversion of declared nuclear material from peaceful nuclear activities and of the absence of undeclared nuclear material or activities in that State Party as a whole. Negotiation of such agreement shall commence within 180 days from the entry into force of this Treaty for that State Party. The agreement shall enter into force no later than 18 months from the entry into force of this Treaty for that State Party. That State Party shall thereafter, at a minimum, maintain these safeguards obligations, without prejudice to any additional relevant instruments that it may adopt in the future.

2. Notwithstanding Article 1 (a), each State Party that owns, possesses or controls nuclear weapons or other nuclear explosive devices shall immediately remove them from operational status, and destroy them as soon as possible but not later than a deadline to be determined by the first meeting of States Parties, in accordance with a legally binding, time-bound plan for the verified and irreversible elimination of that State Party's nuclear-weapon programme, including the elimination or irreversible conversion of all nuclear-weapons-related facilities. The State Party, no later than 60 days after the entry into force of this Treaty for that State Party, shall submit this plan to the States Parties or to a competent international authority designated by the States Parties. The plan shall then be negotiated with the competent international authority, which shall

submit it to the subsequent meeting of States Parties or review conference, whichever comes first, for approval in accordance with its rules of procedure.

3. A State Party to which paragraph 2 above applies shall conclude a safeguards agreement with the International Atomic Energy Agency sufficient to provide credible assurance of the non-diversion of declared nuclear material from peaceful nuclear activities and of the absence of undeclared nuclear material or activities in the State as a whole. Negotiation of such agreement shall commence no later than the date upon which implementation of the plan referred to in paragraph 2 is completed. The agreement shall enter into force no later than 18 months after the date of initiation of negotiations. That State Party shall thereafter, at a minimum, maintain these safeguards obligations, without prejudice to any additional relevant instruments that it may adopt in the future. Following the entry into force of the agreement referred to in this paragraph, the State Party shall submit to the Secretary-General of the United Nations a final declaration that it has fulfilled its obligations under this Article.

4. Notwithstanding Article 1 (b) and (g), each State Party that has any nuclear weapons or other nuclear explosive devices in its territory or in any place under its jurisdiction or control that are owned, possessed or controlled by another State shall ensure the prompt removal of such weapons, as soon as possible but not later than a deadline to be determined by the first meeting of States Parties. Upon the removal of such weapons or other explosive devices, that State Party shall submit to the Secretary-General of the United Nations a declaration that it has fulfilled its obligations under this Article.

5. Each State Party to which this Article applies shall submit a report to each meeting of States Parties and each review conference on the progress made towards the implementation of its obligations under this Article, until such time as they are fulfilled.

6. The States Parties shall designate a competent international authority or authorities to negotiate and verify the irreversible elimination of nuclear-weapons programmes, including the elimination or irreversible conversion of all nuclear- weapons-related facilities in accordance with paragraphs 1, 2 and 3 of this Article. In the event that such a designation has not been made prior to the entry into force of this Treaty for a State Party to which paragraph 1 or 2 of this Article applies, the Secretary-General of the

United Nations shall convene an extraordinary meeting of States Parties to take any decisions that may be required.

ARTICLE 5

National implementation

1. Each State Party shall adopt the necessary measures to implement its obligations under this Treaty.

2. Each State Party shall take all appropriate legal, administrative and other measures, including the imposition of penal sanctions, to prevent and suppress any activity prohibited to a State Party under this Treaty undertaken by persons or on territory under its jurisdiction or control.

ARTICLE 6

Victim assistance and environmental remediation

1. Each State Party shall, with respect to individuals under its jurisdiction who are affected by the use or testing of nuclear weapons, in accordance with applicable international humanitarian and human rights law, adequately provide age- and gender-sensitive assistance, without discrimination, including medical care, rehabilitation and psychological support, as well as provide for their social and economic inclusion.

2. Each State Party, with respect to areas under its jurisdiction or control contaminated as a result of activities related to the testing or use of nuclear weapons or other nuclear explosive devices, shall take necessary and appropriate measures towards the environmental remediation of areas so contaminated.

3. The obligations under paragraphs 1 and 2 above shall be without prejudice to the duties and obligations of any other States under international law or bilateral agreements.

ARTICLE 7

International cooperation and assistance

1. Each State Party shall cooperate with other States Parties to facilitate the implementation of this Treaty.

2. In fulfilling its obligations under this Treaty, each State Party shall have the right to seek and receive assistance, where feasible, from other States Parties.

3. Each State Party in a position to do so shall provide technical, material and financial assistance to States Parties affected by nuclear-weapons use or testing, to further the implementation of this Treaty.

4. Each State Party in a position to do so shall provide assistance for the victims of the use or testing of nuclear weapons or other nuclear explosive devices.

5. Assistance under this Article may be provided, inter alia, through the United Nations system, international, regional or national organizations or institutions, non-governmental organizations or institutions, the International Committee of the Red Cross, the International Federation of Red Cross and Red Crescent Societies, or national Red Cross and Red Crescent Societies, or on a bilateral basis.

6. Without prejudice to any other duty or obligation that it may have under international law, a State Party that has used or tested nuclear weapons or any other nuclear explosive devices shall have a responsibility to provide adequate assistance to affected States Parties, for the purpose of victim assistance and environmental remediation.

ARTICLE 8

Meeting of States Parties

1. The States Parties shall meet regularly in order to consider and, where necessary, take decisions in respect of any matter with regard to the application or implementation of this Treaty, in accordance with its relevant provisions, and on further measures for nuclear disarmament, including:

(a) The implementation and status of this Treaty;

(b) Measures for the verified, time-bound and irreversible elimination of nuclear-weapon programmes, including additional protocols to this Treaty;

(c) Any other matters pursuant to and consistent with the provisions of this Treaty.

2. The first meeting of States Parties shall be convened by the Secretary- General of the United Nations within one year of the entry into force of this Treaty. Further meetings of States Parties shall be convened by the Secretary-General of the United Nations on a biennial basis, unless otherwise agreed by the States Parties. The meeting of States Parties shall adopt its rules of procedure at its first session. Pending their adoption, the rules of procedure of the United Nations conference to negotiate a legally binding instrument to prohibit nuclear weapons, leading towards their total elimination, shall apply.

3. Extraordinary meetings of States Parties shall be convened, as may be deemed necessary, by the Secretary-General of the United Nations, at the written request of any State Party provided that this request is supported by at least one third of the States Parties.

4. After a period of five years following the entry into force of this Treaty, the Secretary-General of the United Nations shall convene a conference to review the operation of the Treaty and the progress in achieving the purposes of the Treaty. The Secretary-General of the United Nations shall convene further review conferences at intervals of six years with the same objective, unless otherwise agreed by the States Parties.

5. States not party to this Treaty, as well as the relevant entities of the United Nations system, other relevant international organizations or institutions, regional organizations, the International Committee of the Red Cross, the International Federation of Red Cross and Red Crescent Societies and relevant non-governmental organizations, shall be invited to attend the meetings of States Parties and the review conferences as observers.

ARTICLE 9

Costs

1. The costs of the meetings of States Parties, the review conferences and the extraordinary meetings of States Parties shall be borne by the States Parties and States not party to this Treaty participating therein as observers, in accordance with the United Nations scale of assessment adjusted appropriately.

2. The costs incurred by the Secretary-General of the United Nations in the circulation of declarations under Article 2, reports under Article 4 and proposed amendments under Article 10 of this

Treaty shall be borne by the States Parties in accordance with the United Nations scale of assessment adjusted appropriately.

3. The cost related to the implementation of verification measures required under Article 4 as well as the costs related to the destruction of nuclear weapons or other nuclear explosive devices, and the elimination of nuclear-weapon programmes, including the elimination or conversion of all nuclear-weapons-related facilities, should be borne by the States Parties to which they apply.

ARTICLE 10

Amendments

1. At any time after the entry into force of this Treaty, any State Party may propose amendments to the Treaty. The text of a proposed amendment shall be communicated to the Secretary-General of the United Nations, who shall circulate it to all States Parties and shall seek their views on whether to consider the proposal. If a majority of the States Parties notify the Secretary-General of the United Nations no later than 90 days after its circulation that they support further consideration of the proposal, the proposal shall be considered at the next meeting of States Parties or review conference, whichever comes first.

2. A meeting of States Parties or a review conference may agree upon amendments which shall be adopted by a positive vote of a majority of two thirds of the States Parties. The Depositary shall communicate any adopted amendment to all States Parties.

3. The amendment shall enter into force for each State Party that deposits its instrument of ratification or acceptance of the amendment 90 days following the deposit of such instruments of ratification or acceptance by a majority of the States Parties at the time of adoption. Thereafter, it shall enter into force for any other State Party 90 days following the deposit of its instrument of ratification or acceptance of the amendment.

ARTICLE 11

Settlement of disputes

1. When a dispute arises between two or more States Parties relating to the interpretation or application of this Treaty, the parties concerned shall consult together with a view to the settlement of the dispute by negotiation or by other peaceful means of the parties'

choice in accordance with Article 33 of the Charter of the United Nations.

2. The meeting of States Parties may contribute to the settlement of the dispute, including by offering its good offices, calling upon the States Parties concerned to start the settlement procedure of their choice and recommending a time limit for any agreed procedure, in accordance with the relevant provisions of this Treaty and the Charter of the United Nations.

ARTICLE 12

Universality

Each State Party shall encourage States not party to this Treaty to sign, ratify, accept, approve or accede to the Treaty, with the goal of universal adherence of all States to the Treaty.

ARTICLE 13

Signature

This Treaty shall be open for signature to all States at United Nations Headquarters in New York as from 20 September 2017.

ARTICLE 14

Ratification, acceptance, approval or accession

This Treaty shall be subject to ratification, acceptance or approval by signatory States. The Treaty shall be open for accession.

ARTICLE 15

Entry into force

1. This Treaty shall enter into force 90 days after the fiftieth instrument of ratification, acceptance, approval or accession has been deposited.

2. For any State that deposits its instrument of ratification, acceptance, approval or accession after the date of the deposit of the fiftieth instrument of ratification, acceptance, approval or accession, this Treaty shall enter into force 90 days after the date on which that State has deposited its instrument of ratification, acceptance, approval or accession.

ARTICLE 16

Reservations

The Articles of this Treaty shall not be subject to reservations.

ARTICLE 17

Duration and withdrawal

1. This Treaty shall be of unlimited duration.

2. Each State Party shall, in exercising its national sovereignty, have the right to withdraw from this Treaty if it decides that extraordinary events related to the subject matter of the Treaty have jeopardized the supreme interests of its country. It shall give notice of such withdrawal to the Depositary. Such notice shall include a statement of the extraordinary events that it regards as having jeopardized its supreme interests.

3. Such withdrawal shall only take effect 12 months after the date of the receipt of the notification of withdrawal by the Depositary. If, however, on the expiry of that 12-month period, the withdrawing State Party is a party to an armed conflict, the State Party shall continue to be bound by the obligations of this Treaty and of any additional protocols until it is no longer party to an armed conflict.

ARTICLE 18

Relationship with other agreements

The implementation of this Treaty shall not prejudice obligations undertaken by States Parties with regard to existing international agreements, to which they are party, where those obligations are consistent with the Treaty.

ARTICLE 19

Depositary

The Secretary-General of the United Nations is hereby designated as the Depositary of this Treaty.

ARTICLE 20

Authentic texts

The Arabic, Chinese, English, French, Russian and Spanish texts of this Treaty shall be equally authentic.

DONE at New York, this seventh day of July, two thousand and seventeen.

Appendix II: Ireland Prohibition of Nuclear Weapons Act

PROHIBITION OF NUCLEAR WEAPONS ACT 2019

An Act to give effect to the Treaty on the Prohibition of Nuclear Weapons done at New York on 7 July 2017 and for those purposes to provide for offences relating to acts prohibited by that Treaty; and to provide for related matters. [11th December, 2019]

Be it enacted by the Oireachtas as follows:

Definitions

1. In this Act—

"act" includes omission and a reference to the committing of an act includes a reference to the making of an omission;

"hostile purpose" means, in relation to a nuclear weapon or other nuclear explosive device, for the purpose of causing, or being likely to cause, death or serious injury to any person or substantial damage to property or the environment;

"nuclear weapon or other nuclear explosive device" means any weapon or other explosive device capable of releasing nuclear energy that is designed for a hostile purpose or for use in armed conflict, and includes such a weapon or device in unassembled or partly assembled forms but does not include the means of transport or delivery of such a weapon or device if separable from, and not an indivisible part of, such a weapon or device;

"transfer" means, in relation to a nuclear weapon or other nuclear explosive device—

(a) the physical transfer or movement of a nuclear weapon or other nuclear explosive device, or
(b) the transfer of title to, or control over, a nuclear weapon or other nuclear explosive device;

"Treaty" means the Treaty on the Prohibition of Nuclear Weapons done at New York on 7 July 2017, the text of which is set out in the Schedule for convenience of reference.

Offences

2. (1) It shall be an offence for a person to—

(a) develop, produce, manufacture, acquire or possess,
(b) transfer, directly or indirectly, to any person,
(c) receive the transfer, directly or indirectly, of,
(d) use or threaten to use, or
(e) station, install or deploy,

a nuclear weapon or other nuclear explosive device.

(2) A person who assists, encourages or induces the commission of an offence under *subsection (1)* shall be guilty of an offence.

(3) A person who seeks or receives assistance from any person to commit an offence under *subsection (1)* shall be guilty of an offence.

(4) In proceedings for an offence under this Act, a weapon or other explosive device capable of releasing nuclear energy is presumed to be designed for a hostile purpose or for use in armed conflict unless the court or jury, as the case may be, is satisfied, having regard to the whole of the evidence, that there is a reasonable doubt that it is so designed.

Offences outside State

3. (1) A person who, in a place outside the State, commits an act that would, if the act occurred in the State, constitute an offence under section 2, shall be guilty of an offence if—

    (a) the act is committed on board an Irish ship within the meaning of section 9 of the Mercantile Marine Act 1955,
    (b) the act is committed on board an aircraft registered in the State, or
    (c) the person is a member of the Defence Forces.

(2) A person to whom *subsection (1)* applies who attempts, in a place outside the State, to commit an offence to which that subsection refers shall be guilty of an offence.

(3) Proceedings for an offence under this section may be taken in any place in the State and the offence may for all incidental purposes be treated as having been committed in that place.

Penalties

4. A person guilty of an offence under section 2 or 3 shall be liable on conviction on

indictment to—

    (a) a fine, or
    (b) imprisonment for life or such lesser term of imprisonment as the court may determine,

or both.

Double jeopardy

5. (1) Where a person has been acquitted of an offence in a place outside the State, he or she shall not be proceeded against for an offence under this Act consisting of the alleged act or acts constituting the first-mentioned offence.

(2) Where a person has been convicted of an offence in a place outside the State, he or she shall not be proceeded against for an offence under this Act consisting of the act Or acts constituting the first-mentioned offence.

Offences by body corporate

6. (1) Where an offence under this Act is committed by a body corporate and it is proved that the offence was committed with the consent or connivance, or was attributable to any wilful neglect, of a person who was a director, manager, secretary or other officer of the body corporate, or a person purporting to act in that capacity, that person shall, as well as the body corporate, be guilty of an offence and may be liable to be proceeded against and punished as if he or she were guilty of the first-mentioned offence.

(2) Where the affairs of a body corporate are managed by its members, *subsection (1)* shall apply in relation to the acts and defaults of a member in connection with his or her functions of management as if he or she were a director or manager of the body Corporate.

Short title and commencement

7. (1) This Act may be cited as the Prohibition of Nuclear Weapons Act 2019.

(2) This Act shall come into operation on such day or days as the Minister for Foreign Affairs and Trade may by order or orders appoint either generally or with reference to any particular purpose or provision and different days may be so appointed for different purposes or different provisions.

Appendix III: Swiss Federal War Materiel Act (part)

Federal Act on War Materiel (War Mat Act, WMA)

of 13 December 1996 (Status as of 1 September 2023)

The Federal Assembly of the Swiss Confederation,

based on the Articles 54 paragraph 1 and 107 paragraph 2 of the Federal Constitution[1, 2]

and having considered the Federal Council Dispatch dated 15 February 19953,

decrees:

Chapter 1 General Provisions

Art. 1 Purpose

This Act has as its aim the fulfilment of Switzerland's international obligations and the respect of its foreign policy principles by means of controlling the manufacture and transfer of war materiel and related technology, while at the same time maintaining an industrial capacity in Switzerland that is adapted to the requirements of its national defence.

Art. 2 Principles

The following require authorisation by the Confederation:

a. the manufacture of war materiel;

b. the trade in war materiel;

c. the brokerage of war materiel;

d. the import, export and transit of war materiel;

e. the transfer of intellectual property, including know-how, and the granting of related rights, provided this relates to war materiel and is intended for private individuals or legal entities that have their domicile or headquarters abroad.

- - - - -

Chapter 2 Prohibited War Materiel[6]

Art. 7 Nuclear, biological and chemical weapons

1 It is prohibited:

a. to develop, produce, broker, acquire, transfer to anyone, import, export, carry in transit, or store nuclear, biological or chemical weapons (NBC weapons) or to possess them in any other way;
b. to incite anyone to carry out an act mentioned in letter a above;
c. to assist anyone to carry out an act mentioned in letter a above.

2 The foregoing prohibition does not apply to acts that are intended:

a. to enable the destruction of NBC weapons by the agencies responsible therefor; or
b. to provide protection against the effects of NBC weapons or to combat such effects.

3 The prohibition also applies to acts carried out abroad, irrespective of the law at the place of commission, if:

a. the acts violate international law agreements to which Switzerland is a party; and
b. the perpetrator is Swiss or is domiciled in Switzerland.

- - - - -

Art. 8*b*[14] Prohibition of direct financing

1 The direct financing of the development, manufacture or acquisition of prohibited war materiel is itself prohibited.

2 Direct financing within the meaning of this Act is the direct granting of credits, loans or gifts or comparable financial advantages in order to pay or advance costs and expenditures that are associated with the development, manufacture or acquisition of prohibited war materiel.

Art. 8c[15] Prohibition of indirect financing

1 The indirect financing of the development, manufacture or acquisition of prohibited war materiel is itself prohibited where the prohibition of direct financing is circumvented thereby.

2 Indirect financing within the meaning of this Act is:

a. participation in companies that develop, manufacture or acquire prohibited war materiel;

b. the acquisition of debt securities or other investment products issued by such companies.

- - - - -

Chapter 6 Criminal Provisions

Art. 34 Offences against the prohibition of nuclear, biological and chemical weapons

1 Any person who wilfully commits any of the following acts without being able to claim an exemption under Article 7 Paragraph 2 is liable to a custodial sentence not exceeding ten years or to a monetary penalty:[41]

a. the development, manufacture, brokerage, acquisition, surrender to another, imports, export, transit, stockpiling, or any other form of possession of nuclear, biological or chemical weapons (NBC weapons);

b. incitement to commit any of the acts listed under letter a; or

c. assisting in the commission of an act listed under letter a.

2 ...[42]

3 If the act is committed through negligence, the penalty is a custodial sentence not exceeding one year or a monetary penalty.[43]

4 An act committed abroad is an offence in terms of these provisions irrespective of the law of the place of commission if:

a. it violates international law agreements to which Switzerland is a contracting party; and

b. the offender is Swiss or is domiciled in Switzerland.

5 Article 7 paragraphs 4 and 5 of the Criminal Code[44] apply.[45]

- - - - - -

Art. 35*b*[51] Offences against the prohibition of financing

1 Any person who wilfully fails to comply with the prohibition of financing under Articles 8b or 8c without being able to claim an exemption under Article 7 paragraph 2, Article 8 paragraph 2 or Article 8a paragraph 3 is liable to a custodial sentence not exceeding five years or to a monetary penalty.

2 ...[52]

3 A person who merely accepts the possibility of an offence against the prohibition of financing under Articles 8b or 8c does not commit an offence.

Art. 36 Contraventions

1 Any person who wilfully commits any of the following acts is liable to a fine not exceeding 100,000 francs:[53]

a. the refusal to provide information, submit documents or permit access to business premises in terms of Articles 27 and 28 paragraph 1 or provides false information in this connection;

b. the violation in any other way of a provision of this Act or of an implementing regulation, the contravention of which is declared to be an offence, or the failure to comply with an order issued with notice of the applicability of the penalties in terms of this Article, unless the criminal conduct constitutes a different offence.

2 Attempts and complicity are offences.

3 If the act is committed through negligence, the penalty is a fine of up to 40 000 francs.

4 The right to prosecute prescribes after five years.[54]

Art. 37 Offences in commercial enterprises

In relation to offences in commercial enterprises, Article 6 of the Federal Act of 22 March 1974[55] on Administrative Criminal Law applies.

---

[1] SR 101

[2] Amended by No II 3 of the FA of 17 Dec. 2021 on the Harmonisation of Sentencing Policy, in force since 1 July 2023 (AS 2023 259; BBl 2018 2827).

[3] BBl 1995 II 1027

[6] Amended by No I of the FA of 16 March 2012, in force since 1 Feb. 2013 (AS 2013 295; BBl 2011 5905).

[14] Inserted by No I of the FA of 16 March 2012, in force since 1 Feb. 2013 (AS 2013 295; BBl 2011 5905).

[15] Inserted by No I of the FA of 16 March 2012, in force since 1 Feb. 2013 (AS 2013 295; BBl 2011 5905).

[41] Amended by No I of the FA of 16 March 2012, in force since 1 Feb. 2013 (AS 2013 295; BBl 2011 5905).

[42] Repealed by No I 17 of the FA of 17 Dec. 2021 on the Harmonisation of Sentencing Policy, with effect from 1 July 2023 (AS 2023 259; BBl 2018 2827).

[43] Amended by No I of the FA of 16 March 2012, in force since 1 Feb. 2013 (AS 2013 295; BBl 2011 5905).

[44] SR 311.0

[45] Inserted by No I of the FA of 16 March 2012, in force since 1 Feb. 2013 (AS 2013 295; BBl 2011 5905).

[51] Inserted by No I of the FA of 16 March 2012, in force since 1 Feb. 2013 (AS 2013 295; BBl 2011 5905).

[52] Repealed by No I 17 of the FA of 17 Dec. 2021 on the Harmonisation of Sentencing Policy, with effect from 1 July 2023 (AS 2023 259; BBl 2018 2827).

[53] Amended by No I of the FA of 16 March 2012, in force since 1 Feb. 2013 (AS 2013 295; BBl 2011 5905).

[54] Amended by No I of the FA of 16 March 2012, in force since 1 Feb. 2013 (AS 2013 295; BBl 2011 5905).

[55] SR 313.0

Appendix IV: Oakland NFZ Ordinance

ORDINANCE No. 11478 C. M. S.

AN ORDINANCE DECLARING THE CITY OF OAKLAND
A NUCLEAR FREE ZONE
AND REGULATING NUCLEAR WEAPONS WORK
AND CITY CONTRACTS WITH AND INVESTMENT
IN NUCLEAR WEAPONS MAKERS

WHEREAS, the residents of the City of Oakland approved an initiative ordinance entitled "OAKLAND NUCLEAR FREE ZONE ACT" ("Act") at the Special Municipal Election held on November 8, 1988; and

WHEREAS, the United States District Court for the Northern District of California invalidated the Act as being in conflict with the United States Constitution and/or federal statutes, regulations and executive orders, with the exception of two provisions that were not challenged; and

WHEREAS, on or about March 9, 1992, the United States Court of Appeals denied an appeal of the District Court opinion on procedural grounds; and

WHEREAS, the City Council, by adopting this Ordinance, intends to reaffirm, to the extent legally permissible, the City's commitment to peace and prosperity as evidenced by the 1989 Act, by the vote of the City's residents in 1982 to support a bilateral freeze on "the testing, production and further development of all nuclear weapons," and by the Council's vote in 1986 to support a comprehensive nuclear test ban; and

WHEREAS, the expenditure of City funds on goods and services produced by nuclear weapons makers, the investment of City funds in nuclear weapons makers, and the presence of nuclear weapons and work on nuclear weapons within the City directly conflict with the maintenance of the City's public health, safety, morals, economic well-being and general welfare; and

WHEREAS, the emergency response services of the City may be unable to fully contain the effects of an accident following a major fire, traffic accident, earthquake or similar disaster involving nuclear weapons, nuclear reactors or shipments of hazardous radioactive materials;

WHEREAS, the allocation of City resources in the form of police, fire and other services to prepare for and contain the effects of an accident involving nuclear weapons, nuclear reactors and shipments of hazardous radioactive materials diverts the City's limited resources from urgently needed human services such as job training, social services for children, the elderly and disabled, shelter for the homeless, health care, education and drug abatement;

WHEREAS, the public morality is affronted by the expenditure of City funds on goods and services produced by nuclear weapons makers, the investment of City funds in nuclear weapons makers, and the presence of nuclear weapons and work on nuclear weapons which may ultimately lead to widespread death and destruction; and

WHEREAS, the presence of nuclear weapons and work on nuclear weapons poses a threat to the residents of the City by increasing the likelihood that the City will be a target of terrorism, violent protest or nuclear attack.

NOW, THEREFORE, BE IT RESOLVED that the City Council adopts the following:

Section 1: Declaration:

The City of Oakland is hereby declared to be a nuclear free zone. This Ordinance shall be known as the Oakland Nuclear Free Zone Ordinance.

Section 2: Definitions:

As used herein, these words are provided the following definitions:

(a) "Person" means any natural person, corporation, institution, or other entity. "Person," unless otherwise specified, does not include the governments of the United States and the State of California, or any agency, department, instrumentality, board, or commission thereof.

(b) "Nuclear Weapon" means any device, the purpose of which is use as a weapon, a weapon prototype, or a weapon test device, the intended detonation of which results from the energy released by reactions involving atomic nuclei, either fission or fusion, or both. "Nuclear weapon" includes the means of deploying, transporting, propelling, guiding, or triggering the weapon if the primary intended function of such means is integral to use of the weapon. "Nuclear Weapon" also includes any device which has the primary intended function of being a component of a nuclear weapon.

(c) "Nuclear Weapons Work" means any work that has as its primary purpose the development, production, possession, maintenance or storage of a nuclear weapon. It does not include theoretical or basic research not having as its primary purpose the development, production, possession, maintenance or storage of a nuclear weapon.

(d) "Nuclear Weapons Maker" means any person knowingly engaged in nuclear weapons work; subsidiaries, affiliates and divisions under operating control of such person; the parent entities that have operating control over such person, and the subsidiaries, affiliates and divisions under operating control of such parent entity.

(e) "Nuclear Reactor" means any device that has as its purpose the release of energy from non-explosive reactions involving the fission of atomic nuclei.

(f) "Hazardous Radioactive Materials" means any material having a specific activity greater than 0.002 microcuries per gram (uCi/g). Specific activity of a radionuclide means the activity of the radionuclide per unit mass of that nuclide. The specific activity of a material in which the radionuclide is essentially uniformly distributed is the activity per unit mass of the material. "Hazardous Radioactive Materials" does not include radioactive materials contained in medical devices, radiopharmaceuticals, and consumer products such as smoke detectors, light-emitting watches and clocks and similar applications.

(g) "City Manager" means the City Manager of the City of Oakland, or any authorized representative of the City Manager.

Section 3: Exclusions:

The provisions of this Ordinance do not apply to the following persons, except as otherwise provided herein:

(a) The government of the United States, its agencies, departments, instrumentalities, boards and commissions;

(b) the government of the State of California, its agencies, departments, boards and commissions;

(c) the Port of Oakland;

(d) the chartered retirement systems of the City of Oakland;

(e) the chartered boards and commissions of the City of Oakland;

(f) the Oakland Housing Authority; and

(g) the Oakland School District.

Section 4: Nuclear Weapons Work Restriction:

(a) Any and all nuclear weapons work within the City of Oakland shall occur on land owned or leased by the government of the United States or the State of California or in other areas as permitted by the City Manager.

(b) A nuclear weapons work permit must be obtained for all nuclear weapons work which will occur on land that is not owned or leased by the United States or the State of California and which is commenced after the effective date of this Ordinance. Existing nuclear weapons work conducted on land other than that owned or leased by governments of the United States or the State of California, shall cease within one hundred twenty (120) days of the effective date of this ordinance unless a permit for such work is obtained.

(c) The City Manager shall consider the following factors, where relevant, in reviewing applications for nuclear weapons work permits:

(i) The proximity of the proposed work site to active earthquake faults;

(ii) the proximity of the proposed work site to residential neighborhoods;

(iii) ease of access to the proposed work site by emergency response personnel; and

(iv) the findings set forth in the preamble hereinabove.

A nuclear weapons work permit shall not be issued unless the City Manager determines that the risk posed by nuclear weapons work occurring at the proposed location is clearly outweighed by the benefit of the work occurring at that location to the residents of the City. Any approval or denial of an application for a nuclear weapons work permit by the City Manager shall be reported to the City Council.

(d) Any interested person is entitled to appeal such approval or denial to the City Council. An appeal must be filed within 30 days from the date of notification to the City Council by the City Manager. The City Council shall review such appeals pursuant to the standards set forth in subpart (c) of this section.

Section 5: Transportation of Nuclear Weapons and Hazardous Radioactive Materials

(a) Transportation of nuclear weapons and hazardous radioactive materials on the streets of the City of Oakland shall occur only on designated routes. Such routes shall be designated by the City Manager upon the effective date of this Ordinance and approved by the City Council after public hearing. The designations shall be reviewed on an annual basis, or more frequently as required, and amended as necessary.

(b) Any deviation from the designated routes requires prior approval by the City Manager. The City Manager shall approve requested deviations unless the alternative route would pose greater risks to the public health and safety than the designated routes.

(c) The City Manager shall request all known transporters of nuclear weapons and hazardous radioactive materials, including the governments of the United States and the State of California, to transport such materials on the designated routes during designated times within the City of Oakland.

(d) The City Manager shall report shipments of nuclear weapons and hazardous radioactive materials to the City Council. Where practicable, the City Manager shall provide the report to the City Council prior to shipments of such weapons and materials.

(e) The provisions of this section do not apply to the transportation of nuclear weapons and hazardous radioactive materials on highways of the State of California and interstate highways of the United States within the City of Oakland.

Section 6: Contracting and Purchasing Preferences:

(a) Pursuant to the findings set forth in the preamble hereinabove, it shall be City policy to minimize the expenditure of City funds on goods and services produced by nuclear weapons makers.

(b) For the purposes of this section, "person" and "sealed bid" are defined as follows:

(1) "person" includes the seller, vendor, distributor, manufacturer and provider of products or services to the City.

(2) "sealed bid" means any bid governed by Section 5 of Ordinance No.7937 C.M.S. or other written bids which pursuant to City administrative procedures have been submitted in sealed envelopes to prevent the contents from being revealed or known before lie deadline for submission of all bids.

(c) Contracts and Purchases Requiring Sealed Bids. Except as provided in subdivisions (d) and (e) of this section, for all contracts and purchases for which sealed bids are submitted, persons not designated as nuclear weapons makers shall receive a 5% preference, unless:

(1) the use of preferences is specifically prohibited by then governments of the United States and/or the State of California, or any party from whom funding for the contract or purchase is received; or

(2) the City Council determines that, for any bid governed by Section 5 of Ordinance No. 7937 C.M.S., the use of preferences would result in an additional cost of $10,000.00 or more to the City.

(d) Sole Source Contracts.

The City shall make every reasonable effort to enter into sole source contracts and sole source purchases with persons not designated as nuclear weapons makers.

(1) All sole source contracts or sole source purchases entered into pursuant to subsection (i)(2) of section

5 of Ordinance No. 7937 C.M.S., shall be made with persons not designated as nuclear weapons makers, unless the City Council finds that no reasonable alternative product or service exists, or that additional costs would exceed $10,000.00 or 5% of the cost of the product or service manufactured or provided by the nuclear weapons maker, whichever is less.

(2) All sole source contracts or purchases which are not governed by the requirements of subsection (i)(2) of section 5 of Ordinance No. 7937 C.M.S., but which exceed $2000, shall be made with persons not designated as nuclear weapons makers, unless the City Manager finds that no reasonable alternative product or service exists or that unreasonable additional costs would result from the use of available alternatives.

(3) For all sole source contracts or sole source purchases under $2,000.00, all efforts will be undertaken to avoid contracting with nuclear weapons makers.

(e) Professional Services Contracts.

The City shall make every reasonable effort to enter into professional service contracts with persons not designated as nuclear weapons makers.

(1) All professional service contracts entered into pursuant to subsection (i)(1) of section 5 of Ordinance No. 7937 C.M.S., shall be made with persons not designated as nuclear weapons makers, unless the City Council finds that no reasonable alternative product or service exists, or that additional costs would exceed $10,000.00 or 5% of the cost of the service provided by the nuclear weapons maker, whichever is less.

(2) All professional service contracts which are not governed by the requirements of subsection (i)(1) of section 5 of Ordinance No. 7937 C.M.S., but which exceed $2,000, shall be made with persons not designated as nuclear weapons makers, unless the City Manager finds that no reasonable alternative product or service exists or that unreasonable additional costs would result from the use of available alternatives.

(3) For all professional services contracts under $2,000.00, all efforts will be undertaken to avoid contracting with nuclear weapons makers.

(f) All public works and construction bid advertisements and contracts shall state the City policy set forth in subdivision (a) of this section and urge contractors to comply with the policy in making purchases and subcontracts.

(g) For contracts and purchases other than those governed by subdivisions (c), (d), (e), and (f) of this section, the City Manager shall promulgate an Administrative Instruction pursuant to section 11 to ensure that City departments comply, to the extent reasonable and practicable, with the intent of this Ordinance.

(h) For the purposes of determining which persons are nuclear weapons makers, the City Manager shall rely on information published by reliable sources and information released by public agencies.

(i) Any person who is identified as a nuclear weapons maker and potentially affected by this section shall be notified of the determination. Any such person shall be entitled to a review of the determination by appeal to the City Manager. Request for such review shall be made within forty five (45) days of notification, or seven (7) days of the date of City advertisement of a pending contract or purchase, of interest to the person seeking review. .Any person so identified or any other interested person may appeal the City Manager's determination to the City Council, within fifteen (15) days of the City Manager's determination.

(j) The City Manager may phase in implementation of this section as necessary for reasonable and practicable effectuation of its requirements.

Section 7: Investment Restrictions

(a) The City of Oakland shall, after the effective date of this section, refrain from making any investments in stocks, bonds, securities, or other obligations issued by nuclear weapons makers.

(b) Within two years after the effective date of this section, the City shall divest itself of any and all investments in stocks, bonds, securities or other obligations issued by nuclear weapons makers, unless the Director of Finance determines, and so reports to Council, that such divestment would result in substantial and immediate losses of investment income, or would require the City to sell investments at prices materially below their fair market value.

Section 8: Siting Of Nuclear Reactors:

The City Manager shall notify the applicable agencies or departments of the State of California and the United States, in response to any proposed siting of a nuclear reactor within the City of Oakland, that, due to seismic dangers and the City's population density, the potential adverse economic effect on the City, and all other relevant factors, the City strongly opposes such siting.

Section 9: Public Hearings and Reports:

(a) Two public hearings before Council shall be held within the first year following the date of passage of this Ordinance to evaluate implementation of and compliance with the provisions of this Ordinance. One public hearing shall be held each year thereafter.

(b) Two weeks prior to each public hearing held pursuant to subsection (a), the City Manager shall issue a report describing the implementation of the provisions of this Ordinance and compliance therewith. The City Manager may recommend amendments to this Ordinance to further its purposes.

Section 10: Severability

This Ordinance shall be enforced to the full extent of the authority of the City of Oakland. If any section, subsection, paragraph, sentence or word of this Ordinance is deemed to be invalid or beyond the authority of the City of Oakland, either on its face or as applied, the invalidity of such provision shall not affect the other sections, subsections, paragraphs, sentences or words of this Ordinance, and the applications thereof; and to that end the section, subsections, paragraphs, sentences and words of this Ordinance shall be deemed severable.

Section 11: Rules and Regulations

The City Manager shall be authorized to promulgate any rules and regulations necessary or appropriate to carry out the purposes and requirements of this Ordinance, effective upon approval of the City Council.

Section 12: Effective Date

The provisions of this Ordinance, except Sections 6 and 7, shall become effective sixty (60) days after its passage. Sections 6 and 7 shall become effective six (6) months after passage of this Ordinance.

Section 13: Enforcement

(a) Any person violating Section 4 of this Ordinance shall be guilty of an infraction. An infraction is punishable upon first conviction by a fine of not more than $100.00 and, for a second conviction within a period of one year, by a fine of not more than $200.00 and, for a third or subsequent violation within a one year period, by a fine of not more than $500.00. A violation beyond the third conviction within a one-year period may be charged as a misdemeanor. Penalty for conviction of the misdemeanor shall be a fine of not more than $1,000.00 or imprisonment in the County Jail for a period of not more than six months or by both.

(b) Any person violating Section 5 of this Ordinance or knowingly supplying false information in connection with a designation of nuclear weapons makers under sections 6 and 7 of this Ordinance shall be guilty of a misdemeanor and punishable therefor pursuant to subsection (a) above.

(c) The City shall refrain from conducting business with persons found to have knowingly supplied false information used in fulfillment of the requirements of this Ordinance.

Section 14:

The City shall make all reasonable attempts to insure that the information required to be provided by this Ordinance is accurate. However, the City shall not be responsible for the accuracy of information provided by entities and individuals pursuant to this Ordinance, or for the accuracy of information obtained from the public record or released by public agencies.

IN COUNCIL, OAKLAND, CALIFORNIA, JUN 30, 1992

PASSED BY THE FOLLOWING VOTE:

AYES— BAZILE, CANNON, GIBSON HASKELL, MILEY, MOORE, OGAWA, RILES, SPEES, and PRESIDENT HARRIS , - 9

NOES— NONE

ABSENT— NONE

ABSTENTION— NONE

Appendix V: Spokane Nuclear Free Zone ordinance

Spokane, Washington – Municipal Code

Title 18 Human Rights

Chapter 18.09 Nuclear Weapons Free Zone

Section 18.09.010 Purpose

The purpose of this title is to establish the City of Spokane as a zone free of nuclear weapons, prohibiting work on nuclear weapons and limiting harmful exposure to high-level nuclear waste within City limits. Residents and representatives are urged to redirect resources previously used for the production of nuclear weapons towards endeavors which promote and enhance life, including economic development, childcare, housing, schools, health care, emergency services, public transportation, energy conservation, small business support and jobs.

Section 18.09.020 Definitions

As used in this chapter, the following terms shall have the meanings indicated:

A. "Component of a nuclear weapon" is any device, radioactive substance or nonradioactive substance designed knowingly and intentionally to contribute to the operation, launch, guidance, delivery, or detonation of a nuclear weapon.

B. "Nuclear weapon" is any device with the sole purpose of the destruction of human life and property by an explosion resulting from the energy released by a fission or fusion reaction involving atomic nuclei.

C. "Nuclear weapons producer" is any person, firm, corporation, limited liability company, institution, facility, parent, or subsidiary thereof, engaged in the production of nuclear weapons or their components.

D. "Production of nuclear weapons" includes the knowing or intentional research, design, development, testing, manufacture, evaluation, maintenance, storage, transportation, or disposal of nuclear weapons or their components.

E. A "product produced by a nuclear weapons producer" is any product which is made wholly or primarily by a nuclear weapons producer, except that products which, prior to their intended purchase by the City, have been previously owned and used by an entity other than the manufacturer or distributor; such products shall not be considered produced by a nuclear weapons producer if, prior to their purchase by the City, more than 25% of the useful life of such product has been used or consumed, or within one year after it has been put into service by the previous nonmanufacturer owner. The "useful life of a product" shall be defined, where possible, by the applicable rules, regulations or guidelines of the United States Internal Revenue Service.

Section 18.09.030 Nuclear Facilities Prohibited

A. The production of nuclear weapons shall not be allowed in the City. No facility, equipment, components, supplies, or substance used to produce nuclear weapons shall be allowed in the City.

B. No person, corporation, university, laboratory, institution, or other entity in the City knowingly and intentionally engaged in the production of nuclear weapons shall commence any such work within the City after adoption of this chapter.

Section 18.09.040 Investment of City Funds

The City Council shall consider a socially responsible investment policy, specifically addressing any investments the City may have or may plan to have in industries and institutions which are knowingly and intentionally engaged in the production of nuclear weapons.

Section 18.09.050 Eligibility for City Contracts

A. The City and its officials, employees or agents shall not knowingly or intentionally grant any award, contract, or purchase order, directly or indirectly, to any nuclear weapons producer.

B. The City and its officials, employees or agents shall not knowingly or intentionally grant any award, contract or purchase order, directly or indirectly, to purchase or lease products produced by a nuclear weapons producer.

C. The recipient of a City contract, award or purchase order shall certify to the City Clerk by a notarized statement that it is not knowingly or intentionally a nuclear weapons producer.

D. The City shall phase out the use of any products of a nuclear weapons producer which it owns or possesses. Insofar as nonnuclear alternatives are not available, for the purpose of maintaining a product during its normal useful life and for the purpose of purchasing or leasing replacement parts, supplies and services for such products, subsections (A) and (B) of this section shall not apply.

E. The City shall identify a source annually that maintains a list of nuclear weapons producers to guide the City, its officials, employees and agents in the implementation of subsections (A) through (C) of this section. The list shall not preclude application or enforcement of these provisions to or against any other nuclear weapons producer.

F. Waivers.

1. The provisions of subsections (A) and (B) of this section may be waived by resolution passed by a majority vote of the City Council; provided that:

i. After a diligent good-faith search, it is determined that a necessary good or service cannot reasonably be obtained from any source other than a nuclear weapons producer;

ii. A resolution to consider a waiver be on file with the City Clerk under the normal timing as laid out in Council's Rules and shall not be added by a suspension of those Rules.

2. The reasonableness of an alternative source shall be determined upon the consideration of the following factors:

   i. The intent and purpose of this chapter;

   ii. Documented evidence establishing that the necessary good or service is vital to the health or safety of the residents or employees of the City, with the understanding that the absence of such evidence shall diminish the necessity for waiver;

   iii. The recommendations of the Mayor and/or City Administrator;

   iv. The availability of goods or services from a non-nuclear-weapons producer reasonably meeting the specification or requirements of the necessary good or service;

   v. Quantifiable substantial additional costs that would result from the use of a good or service of a non-nuclear-weapons producer; provided, that this factor shall not become the sole consideration.

Section 18.09.060 Exclusions

A. Nothing in this chapter shall be construed to prohibit or regulate the research and application of nuclear medicine or the use of fissionable materials for smoke detectors, light-emitting watches and clocks and other applications where the purpose is unrelated to the production of nuclear weapons. Nothing in this chapter shall be interpreted to infringe upon the rights guaranteed by the First Amendment to the United States Constitution nor upon the power of Congress to provide for the common defense.

B. Nothing in this chapter shall be interpreted, construed or applied to prevent the City Council, Mayor or the City Administrator or their designee from acting to remedy, ameliorate or prevent an emergency situation presenting a clear and present danger to the public health, safety and general welfare, as defined in Chapter 2.04 of the Spokane Municipal Code; provided, that should any such emergency situation require the purchase of products or services from or entry into a contract with a nuclear weapons producer then the Mayor or City Administrator shall notify the City Council within three working days of the City's actions.

C. Nothing in this chapter shall be interpreted, construed, or applied to supersede or bypass any procurement regulations, whether those regulations are legislative or administratively promulgated; provided, however, that no procurement regulations pertaining to the granting of any award, contract or purchase order shall alter or abrogate the intent or requirements of this chapter.

Section 18.09.070 Violations and Penalties

A. Any violation of this chapter shall be a Class 1 Civil Infraction.

B. Without limitation or election against any other available remedy, the City or any of its residents may apply to a court of competent jurisdiction for an injunction enjoining any violation of this chapter. The court shall award attorney's fees and costs to any party who succeeds in obtaining an injunction hereunder.

Date Passed: Monday, November 7, 2022

Effective Date: Wednesday, December 21, 2022

Appendix VI: Oregon's failed ballot initiative

Proposed by Initiative Petition, voted on at the General Election, November 4,1986. FAILED 400,119 votes to 590,971 votes.

Measure No. 16: PHASES OUT NUCLEAR WEAPONS MANUFACTURE WITH TAX CREDITS, CIVIL PENALTY

AN ACT Relating to nuclear weapons.

Be It Enacted by the People of the State of Oregon:

Section 1. It is the policy of the State of Oregon to assist businesses in the conversion from nuclear weapons production. This policy shall be implemented through tax relief to Oregon businesses that convert from manufacture of nuclear weapons or nuclear weapon components to manufacture of consumer products.

Section 2. Any person who manufactures nuclear weapons or nuclear weapon components may apply for a tax credit as provided in sections 3 and 4 of this Act if:

(1) That person makes an expenditure in Oregon for retraining of Oregon employes specifically to convert from manufacture of nuclear weapons or nuclear weapon components to manufacture of a consumer product;

(2) That person makes a capital investment in Oregon specifically to convert from manufacture of nuclear weapons or nuclear weapon components to manufacture of a consumer product; and

(3) The cost of conversion is certified as specified in section 3 of this Act.

Section 3. (1) There is created a Governor's Task Force on Nuclear Weapons Conversion. The Governor shall appoint nine members to the task force. The term of office of each member is four years, except as such term may be interrupted by retirement of the task force as provided in this section. If there is a vacancy for any cause, the Governor shall make an appointment for the unexpired term. Task force members shall serve without pay, but shall be compensated as provided in ORS 292.495. Staff work necessary to task force operation shall be provided by a member of the Governor's staff. The task force shall be retired on January 1,1991.

(2) The task force shall identify those businesses that manufacture nuclear weapons or nuclear weapon components in Oregon, and shall advise those businesses of the tax credit available through conversion to manufacture of consumer products.

(3) Upon written application containing the necessary information, the task force shall certify those costs of conversion that it determines qualify for a tax credit under section 4 of this Act and the tax year of the taxpayer for which the certification is first issued.

Section 4. (1) Upon certification of the costs of conversion pursuant to section 3 of this Act, a taxpayer shall be allowed a tax credit against taxes otherwise due under ORS chapter 316, 317 or 318 in an amount that is the lesser of:

(a) Thirty percent of the certified costs of conversion actually paid or incurred by the taxpayer; or

(b) The total tax liability of the taxpayer determined without regard to this section for three successive tax years beginning with the tax year for which certification is first issued as specified by the task force under subsection (3) of section 3 of this Act.

(2) A credit pursuant to this section may be claimed only on the basis of costs of conversion certified by the task force on or after January 1,1987, and before January 1,1990.

(3) Any amount of the tax credit allowable under this section which is not used by the taxpayer for the tax year for which a certification is first issued by the task force may be carried forward and offset against tax liability for the second and third succeeding tax years, but may not be carried forward for any year thereafter.

(4) The credit allowed by sections 1 to 7 of this Act shall be in addition to any other tax benefit and shall not affect basis.

Section 5 . (1) A claim for a tax credit pursuant to a certification shall be substantiated as prescribed by rule of the Department of Revenue.

(2) Any amount of unused tax credit, up to the amount of tax liability of the transferee, may be transferred in the event of sale, exchange or other transfer of a business that has received certification.

Section 6. As used in sections 1 to 5 of this Act:

(1) " Capital investment" means the amount of money a person invests to acquire, retool or construct equipment or machinery necessary to manufacture a consumer product. " Capital investment" does not include purchase of land or buildings.

(2) " Consumer product" means a product for individual, industrial or business use.

(3) " Costs of conversion" includes all expenditures for retraining Oregon employes and any capital investment in Oregon made specifically to convert from the manufacture of nuclear weapons or nuclear weapon components to the manufacture of a consumer product.

(4) " Task force" means the Governor's Task Force on Nuclear Weapons Conversion established under section 3 of this Act.

Section 7. As used in sections 1 to 9 of this Act:

(1) " Nuclear weapon component" means:

(a) Any part of a nuclear weapon that is designed specifically and exclusively for use in a nuclear weapon; or

(b) Materials which are refined or manufactured to be used in devices described in subsection (2) of this section, if the by-products of those materials include radioactive wastes as defined in ORS 469.300.

(2) " Nuclear weapon" means any device the intended explosion of which results from the energy released by reactions involving atomic nuclei by either fission or fusion or by both, including the means of propelling, guiding or triggering the device if the means is destroyed or rendered useless in propelling, guiding, triggering or detonation of the device.

(3) " Person" includes individuals, corporations, associations, firms, partnerships, joint stock companies, and public and private institutions.

Section 8. Any individual shall have the right to enforce provisions of section 9 of this Act by an appropriate action for declaratory or injunctive relief. Reasonable attorney fees and costs shall be awarded to a prevailing plaintiff in such an action.

Section 9. (1) No person shall knowingly engage in the manufacture of nuclear weapons or nuclear weapon components after January 1,1990.

(2) In addition to any other liability or penalty imposed by law, the State Fire Marshal may impose a civil penalty in an amount not to exceed $5,000 for each day of each violation against any person who violates subsection (1) of this section. The provisions of ORS 453.357 shall apply to such civil penalties.

Section 10. Notwithstanding the provisions of section 9 of this Act, that section does not prohibit the manufacture of nuclear weapons or nuclear weapon components pursuant to a contract entered into before the effective date of this Act. However, section 9 of this Act does apply to the extension or renewal of a contract on or after the effective date of this Act if the original contract was entered into before the effective date of this Act.

ACKNOWLEDGEMENTS

My thanks go first of all to the people who generously agreed to be interviewed for this book and provided feedback. They are all listed at the beginning of the book. Without them, this book would have been pretty boring!

And for the final product, I am especially indebted to my wife and editor-in-chief, Vicki Elson, who painstakingly proofread, corrected and re-worked every page. Vicki is also responsible for the cover design and other graphics in the book.

I am also deeply grateful to Anduin DeVos, who helped with research, indexing and other details of the book; Phoebe Meskill, who produced all the maps; and Joanne Dufour and Anthony Donovan, for their editing and proofreading.

Many others contributed to the research, writing, editing and design of *Warheads to Windmills*, which forms the basis of this book, including Asher Supernaw, Dan Bullen, Sheila Siragusa, Sarah Bloomgarden, Janet McKenna Lowry, Nancy Horn, Nathalie Reinstein, Dan Smith and Nora Bajor.

Finally, I am thankful for the encouragement and support I have received from Cynthia Lazaroff, Ivana Hughes, Susi Snyder, Ward Wilson and many others – most especially Randy Kehler and David Hartsough. Sadly, both died before seeing the final product.

None of these people necessarily agree with or have endorsed the contents, style or tone of this book. As the named author, I take full responsibility for that, as well as for any errors or misrepresentations that may still remain in it.

T.W.

LIST OF ABBREVIATIONS

ABM Anti-Ballistic Missile Treaty
APMBC Anti-Personnel Mine Ban Convention
BRICS Brazil, Russia, India, China, and South Africa
CAP Center for American Progress
CBM Confidence Building Measures
CBO Congressional Budget Office
CCM Convention on Cluster Munitions
CD Conference on Disarmament
CDU Christian Democratic Party of Germany
CEP Circular Error Probable
CIA Central Intelligence Agency
CRS Congressional Research Service
CTBT Comprehensive Test Ban Treaty
CWC Chemical Weapons Convention
DCA Dual Capable Aircraft (nuclear and conventional weapons)
DOD Department of Defense
DOE Department of Energy
DRC Democratic Republic of the Congo
DTRA Defense Threat Reduction Agency
END Extended Nuclear Deterrence
ESG Environment, Social and Governance
EU European Union
FFT Fossil Fuel (Non-Proliferation) Treaty
FMCT Fissile Material Cut-Off Treaty
GDP Gross Domestic Product
GNP Gross National Product
GRIT Graduated, Reciprocal Initiatives for Tension-reduction
HEU Highly-Enriched Uranium
HFC Hydrofluorocarbon
HLW High-Level Radioactive Waste
ICAN International Campaign to Abolish Nuclear Weapons
ICBM Intercontinental Ballistic Missile
ICJ International Court of Justice
IAEA International Atomic Energy Agency
INF Intermediate-Range Nuclear Forces Treaty
ILO International Labor Organization
IPPNW International Physicians for the Prevention of

Nuclear War

IRS	Internal Revenue Service
KT	Kiloton (1 thousand tons) of TNT
MOAB	Mother of All Bombs, the GBU-43
MIRV	Multiple Independently-targeted Re-entry Vehicles
MSP	Meeting of States Parties (to the TPNW)
MT	Megaton (1 million tons) of TNT
NATO	North Atlantic Treaty Organization
NPT	Nuclear Non-Proliferation Treaty
NRA	National Rifle Association
NRC	Nuclear Regulatory Commission
NRDC	Natural Resources Defense Council
NWC	Nuclear Weapons Convention
OSCE	Organization for Security and Cooperation in Europe
PERI	Political Economy Research Institute
PNI	Presidential Nuclear Initiative
PTBT	Partial Test Ban Treaty
SALT	Strategic Arms Limitation Treaty
SPD	Social Democratic Party of Germany
START	Strategic Arms Reduction Treaty
SIPRI	Stockholm International Peace Research Institute
STEM	Science, Technology, Engineering, and Mathematics
TNT	The standard used to measure size of explosives
TPNW	Treaty on the Prohibition of Nuclear Weapons
WMD	Weapons of Mass Destruction
UN	United Nations
UNGA	UN General Assembly
XR	Extinction Rebellion

NOTES

Preface

[1] See Milton Leitenberg, *Deaths in Wars and Conflicts in the 20th Century* for one researcher's estimates of war dead, and a good explanation of the difficulties of determining what the numbers actually are: https://www.clingendael.org/sites/default/files/pdfs/20060800_cdsp_occ_leitenberg.pdf

Prologue

[1] This was the case in 2016, when Trump won those three states but secured 3 million fewer votes nationally than Hillary Clinton.

[2] Just over 86 million eligible voters did not vote in 2024, compared to just under 78 million who did not vote in 2020. See more details at Ballotpedia.org: https://ballotpedia.org/Election_results,_2024:_Analysis_of_voter_turnout_in_the_2024_general_election

[3] See PRRI *Post-Election Survey Results:* https://www.prri.org/spotlight/understanding-the-2024-election-uncovering-the-key-factors-influencing-americans-presidential-votes/

Chapter 1: Turning back the doomsday clock

[1] See https://thebulletin.org/doomsday-clock/

[2] For a full discussion of nuclear 'deterrence' claims, see Chapter 3, in Wallis, T. M. (2017). *Disarming the Nuclear Argument: The Truth About Nuclear Weapons* (p. 41). Luath Press.

[3] Lewis, P., Williams, H., Pelopidas, B., & Aghlani, S. (2014). *Too Close for Comfort: Cases of Near Nuclear Use and Options for Policy*. Chatham House. https://www.chathamhouse.org/sites/default/files/field/field_document/20140428TooCloseforComfortNuclearUseLewisWilliamsPelopidasAghlani.pdf

[4] This is evident from Reagan's memoirs and other Western intelligence reports, although no archives have been forthcoming from the Russian side to confirm what Soviet leaders were thinking. See Chatham House, *op cit*, pp. 13–16.

[5]Lewis, P., Williams, H., Pelopidas, B., & Aghlani, S. (2014). Too Close for Comfort: Cases of Near Nuclear Use and Options for Policy. In *Chatham House* (p. vi). https://www.chathamhouse.org/sites/default/files/field/field_document/20140428TooCloseforComfortNuclearUseLewisWilliamsPelopidasAghlani.pdf

[6] Lewis, P. et al, (2014) *op cit*, pp. 16–17.

[7] See IPPNW (1991), *Radioactive Heaven and Earth: The Health and Environmental Effects of Nuclear Weapons Testing In, On and Above the Earth:* https://ieer.org/wp/wp-content/uploads/1991/06/RadioactiveHeavenEarth1991.pdf

[8] Robock, A. et al (2022), "Global Food Insecurity and Famine from Reduced Crop, Marine Fishery and Livestock Production Due to Climate Disruption from Nuclear War Soot Injection," in *Nature Food*, 3, p 586-596: https://www.nature.com/articles/s43016-022-00573-0

[9] Lewis, P. et al (2014), *op cit.*

[10] Pilkington, E. (2013, September 20). US nearly detonated atomic bomb over North Carolina – secret document. *The Guardian*.

https://www.theguardian.com/world/2013/sep/20/usaf-atomic-bomb-north-carolina-1961

[11] See Schlosser, E. (2013). *Command and Control*. Penguin Books, and also this account here: https://blog.nuclearsecrecy.com/2013/09/27/final-switch-goldsboro-1961/

[12] According to papers released in 2013 under a FOI request. See Johnson, M. A. (2013, September 21). *One cheap switch saved US from nuclear catastrophe in 1961, declassified document reveals*. NBC News. https://www.nbcnews.com/news/us-news/one-cheap-switch-saved-us-nuclear-catastrophe-1961-declassified-document-flna4b11221026. See also Schlosser, E. (2013). *Command and Control*. Penguin Books.

[13] See Jorgensen, T. J. (2018, January 23). *50 years ago, a B-52 crashed in Greenland ... with 4 nuclear bombs on board*. Air Force Times. https://www.airforcetimes.com/news/your-air-force/2018/01/23/50-years-ago-a-b-52-crashed-in-greenland-with-4-nuclear-bombs-on-board/

[14] See Schlosser, E. (2013). *Command and Control*. Penguin Books. Also Lewis, P., Williams, H., Pelopidas, B., & Aghlani, S. (2014). Too Close for Comfort: Cases of Near Nuclear Use and Options for Policy. In *Chatham House*. https://www.chathamhouse.org/sites/default/files/field/field_document/20140428TooCloseforComfortNuclearUseLewisWilliamsPelopidasAghlani.pdf

[15] Nuclear weapons at the bottom of the ocean are not at risk of causing a thermonuclear explosion, however as the metals corrode and rust, the risk of radioactive leakage is very high and will inevitably affect radiation levels in fish and on up the food chain. Scott, J. (2006, April 2). *Broken Arrow Nuclear Weapon Accidents*. Aerospaceweb.org. https://aerospaceweb.org/question/weapons/q0268.shtml

[16] Scott, J. (2006, April 2). *Broken Arrow Nuclear Weapon Accidents*. Aerospaceweb.org. https://aerospaceweb.org/question/weapons/q0268.shtml

[17] A depth charge is dropped from a ship to try to destroy a submarine below. In the case of nuclear-tipped depth charge, it is unlikely that the ship above would escape the blast.

[18] See Sudakov, D. (2012, October 9). *K-219: The sub that scared Reagan and Gorbachev*. PRAVDA.Ru. https://english.pravda.ru/russia/122396-submarine_reagan_gorbachev/

[19] Foreign staff and agencies. (2001, April 5). Kursk "carried nuclear weapons." *The Guardian*. http://www.theguardian.com/world/2001/apr/05/kursk.russia

[20] See Associated Press. (2014, January 30). Air Force: 92 implicated in nuke cheating scandal. *AP News*. https://apnews.com/united-states-government-b942adacae524dcfa7fbc85ed6292433

[21] Schlosser (2013), *op cit*, p. 472.

[22] Wikipedia contributors. (2020, August 27). *2007 United States Air Force nuclear weapons incident*. Wikipedia, the Free Encyclopedia. https://en.wikipedia.org/wiki/2007_United_States_Air_Force_nuclear_weapons_incident

[23] Rushe, D. (2013, May 8). US air force strips 17 officers of power to launch nuclear missiles. *The Guardian*. https://www.theguardian.com/world/2013/may/08/us-airforce-nuclear-missiles

[24] Martin, D. (2018, May 24). *U.S. troops guarding nuclear missiles took LSD, Air Force records show*. CBS News. https://www.cbsnews.com/news/us-air-force-airment-lsd-cocaine-warren-air-force-base-wyoming-nuclear-missile-sites-records-show/

[25] Copp, T. (2023, March 1). Minot firings due to failed nuclear safety inspection. *Air Force Times*. https://www.airforcetimes.com/news/your-air-force/2023/03/02/minot-firings-due-to-failed-nuclear-safety-inspection/

[26] U.S. NRC. (1975). *Reactor safety study. An assessment of accident risks in US commercial nuclear power* (No. WASH1400). http://inis.iaea.org/search/search.aspx?orig_q=RN:35053391

[27] Since then, of course, there have also been the accidents at Chernobyl in Ukraine and Fukushima in Japan. And the vulnerability of the Zaporizhshia nuclear power plant in

war-torn Ukraine reminds us that all nuclear power plants are potential stationary nuclear bombs.

[28] US, Russia, UK, France, China, India, Pakistan, Israel and North Korea.

[29] However, to get from uranium ore in the ground to weapons-grade uranium requires advanced technologies and a lot of money.

[30] Israel may have managed to do that, although they probably tested their first weapon jointly with South Africa.

[31] Intermediate-Range Nuclear Forces Treaty. For explanation of acronyms used in this book, see List of Abbreviations at the back of the book.

Chapter 2: Why abolition?

[1] Kristensen, Hans and Korda, Matt (2022), "World Nuclear Forces," Chapter 10 in *SIPRI Yearbook 2022* (p. 342). Oxford University Press.
https://www.sipri.org/sites/default/files/YB22%2010%20World%20Nuclear%20Forces.pdf

[2] See Deputy Assistant Secretary of Defense for Nuclear Matters. (2020). *Nuclear Matters Handbook 2020 [Revised]*. Nuclear Matters Handbook.
https://www.acq.osd.mil/ncbdp/nm/NMHB2020rev/chapters/chapter2.html

[3] Missile Defense Project. (2021, August 2). *Minuteman III*. Missile Threat. https://missilethreat.csis.org/missile/minuteman-iii/

[4] See Kristensen, H. M., McKinzie, M., & Postal, T. A. (2017, March 1). *How US nuclear force modernization is undermining strategic stability: The burst-height compensating super-fuze - Bulletin of the Atomic Scientists*. Bulletin of the Atomic Scientists. https://thebulletin.org/2017/03/how-us-nuclear-force-modernization-is-undermining-strategic-stability-the-burst-height-compensating-super-fuze/

[5] This section, revised and updated, taken directly from Wallis, T (2017), *Disarming the Nuclear Argument*, Luath Press, Chapter 3, pp.41ff.

[6] See complete timetable of revised estimates for "minimum deterrence" in the UK at Nick Richie, *A Nuclear Weapons Free World? Britain, Trident and the Challenge Ahead*, Palgrave MacMillan, London, 2012, p. 12.

[7] In their book, *Nuclear Weapons and Coercive Diplomacy*, Sechser and Fuhrmann examined 348 international territorial disputes between 1919 and 1995 to see whether possession of nuclear weapons had any impact on the outcome of such disputes. They found no statistical correlation at all. In other words, the countries now possessing nuclear weapons are no more likely than they were before having nuclear weapons to "win" a dispute or get what they want from other countries. They are also no more likely to "win" a dispute or get what they want than are the countries which do not have nuclear weapons. See Sechser, T. S., & Fuhrmann, M. (2017). *Nuclear weapons and coercive diplomacy*. Cambridge University Press. https://doi.org/10.1017/9781316227305

[8] Smith, A. (2021, April 15). *Chairman Smith, Senator Warren introduce "No first use" bill for nuclear weapons* [Press release]. https://adamsmith.house.gov/2021/4/chairman-smith-senator-warren-introduce-no-first-use-bill-for-nuclear-weapons

[9] See Kennedy's American University speech of June 10, 1963, in which he outlined his proposal for negotiations with the Soviets to bring the nuclear arms race to an end, starting with his unilateral halt to above ground testing: Kennedy, J. F. (1963, June 10). American University Commencement Address. In *C-SPAN.org*. American University Commencement Address. https://www.c-span.org/video/?153206-1/american-university-commencement-address#

[10] Each treaty has its own requirements for entering into force, and for the CTBT, a specific list of countries that include all those known to have nuclear weapons or the means to make nuclear weapons must ratify the treaty for it to enter into force. Russia,

the UK and France have signed and ratified the CTBT, but not the US, China, India, Pakistan, Israel or North Korea.

[11] See summary of recent developments in all nuclear states at: SIPRI. (2021). Military Spending and Armaments, 2021. In *SIPRI*. https://sipri.org/sites/default/files/YB22%2010%20World%20Nuclear%20Forces.pdf

[12] See Fact Sheet on US Nuclear Weapon Computer Simulations at U.S. Department of State. (n.d.-b). *U.S. nuclear weapon computer simulations*. https://2009-2017.state.gov/t/avc/rls/202014.htm

[13] See Von Hippel, F. (2012, December 14). *Subcritical experiments - Bulletin of the Atomic Scientists*. Bulletin of the Atomic Scientists. https://thebulletin.org/2012/12/subcritical-experiments/

[14] UK Parliament. (n.d.). GS (UK/US) 6: Written evidence from the British Pugwash Group. In *UK Parliament*. https://publications.parliament.uk/pa/cm200809/cmselect/cmfaff/memo/ukus/ucm602.htm

[15] From 1972 to 1980, US nuclear stockpile increased from 5,800 warheads to 10,000. The Soviet nuclear stockpile increased from 2,100 warheads to 7,200 warheads during that same period. See Wikipedia contributors. (2023, August 23). *Nuclear Arms Race*. Wikipedia, the Free Encyclopedia. https://en.wikipedia.org/w/index.php?title=Nuclear_arms_race&oldid=1171779693

[16] See MacKenzie, D., & Spinardi, G. (1988). The Shaping of Nuclear Weapon System Technology: US Fleet Ballistic Missile Guidance and Navigation: II: `Going for Broke' — The Path to Trident II. *Social Studies of Science*, *18*(4), 581–624. https://doi.org/10.1177/030631288018004002

[17] Strategic Arms Reduction Treaty (START I). (2023). In *Center for Arms Control and Non-Proliferation*. https://armscontrolcenter.org/strategic-arms-reduction-treaty-start-i/

[18] See Koch, S. J. (1991). *The Presidential Nuclear Initiatives of 1991–1992*. Center for the Study of Weapons of Mass Destruction National Defense University. https://ndupress.ndu.edu/portals/68/documents/casestudies/cswmd_casestudy-5.pdf

[19] National Park Service. (2020, October 20). *Strategic Arms Reduction Treaty of 1991*. https://www.nps.gov/articles/start-treaty-1991.htm

[20] Air Force Center for Studies and Analyses. (1985). *Effectiveness of the Minuteman II Stage III Refurbishment Program*. https://apps.dtic.mil/sti/pdfs/ADA363899.pdf

[21] See, for example, the description here: Baker, J. C. (2018, February 21). *The Nuclear Freeze Movement*. Outrider. https://outrider.org/nuclear-weapons/articles/nuclear-freeze-movement

[22] It finally passed in the US House of Representatives but then failed in the Senate by a vote of 58-40. See Chapter 16 for more background on the Freeze campaign of the 1980s.

[23] Ed Markey's HALT Act, S.1499, calls for "a verifiable freeze on the testing, production, and further deployment of all nuclear weapons and delivery vehicles for such weapons" among other things: S.1499 - 118th Congress (2023-2024): HALT Act of 2023. (2023, May 9). https://www.congress.gov/bill/118th-congress/senate-bill/1499

[24] See David Cortright's review of Henry Marr, *Freeze! The Grassroots Movement to Halt the Arms Race and End the Cold War*, 2022, in Cortright, D. (2022, September). *Freeze! The grassroots movement to halt the arms race and end the Cold War*. Arms Control Association. https://www.armscontrol.org/act/2022-09/features/freeze-grassroots-movement-halt-arms-race-end-cold-war

[25] See National Nuclear Security Administration. (n.d.). *Maintaining the stockpile*. Energy.gov. https://www.energy.gov/nnsa/maintaining-stockpile

[26] ICBM Act of 2021, S.982, Section 2, paragraph 9. Text - S.982 - 117th Congress (2021-2022): ICBM Act. (2021, March 25). https://www.congress.gov/bill/117th-congress/senate-bill/982/text

Chapter 3: Pressure, politics and profiteers

[1] Fossil Fuel companies that spent more than $1million on lobbying in 2022 from Open Secrets: https://www.opensecrets.org/industries/lobbying.php?cycle=&ind=E01. Profit information from company's fy2022 financial reports. See also *Wasted: 2022 Global Nuclear Weapons Spending*. (June, 2023). ICAN. https://www.icanw.org/wasted_2022_global_nuclear_weapons_spending

[2] Graphic by Vicki Elson (2023)

[3] There is also "dark money" going to candidates, not all of which can be identified (see section below), but OpenSecrets does a pretty good job of monitoring the money that they can find out about: OpenSecrets. (n.d.). *Defense*. https://www.opensecrets.org/industries/indus.php?Ind=D

[4] See employment history of Lloyd Austin at https://www.opensecrets.org/revolving/rev_summary.php?id=82688

[5] See Giorno, Taylor (2023), "Revolving Door lobbyists help defense contractors get off to a strong start in 2023" in *Open Secrets*: https://www.opensecrets.org/news/2023/05/revolving-door-lobbyists-help-defense-contractors-get-off-to-strong-start-in-2023/

[6] Smithberger, M. (2018). Brass parachutes: The problem of the Pentagon revolving door. In *Project on Government Oversight*. https://www.pogo.org/report/2018/11/brass-parachutes

[7] *Wasted: 2022 global nuclear weapons spending*. (June 2023). ICAN. https://www.icanw.org/wasted_2022_global_nuclear_weapons_spending

[8] https://www.cbsnews.com/news/60-minutes-are-members-of-congress-becoming-telemarketers/

[9] OpenSecrets. (n.d.). *Defense lobbying profile*. https://www.opensecrets.org/federal-lobbying/sectors/summary?cycle=2021&id=D

[10] Beckel, M. (2018). Dark Money Illuminated. In *Issue One*. https://www.issueone.org/wp-content/uploads/2018/09/Dark-Money-Illuminated-Report.pdf

[11] https://www.cambridge.org/core/journals/perspectives-on-politics/article/testing-theories-of-american-politics-elites-interest-groups-and-average-citizens/62327F513959D0A304D4893B382B992B

[12] Citizens United gave corporations first amendment rights, thus allowing unlimited campaign contributions as a form of "free speech." See Campaign Legal Center (2022), "How Does the Citizens United Decision Still Affect Us in 2022?" https://campaignlegal.org/update/how-does-citizens-united-decision-still-affect-us-2022

[13] See for example the arguments put forward by MacAskill, W. (2015, October 20). Does Divestment Work? *The New Yorker*. https://www.newyorker.com/business/currency/does-divestment-work

[14] A number of research studies have stressed that the main and most important effect of divestment is stigmatization of the companies concerned and what that does to their reputation and their overall value (market capitalization). Ansar, A., Caldecott, B., & Tilbury, J. (2013). Stranded assets and the fossil fuel divestment campaign: what does divestment mean for the valuation of fossil fuel assets? In *Stranded assets and the fossil fuel divestment campaign*. Smith School of Enterprise and the Environment, University of Oxford.

[15] See, for instance, Hasan, S., Kumar, A., & Taffler, R. (2021). Anxiety, Excitement, and Asset Prices. *SSRN Electronic Journal*. https://doi.org/10.2139/ssrn.3902654

[16] See *What are stranded assets?* (2022, July 27). Grantham Research Institute on Climate Change and the Environment. https://www.lse.ac.uk/granthaminstitute/explainers/what-are-stranded-assets/

[17] See Sharma, R. (2023, October 26). Top 10 Impacts of Social Media on Business. *Emeritus* https://emeritus.org/in/learn/impact-of-social-media-on-businesses/

[18] Ronald Reagan and Mikhail Gorbachev negotiated the Intermediate-Range Nuclear Forces Treaty (INF) in 1987. They talked about abolishing nuclear weapons altogether, but when Reagan insisting on keeping his Star Wars program, those talks came to end.

[19] Private communication. See Jezer, Marty, Kehler, Randy and Senturia, Ben, (1993) "A Proposal for Democratically Financed Congressional Elections," in *Yale Law and Policy Review*, Vol.11, no.2, pp.333-360.

[20] See https://www.nytimes.com/1987/09/20/magazine/the-company-as-target.html and also: https://scispace.com/pdf/taming-the-new-breed-of-nuclear-free-zone-ordinances-447upr68k4.pdf

[21] For more on the Orange County bankruptcy: https://merage.uci.edu/~jorion/oc/case.html; Information about how it led to a change in the law at: https://www.cacities.org/UploadedFiles/LeagueInternet/df/df0d301a-89ee-4cfe-be53-3e06b5985199.pdf and the CA law on municipal investments: https://law.justia.com/codes/california/code-gov/title-5/division-2/part-1/chapter-4/article-2/section-53630-1/

[22] According to *New Abolitionist*, February 1987, pg 12.

[23] They were also blamed for the space shuttle disaster which took place in the interim. Greenhouse, S. (1986, February 3). *THIOKOL: CONTRACTOR AT BIGGEST RISK. The New York Times.* https://www.nytimes.com/1986/02/03/business/thiokol-contractor-at-biggest-risk.html

[24] Quoted in Wallis, T (1992), "The Road to Reykjavik: The Impact of European and American Peace Movements on the Decision to Remove Land-Based Missiles from Europe," a paper for *Peace Movements in the Cold War and Beyond*, international conference, LSE, London, Jan 2008. p.10.

[25] Mintz, J. (1992, May 6). ATT TO CUT ITS TIES WITH SANDIA LAB. *Washington Post.* https://www.washingtonpost.com/archive/business/1992/05/06/att-to-cut-its-ties-with-sandia-lab/c980765e-dda5-45b4-a991-fa7240466b54/

[26] Quoted in the documentary, *Dangerous Deception:*

[27] I did my PhD research on the different tactics of the peace movement of the 1980s and their impact on the Reagan Administration. For a summary of my findings, see T. Wallis, "How Boycott and Divestment Campaigns Helped Halt the Nuclear Arms Race in the 1980s," on NuclearBan.US: https://www.nuclearban.us/economic-pressures-and-the-inf-treaty/ For the full account, see Timmon Wallis, "Dialogue and Resistance: Two Approaches to Peace Campaigning at RAF Molesworth (1980-1987), unpublished PhD thesis, Bradford University, Bradford, UK, 1991.

[28] See, for example, Ralph Nader's commentary on the Reagan Presidency from 1984: https://www.multinationalmonitor.org/hyper/issues/1984/07/nader.html

[29] *Countries Ban Investment in Cluster Munitions* (2009). Arms Control Association. https://www.armscontrol.org/act/2009-12/countries-ban-investment-cluster-munitions

Chapter 4: From Mali to Australia

[1] So long as there are five permanent members of the UN Security Council, each with veto power over any decision and each with its own arsenal of nuclear weapons, the UN is powerless to act on its own resolutions calling for nuclear weapons to be abolished. Nevertheless, resolutions play a role in moving issues forward and keeping them in the public eye. In the case of nuclear weapons, 75 years of resolutions at the UN finally yielded a new treaty that now has the potential to abolish these weapons.

[2] The countries no longer voting in favor of the TPNW, for different complex reasons are: Argentina, Marshall Islands, Moldova, Saudi Arabia, Sweden, and Switzerland. Countries that did not take part in the negotiations but are now fully supporting it are: Andorra, Eswatini, Guinea, Mali, Rwanda, Somalia, Turkmenistan and Uzbekistan.

[3] There are four more countries that have already joined the TPNW but *cannot* vote at the UN, bringing the total to 140 of countries that positively support the TPNW. Palestine and the Holy See have "observer" states at the UN, meaning they cannot vote, but they can sign treaties. Cook Islands and Niue are semi-autonomous islands that can sign treaties but do not as yet have status as a member state of the UN.

[4] Smaller countries, and countries facing natural disasters, civil war or other major challenges at home, cannot always be present for every vote at the UN in New York. So the numbers on these votes fluctuate somewhat from year to year. At the UN vote in October 2024, for instance, seven countries who have been supporting the TPNW were not present for the vote, which would have brought the total up to 134.

[5] In the case of UN General Assembly resolutions, the only entity capable of *implementing* the will of the majority is the UN Security Council. And the Security Council makes its own decisions about what it wants to implement. The Security *can* issue enforceable resolutions, but only when explicitly basing them on Article VII of the UN Charter, which authorizes the Security Council to make decisions relating to world peace and security that are binding on all Members of the UN.

[6] Only nine countries have their own nuclear weapons: US, Russia, China, UK, France, India, Pakistan, Israel and North Korea. Five European countries have US nuclear weapons based in their country: Germany, Belgium, Netherlands, Italy andTürkiye (Turkey). Belarus now also has Russian nuclear weapons based there. Other NATO members, plus Japan, South Korea and Australia, claim to be under the US "nuclear umbrella."

[1] The Marshall Islands consists of five main islands, 29 coral "atolls" and over 1,000 smaller atolls which are mostly uninhabited.

[2] Other Pacific islands where high levels radioactive fallout were detected include the Cook Islands, New Zealand, Niue, Fiji, Tokelau, Samoa, and Tonga. French nuclear testing in the Pacific continued until 1996.

[3] See the Pacific Nuclear Test Archive: https://disarmament.blogs.pace.edu/nuclear-test-archive/

[4] deBrum was also a champion of the fight against climate change and is credited with being a key role in the negotiations which led to the Paris Climate Agreement of 2015.

[5] See https://reachingcriticalwill.org/images/documents/Disarmament-fora/npt/NIR2025/NIR20.2.pdf

[6] IPSOS poll: ICAN. (2022, May 13). *New poll results*. ICAN Australia. https://icanw.org.au/new-poll-results/

[7] The text of the ICAN Parliamentary Pledge, and the list of signers is at https://pledge.icanw.org/

[8] ICAN. (2018, December 18). *Australian Labor Party commits to joining Nuclear Ban Treaty*. https://www.icanw.org/australian_labor_party_commits_to_joining_nuclear_ban_treaty

[9] The Australia-UK-US (AUKUS) Agreement was announced in September 2021 and involves Australia buying nuclear-powered submarines from the US and sharing other military technology and resources with the US and the UK.

[10] See Doherty, B., & Hurst, D. (2023, March 14). What is the Aukus submarine deal and what does it mean? – the key facts. The Guardian. https://www.theguardian.com/world/2023/mar/14/what-is-the-aukus-submarine-deal-and-what-does-it-mean-the-key-facts

[11] https://icanw.org.au/wp-content/uploads/Complementarity-Open-Letter-to-PM-DPM-and-foreign-minister-090824.pdf

[12] See https://www.theguardian.com/world/2022/nov/09/us-warns-australia-against-joining-treaty-banning-nuclear-weapons

[13] This is the "moveable trailing edge" part of the aircraft wing, made with a unique technology developed in Australia. See https://www.boeing.com.au/content/dam/boeing/en-au/pdf/bck_Boeing_Aerostructures_Australia.pdf

[14] Photo: MilborneOne, CC BY-SA 3.0 <https://creativecommons.org/licenses/by-sa/3.0>, via Wikimedia Commons

[15] KPMG, *Northrop Grumman's Contribution to Australia*: https://cdn.northropgrumman.com/-/media/wp-content/uploads/northrop-grummans-contribution-to-australia.pdf?v=1.0.0

Chapter 5: From Sierra Leone to Egypt

[1] The process for joining a treaty varies from country to country. Most have a two-step process of signing and then ratifying, but if allowed in the treaty itself (which in the case of the TPNW it is) some countries use the one-step process of "acceding" to the treaty.

[2] The Geneva Conventions make it illegal to target civilians (i.e. cities), to cause unnecessary suffering (i.e. with radiation poisoning), to harm neutral parties (i.e. with fall-out drifting hundreds of miles away), to cause damage disproportionate to the military objective (i.e. with bombs that are hundreds or even thousands of times more destructive than the bombs dropped on Hiroshima and Nagasaki)...

[3] See https://www.youtube.com/watch?v=FnjcbgH4Gu4

[4] https://d3n8a8pro7vhmx.cloudfront.net/ican/pages/821/attachments/original/1590165765/NATO_OCT2016.pdf?1590165765

[5] https://peaceandhealthblog.com/2016/11/03/under-pressure/

[6] https://apnews.com/article/nuclear-weapons-disarmament-latin-america-united-nations-gun-politics-4f109626a1cdd6db10560550aa1bb491

[7] Because one of CHRDI's goals is to root out corruption in the government and the judiciary, they are very strict about sticking to a few basic principles – like not accepting any money or gifts from government officials, so as to remain impartial and beyond reproach.

[8] At that point, seven West African countries had by then signed the TPNW (Benin, Cabo Verde, Côte d'Ivoire, Ghana, Guinea-Bissau, Nigeria and Togo) and one had ratified it (Gambia).

[9] FGM is a widespread practice in West Africa as well as in many other parts of the world. It is traumatic, dangerous, and a violation of women's rights. The practice is universally condemned by governments across the world, including in Guinea, and a global effort hopes to eradicate FGM by 2030.

[10] Six countries that voted for the TPNW in 2017 but have since abstained or even voted no in resolutions supporting the treaty are Argentina, Marshall Islands, Moldova, Saudi Arabia, Sweden and Switzerland. Meanwhile, eight countries who did not take part in the 2017 vote but have since been a consistent supporter of the treaty are Andorra, Guinea, Mali, Rwanda, Somalia, Eswatini, Turkmenistan and Uzbekistan. United Nations General Assembly. (2017). *United Nations conference to negotiate a legally-binding instrument to prohibit nuclear weapons: Second session.* https://s3.amazonaws.com/unoda-web/wp-content/uploads/2017/07/A.Conf .229.2017.L.3.Rev .1.pdf

[11] See a history of Egypt's relationship with all matters nuclear in Hebatalla Hata, "Egypt's Quest for a Nuclear Future," *Special Report, January 2021*, South African Institute for International Affairs: https://saiia.org.za/wp-content/uploads/2021/01/Special-Report-taha.pdf

[12] https://www.washingtonpost.com/archive/politics/1995/04/21/egypt-opposes-indefinitely-extending-non-proliferation-treaty/419d5dcb-4ce1-4b01-9493-82e7f9d5ba0b/

[13] Saudi Arabia voted in favor of the UN resolutions calling on all countries to sign the TPNW until 2021, and since then has abstained on those resolutions, but still claims to support it.

[14] Northrop Grumman has 68,000 employees working in at least 14 other countries. These include 6 countries in Europe (not in the TPNW), 6 countries in Asia and the Pacific (none of them currently in the TPNW), plus Saudi Arabia and the UAE.

[15] *Bechtel in Egypt,* Accessed via the Wayback Machine, April 6, 2024: https://web.archive.org/web/20240406050821/https://www.bechtel.com/getmedia/4c174b1a-059c-4456-bf0c-75fb2003a0f6/Bechtel-in-Egypt.pdf

[16] Bechtel lost the contract for managing the Pantex plant, for "failing to meet safety and security standards." See https://www.dontbankonthebomb.com/bechtel/

Chapter 6: From Guatemala to Brazil

[1] It is slightly more complicated than that, because while most countries go through a two-step process of signing and then ratifying a treaty like this, others join the treaty with just one step, called "accession" to the treaty. So far, four of the countries that are now parties to the TPNW skipped the signing step and acceded to the treaty, meaning that the total who have "signed" is actually 94, not counting the additional four who acceded to the treaty.

[2] Mexico is considered part of North America, and Belize is sometime included as a country in Central America and sometimes not. The Dominican Republic is an island in the Caribbean, but also a member of SICA.

[3] All treaties set their own requirement for what it will take for that treaty to enter into force. Usually this is when a certain number of countries have ratified or acceded to it, but sometimes, as in the case of the Comprehensive Test Ban Treaty, it must be certain countries that join before the treaty enters into force. In the case of the TPNW, it was agreed that it would enter into force once 50 countries, no matter which ones, ratified or acceded to it.

[4] Not to be confused with CELAC, which is the Community of Latin American and Caribbean States. CELAC is an official government body consisting of 33 countries in Latin America and the Caribbean, while SEHLAC is a non-governmental network working through Latin America and the Caribbean to promote human security and advocate for humanitarian disarmament.

[5] For an overview of humanitarian disarmament, see https://humanitariandisarmament.org/

[6] Article 81 of Colombia's 1991 constitution prohibits "the manufacture, importation, possession, and use of chemical, biological, or nuclear weapons" as well as "the introduction into the national territory of nuclear and toxic wastes."

[7] See https://fossilfueltreaty.org/colombia

[8] For full text of the TPNW, see Appendix I.

[9] "As long as nuclear weapons exist, there will always be the possibility of their use," he said. See Da Silva, L. I. L. (2023, May 21). Speech by President Lula at the G7 working session: "Towards a Peaceful, Stable and Prosperous World." In *Planalto*. G7 Working Section, Hiroshima, Japan. https://www.gov.br/planalto/en/latest-news/speech-by-president-lula-at-session-8-of-g7

[10] https://reachingcriticalwill.org/images/documents/Disarmament-fora/1com/1com23/statements/16Oct_Brazil.pdf

[11] See COMISSÃO DE RELAÇÕES EXTERIORES E DE DEFESA NACIONAL MENSAGEM No 516, DE 2018

[12] See, for instance, Parth Satam and David Cenciotti, "KC-135 Tankers Take Part in "No Notice" Nuclear Operational Readiness Drills," in *The Aviationist*, August 1, 2024: https://theaviationist.com/2024/08/01/nori-fairchild-afb/

[13] https://breakingdefense.com/2024/10/exclusive-l3harris-embraer-no-longer-working-together-to-pitch-c-390-to-us/

Chapter 7: From Ireland to Mexico

[1] Article 5 of the TPNW (see Appendix I) states that parties to the treaty "shall take all appropriate legal, administrative and other measures, including the imposition of enal sanctions, to prevent and suppress any activity prohibited to a State Party under this Treaty undertaken by persons or on territory under its jurisdiction or control."

[2] The only mechanism available to enforce international law is the UN Security Council, which can impose sanctions on a country or ultimately go to war with it. This latter option has been used only twice in UN history, when the UN went to war against North Korea and more recently when it pushed Iraq out of Kuwait in 1991. Since any one of the five permanent members can block any decision of the Security Council, and those five all possess nuclear weapons, it is unlikely that the Security Council would be willing to enforce anything to do with the TPNW.

[3] In most jurisdictions, "person" can mean both an individual ("natural" person) and a corporation ("legal" person). Sometimes this is explicitly defined in laws or treaties, and other times it may be implied. Where the term is more ambiguous, it may require a legal case to determine whether corporations are also included in the definition. And in some countries this may not be the case at all.

[4] And if the offense is committed "with the consent or connivance, or was attributable to any willful neglect, of a person who was a director, manager, secretary or other officer of the body corporate, or a person purporting to act in that capacity, that person shall, as well as the body corporate, be guilty of an offence and may be liable to be proceeded against and punished as if he or she were guilty of the first-mentioned offense."

[5] When Malta ratified the Chemical Weapons Convention, they passed a similar Act in 1997, implementing the CWC prohibitions into Maltese law. This law was later repealed (Act V of 2000) in favor of giving the Prime Minister authority to implement "regulations necessary or expedient for the implementation of international treaties." However, since 2000, Malta has continued to pass specific pieces of legislation to implement the Anti-Personnel Landmines Treaty in 2001, Security Council Resolution 1540 in 2005, and the Comprehensive Test Ban Treaty in 2007.

[6] The Comprehensive Nuclear-Test Ban Treaty Regulations, Subsidiary Legislation no. 365.11: https://legislation.mt/eli/sl/365.11/eng/pdf

[7] Malta's comprehensive anti-terrorist laws are found in Chapter 9 of the Criminal Code, Articles 328A-328M. https://legislation.mt/eli/cap/9/eng/pdf

[8] The Core Group of countries that shepherded the TPNW through the process of being negotiated and adopted were Mexico, Ireland, Brazil, Austria, New Zealand and South Africa. Since entry into force of the treaty, this group has grown to include others that are taking a lead on one or another issue or Working Group between meetings of the States Parties. These countries now form a Coordination Group, led by the country elected to preside over the next meeting. From 2023 to 2025, this was led by Kazakhstan and also included, in addition to the original six countries, Kiribati, Malaysia, Uruguay, and Thailand. This group now includes Philippines and Malta.

[9] The Antarctic Treaty (1961) was the first treaty ensuring an entire continent would remain free of nuclear weapons. But the Treaty of Tlatelolco (1969) was the first such treaty to cover a densely-populated part of the world. Since then, similar treaties have been agreed covering the whole of Africa, Southeast Asia, Central Asia and the Pacific.

[10] Mexico also has a unitary legal system with "automatic treaty incorporation," meaning that international treaties that Mexico joins are automatically incorporated into national law in Mexico.

[11] See https://kcnsc.doe.gov/about-us/nuclear-weapons-program/

[12] These laws apply to all federal agencies (with certain exceptions), including the Pentagon, and have been on the books since 1978. See https://www.gao.gov/products/105519

[13] The most up-to-date list of major nuclear weapons contractors is kept at https://www.dontbankonthebomb.com/nwproducers/. The public websites of most of these contractors either list or show on maps where they have offices, plants or major projects, and according to these, Airbus, Bechtel, Fluor, General Dynamics, Honeywell, Safran, and Thales are all currently operating in Mexico.

Chapter 8: From Cuba to the Holy See

[1] Quoted in the December 2018 Update from Pax, *Worldwide Investments in Cluster Munitions: A Shared Responsibility*: https://stopexplosiveinvestments.org/wp-content/uploads/sites/6/latest-report-worldwide-investments.pdf

[2] https://www.msci.com/indexes/documents/methodology/2_MSCI_Global_ex_Controversial_Weapons_Indexes_Methodology_20241216.pdf

[3] See https://www.sustainablefinance.ch/upload/cms/user/Controversial_Weapons_Letter_FINAL_2019_01_31.pdf

[4] https://www.marketplace.org/2023/02/10/how-much-money-does-catholic-church-have/

[5] For example, in Germany, Catholics, Protestants and Jews pay a "church tax" as a percentage of their national income tax that goes directly to those religious institutions

[6] https://www.usccb.org/resources/Socially%20Responsible%20Investment%20Guidelines%202021%20(003).pdf

[7] https://www.avemariafunds.com/about-us/investment-process.html

Chapter 9: From Switzerland to South Africa

[1] See https://www.icanw.org/both_houses_of_swiss_parliament_call_on_government_to_join_the_nuclear_ban_treaty_immediately

[2] UBS currently provides loans to six of the major nuclear weapons companies, according to Don't Bank on the Bomb. It gets away with this by claiming that the prohibition of "direct" financing in Article 8b of the Law allows it to continue financing *other* activities of those companies, so long as none of their funds go towards the "direct" financing of nuclear weapons activities by those companies. Meanwhile, UBS has more than $3.5 billion dollar's worth of shares in four other nuclear weapons companies. The holding of shares constitutes "indirect" financing and is prohibited by Article 8c of the War Materiel Act. In this case, however, there is another clause in the Act that says indirect financing is prohibited, "where the prohibition of direct financing is circumvented thereby..." What is exactly is meant by that phrase is unclear. But so far, UBS has managed to get away with it meaning whatever they want it to mean.

[3] These were Ireland, Italy, Liechtenstein, Luxembourg, Netherlands, New Zealand, St Kitts and Nevis, Samoa, Spain and Switzerland. See 2024 Cluster Munition Monitor: https://backend.icblcmc.org/assets/reports/Cluster-Munition-Monitors/CMM2024/Downloads/Cluster-Munition-Monitor-2024-Web.pdf

[4] See https://www.irishstatutebook.ie/eli/2018/act/29/enacted/en/html#:~:text=An%20Act%20to%20impose%20certain,are%20not%20directly%20invested%20in

[5] According to their 2023 report to parliament, ISIF "maintains an exclusionary strategy around... direct investment in companies involved in the manufacture and testing of

nuclear weapons or their critical component parts. https://isif.ie/uploads/publications/Ireland-Strategic-Investment-Fund-2023-Annual-Report-Extract.pdf

[6] Bank of America, Barclay's, CitiBank, Wells Fargo and other international banks are also operating in Ireland, and all of those banks have known investments in nuclear weapons companies. See DontBankontheBomb.com/investors and the most recent 2025 Don't Bank on the Bomb report: *At Great Cost: The companies building nuclear weapons and their financiers*, PAX/ICAN: https://www.dontbankonthebomb.com/wp-content/uploads/2025/02/72025004_PAX_-_DONT-BANK-ON-THE-BOMB_FINAL_WEB.pdf

[7] See pp. 54 ff for a discussion of the context, plus full text of the pledge in Alexander Kmentt, *The Treaty on the Prohibition of Nuclear Weapons: How it was Achieved and Why it Matters*, Routledge, 2021.

[8] *Ibid*

[9] Don't Bank on the Bomb is the most up-to-date and reliable source of information on the major nuclear weapons companies and their investors. See https://www.dontbankonthebomb.com/

[10] Ninety One Limited is registered in South Africa, but the investment in Jacobs Solutions (formerly Jacobs Engineering) comes from a UK-based subsidiary. Meanwhile, Jacobs Solutions has spun off all its US nuclear weapons related work and only retains a small contract for maintaining UK nuclear submarines.

[11] South Africa also hosts UK-based Babcock International, which has just been added to Don't Bank on the Bomb's list of nuclear weapons contractors for their involvement in UK Trident and Vanguard-class nuclear-armed submarines. Jacobs' and Babcock's operations in South Africa are not directly related to their work on nuclear weapons in the US or the UK. Jacobs currently has a 20-year contract worth $1.2 billion with the state-owned public utility company, Eskom, to carry out essential modifications to South Africa's only nuclear power plant, at Koeberg. Babcock Africa offers construction and engineering equipment and services.

[12] Many investors who don't want to divest will instead retain stock in order to "engage" with the offending companies, through shareholder resolutions and other direct communications with the company.

[13] See country tables at the end of PAX/ICAN, *At Great Cost: The Companies Building Nuclear Weapons and Their Financiers*, 2025: https://www.dontbankonthebomb.com/wp-content/uploads/2025/02/72025004_PAX_-_DONT-BANK-ON-THE-BOMB_FINAL_WEB.pdf

[14] Like most of the other nuclear weapons companies, Jacobs gets most of its financing from large US investment firms. State Street Bank owns more than $1 billion worth of shares in Jacobs and Wells Fargo almost $2 billion worth. But other major investors include BBVA in Spain, Barclays in the UK, and BNP Paribas in France. These are all financial institutions scheduled to join the growing divestment movement in this scenario.

Chapter 10: From Venezuela to the Philippines

[1] From Section 314: *"No department, agency or any other entity of the United States Government may enter into a contract for the procurement of goods or services from parastatal organizations (except for items necessary for diplomatic and consular purposes)* See full text of the Comprehensive Anti-Apartheid Act: https://www.congress.gov/99/statute/STATUTE-100/STATUTE-100-Pg1086.pdf. Note that there are various and inconsistent definitions of what constitutes a parastatal corporation. Some definitions insist that the corporation must be at least part *owned* by a government. In most contexts, however, that would describe a "public" or state-owned company as opposed to a "para" state company. Given the intensely close relationship of

the nuclear weapons corporations to the government that funds them, as described in Chapter 3, it seems appropriate to give these corporations a parastatal status.

[2] In 2024, the Venezuelan National Assembly passed the "Organic Law of the Liberator Simon Bolivar against the Imperialist Blockade and in Defense of the Bolivarian Republic of Venezuela." This law gave sweeping powers to the government to control and crack down on individuals, organizations and media outlets supporting or promoting the economic sanctions imposed on Venezuela by the United States. And in response to Trump's Executive Order 13692 in March 2025, imposing a secondary tariff on countries importing oil from Venezuela, and his decision to rescind Chevron's license to sell Venezuelan oil to the United States, Venezuela announced its "Absolute Productive Independence Plan Amid Sanctions" to ensure continued production of Venezuela's oil and gas reserves.

[3] See https://nzhistory.govt.nz/page/uss-buchanan-refused-entry-new-zealand

[4] Quoted in Ollie Neas, "Mahia, We Have a Problem," in *North & South*, April, 2021: https://northandsouth.co.nz/2021/03/14/rocket-lab-military/

[5] Quoted in Ollie Neas, "Mahia, We Have a Problem," in *North & South*, April, 2021: https://northandsouth.co.nz/2021/03/14/rocket-lab-military/

[6] See Ollie Neas, "Mahia, We Have a Problem," in *North & South*, April, 2021: https://northandsouth.co.nz/2021/03/14/rocket-lab-military/

[7] https://thespinoff.co.nz/politics/21-06-2021/mahia-residents-descend-on-auckland-to-protest-rocket-lab-links-with-us-military

[8] *Ibid*

[9] See https://www.spacecom.mil/Newsroom/News/Article-Display/Article/4154114/new-zealand-joins-space-multinational-force-operation-olympic-defender/

[10] https://thespinoff.co.nz/business/06-06-2019/managing-risk-and-reward-in-new-zealands-emerging-space-sector

[11] Quoted in https://www.nzherald.co.nz/gisborne-herald/news/protesters-threaten-rocket-lab-launch-pad-with-disruption-time-to-damage-property/WYM3PCFI4NCIVIVOV56FB4Y6VI/

[12] See https://www.reuters.com/world/asia-pacific/us-tariffs-philippines-could-affect-weapons-deal-ambassador-says-2025-04-10/ accessed through archive.ph.

[13] See https://asiatimes.com/2022/12/marcos-jr-shows-the-way-to-balance-us-and-china/#

Chapter 11: From Norway to Spain

[1] The original 12 were the US, Canada, UK, France, Belgium, Netherlands, Luxembourg, Denmark, Norway, Italy, Portugal and Iceland. Greece, Türkiye (Turkey) and West Germany then joined the Alliance in the 1950s. Spain joined in 1982, after the death of Franco and a return to democracy.

[2] https://www.nato.int/nato_static_fl2014/assets/pdf/2022/6/pdf/290622-strategic-concept.pdf

[3] General Charles de Gaulle took France out of the military structures of NATO in 1966. France returned in 2009, but has remained outside the Nuclear Planning Group for its own political reasons.

[4] The last US nuclear weapons were removed from the UK in 2008, but the UK is getting ready to have them back again at RAF Lakenheath in Suffolk.

[5] Norway secretly allowed the US to deploy nuclear-capable artillery and missiles in the north of Norway, which remained there until 1965, but without the nuclear warheads installed.

[6] At its 1957 annual conference, the Norwegian Labor Party, *Arbeiderpartiet,* declared that nuclear weapons "shall not be placed on Norwegian territory." And later that year,

the Labor Prime Minister, Einar Gerhardsen, announced at a NATO summit that Norway would not allow the stationing of US nuclear weapons on its soil.

7 See Kjølv Egeland, "The 'Cosmic Bluff' Revisited: Extended Nuclear Deterrence in the US–Norway Alliance," in *Cold War History*, Dec 11, 2023, vol 25 (1), pp 43-66.

8 Minister for Agriculture and Fisheries Svandís Svavarsdóttir and Minister for Social Affairs Gudmundur Ingi Gudbrandsson. See ICAN. (n.d.-a). *Full list of pledge takers.* https://pledge.icanw.org/full_list_of_pledge_takers

9 ICAN. (n.d.-c). *Iceland.* https://www.icanw.org/iceland#:~:text=Public%20opinion,per%20cent%20opposed%20to%20joining

10 Burr, W. (2016, August 15). *U.S. government debated secret nuclear deployments in Iceland.* National Security Archive. https://nsarchive.gwu.edu/briefing-book/nuclear-vault/2016-08-15/us-government-debated-secret-nuclear-deployments-iceland

11 Ministry of Foreign Affairs. (n.d.). *National Security.* Government of Iceland. from https://www.government.is/topics/foreign-affairs/national-security/

12 Oskarsson, T. A. (2022, August 2). *Statement at the 10th NPT Review Conference.* 10th NPT Review Conference General Assembly 76th session. https://www.government.is/diplomatic-missions/embassy-article/2022/08/02/Statement-at-the-10th-NPT-Review-Conference-/

13 Laitinen, E. (2019). 84% of Finns want the government to join the TPNW. *Rauhanliitto.* https://rauhanliitto.fi/en/rauhanliitto-en/articles/press-releases/84-of-finns-want-the-government-to-join-the-tpnw

14 Pekka Haavisto was Foreign Minister of Finland from 2019-2023. He has served in the Finnish government in a number of other capacities and has run for President of Finland three times, most recently in 2024 (coming in second). As well as being a politician, Pekka has been an active peace campaigner and has signed the ICAN Pledge.

15 Reuters. (2023, April 13). New member Finland to take part in NATO's nuclear planning. *Reuters.* https://www.reuters.com/world/europe/new-member-finland-take-part-natos-nuclear-planning-2023-04-13/

16 See remarks quoted here: Wright, T. [@TimMilesWright]. (2020, December 16). *The former Swedish foreign minister @margotwallstrom expressed regret today at having failed to convince the Swedish parliament to agree to...* [X post]. X. https://twitter.com/TimMilesWright/status/1339319467965358080?s=20

17 ICAN. (2021, November 9). *Ruling party in Sweden: the goal is to join the TPNW.* https://www.icanw.org/sweden_social_democrats_goal_to_join_tpnw

18 Reuters. (2022, November 11). Sweden to spurn nuclear weapons as NATO member, foreign minister says. *Reuters.* https://www.reuters.com/world/europe/sweden-spurn-nuclear-weapons-nato-member-foreign-minister-says-2022-11-11/

19 Survey conducted January 2021, see Portela, C. (2021, July 15). *Weapons of Mass Debate - Spain: a dispassionate supporter of nuclear deterrence.* Institut Montaigne. https://www.institutmontaigne.org/en/expressions/weapons-mass-debate-spain-dispassionate-supporter-nuclear-deterrence

20 See above for history.

21 France and Germany each have an 11% stake in the company, and the rest of the shares are mainly owned by large US investment banks like Capital Group, Blackrock, Vanguard and Fidelity. Nevertheless, Spain's share of Airbus is crucial to its viability as a European airplane manufacturer.

22 Airbus has a 50% stake in the ArianeGroup and a 37.5% stake in MBDA France. ArianeGroup is the prime contractor for France's M51 submarine-launched ballistic missile and its latest iteration, the M51.3. MBDA France is the prime contractor for France's ASMPA air-launched nuclear cruise missile and its successor, the ASN4G, currently under development.

[23] In the end, ESG criteria, including involvement with controversial weapons, was removed from being a qualifying factor in which companies would be part of the DAX index in Germany. See https://www.klgates.com/Reform-of-the-DAX-the-German-Blue-Chip-Stock-Market-Index-1-12-2021

[24] See https://www.reuters.com/business/aerospace-defense/exclusive-airbus-reviews-defence-business-pressures-mount-2022-02-16/

[25] At the moment, movement by financial institutions in Europe is going in the opposite direction. Policies that prohibited investments in controversial weapons are being relaxed in response to political demands to increase defense spending following Russia's invasion of Ukraine. But in this scenario, other factors are pushing them back in a more positive direction.

Chapter 12: From Italy to Germany

[1] see https://www.npr.org/2025/04/23/nx-s1-5366685/trump-populism-right-wing-world-canada-australia

[2] see https://www.defensenews.com/global/europe/2025/04/18/behind-italys-defense-spending-hike-pushback-at-home/

[3] https://www.icanw.org/italy

[4] Francesco Vignarca, *Disarmo Nucleare*, Altra Economia, Milan, 2023.

[5] https://sgi-peace.org/latest/new-senzatomica-exhibition-in-italy-features-vr-experience

[6] See ICAN poll, conducted by YouGov in 7 European countries: https://d3n8a8pro7vhmx.cloudfront.net/ican/pages/234/attachments/original/1611134933/ICAN_YouGov_Poll_2020.pdf

[7] ICAN. (n.d.-a). *Belgium*. https://www.icanw.org/belgium

[8] See https://www.washingtonpost.com/archive/politics/1983/12/15/dutch-peace-movement-maintains-broad-support/a5303a37-58fe-42d6-9e9b-99071819f511/?_pml=1

[9] See Stelzenmüller, C. (2021, November 19). *Nuclear weapons debate in Germany touches a raw NATO nerve.* Brookings. https://www.brookings.edu/articles/nuclear-weapons-debate-in-germany-touches-a-raw-nato-nerve/

[10] All of the B61 bombs deployed in Europe are currently being upgraded to the B61-12 version, which has a maximum yield of 50 Kt rather than 170 Kt. These are designed to be more accurate, however, and to be dropped from further away for safety of air crews. In January, 2025, it was inadvertently announced that deployment of the B61-12s was already underway: https://www.newsweek.com/us-deploys-b61-12-gravity-bombs-europe-tactical-nuclear-weapons-2017485

[11] https://www.dw.com/en/germany-no-return-to-compulsory-military-service/a-72213817

[12] See ICAN. (2021a). NATO Public Opinion on Nuclear Weapons. In *ICAN*. https://d3n8a8pro7vhmx.cloudfront.net/ican/pages/234/attachments/original/1611134933/ICAN_YouGov_Poll_2020.pdf

[13] https://x.com/ican_de/status/1301110556074692609?s=20

[14] See The Economist. (2021, November 18). Allies fear Germany's incoming government will go soft on nukes. *The Economist*. https://www.economist.com/europe/2021/11/20/allies-fear-germanys-incoming-government-will-go-soft-on-nukes

[15] U.S Government Accountability Office. (2023). F-35 Joint Strike Fighter. In *U.S Government Accountability Office* (GAO-23-106047). (p. 7) https://www.gao.gov/assets/gao-23-106047.pdf

[16]Losey, S. (2022, November 18). *F-35 costs have been declining. That's about to change.* Defense News. https://www.defensenews.com/industry/2022/11/18/f-35-costs-have-been-declining-thats-about-to-change/

[17] Sprenger, S. (2022, December 14). *Germany clinches $8 billion purchase of 35 F-35 aircraft from the US*. Defense News. https://www.defensenews.com/global/europe/2022/12/14/germany-clinches-8-billion-purchase-of-35-f-35-aircraft-from-the-us/

[18]Kadam, T. (2022, December 23). Canada To Pay A Whopping $450 Million Per F-35 Stealth Fighter When Actual Cost Of US Aircraft Is Less Than 100M? *The EurAsian Times*. https://www.eurasiantimes.com/canada-to-pay-a-whopping-450-million-per-f-35-stealth-fighter-when-actual-cost-of-us-aircraft-is-less-than-100m/

[19] This is known as the "block 4" upgrade and includes other upgraded capabilities of the aircraft. Congressional Research Service. (2022). F-35 Joint Strike Fighter (JSF) Program. In *Congressional Research Service* (No. RL30563). (p. 23). https://crsreports.congress.gov/product/pdf/RL/RL30563/85

[20]*Flight tests to show B61-12 will work on Air Force's newest fighter jet*. (2020, November 23). Sandia National Laboratories https://newsreleases.sandia.gov/b61-12_flight/
Image here: F-35A with 2B61-12 bombs. https://commons.wikimedia.org/wiki/File:F-35A_with_2_B61-12_bombs.jpg
Defense Acquisition Management Information Retrieval. (2019). *F-35 Lightning II Joint Strike Fighter (JSF) Program (F-35)*. (p. 18). https://www.esd.whs.mil/Portals/54/Documents/FOID/Reading%20Room/Selected_Acquisition_Reports/FY_2019_SARS/20-F-0568_DOC_32_F-35_SAR_Dec_2019_Full.pdf

[21] U.S Government Accountability Office. (2023). F-35 Joint Strike Fighter. In *U.S Government Accountability Office* (GAO-23-106047). (p. 1) https://www.gao.gov/assets/gao-23-106047.pdf Congressional Research Service. (2022). F-35 Joint Strike Fighter (JSF) Program. In *Congressional Research Service* (No. RL30563). (p. 36). https://crsreports.congress.gov/product/pdf/RL/RL30563/85

[22] See https://bulgarianmilitary.com/2025/03/25/heavy-haulage-transforms-weeze-into-an-f-35-manufacturing-hub/

[23] Full details of the F-35 program at https://www.congress.gov/crs-product/R48304

Chapter 13: From Syracuse to Phoenix

[1] Waller, Douglas (1987). *Congress and the Nuclear Freeze: An inside look at the politics of a mass movement*. UMass Press. pg.163

[2]Waller (1987), pg.291

[3] A 2016 poll by YouGov for the Huffington Post showed that a clear 50% of Americans supported the US using nuclear weapons "only in response to a nuclear attack." And a 2019 poll conducted by the University of Maryland showed that 74% of Democrats support a bill limiting presidential first use of nuclear weapons. See https://today.yougov.com/topics/politics/articles-reports/2016/08/11/poll-results-nuclear-weapons and http://www.publicconsultation.org/wp-content/uploads/2019/05/Nuclear_Weapons_Report_0519.pdf

[4] See more background on this poll at https://www.nuclearban.us/us-opinion-on-nuclear-weapons-september-2019/ and full poll breakdown at https://www.nuclearban.us/us-opinion-on-nuclear-weapons-september-2019/

[5] See poll details at https://www.nuclearban.us/ma-state-poll/

[6] In the previous session of Congress (2023-2024), only 13 Members of the House of Representatives specifically endorsed the bill calling for the US to sign the TPNW and another 30 endorsed the resolution calling for the US to "embrace" the goals and provisions of the TPNW and work towards the abolition of nuclear weapons. No Senators have so far been willing to support anything that mentions abolition. The main reason for this was spelled out in Chapter 3: the undue influence of the nuclear weapons industry on Members of Congress and the Administration, ensuring continued bipartisan support for nuclear weapons, regardless of the views of the general public.

[7] Washington, DC and Tuscon, AZ have joined BftB, Austin, Seattle, Denver, Detroit, Louisville, KY, Fresno, Sacramento, Kansas City and Atlanta are in MfP, and San Francisco, Boston, Portland, OR, Baltimore and Mikwaukee are in both.

[8] https://www.mayorsforpeace.org/wp-content/uploads/2021/file-PX_Vision_Action_Plan_en.pdf

Chapter 14: From Milwaukee to Kansas City

[1] In some cases, a city or town has passed a resolution but not yet joined Mayors for Peace, so it is a bit more complicated than it looks.

[2] See https://www.preventnuclearwar.org

[3] https://psr.org/issues/nuclear-weapons-abolition/

[4] See, for example: https://www.jsonline.com/story/news/politics/analysis/2024/07/15/milwaukee-is-a-democratic-city-but-it-also-has-a-lot-of-republicans/74126989007/

[5] The Golden Rule is a 30-foot sailboat that set sail for the Marshall Islands in 1958, skippered by Quaker Albert Bigelow. Their goal was to stop US nuclear testing by sailing into the test zone, but they were arrested before reaching it. The boat was restored by Veterans For Peace and set sail again in 2015 to promote peace and nuclear disarmament. In 2022-2023, the Golden Rule sailed the 11,000 mile Great Loop around the US and through the Great Lakes.

[6] Alders are the elected representatives on the Milwaukee Common Council, which is the body responsible for the municipality.

[7] The first to go was the thermostat and "home" division, which became a separate company in 2018, with the name Resideo. Resideo continues to use the Honeywell brand name under license from Honeywell. But Honeywell itself no longer makes home thermostats. Honeywell then sold its Muck Boot brand and other boot and footwear products to a company called Rocky Brands in 2021. These were not branded as Honeywell, but in any case are no longer produced by Honeywell. The next to go was Honeywell's Personal Protective Equipment (PPE) division. This produces the safety goggles, COVID masks and other safety products. This was sold to Protective Industrial Products, Inc. for $1.3 billion in 2024. So Honeywell no longer makes the Honeywell branded PPE, either. In early 2025, Honeywell announced plans to sell off its Advanced Materials division by the end of the year. It then announced spinning off two more of its divisions in 2026: Aerospace and Automation will then be separate, independently traded companies.

[8] https://careers.honeywell.com/us/en/High-School-STEM-Internships

Chapter 15: From Evanston to Washington

[1] See https://prop1.org/prop1/index.html

[2] DC does not have representation in Congress, so Norton is a "delegate" rather than a US Representative. She is allowed to introduce bills, but cannot vote on them. Her priority, in addition to nuclear abolition, has been a bill to give statehood to DC and thus official representation in Congress. If DC were a state, it would still be larger in population than Wyoming or Vermont, both fully recognized states with voting representation in Congress.

[3] https://boeing.mediaroom.com/2022-05-05-Boeing-Names-Northern-Virginia-Office-Its-Global-Headquarters-Establishes-Research-Technology-Hub

Chapter 16: From Spokane to Providence

[1] Hanford in Washington State was one of the sites where plutonium was produced for the original Manhattan Project. During the Cold War period, it expanded into a massive complex with nine nuclear reactors and other facilities for the production of plutonium for the rapidly growing US nuclear arsenal. By the 1960s, parts of the site were being

shut down, but decommissioning of the final reactor was not complete until 2022. There is still enormous amounts of dangerous radioactive waste on the site, and what has been labeled the world's largest environmental cleanup operation is still ongoing.

[2] These included Pax Christi RI, East Bay Citizens for Peace, Action Corps RI, No Endless War or Excessive Militarism, CodePink, War Watch, Sisters of Mercy Justice Team, RI Poor People's Campaign, Direct Action for Rights and Equality, ANSWER Coalition, RI Anti-war Committee, Westerly Area Peace and Justice, BLM RI PAC, and ProvDSA.

Chapter 17: From New York to Philadelphia

[1] Wander, N., & Malone, R. E. (2006). Fiscal versus social responsibility: how Philip Morris shaped the public funds divestment debate. *Tobacco control, 15*(3), 231–241.

[2] This is the most comprehensive list of fossil fuel divestment commitments available at present, but even this database cannot keep up with the pace of divestment worldwide, so the totals are likely higher in all categories and continuing to rise: https://divestmentdatabase.org/

[3] Based on percentages at https://divestmentdatabase.org/

[4] See list of Nuclear Free Zone ordinances in the US with links to some city codes at: https://www.nuclearban.us/nfz-ordinances-and-city-codes/

[5] Tegmark, M. (2016, April 4). Hawking Says 'Don't Bank on the Bomb' and Cambridge Votes to Divest $ 1Billion From Nuclear Weapons. *Future of Life Institute.* (n.d.). https://futureoflife.org/nuclear/hawking-says-dont-bank-on-the-bomb-and-cambridge-votes-to-divest-1billion-from-nuclear-weapons/

[6] See very detailed history of New York's nuclear weapons legacy by Matthew Bolton, *From Manhattan Project to Nuclear Free*: https://bpb-us-w2.wpmucdn.com/blogs.pace.edu/dist/0/195/files/2020/01/From-Manhattan-Project-to-Nuclear-Free-011620.pdf

[7] *The New York City Council—File #: Res 0976-2019.* (2019, June 26).

[8] In the 1980s, it was not so much the actual amounts of money being divested that worried the companies, but the fear that this was just the tip of an iceberg that would melt over them if they were not able to nip it in the bud. See Dugger, Ronnie (1987), "The Company as Target: Antinuclear Campaigners Across the Country are Interfering with Business as Usual," in *New York Times Magazine*, Sept. 20, 1987. (p.30ff) https://www.nytimes.com/1987/09/20/magazine/the-company-as-target.html

[9] See, for example, this article in the local paper from 2009: https://www.dailycamera.com/2009/11/17/boulder-tackles-global-climate-change-nuclear-weapons/

[10] See DontBankontheBomb.com/investors and the most recent 2025 Don't Bank on the Bomb report: *At Great Cost: The companies building nuclear weapons and their financiers*, PAX/ICAN: https://www.dontbankonthebomb.com/wp-content/uploads/2025/02/72025004_PAX_-_DONT-BANK-ON-THE-BOMB_FINAL_WEB.pdf

Chapter 18: From Northampton to Boston

[1] Narkewicz, D. (2018, September 26) Northampton Executive Policy Order: *Supporting the Mitigation and Abolition of Nuclear Weapons* https://northamptonma.gov/DocumentCenter/View/11503/Executive-Policy-Order---Supporting-the-Mitigation--Abolition-of-Nuclear-Weapons---Sept-26-2019-PDF?bidId=

[2] Dunau, B. (2019, August 20). Northampton City Council takes stand against companies involved with nuclear weapons. *Daily Hampshire Gazette.* https://www.gazettenet.com/City-Council-passes-home-rule-petition-to-forbid-city-from-doing-business-with-nuclear-weapons-makers-27862171

[3] City of Northampton, MA. *Act No. H.4102* (2020, June 25). An Act Regulating City Contracts in the City of Northampton. Retrieved from, https://www.nuclearban.us/wp-content/uploads/2020/07/H4102.-HOme-Rule-Northampton.pdf
[4] https://www.documentcloud.org/documents/24097515-2020-city-of-boston-disparity-study-final-report/#document/p10/a2398896

Chapter 19: From Oregon to California

[1] https://www.cambridgeday.com/2024/08/28/elbit-company-that-was-protested-weekly-confirms-it-is-moving-out-of-cambridge/
[2] See Title 18 § 2332a(c)(2) of the US Code, which defines "weapon of mass destruction" along with the definition of "destructive device" at Title 18 § 921(a)(4).
[3] This was a Back from the Brink resolution, calling on the our federal leaders "and our nation" to embrace the TPNW: https://legiscan.com/CA/text/AJR33/id/1818253

Chapter 20: From AOC to the DNC

[1] AOC agreed to cosponsor the Norton Bill during the final days of the 2021-22 session of Congress, but her co-sponsorship was snuck in under the radar of the media and the public and went unnoticed. She failed to renew her co-sponsorship in the 2023-24 session. This time, however, she is going to make it a big deal (in this scenario).
[2] https://www.newyorker.com/tech/annals-of-technology/the-most-radioactive-place-in-new-york-city
[3] https://www.youtube.com/watch?v=N-5d7V4Sbqk
[4] See www.warheadstowindmills.org and Timmon Wallis, *Warheads to Windmills: Preventing Climate Catastrophe and Nuclear War*, Indispensable Press, 2023.
[5] Senator Ed Markey is considered the Senate's leading spokesperson on nuclear weapons issues. He spoke in favor of the Nuclear Freeze at the 1982 rally in Central Park in front of a million people and wrote a book entitled *Nuclear Peril: The Politics of Proliferation*. He has introduced a number of bills over the years, calling for No First Use, reductions in nuclear spending, urging the government back to the negotiating table and other such measures. But he talks about arms control and non-proliferation, never about nuclear abolition. He refuses to support the TPNW and will not put his name to anything calling on the US to join it.
[6] DNC can stand for the Democratic National *Committee*, which runs the Democratic Party, as used here, or for the Democratic National *Convention*, which takes place every four years to nominate the Democratic candidate for President (but does little else).

Chapter 21: The US signs the TPNW

[1] Some climate activists see nuclear power as a "clean" alternative to burning fossil fuels. However, nuclear power is already the most expensive form of electricity, with wind and solar getting cheaper by the day. Nuclear power's main advantage over wind and sun is that it runs all the time, but this also now being undercut by cheaper battery storage. Building nuclear plants can also take decades, whereas the climate crisis needs addressing now. There are many other reasons why nuclear power is not a "solution" to the climate crisis. For a summary of these, see pp 41-50 in T. Wallis, *Warheads to Windmills: Preventing Climate Catastrophe and Nuclear War*, Indispensable Press, 2023.
[2] See Vicki Elson, "Inside the Doomsday Machine" in *Pressenza,* 5/3/23 (in three parts): https://www.pressenza.com/2023/03/inside-the-doomsday-machine-the-2023-deterrence-summit-part-1/
[3] See ICAN (2019), *Schools of Mass Destruction*: https://d3n8a8pro7vhmx.cloudfront.net/ican/pages/430/attachments/original/1574113227/ICAN-Schools-of-mass-Destruction_nov2019.pdf?1574113227
[4] See Reagan diary: https://www.reaganfoundation.org/ronald-reagan/white-house-diaries/diary-entry-10211983. October 22, 1983 was the day that over a million people

demonstrated in Germany against plans to bring a new generation of US nuclear missiles to Europe. Another 400,000 demonstrated in London, 350,000 in Rome, 100,000 in Vienna and huge numbers in many other cities across Europe. See https://www.nytimes.com/1983/10/23/world/vast-crowds-hold-rallies-in-europe-against-us-arms.html

5 It was the largest demonstration in that country's post-war history: 400,000 in Bonn; 200,000 in Hamburg; 200,000 in Stuttgart; 75,000 in West Berlin. See https://www.washingtonpost.com/archive/politics/1983/10/23/more-than-a-million-protest-missiles-in-western-europe/9d703245-36fa-40ce-8714-e281f796a472/

6 With Reagan's help, Jack Welch took GE from being a $14 billion industry in 1981 to a $400 billion industry by 2001. See https://www.washingtonpost.com/archive/business/1986/03/23/welch-sees-new-era-for-us-manufacturers/127bc84f-001a-47cc-a77e-33bdd12a9b67/ But GE also reputedly suffered losses of $30 million from hospital boycotts alone. See See Janet Lowe, *Jack Welch Speaks*, Wiley and Sons, Hoboken, NJ, 2008. P. 201: https://familiapinto.wordpress.com/wp-content/uploads/2008/09/jack-welch-speaks.pdf

7 See Chapter 11.

Chapter 22: UK, France and Israel

1 Meanwhile, the USSR had tested its first bomb in 1949, so the UK was the third nuclear-armed nation.

2 CND UK. (2021, April 23). *Trident: The US connection*. https://cnduk.org/resources/trident-us-connection/

3 See T. Wallis, *The Truth About Trident*, Luath Press, Edinburgh, 2016, especially chapter 10, pp 108-111 and footnotes.

4 They are made and maintained, however, in the south of England, which means a regular stream of military convoys carrying nuclear warheads travel up and down the country, passing through towns and villages, parking up outside of schools and churches, and getting into traffic accidents... See https://www.nukewatch.org.uk/convoys/nuclear-weapon-convoy-accidents/

5 A report looking at alternative sites to base the UK's Trident submarines found none in England or Wales that meet the requirements and suggested the most likely alternative to Faslane would be co-locate the UK submarines together with the US submarine fleet based in King's Bay, Georgia on the US east coast. See John Ainslie (2013), *Nowhere to Go*, Scottish CND: https://www.banthebomb.org/wp-content/uploads/2021/07/2013-02-TridentNowheretoGoMarch2013.pdf

6 They could base them with US Trident submarines in Kings Bay, Georgia, or with the French nuclear submarines in Toulon, but both these options would be hugely embarrassing for the UK and would seem to defeat the purpose of having a so-called "independent deterrent."

7 UK devolution set up separate parliaments in Scotland, Wales and Northern Ireland. These are responsible for many decisions affecting those nations, but not for defence matters. See Scottish Parliament. (n.d.). *Devolved and reserved powers*. https://www.parliament.scot/about/how-parliament-works/devolved-and-reserved-powers

8 See summary of recent polls at https://www.statista.com/statistics/1170409/scottish-independence/

9 The UK continues to depend heavily on US technology and assistance for its own Trident nuclear weapons program (see next page), but the initial impetus for the UK to develop its own nuclear weapons was the "breakdown in the exchange of information" between the US and the UK, according to Churchill, in *Hansard*, 1 March, 1955, p.1892. See https://www.parliament.uk/about/living-heritage/transformingsociety/private-lives/yourcountry/collections/churchillexhibition/churchill-the-orator/hydrogen/.

Once the Soviets had their own Bomb, it seemed increasingly unlikely that any US President would risk destruction of the US homeland by using nuclear weapons against the Soviet Union in defense of the UK or any other European ally. But were the UK or France to launch nuclear weapons against Russia, it would be equally self-destructive.

[10] Then Foreign Secretary Ernest Bevin famously exclaimed in a Cabinet meeting where the decision was taken: "We've got to have this thing over here, whatever it costs. We've got to have the bloody Union Jack on top of it." The formal minutes of the meeting on 8 January 1947 are printed in Documents on British Policy Overseas (DBPO), Series I, Vol. XI, No. 36, and record Bevin's views in a more measured way. See also Peter Hennessy, *The Secret State: Preparing for the Worst 1945-2010* (Penguin revised edn, 2010).

[11] BBC News. (2018, November 6). France's Macron pushes for "true European army." *BBC News*. https://www.bbc.com/news/world-europe-46108633

[12] Bugos, S. (2020, March). *France Offers Nuclear Deterrent to All Europe*. Arms Control Association. https://www.armscontrol.org/act/2020-03/news/france-offers-nuclear-deterrent-europe

[13] See https://www.mvtpaix.org/wordpress/wp-content/uploads/2018/07/CP-05.07.2018-Sondage-TIAN_EN.pdf

[14] See: Center for Arms Control and Non-Proliferation. (2020, March 31). *Fact Sheet: Israel's Nuclear Inventory*. https://armscontrolcenter.org/fact-sheet-israels-nuclear-arsenal/

[15] The Glenn Amendment, passed by the US Congress in 1977, prevents US arms sales to any country deemed to possess nuclear weapons outside of the NPT. If Israel were to admit to possessing nuclear weapons, that would theoretically cut off their largest supplier of military aid, so both countries continue to pretend that Israel does not have nuclear weapons and the US military aid continues to flow. See https://carnegieendowment.org/2023/04/20/would-u.s.-sanction-allies-seeking-bomb-pub-89587

[16] NTI. (2023, January 23). *Nuclear disarmament Israel*. The Nuclear Threat Initiative. https://www.nti.org/analysis/articles/israel-nuclear-disarmament/

Chapter 23: India and Pakistan

[1] The Kargil War in 1999 was fought between India and Pakistan after they both had nuclear weapons.

[2] Kimball, D. G. (2022, April). *India Accidentally Fires Missile Into Pakistan*. Arms Control Association. https://www.armscontrol.org/act/2022-04/news/india-accidentally-fires-missile-into-pakistan

[3] https://economictimes.indiatimes.com/news/international/world-news/panic-in-pakistan-as-india-vows-to-cut-off-water-supply-over-kashmir/articleshow/120683286.cms?from=mdr

[4] https://english.alarabiya.net/News/world/2025/04/28/pakistan-defense-minister-says-a-military-incursion-by-india-is-imminent

Chapter 24: China and North Korea

[1] Greve, J. E., & Gambino, L. (2023, February 26). Capitol Hill finds rare bipartisan cause in China – but it could pose problems. *The Guardian*. https://www.theguardian.com/us-news/2023/feb/26/chinese-balloon-bipartisan-capitol-hill-risk

[2] See above.

[3] SIPRI. (2023, June 12). *States invest in nuclear arsenals as geopolitical relations deteriorate*. SIPRI. https://www.sipri.org/media/press-release/2023/states-invest-nuclear-arsenals-geopolitical-relations-deteriorate-new-sipri-yearbook-out-now

[4] 567 troops were reportedly killed during the First Taiwan Strait Crisis of 1954-55. Another 440 troops were killed during the Second Taiwan Strait Crisis of 1958. No

troops were killed during the so-called "Third" Taiwan Strait Crisis of 1995-96. This third crisis involved a series of missile tests and military exercises by China that were "aimed" at Taiwan but did not kill anyone or damage any property.

[5] See Xinhuanet. (2017, January 19). *Backgrounder: 10 key quotes from Xi's speech at UN Office at Geneva*. http://www.xinhuanet.com/english/2017-01/19/c_135994782.htm

[6] This section taken from Wallis, T., *Disarming the Nuclear Argument*, chapter 7, p.83.

[7] See ICAN. (n.d.-e). *North Korea*. https://www.icanw.org/north_korea

[8] The armed conflict ended in 1953 with an armistice, but there has never been a peace treaty.

[9] He is now perhaps being superseded in this role by the Mullahs of Iran, however there are no "safe hands" for unsafe weapons. And Donald Trump is arguably even more unhinged than Kim Jong-un.

[10] Some say his only priority is his own survival or that of his family, or of the regime. But neither he nor his regime can survive if his country does not.

Chapter 25: Russia

[1] Bush claimed the invasion of Iraq was justified as "pre-emptive self-defense" but this is not a legal justification for war. Officially it was claimed that the invasion was "allowed" under UN Security Council resolution 678, but the UN Security Council itself refused to accept that interpretation. See https://scholarship.law.gwu.edu/cgi/viewcontent.cgi?article=1898&context=faculty_publications

[2] President Trump's threat to rain down "fire and fury" on North Korea if it conducted any more nuclear tests was an unambiguous reference to the use of nuclear weapons by the United States. See https://mynbc15.com/news/nation-world/white-house-trumps-fire-and-fury-warning-is-clear

[3] The Iraq War was officially called "Operation Iraqi Freedom" https://www.brookings.edu/articles/operation-iraqi-freedom-and-the-future-of-the-u-s-military/

[4] In Iraq, these include torture of prisoners at Abu Ghraib, torture at Guantanamo Bay, the Haditha massacre of 24 women and children and other incidents.

[5] In the Kosovo War, US forces bombed bridges, factories, power stations, telecommunications facilities and the Chinese embassy in Belgrade. See Shue, Henry (2016), Fighting Hurt: Rule and Exception in Torture and War, pp.277-294. https://doi.org/10.1093/acprof:oso/9780198767626.003.0014

[6] Kosovo is still not recognized as an independent country by Russia or by several other states, and it is not a member of the UN.

[7] See history of Hawaii becoming a US state in 1959 at https://billofrightsinstitute.org/essays/the-annexation-of-hawaii

[8] *Russian Federation, Presidential Election, 18 March 2018: Final Report*. (2018, June 6). Organization for Security and Co-operation in Europe. https://www.osce.org/files/f/documents/2/4/383577_0.pdf

[9] See Wallis (2022), *Op. Cit.*

[10] Weisberg, J. (2016, January 1). Ronald Reagan and Mikhail Gorbachev and disarmament. *The Atlantic*. https://www.theatlantic.com/politics/archive/2016/01/ronald-reagans-disarmament-dream/422244/

[11] Still devastating to the people trying to survive through those wars.

[12] This one may have just ended in September 2023, but it's too early to know for sure.

[13] See: OSCE. (n.d.). *Participating States*. OSCE. https://www.osce.org/participating-states

[14] There are signs that this could change, however, especially with world attention shifting to the Middle East.

[15] Russia's current military forces and capacity for military production vastly outweighs that of Ukraine. Statista Research Department. (2023, February 8). *Russia vs Ukraine military comparison 2023.*
Statista. https://www.statista.com/statistics/1296573/russia-ukraine-military-comparison/

[16] See Roth, C., & Abbany, Z. (2023, June 6). Zaporizhzhia: What would happen if there was an accident? *dw.com*. https://www.dw.com/en/zaporizhzhia-what-would-happen-if-there-was-an-accident/a-63686362

[17] There has been a huge amount of unsubstantiated speculation about the possibility of Russia using so-called tactical nuclear weapons in Ukraine. The reality is that, apart from missiles designated for air defenses, the smallest nuclear warheads in the Russian arsenal are believed to be in the 10 Kt range, which is just slightly less than the destructive power of the bomb that destroyed Hiroshima. See inventory: Kristensen, H. M., Korda, M., & Reynolds, E. (2023). Russian nuclear weapons, 2023. *Bulletin of the Atomic Scientists*, *79*(3), 175. https://doi.org/10.1080/00963402.2023.2202542 If used in Ukraine, the civilian casualties would be extremely large and the radiation would almost certainly affect civilians in Russia as well in other countries across Europe.

[18] Wikipedia contributors. (2019, May 22). *Languages of Russia*. Wikipedia, the Free Encyclopedia; Wikimedia Foundation.
https://en.wikipedia.org/wiki/Languages_of_Russia

[19] Frye, T., et al. (2015). Is Putin's popularity real? *Post-Soviet Affairs*, *33*(1), 1–15.
https://doi.org/10.1080/1060586x.2016.1144334

[20] Frye, T., et al. (2015). Is Putin's popularity real? *Post-Soviet Affairs*, *33*(1), 8.
https://doi.org/10.1080/1060586x.2016.1144334

[21] NATO Information Service. (1984). *NATO and the Warsaw Pact: Force Comparisons.*
https://archives.nato.int/uploads/r/null/1/3/137795/0228_NATO_and_the_Warsaw_Pact_1984-Force_Comparisons_ENG.pdf

[22] See Véron, N. (2022, April 8). Putin's Russia is a minnow compared to the Cold War Soviet Bloc. *Bruegel*. https://www.bruegel.org/blog-post/putins-russia-minnow-compared-cold-war-soviet-bloc

[23] Statista. (2023). *NATO Russia military comparison 2023*. Statista.
https://www.statista.com/statistics/1293174/nato-russia-military-comparison/

[24] See OSCE. (n.d.). *History*. https://www.osce.org/history

[25] Article 51 of the UN Charter only allows for self-defense only "if an armed attack *occurs* against a Member of the United Nations, *until* the Security Council has taken measures necessary to maintain international peace and security." The United States, Russia, and other countries have tried to claim that self-defense is justified if an armed attack is considered *imminent* or even a *possibility*, which is not what the UN Charter says. They also try to claim that a war, justified on the grounds of "self-defense," can go on more or less indefinitely, which is also not what the UN Charter says. Self-defense from an actual attack is only allowed under the UN Charter *until* the Security Council is able to take some action to stop the attack.

[26] See ongoing discussion, for instance, in Delahunty, Robert (2007), "Paper Charter: Self-Defense and the Failure of the UN Collective Security System," *Catholic University Law Review*, 56:3:
https://scholarship.law.edu/cgi/viewcontent.cgi?article=1127&context=lawreview

[27] See McCogwire, M. (1998). NATO Expansion: "A Policy Error of Historic Importance." *Review of International Studies*, *24*(1), 23–42. http://www.jstor.org/stable/20097504

[28] There has been much confusion around the different proposals put forward at the UN in recent years. Russia and China have proposed banning *all* weapons in space, which has been consistently blocked by the US. Meanwhile, the US proposed reaffirming the ban on deploying *nuclear weapons* in space (which is already banned by the Outer Space Treaty), which was blocked by Russia – supposedly on the grounds that it did not go far

enough. See https://apnews.com/article/nuclear-arms-space-un-russia-us-japan-561ab8ae569afd7ee79789588ca34033

[29] See https://www.nytimes.com/2009/06/28/world/28cyber.html

Chapter 26: Final steps to abolition

[1] See Osgood, Charles, *An Alternative to War or Surrender*, University of Illinois Press, 1962.

[2] See Lindskold, S. (1978). Trust development, the GRIT proposal, and the effects of conciliatory acts on conflict and cooperation. *Psychological Bulletin*, 85(4), 772–793. https://doi.org/10.1037/0033-2909.85.4.772 and Psychology. (n.d.). *GRIT Tension Reduction Strategy*. https://psychology.iresearchnet.com/social-psychology/antisocial-behavior/grit-tension-reduction-strategy/

[3] For instance, both sides would first cut their arsenals in half by the end of phase one, then cut them in half again by the end of phase two, etc. See Global Zero. (n.d.). *The Global Zero Action Plan*. Global Zero. http://www.globalzero.org/reaching-zero/

[4] Urbina, J., & Ali, H. (2007). Letter dated 17 December 2007 from the Permanent Representatives of Costa Rica and Malaysia to the United Nations addressed to the Secretary-General. In *International Network of Engineers and Scientists Against Proliferation*. http://inesap.org/sites/default/files/inesap_old/mNWC_2007_Unversion_English_N0821377.pdf

[5] Out of the trillions of dollars budgeted for nuclear weapons over the coming decades, as much as $500 billion, or $10 billion per year, will need to be set aside for their elimination and final disposal. Nevertheless, the savings will begin immediately and will be substantial.

[6] See, for instance, Findlay, Trevor (1999), *The Verification and Compliance Regime for a Nuclear Weapon-Free World*, VERTIC Briefing Paper 99/5: https://www.vertic.org/media/Archived_Publications/Briefing_Papers/Briefing_Paper_99_5.pdf

[7] See Figure 26.4 below.

[8] Data obtained from websites of the different nuclear weapon facilities and local newspaper reports.

[9] See Chapter 3 for a list of the main companies involved.

[10] Map by Nancy Horn. Data from multiple sources.

[11] See footnote 1 in Chapter 21.

[12] Oak Ridge Institute for Science and Education. (2019). *Nuclear Engineering Enrollments and Degrees Survey*. U.S. Department of Energy Office of Science. https://orise.orau.gov/stem/workforce-studies/nuclear-engineering-enrollments.html

[13] Prichard, I. (2014). Arms to Renewables: Work for the Future. Campaign Against Arms Trade. https://caat.org.uk/app/uploads/2020/03/arms-to-renewables-background-briefing.pdf

[14] See, for example, Pollin, et al. (2014), *op.cit.* and also International Trade Union Confederation. (n.d.). *Growing green and decent jobs*. https://www.ituc-csi.org/growing-green-and-decent-jobs,11011,
Mahan, S., Pearlman, I., & Suavity, J. (2010, September 28). *Untapped wealth: Offshore wind can deliver cleaner, more affordable energy and more jobs than offshore oil*. Oceana. https://oceana.org/reports/untapped-wealth-offshore-wind-can-deliver-cleaner-more-affordable-energy-and-more-jobs/

Epilogue

[1] See https://psr.org/what-are-donald-trumps-thoughts-about-the-threat-of-nuclear-weapons/

[2] See https://apnews.com/article/trump-china-russia-nuclear-bbc1c75920297f1e5ba5556d084da4de

[3] For example, see https://www.armscontrol.org/act/2018-05/news/denuclearization-poses-summit-challenge

[4] Trump then lost the election to Biden, who renewed the New START treaty for a further 5 years, from Feb 2021 to Feb 2026. Under the terms of the treaty itself, it cannot be extended further but must be re-negotiated as a new treaty.

[5] The federal discretionary budget amounted to about $1.7 trillion in 2024. This is spending that congress has control over each year. An additional $4.3 trillion is considered "mandatory" spending that is based on social security contributions withheld from millions of paychecks, etc., plus another $1 trillion or so that is the interest owed on the national debt.

[6] https://www.wsj.com/politics/policy/doge-government-efficiency-ideas-musk-ramaswamy-3b554b97

[7] https://www.washingtonpost.com/news/the-fix/wp/2017/10/11/trumps-loose-rhetoric-on-nuclear-weapons-has-become-a-very-real-concern/

REFERENCES

Acheson, Ray. (2021). *Banning the Bomb, Smashing the Patriarchy,* Rowman and Littlefield, Lanham, Maryland.

Air Force Center for Studies and Analyses. (1985). *Effectiveness of the Minuteman II Stage III Refurbishment Program.* https://apps.dtic.mil/sti/pdfs/ADA363899.pdf

Bird, Kai and Sherwin, Martin (2006), *American Prometheus: The Triumph and Tragedy of J. Robert Oppenheimer,* Vantage Books.

Bolton, Matthew (2020), *From Manhattan Project to Nuclear Free New York.* https://bpb-us-w2.wpmucdn.com/blogs.pace.edu/dist/0/195/files/2020/01/From-Manhattan-Project-to-Nuclear-Free-011620.pdf

Center for Arms Control and Non-Proliferation. (2021, April 20). *No first use - Center for Arms Control and Non-Proliferation.* https://armscontrolcenter.org/issues/no-first-use/

Chenoweth, Erica and Stephan, Maria (2011), *Why Civil Resistance Works: The Strategic Logic of Nonviolent Conflict.* Columbia University Press.

Cortright, D. (2022, September). *Freeze! The grassroots movement to halt the arms race and end the Cold War.* Arms Control Association. https://www.armscontrol.org/act/2022-09/features/freeze-grassroots-movement-halt-arms-race-end-cold-war

Crawford, N. (2019). Pentagon Fuel Use, Climate Change, and the Costs of War. In *Watson Institute for International and Public Affairs.* Brown University. https://watson.brown.edu/costsofwar/files/cow/imce/papers/Pentagon%20Fuel%20Use%2C%20Climate%20Change%20and%20the%20Costs%20of%20War%20Revised%20November%202019%20Crawford.pdf

Ellsberg, Daniel (2017), *The Doomsday Machine: Confessions of a Nuclear War Planner,*Bloomsbury.

Fact Sheet: Fissile Material Cutoff Treaty (FMCT). (2023, May 19). Center for Arms Control and Non-Proliferation. https://armscontrolcenter.org/fact-sheet-fissile-material-cutoff-treaty-fmct/

Frye, T., et al. (2015). Is Putin's popularity real? *Post-Soviet Affairs, 33*(1), 1–15. https://doi.org/10.1080/1060586x.2016.1144334

Glasstone, S., & Dolan, P. J. (1977). The Effects of Nuclear Weapons. Third edition. https://doi.org/10.2172/6852629

Harrison, T., & Montgomery, E. B. (2015). The Cost of U.S. Nuclear Forces from BCA to Bow Wave and Beyond. In *CSBA*. Center for Strategic and Budgetary Assessments. https://csbaonline.org/uploads/documents/CSBA-NCS_Resize_FINAL_WEB.pdf

Helfand, I. (2013). *Nuclear Famine: Two Billion People at Risk?* International Physicians for the Prevention of War. https://psr.org/wp-content/uploads/2018/04/two-billion-at-risk.pdf

ICAN. (n.d.-a). *History of the TPNW*. Retrieved September 22, 2023, from https://www.icanw.org/history_of_the_tpnw

IPPNW. (1991). *Radioactive Heaven and Earth* (p. 164). Zed Books. https://ieer.org/wp/wp-content/uploads/1991/06/RadioactiveHeavenEarth1991.pdf

Jacobsen, Annie. (2024). *Nuclear War: A Scenario*, Penguin/Random House, London.

Kaplan, Fred (2020), *The Bomb: Presidents, Generals and the Secret History of Nuclear War*. Simon and Schuster.

Katz, Milton (1986). *Ban the Bomb: A History of SANE*, Greenwood Press, New York.

Kennedy, J. F. (1963, June 10). American University Commencement Address. In *C-SPAN.org*. American University Commencement Address. https://www.c-span.org/video/?153206-1/american-university-commencement-address#

Kmentt, Alexander (2021). *The Treaty Prohibiting Nuclear Weapons: How It Was Achieved and Why It Matters*. Routledge, Abingdon.

Koch, S. J. (1991). *The Presidential Nuclear Initiatives of 1991–1992*. Center for the Study of Weapons of Mass Destruction National Defense University. https://ndupress.ndu.edu/portals/68/documents/casestudies/cswmd_casestudy-5.pdf

Krall, L. M., Macfarlane, A. M., & Ewing, R. C. (2022). Nuclear waste from small modular reactors. *Proceedings of the National Academy of Sciences, 119*(23). https://doi.org/10.1073/pnas.2111833119

Lewis, P., Williams, H., Pelopidas, B., & Aghlani, S. (2014). Too Close for Comfort: Cases of Near Nuclear Use and Options for Policy. In *Chatham House*. https://www.chathamhouse.org/sites/default/files/field/field_document/20140428TooCloseforComfortNuclearUseLewisWilliamsPelopidasAghlani.pdf

Lockard, J. (2000). Desert(ed) geographies: cartographies of nuclear testing. *Landscape Review, 6*(1), 3–20. https://doi.org/10.34900/lr.v6i1.77

Maar, Henry Richard (2021), *Freeze! The Grassroots Movement to Halt the Arms Race.* Cornell University.

MacKenzie, D., & Spinardi, G. (1988). The Shaping of Nuclear Weapon System Technology: US Fleet Ballistic Missile Guidance and Navigation: II: `Going for Broke' — The Path to Trident II. *Social Studies of Science, 18*(4), 581–624. https://doi.org/10.1177/030631288018004002

Markey, Ed. (1982). *Nuclear Peril: The Politics of Proliferation.* Ballinger, Cambridge.

Michael J. Mills, Owen B. Toon, Julia Lee-Taylor, Alan Robock, (2014) "Multidecadal global cooling and unprecedented ozone loss following a regional nuclear conflict," *Earth's Future,* AGU, Vol.2 no.4, April 2014, 161-176: https://doi.org/10.1002/2013EF000205.

National Research Council. (2010). Examination of the U.S. Air Force's Science, Technology, Engineering, and Mathematics (STEM) Workforce Needs in the Future and Its Strategy to Meet Those Needs. The National Academies Press. https://doi.org/10.17226/12718

NATO Information Service. (1984). *NATO and the Warsaw Pact: Force Comparisons.* https://archives.nato.int/uploads/r/null/1/3/137795/0228_NATO_and_the_Warsaw_Pact_1984-Force_Comparisons_ENG.pdf

NCEI. (2022). *Billion-Dollar Weather and Climate Disasters.* National Centers for Environmental Information; NOAA. https://www.ncei.noaa.gov/access/billions/

Newell, P., & Simms, A. (2019). Towards a fossil fuel non-proliferation treaty. *Climate Policy, 20*(8), 1043–1054. https://doi.org/10.1080/14693062.2019.1636759

Obama, B. (2015, June 13). Remarks By President Barack Obama In Prague As Delivered. In *whitehouse.gov.* https://obamawhitehouse.archives.gov/the-press-office/remarks-president-barack-obama-prague-delivered

Office of General Counsel. (2023). *Law of War Manual.* Department of Defense. https://media.defense.gov/2023/Jul/31/2003271432/-1/-1/0/DOD-LAW-OF-WAR-MANUAL-JUNE-2015-UPDATED-JULY%202023.PDF

Ostern, G., ed., (2025). *Nuclear Weapons Ban Monitor 2024,* Norwegian People's Aid/ICAN, Oslo.

Perry, W.J. and Collina, T.Z. (2020). *The Button: The New Nuclear Arms Race and Presidential Power from Truman to Trump.* BenBella Books, Dallas.

Pollin, R. (2019). Green Economics and Decent Work: A Viable Unified Framework. *Development and Change, 51*(2), 711-726. https://doi.org/10.1111/dech.12559

Pollin, R., et al. (2014). Green Growth: A U.S. Program for Controlling Climate Change and Expanding Job Opportunities. In *Political Economy Research Institute*. Center for American Progress. http://www.peri.umass.edu/fileadmin/pdf/Green_Growth_2014/GreenGrowthReport-PERI-Sept2014.pdf

Quinlan, M. (2005). *Thinking about nuclear weapons* (2nd ed.). Royal United Services Institute For Defence Studies. https://fisherp.scripts.mit.edu/wordpress/wp-content/uploads/2017/03/Thinking-about-Nuclear-Weapons-RUSI-WHP41_QUINLAN1.pdf

Richie, Nick (2012), *A Nuclear Weapons Free World? Britain, Trident and the Challenge Ahead*, Palgrave MacMillan, London.

Robock, A., & Toon, O. B. (2012). Self-assured destruction: The climate impacts of nuclear war. *Bulletin of the Atomic Scientists, 68*(5), 66–74. https://doi.org/10.1177/0096340212459127

Robock, A., Oman, L., & Stenchikov, G. L. (2007). Nuclear winter revisited with a modern climate model and current nuclear arsenals: Still catastrophic consequences. *J. Geophys. Res, 112*(D13), 1–14. https://doi.org/10.1029/2006JD008235

Sachs, Jeffrey (2018), *A New Foreign Policy: Beyond American Exceptionalism*. Columbia University Press.

Scarry, Elaine (2014), *Thermonuclear Monarchy: Choosing Between Democracy and Doom*, W.W. Norton.

Schlosser, E. (2013). *Command and Control*. Penguin Books.

Schwartz, S. I. (1998). *Atomic audit: The Costs and Consequences of U.S. Nuclear Weapons Since 1940*. Brookings Intitution Press.

Scott, J. (2006, April 2). *Broken Arrow Nuclear Weapon Accidents*. Aerospaceweb.org. https://aerospaceweb.org/question/weapons/q0268.shtml

Sechser, T. S., & Fuhrmann, M. (2017). *Nuclear weapons and coercive diplomacy*. Cambridge University Press. https://doi.org/10.1017/9781316227305

Smithberger, M. (2018). Brass parachutes: The problem of the Pentagon revolving door. In *Project on Government Oversight*. https://www.pogo.org/report/2018/11/brass-parachutes

Snyder, S. (2021). Perilous Profiteering. In *ICAN*. PAX and ICAN. https://d3n8a8pro7vhmx.cloudfront.net/ican/pages/2331/attachments/original/1637141262/2021_Perilous_Profiteering_Final.pdf?1637141262

Stand.earth. (2023). *Global Fossil Fuel Commitments Database* [Dataset]. https://divestmentdatabase.org/

Stockholm International Peace Research Institute. (2022). SIPRI Yearbook 2022. In *SIPRI*. Oxford University Press. https://www.sipri.org/yearbook/2022

Strategic Arms Reduction Treaty (START I). (2023). In *Center for Arms Control and Non-Proliferation*. https://armscontrolcenter.org/strategic-arms-reduction-treaty-start-i/

U.S. Department of Defense. *2022 National Defense Strategy of The United States of America*. (2022, October 27). https://apps.dtic.mil/sti/trecms/pdf/AD1183539.pdf

U.S. NRC. (1975). *Reactor safety study. An assessment of accident risks in US commercial nuclear power* (No. WASH1400). http://inis.iaea.org/search/search.aspx?orig_q=RN:35053391

UK Government. (2006). The Future of the UK's Nuclear Deterrent. *White Paper*.

United Nations. (2022, March 30). *"War's Greatest Cost Is Its Human Toll", Secretary-General Reminds Peacebuilding Commission, Warning of "Perilous Impunity" Taking Hold | UN Press*. United Nations. https://press.un.org/en/2022/sgsm21216.doc.htm

United States Government Accountability Office. (2019). *Department of Energy: Program-Wide Strategy and Better Reporting Needed to Address Growing Environmental Cleanup Liability*. GAO. https://www.gao.gov/assets/700/696632.pdf

Waller, Douglas (1987). *Congress and the Nuclear Freeze: An inside look at the politics of a mass movement*. UMass Press.

Wallis, T. M. (2017). *Disarming the Nuclear Argument: The Truth About Nuclear Weapons*. Luath Press.

Wallis, T. M. (2023). *Warheads to Windmills: Preventing Climate Catastrophe and Nuclear War*. Indispensable Press.

Wilson, Ward Hayes (2014), *Five Myths About Nuclear Weapons*, Mariner Books.

Wilson, Ward Hayes (2023). *It Is Possible: A Future Without Nuclear Weapons*. Avenues the World School Press, New York.

Wittner, Lawrence S. (2009). *Confronting the Bomb: A Short History of the World Nuclear Disarmament Movement*, Stanford University Press.

World Nuclear Association. (2023, August). *Uranium Supplies: Supply of Uranium*. World Nuclear Association. https://www.world-nuclear.org/information-library/nuclear-fuel-cycle/uranium-resources/supply-of-uranium.aspx#ECSArticleLin

INDEX

www.ingramcontent.com/pod-product-compliance
Lightning Source LLC
LaVergne TN
LVHW100250210926
848480LV00003B/882
9798218697181